Shots in the Dark

World War II: The Global, Human, and Ethical Dimension
G. Kurt Piehler, *series editor*

Shots in the Dark

Experimentation, Success, and Failure in the Second World War

Jadwiga Biskupska and Sara B. Castro, Editors
Foreword by **Robert Citino, The National World War II Museum**

Fordham University Press | New York 2025

Copyright © 2025 Fordham University Press

All rights reserved. No part of this publication may be reproduced, stored in a retrieval system, or transmitted in any form or by any means—electronic, mechanical, photocopy, recording, or any other—except for brief quotations in printed reviews, without the prior permission of the publisher.

Fordham University Press has no responsibility for the persistence or accuracy of URLs for external or third-party Internet websites referred to in this publication and does not guarantee that any content on such websites is, or will remain, accurate or appropriate.

Fordham University Press also publishes its books in a variety of electronic formats. Some content that appears in print may not be available in electronic books.

Visit us online at www.fordhampress.com.

For EU safety / GPSR concerns: Mare Nostrum Group B.V., Mauritskade 21D, 1091 GC Amsterdam, The Netherlands, gpsr@mare-nostrum.co.uk

Library of Congress Cataloging-in-Publication Data available online at https://catalog.loc.gov.

Printed in the United States of America

27 26 25   5 4 3 2 1

First edition

Contents

Foreword
Robert Citino ix

Introduction: Taking Our First Shots in the Dark
Jadwiga Biskupska 1

Part I   Institutional Adaptation

1. **The Dixie Mission(aries):
   The Protestant Roots of US Intelligence Officers
   in Wartime China**
   Sara B. Castro 13

2. **The Diversity and Versatility of British Intelligence
   in Iraq, 1939–1945**
   Adrian O'Sullivan 35

3. **Prelude to Barbarossa? The 4th Mountain Division War
   in Yugoslavia, April–May 1941**
   Jeff Rutherford 61

4. **"Believed Reliable": The "Morale and Opinions"
   of German Prisoners of War in the United States,
   February 1944–June 1945**
   Derek R. Mallett 85

Part II Totalization: The Militarization of Civilians

5. **Montélimar's Phony War: Requisitions, Mobilization, and French Civilians**
   Cameron Zinsou — 113

6. **Red Army Divisions' Growing Demand for Artistic Service: Entertainment at the Front, 1941–1945**
   Erina Megowan — 134

7. **From Covert Reports to Front-Page News: How North American Newspaper Reports Contributed to Views on Reconnaissance Actions in Northwest Europe**
   Victoria Sotvedt — 158

8. **"Everything We Can Lay Hands On": Canadian Soldiers and Sexual Violence in Germany in 1945**
   Claire Cookson-Hills — 179

Part III Cultural Transformation

9. **"The Men of Bataan Lived Up to the Best American Tradition": Journalists, Civilians, Politicians, and the Meaning of Surrender during World War II**
   Elena M. Friot — 207

10. **Who Do You Believe? Loyalty and Asian Americans in the OSS during World War II**
    Brian Masaru Hayashi — 230

11. **World War II and Soviet Intelligence and State Security Officer Defectors**
    Kevin P. Riehle — 250

12. **The Space Between: Hildegard Beetz, Espionage, and Gender, 1944–1949**
    Katrin Paehler — 278

Acknowledgments	305
Acronyms and Abbreviations	307
Contributors	311
Index	315

Foreword

Back in 2007, I published an article in the *American Historical Review*, "Military Histories Old and New: A Reintroduction," which addressed the contemporary state of military history. The article intended to address military history's relative decline within the scholarly ranks, to show the diversity of approaches and methodologies—social, cultural, anthropological—that informed the work of military historians, and to argue for the continued importance of war studies within the modern academy. It was an *apologia* in the classic sense: not only a defense of our beloved subfield, but a friendly invitation to historians of other stripes to check us out.

Looking back, I can see something that was left unsaid in that article: Military history itself had split, perhaps even splintered, into different camps. Those who wrote campaign history, such as myself, often felt estranged from those attempting to place war within the burgeoning field of the history of memory, and I have no doubt that the feeling was mutual. Military historians who focused their works on categories of race or gender—the "new military history" of the 1960s—probably dominated the field numerically and yet still often had the sense that they were not accepted as "real" military historians by many of their colleagues who studied actual warfighting. Military historians often complained that they were not taken seriously within the broader profession, but often they failed to take their own colleagues seriously enough.

That's just one reason why the volume you are about to read is so impressive to me, and so valuable to the field. The offspring of a new intellectual project, the Second World War Research Group, North America (itself an offshoot of the Second World War Research Group, founded in the United Kingdom), *Shots in the Dark* breathes the spirit of scholarly diversity and multiplicity of approaches. It is a volume of intellectual cooperation and collaboration, *con brio*. Editors Jadwiga Biskupska and Sara B. Castro have chosen a diverse group of younger scholars and more established ones who analyze the war in its totality: military intelligence and global operations, civilian mobilization, media coverage, culture, and more.

Volume entries certainly discuss the front-line experience. We read about "what soldiers do," usually involving sex (and all too often sexual violence), how they train and fight, how newspapers mediate their exploits to the folks back home, and what happens when they are taken prisoner. But the home front also takes a bow, from French civilians being prepped (or not) for war in 1939–40 to the experience of Japanese Americans caught in the crosshairs of illegal internment and the desire to serve.

The great Prussian philosopher of war, Carl von Clausewitz, once stated something that should be obvious:

> The first, the supreme, the most far-reaching act of judgment that the statesman and commander have to make is to establish by that test the kind of war on which they are embarking; neither mistaking it for, nor trying to turn it into, something that is alien to its nature. (*On War*, book I, chapter 1)

Commanders should understand what kind of war they're dealing with, in other words, but if recent history has shown us anything, it is that they haven't always looked at things clearly.

Historians, too, need to comprehend the nature of the war they're studying. Those who insist that that there can only be one approved scholarly approach to the study of World War II are ignoring the conflict's most obvious characteristics: sheer size and vast complexity. World War II itself was the very realm of uncertainty, another concept from Clausewitz, and trying to comprehend it, even at the time, was no easy matter.

So, too, for history and historians. We will never exhaust the available topics, and the approaches to studying them are limited only by our imaginations. Battlefields matter, of course, but so do the home fronts and factories that feed them. The cultural lens through which individual nations and armies view their war is crucial; so too is the interplay of social class, race, and gender. Who won World War II? How do (and should) we remember and memorialize it? How can World War II help us understand our current situation? How can it lead us astray?

We will never "understand" World War II completely, never put it in a box and tie a bow. We can only continue to strive, and the best way forward is to read the work of other scholars who may disagree with us or who use analytical categories with which we might not be completely comfortable.

That's why this volume is so useful. Remember, the "shot in the dark" may be an uncertain act, but it also can also offer a striking moment of light, elucidation, and clarity.

    Robert Citino
    The National World War II Museum

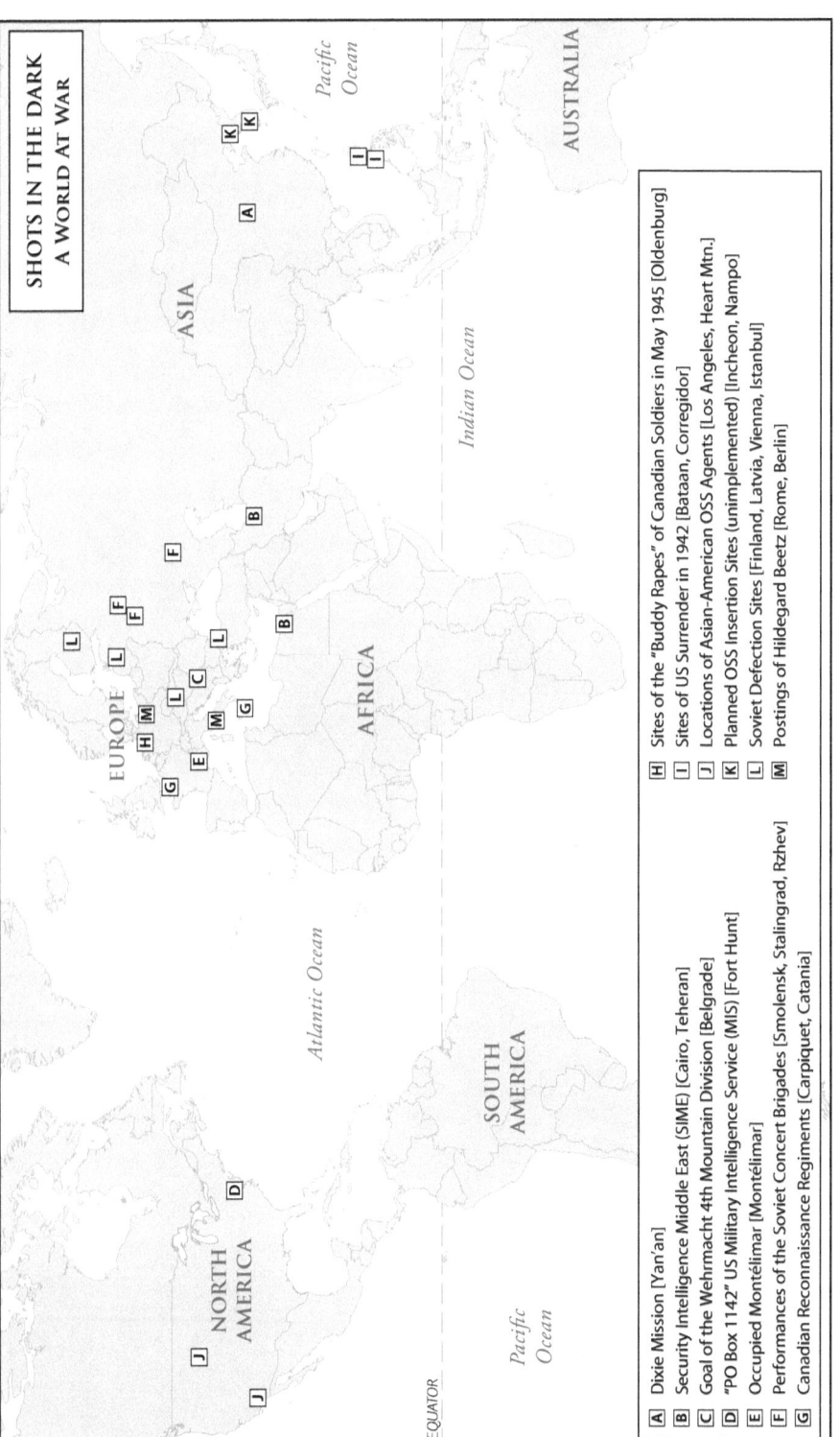

Shots in the Dark

Introduction
Taking Our First Shots in the Dark
Jadwiga Biskupska

More than two generations after its combatants slowly demobilized and began to integrate back into their changed societies, World War II means less and more than it did to those who fought and witnessed it. It is currently in the process of being taken for granted and hence forgotten or at best misremembered. The war is now a historical event rather than a formative experience for authors addressing it, which is an important transition that requires reflection.[1] We cannot assume that we intuitively understand this complex conflict without continued study. Conversely, emotional separation from the war offers today's historians a different perspective than that of our predecessors. The passage of time has not decreased the relevance of Second World War history. On the contrary, not only does the war have new lessons to teach in the present, but we also continuously learn new things about it, particularly as new sources are revealed, new research methods arise, and new collaborations become possible.

This volume emerges out of an intellectual project launched in the United Kingdom in 2014 as the Second World War Research Group (SWWRG) to reestablish the scholarly study of the Second World War, understanding the war as having been a global and collaborative endeavor that therefore requires global and collaborative study. The North American branch of this young institution set out to expand the SWWRG mission in the United States and Canada, drawing on scholars there to discuss the war anew. Built out of three thematic workshops that brought together small groups of historians at different stages in their careers and with different geographical expertise and methodological approaches, the supposition was that new combinations of insight and focus would yield new knowledge. That expectation has happily been fulfilled in the chapters combined in this volume, which offer fresh insights into how the long, global Second World War changed nearly everything about the institutions, armies, and societies that fought it, for good or for ill.

The volume builds on a robust literature on military innovation and adaptation, and a library of studies that have assessed how armies and states learn and develop during wartime.[2] It is nevertheless more open in its scope than this work has traditionally been, drawing in civilians, auxiliaries, and "ordinary" actors as adapters and innovators whose behavior had the ability to shape the Second World War. Not confining itself just to questions about military effectiveness, the chapters consider what it means to be effective and successful in wartime beyond and before final victory and suggests answers that should be of interest to the wide community of experts and students of the war.

Shots in the Dark posits that this war and its consequences powerfully shaped the world we live in today and offers three broad frameworks for understanding the war as a source of innovation, adaptation, and change: 1. institutional adaptation, 2. "totalization" or the militarization of civilians, and 3. cultural transformation. For each framework, four essays address different problems with different methodologies and geographies, zeroing in on different actors. Unfolding in a loose chronology that respects the different timelines of war and violence in different spaces, each section expands where and who we understand to be the "proper" actors in the war, moving from changes in specific institutions and tactics to shifts in more diffuse topics of personal identity and group loyalty.

Part I: Institutional Adaptation

The first part is the most concrete, examining institutions revolutionized by the war and the personnel who kept them afloat and then made them successful. It opens with co-editor Sara Castro's chapter on the "mish kids," an unlikely group of people to provide expertise to the United States government and inform its developing policy vis-à-vis China as the world collapsed into war. The children of Protestant Christian missionaries in east Asia and some of the few Americans with deep knowledge of Chinese language and culture, they provided the first—and only—source of information on domestic political conflicts in China, at war with Japan, to the United States government before Pearl Harbor. The "mish kids," however, had ideas of their own about how US-China relations should operate, ideas that took on increasing significance as the Asia-Pacific War escalated and General Joseph "Vinegar Joe" Stilwell, the US commander in the China-Burma-India (CBI) theater, both needed and suspected their advice and their patriotism.

Adrian O'Sullivan's chapter also looks at precedent and tradition, the people "on the ground" who were forced to rise to the occasion as the war took over their lives: the personnel of the British intelligence community in Iraq.³ Breaking new ground in the intelligence history of the war, O'Sullivan argues that British intelligence personnel in Iraq performed their jobs well, despite the frequent bungling of higher-ups in Cairo and London. Overlapping personnel and institutions and widely separated operatives drew on long-standing personal connections and experience to keep information moving and undermine the Axis. It has become a truism to discuss institutional rivalry and infighting as a source of failure, but O'Sullivan demonstrates that groups and individuals working for the same cause also collaborated effectively, even triumphantly, during the war.

Jeff Rutherford turns our attention to the military that ultimately lost the war—the German *Wehrmacht*—but at a moment in spring 1941 and in a place, Yugoslavia, where it was adapting and innovating toward victory. Rutherford's case study of the 4th Mountain Division "before Barbarossa," when scholars generally agree that Nazi Germany's war turned genocidally ideological,⁴ demonstrates the nuts and bolts of *how* an army made the war total as it fought, how, as Rutherford phrases it, it "merg[ed] the operational and occupation practices of the German way of war." The Wehrmacht was not the only military that escalated its behavior, increasingly targeting civilians and those on the periphery of combat, as other chapters detail, but it was the first and may have been the most brutal of these adapting institutions.

Derek R. Mallett also examines men of the Wehrmacht as his subject, but in a very different time and place: after their defeat and through the eyes of "PO Box 1142," the US Military Intelligence Service (MIS) operation at Fort Hunt, Virginia, that interrogated German POWs from 1942 until the end of the war. PO Box 1142 was also learning as it went, its analysts suddenly in possession of a huge amount of intelligence sourced from its prisoners, figuring out what do with this information, how to categorize and prioritize it, and how to weaponize it toward Allied victory. Like O'Sullivan's operatives in Iraq, PO Box 1142 was in communication with a dizzying variety of US and British military organizations. Through analysis of surviving interrogation reports, Mallett reveals the volatility of German morale and how German soldiers assessed the United States as it began to win the war. Extracting that information was one difficulty; putting it to concrete use in wartime was another: The process was tentative and halting even for an alliance like the Anglo-American one, which was more harmonious than others.⁵

The institutions in Part I are ascending: Each is in the process of figuring out how to operate to win in the short and long term. We should not take these institutional successes for granted or assume they were inevitable in retrospect. Castro's mish kids provided the foundation for US military cooperation with China's Communist leaders, but in a way few of them supported by 1945. O'Sullivan's intelligence community kept its corner of the British Empire operational on a shoestring despite German endeavors to undermine it, but British wartime successes were not predetermined, and the British Empire would itself disintegrate within a decade after the conclusion of hostilities. This success is thus easy to ignore or forget. Rutherford's German soldiers were as flexible as they were brutal in 1941, and their developments would sustain them through several years of combat and atrocity in the Soviet Union, but they would ultimately lose that campaign. Mallett's US Navy and US Army personnel figured out how to classify and prioritize information in a war that they, along with their British allies, had begun to win, but plenty of this information showed the combat performance of their own troops in an uneven, even embarrassing, light. For each of these institutions, surprises punctuated achievements. These institutions were revolutionized by what the war required of them, establishing norms that persisted into the Cold War and in some cases into the present.

Part II: Totalization: The Militarization of Civilians

The second part expands our gaze to include civilians and civilian institutions in this story of adaptation and innovation, examining the way that the war militarized those who did not fight, curtailed and expanded their agency, and put them in positions where their actions and opinions changed the war and how it was remembered. This part thus confronts the idea of total war but takes the approach Rutherford introduced in Part I, not assuming that the war was total, but assessing precisely how it became that way, and for whom. It begins with Cameron Zinsou's case study of the shifting social contract in Montélimar, a sleepy corner of southeastern France, during the "Phony War" between the German invasion of Poland in fall 1939 and the arrival of war in western Europe in May 1940. Raising tricky questions about patriotism, property rights, and the obligations of both citizens and their governments in wartime, Zinsou details how French civilians, including a widow, a farmer, and an equestrian club, haggled over how to accommodate the new and expanding needs of their army—indeed, it raises questions about *whose* army the French army was. Retrospective studies of this period and its importance for the later course of the war have opined about the horrors of World War I, the Maginot Line, and the rapid course of the 1940 campaign, but Zinsou convinces us that the fight over the use of a laundry room or a truck provide in microcosm a portrait of the violent, contested transition from peace to war.⁶

Erina Megowan details the process of self-mobilization of another group of civilians swept up in war: the artists, musicians, poets, and actors of the "concert brigades" who organized entertainment for Red Army soldiers from the opening of the Eastern Front in 1941, often not far from combat. Massively larger than the United Service Organizations (USO) better known in the West, these concert brigades provided more than 1.2 million performances over four years. Both spontaneously organized by patriotic civilians—including Soviet women—and increasingly demanded by the state, the concert brigades were pulled in different directions, in high demand but torn between conflicting agendas of propagandizing the soldiers with Stalinist content and comforting and distracting them in some of the worst moments of the war. Their repertoire was hotly contested, each song and skit a battle of its own. The eventual success of these troupes helped to fuse front lines and home front in the Soviet Union, putting civilians in uniform. Megowan argues that careful analysis of official surveys demonstrates that concert brigades ultimately buoyed the morale of Red Army soldiers at crucial moments, but that this success was a complex and contested process.

Victoria Sotvedt's chapter tackles the role of civilians in wartime from a new angle: She mines Canadian and US newspapers to draw a fuller portrait of armored reconnaissance units operating in western Europe late in the war. Often neglected and misunderstood for reasons Sotvedt details, these tank groups were crucial to the conduct of war and the Western Allied advance across France. Canadian and American readers, however, read nothing about them and thus built a skewed picture of the nature of the war "their boys" were fighting. Sifting through articles and memoirs, the author traces the emerging disconnect between what civilian readers thought combat entailed and what was actually happening on the battlefield, demonstrating the agency of North American civilian home fronts during and after the war, in this case to misunderstand and misremember its course. Sotvedt's chapter promises to provoke a reexamination of both combat support units and how civilian publics assess war as it is happening.

Claire Cookson-Hills's chapter provides a brutal coda to this discussion of the totalization of war and the adaptation of civilians to its unfolding. A fine-grained case study of two Canadian soldiers put on trial for the rape of German women in spring 1945, Cookson-Hills carefully contextualizes and weighs the trial testimony and sentencing of those accused of "buddy rape." Her analysis explains how German civilians, especially German women, were treated in defeat, and the way their entanglement with the Wehrmacht in which their brothers, fathers, and husbands fought made them into spoils of war for the Western Allied victors. Expanding on the wider body of work on sexual violence and American soldiers, Cookson-Hills assesses how Canadian soldiers compare in these cases and with what consequences for European civilian women at the end of the war and beginning of the postwar period.[7]

Total war may be a development of modernity, but it is not a happy one. These four chapters assess how people once far from combat changed what was happening on the battlefield and were changed by it. Zinsou's French civilians pushed back against the impositions of their army on their personal property and sense of home—for a brief moment before invasion and occupation again altered what was possible. Megowan's artists and musicians leaped into the war effort headfirst and found that artistic expression, too, was fully subordinated to state interests but that they could still turn their talents to productive use. Art was always political in the Soviet Union, but uniquely so in wartime. Sotvedt's newspaper-reading public fundamentally misunderstood reconnaissance, but for reasons that were not their fault; their assumptions must now be laboriously revised. Cookson-Hills's rapists were combatants whose war taught them that German civilians did not deserve humane treatment, even after the declaration of victory and the surrender of the Wehrmacht. The war spilled out into villages and homes and professions far from the front, drawing an increasingly large number of people into its horrors.

Part III: Cultural Transformation

The third part is the most diffuse and examines a phenomenon enabled by the shift in institutions toward a war footing and the militarization of civilians: cultural transformation, or the changing identities of individuals, nations, and societies because of the war. Above all, this part examines changing narratives. Participation did not merely change what soldiers and civilians did, but who they understood themselves to be, and how they explained to themselves and others what the war was about. Elena Friot leads this section with her examination of the shifting meaning of surrender after the US defeat to the Japanese at Bataan in spring 1942. Assembling an impressive array of sources, Friot shows how the US Army, journalists, politicians, and the families of those who fought and lost at Bataan explained to themselves what had happened and how that might still reflect well on the United States' cause and American soldiers, rhetorically snatching victory from the jaws of defeat.

Brian Masaru Hayashi's chapter returns to the idea of loyalty and patriotism, investigating the cases of Joe Koide and Kunsung Rie, men of Japanese and Korean descent who worked with the United States Office of Strategic Services (OSS) during the war. Suspected of divided loyalties (or of serving the Japanese Empire outright), Koide and Rie used their connections with and knowledge of east Asia to serve many causes: their own interests, the communist movement, and ultimately the war effort of the United States. Like the situation of Castro's mish kids, the OSS relied on these men because they had few better options, but neither was ever the double agent he was suspected of being. In fact, Hayashi demonstrates how each man grew into a deep sense of engagement with and loyalty to the American wartime project, raising important questions about the changing identities of immigrant communities in societies at war.

In contrast, Kevin Riehle's Soviet defectors grew out of their Soviet loyalties during the war. His chapter considers several dozen Soviet intelligence and state security officers who defected and assesses why they did so, how they were motivated by both wartime factors and their formative experiences in Soviet society. Such defectors were extremely unusual but nevertheless their decisions give us a window onto the enormous strain on the socialist project during wartime, a contrast to the view Megowan provides of those who came to embrace it in new ways. Rejecting an oversimple explanation that defectors were Nazi sympathizers, Riehle examines how and when these men abandoned the Soviet Union and what they expected in return. A common element in many of their accounts was the opportunity that imprisonment provided for a period of reflection and reassessment, rare during an overwhelming conflict. Some were Russian patriots and others anti-Stalin. One was part of a religious minority—a Muslim. All were forced to reassess during the war where their loyalties lay, and, when the opportunity arose, they changed sides.

The last chapter in the volume, Katrin Paehler's study of Hildegard Beetz, provocatively pulls the story into the postwar. Beetz wore many hats or, rather, changed her identity as circumstances required. She worked for both the Nazi SS and then in postwar Berlin for United States intelligence, becoming a "well-respected American asset." Beetz was not merely flexible in her political and state loyalties but fundamentally reinvented herself multiple times, using her personal contacts and position as a pretty young woman to escape the consequences of her wartime loyalties and ingratiate herself to new employers and a new political system. Paehler interrogates Beetz's CIA files to draw a portrait of her work across multiple intelligence regimes, raising larger questions about gender identity, the durability of Nazism, and whose agency mattered in wartime.

This last part ponders new narratives coming into being, fundamental reassessments of what was happening and why. Whether they were right or wrong, misleading or accurate is clearly less important than the persuasive power of the narratives and the consequences when those narratives were embraced—by the American public, OSS decision-makers, individual Soviet defectors in their cells, or Hildegard Beetz's woefully underprepared male handlers. The war did things to these people: Perhaps it provided them the opportunity to reassess who they were and what they were loyal to, perhaps it forced such reconsiderations in circumstances of danger and duress. Whether forced or chosen or something in between, these shifts in loyalty and identity had durable consequences.

Methodology and Sources

Although questions remain unanswered and topics and themes unexplored, today's historians of the Second World War have some advantages over predecessors in terms of sources and methodological approaches. The governments of the former belligerent states and their successors have slowly released official records and declassified sensitive documents pertaining to now completed (or abandoned) projects and deceased human subjects. Authors in this volume like Mallett, Paehler, Megowan, Riehle, and O'Sullivan benefit from access to official records that the first generations of those analyzing the war could not access. The end of the Cold War, too, gave scholars from different corners of the globe access to materials and historiography that had once been out of reach, and made it possible for them to collaborate and modify one another's assumptions in ways that were much more difficult before. The field is still integrating and expanding to include insights from the Soviet Union, China, and other wartime battle spaces in ways that are reshaping our thinking. Sotvedt's and Friot's close textual analyses of newspapers also demonstrate how even public records can be reexamined in the light of new questions and new methodologies. Despite the time that has passed since the end of the conflict, the source base has become both wider and deeper.

Our authors have profited from the methodological openness of the "new military history," borrowing techniques and approaches from cultural, diplomatic, and social history, and gender theory, genocide studies, and research on memory and trauma.[8] Jeff Rutherford's study of Wehrmacht behavior, for instance, interweaves operational history with questions of ideology and new work on the Holocaust and wartime ethnic cleansing. O'Sullivan's research focuses on how British intelligence personnel succeeded in their mission in wartime Iraq, successes that he explains with reference to what he calls "diversity" and "versatility"—modes of human adaptation. Castro's and Mallett's chapters describe in contrast the growing pains of organizations rising to challenges never before faced by their governments. Several authors in the volume experiment with narrowing the historical scope, such as Zinsou's hyper-local view of southeastern France and Cookson-Hills's dissection of the trial of two Canadian soldiers, while others expand to include new international, interagency, or alliance-wide perspectives. The question of original language source material is also crucial to the current generation of scholarship, which does not rely on translation and pursues sources wherever they might be valuable. This includes ego documents and the perspectives of those left out of early work, asking what the war looked like from the bottom up and the peripheries in. The problem of Hayashi's and Castro's subjects, of ignorance of the relevant languages with which to prosecute the war, is no longer the problem of the field. Material originally composed in English, German, French, Chinese, Japanese, and Russian undergirds the arguments presented here. Subjects like Katrin Paehler's young female spy, Megowan's artists in uniform, Cookson-Hills's Canadian infantrymen, and Zinsou's French provincials have only begun to be conceptualized as wartime agents. *Shots in the Dark* demonstrates the opportunity of considering the widest possible swath of the human population during wartime, to assess how the war changed their lives, and how their actions shaped the war.

The goal of this volume is simultaneously to present the intellectual work done across multiple scholarly workshops of the Second World War Research Group North America and to demonstrate the value of continuing to think about this conflict thematically, bringing together geographies and methodologies often kept apart by the difficulties of researching such a broad-ranging topic as the war. Some of these chapters revise consensus or put myths to rest, others shine light on spaces unexamined by their predecessors; most of our authors raise questions that we cannot yet answer fully. Collaboration helps us refine research questions, and even tentative answers advance our knowledge and animate future projects. The hope is that these chapters encourage this conversation to continue and enable us to ask new and better questions about the war, what we can do with the knowledge we already have, and how we can continue to learn what we did not know and could not appreciate before.

Notes

1. For some of this sort of reflection, see, for example, Mark A. Stoler, "The Second World War in US History and Memory," *Diplomatic History* 25, no. 3 (Summer 2001): 383–92.

2. An excellent example: Williamson Murray, *Military Adaptation in War: With Fear of Change* (Cambridge: Cambridge University Press, 2011), which devotes three crucial chapters to Second World War cases.

3. Adrian O'Sullivan is well known among intelligence historians as an expert on World War II in Iran and Iraq. His books *Nazi Secret Warfare in Occupied Persia (Iran): The Failure of German Intelligence Services, 1939–1945* (Basingstoke: Palgrave Macmillan, 2014); and *Espionage and Counterintelligence in Occupied Persia (Iran): The Success of the Allied Secret Services, 1941–45* (New York: Springer, 2015) are the key books on the topic. Since the publication of those two earlier volumes, O'Sullivan has turned his focus to Iraq, which is featured in this volume.

4. Cf. Christopher R. Browning, *The Origins of the Final Solution: The Evolution of Nazi Jewish Policy, September 1939–March 1942* (Lincoln: University of Nebraska Press/The United States Holocaust Memorial Museum, 2007); Geoffrey Megargee, *War of Annihilation: Combat and Genocide on the Eastern Front, 1941* (Lanham, MD: Rowman & Littlefield, 2007), and Stephen G. Fritz, *Ostkrieg: Hitler's War of Extermination in the East* (Lexington: University Press of Kentucky, 2015).

5. Cf. Richard Overy, *Why the Allies Won* (New York: W. W. Norton, 1997); and Niall Barr, *Eisenhower's Armies* (Cambridge: Pegasus Books, 2015).

6. Cf. Marc Bloch, *Strange Defeat: A Statement of Evidence Written in 1940* (New York: W. W. Norton, 1968); Julian Jackson, *France: The Dark Years, 1940–1944* (New York: Oxford University Press, 2001); and Robert Forczyk, *Case Red: The Collapse of France* (Oxford: Osprey, 2017).

7. J. Robert Lilly, *Taken by Force: Rape and American GIs in Europe during World War II* (London: Palgrave Macmillan, 2007); and Mary Louise Roberts, *What Soldiers Do: Sex and the American GI in World War II France* (Chicago: University of Chicago Press, 2013).

8. Robert M. Citino, "Military Histories Old and New: A Reintroduction," *American Historical Review* 112, no. 4 (October 2007): 1070–90.

Part I
Institutional Adaptation

1

The Dixie Mission(aries)
The Protestant Roots of US Intelligence Officers in Wartime China

Sara B. Castro

US Foreign Service officer John S. Service, who asked everyone he met to call him "Jack," worked as a political officer at the US Embassy in China for nearly a decade before the United States became involved in World War II. Service was born in China in 1909 to American Protestant missionary parents who directed the YMCA branch in Chengdu, a large city in China's far west province of Sichuan.[1] Chengdu was a city of just shy of a million residents when Service lived there, and it had a reputation for sophistication and for its teahouses, where residents would gather to discuss the news and play board games.[2] Americans and Europeans in China before World War II nevertheless considered Chengdu to be a remote location. Few foreigners except Protestant missionaries settled there. Growing up in Chengdu, Service became fluent in several Chinese dialects. His family moved to northern California in the 1920s, and he completed high school and college in the United States. After his graduation from Oberlin College in 1927, he entered the Foreign Service and spent the next two decades, through the Second World War, as a US diplomat in China.[3]

Service was a typical example of what became known as a "mish kid"—the offspring of American Protestant missionaries who grew up abroad in the first decades of the twentieth century and then entered public service or became public intellectuals in the 1930s and 1940s. Pearl Buck and Henry Luce were part of this demographic and became famous writers and public intellectuals. Many lesser-known mish kids like Service worked for the US government. The largest cohort of Americans who had experienced cultural immersion in mainland China in the decades prior to World War II were mish kids like Service, and his career path in diplomacy was common.

Mish kids were particularly essential in the staff of Gen. Joseph "Vinegar Joe" Stilwell, whom President Roosevelt dispatched to China shortly after the attack on Pearl Harbor in 1941. Stilwell went to China's wartime capital, Chongqing, to serve as head of the China-Burma-India (CBI) Theater and aide to Chiang Kai-shek, then president of China.[4] Stilwell staffed his office with as many Americans as he could find who had expertise on Chinese language and culture. Stilwell's need for officials with deep cultural and linguistic expertise was hardly unique for US military leaders serving around the world in 1941, but it made him a logical recruiter of mish kids who were the only cohort of Americans who already had these skills.

As the United States assumed a role in the Second World War, the expanding US diplomatic, military, and intelligence organizations required personnel who could quickly be deployed abroad. US government officials needed linguistic and cultural fluency in parts of the world that were remote and foreign to most Americans. Mish kids like Service filled this need, but their collective characteristics and values inflected US diplomatic and intelligence work during World War II in ways that historians are only beginning to recognize. Children in missionary families in the late nineteenth and early twentieth centuries lived abroad with their parents and often absorbed their parents' religious, moral, and social values as well as deep knowledge of the places where they lived, including linguistic capabilities. Patriotism and American-style liberal values that respected democracy, citizenship, independence, and self-determination became intertwined with Protestant messages, as did views that rejected autocracy, corruption, or the violation of certain human rights.[5] When they came of age, mish kids carried these values into their work, even as their generation moved away from explicitly religious proselytizing. These political values made jobs in diplomacy and foreign intelligence a natural draw for mish kids like Service.

A growing body of scholarship has demonstrated that the mish kid cohort subtly shaped US foreign policy and intelligence operations during the war.[6] These findings illuminate an episode in US-China relations that has puzzled historians for decades: the US Army Observer Group to Yan'an, the so-called Dixie Mission, in which at least three mish kids played an influential role as the first US officials to have sustained contact with the leaders of the Chinese Communist Party (CCP).[7]

The US Army Observer Group to Yan'an initially dispatched a cohort of eighteen US military officers, diplomats, and intelligence officials to the CCP headquarters in rural north China in July 1944. China's central government at the time, under the leadership of Chiang Kai-shek and the Nationalist Party, considered the CCP to be a disruptive opposition party that threatened the ability of the relatively new national republican government to rule China. The Nationalist Party maintained a shaky agreement with the CCP leaders in the early 1940s to cooperate in the fight against Japanese occupation, but Chiang and other Nationalist leaders had attempted to eliminate the CCP in the prior decade, pushing them on the so-called Long March across China to Yan'an. Given the location of the US Observer Group in what the Nationalist Chinese government had declared to be a rebel area, the observer group was known colloquially as the "Dixie Mission," in a loose reference to the US Civil War. The US Army maintained some presence at the Yan'an base until March 1947, when US-led efforts to mediate domestic political conflict between Nationalist and CCP leaders failed.[8] The mission served as a base for observation, intelligence operations, and as a potential incubator for collaboration with the Chinese communists against Japanese troops.

Three mish kids strongly influenced the establishment and initial trajectory of the Dixie Mission. Jack Service was among the first to deploy to Dixie, and at least one other official in the initial cohort was a mish kid: Charles Stelle of the Office of Strategic Services (OSS), an intelligence officer operating on behalf of the Research and Analysis division.[9] Another mish kid, Foreign Service Officer John Paton Davies Jr., conceived of the observer group with Service and was instrumental in its operations though he never permanently deployed to Yan'an.

Davies began working for Stilwell's staff in 1942 after Stilwell requested support from the State Department. Service arrived on the staff a bit later than Davies, in 1943 (along with Raymond Ludden and John Emmerson, who were not mish kids).[10] Davies was born to American missionary parents in 1908, one year before Service. Like Service, Davies embraced US citizenship and considered himself American even though he was born in a remote part of China. Davies's family served in the China Inland Mission in Sichuan Province. The China Inland Mission, a Presbyterian ministry mostly run by British missionaries, was decidedly more politically conservative than YMCA missions and other educational or medical missions elsewhere, according to David A. Hollinger.[11] Davies was educated both in the United States and China, and he graduated from Columbia University in 1931 before he joined the Foreign Service. He began his diplomatic career in China. After the attack on Pearl Harbor, Davies served as a political attaché to Stilwell's CBI command from 1942 to 1944. During the early years of CBI, Davies served in India and Kunming, a city in southwestern China, before he moved to Chongqing, where Chiang Kai-shek and the Chinese central government had relocated after Japan's occupation of the eastern provinces.[12]

In working with Davies and Service, Stilwell found that mish kids tended to have similar skills for working in China as the military officers he had trained. Because proficiency in Chinese language was a requirement for most jobs on Stilwell's CBI staff, most CBI officials serving Stilwell had either grown up in China as mish kids or had been assigned to serve with the US military, such as in the China-based Fifteenth Infantry Regiment of the US Army, where Stilwell himself had served.[13] Stilwell served in China for years, and he was the US military attaché from 1935 to 1939.[14] Officers in the Fifteenth participated in a US Army-run language immersion training program to learn Chinese.[15] The Army colonel selected to lead the Dixie Mission, Col. David Barrett, had become fluent in Chinese in an early immersion program while serving in the Fifteenth. CCP leaders years later remembered Barrett for his excellent Chinese, including his frequent use of classical Chinese literary references and idioms.[16]

Officers from the Fifteenth like Barrett had good Chinese, but they were too few to meet the expanding needs of CBI generals for China experts, which made mish kids like Service, Stelle, and Davies desirable hires. The US government's hiring needs were far too urgent to train the entire staff in Chinese language; recruiters preferred to hire American citizens who were already familiar with remote areas and could operate in foreign cities immediately. The pool of such individuals was shallow, especially for Chinese speakers, and mish kids were the majority of those available.

Before the 1930s, there were few other reasons besides missionary work for Americans to relocate to remote parts of the world, live and work there for extended periods, and develop deep knowledge about those areas. The numbers of Americans based in China from 1860 to 1930 most likely never exceeded a four-digit number. Americans in China in these decades fell into four professional cohorts: Christian missionaries, traders, diplomats and military personnel, and journalists. Christian missionaries were by far the largest group, and they were the most likely to live beyond China's major coastal cities. Many American expatriates in China sought to make their fortune in trade, but these entrepreneurs rarely learned to speak Chinese and often never left posh cantons in urban ports.[17] In the early decades of the twentieth century, the United States had a small military presence in China, designed to help protect the Open Door policy and American consular affairs in China. Journalists made up a fourth cohort of American expatriates in China, but they were relatively few.

Fortunately for the US government, jobs in the State Department, OSS, and CBI were attractive to mish kids, satisfying their need to represent their values in the world. Public service in US government agencies or the military forbade mish kids from formal proselytizing while holding federal jobs. However, relatively few of them followed their parents into such work.

Instead, their missionary family backgrounds frequently shaped foreign policy vocations. In the decades before World War II, the ideas that American Protestant missionaries held about morality, human rights, justice, and democracy became a platform for action abroad, attainable due to the global political upheavals in the 1930s and the outbreak of the Second World War. Historian Matthew Avery Sutton referred to the missionaries and their progeny as "an unofficial foreign service" in the late nineteenth and early twentieth centuries for their tendency to represent the United States and American values among communities of people far from North America.[18] Sutton demonstrated that the effect was a unique brand of cultural imperialism that eschewed force and armies but embraced specific missionary values. Before World War II, missionaries used empathy, conversation, and social welfare organizations to model what their religion meant to them, hoping to convince those around them to embrace their religious ideas.

Although their efforts to convert people in Asia, Africa, and the Middle East were often unsuccessful by quantitative measures, as was the case in China, American Protestant missionaries had a significant social impact. In China, Protestant missionaries established social welfare organizations from orphanages to hospitals to schools. These entities frequently met a need, providing services that the Chinese government at the time was unable to deliver.[19] Contact with these organizations offered Chinese people exposure to Protestant Christianity, which many disregarded, but also to other principles of American citizenship and cultural beliefs. It was these other values that mish kids, a generation younger than their missionary parents, carried into public service, including in the Dixie Mission.

The nuance with which Davies and Service understood Chinese politics was precisely the expertise the US government sought from them, but it also clashed with the talking points Chinese Nationalist leaders used to lobby American policymakers for aid and support. Service's and Davies's direct observations from the 1930s and early 1940s contrasted sharply with the sophisticated and urbane version of themselves that Chiang and his American-educated wife Song Mei-ling presented to the Roosevelt administration. In correspondence with FDR aide Harry Hopkins in 1943, Davies wrote: "The Generalissimo is probably the only Chinese who shares the popular American misconception that Chiang Kai-shek is China."[20] The contrast between the views of the tiny crew of China experts in the field and the image that Chiang and Guomindang elites projected abroad was striking. Dixie Mission reports challenged policymaker biases, but to no avail.

When Davies was working with him in 1943, Stilwell was frustrated with the Chinese central government's sluggish cooperation in the war against

Japan. Stilwell and Chiang disagreed on CBI strategy throughout 1943. Historians since have shown both men to be at least partially correct in their views of the other. Stilwell argued that Chinese military leaders were too risk averse to embrace his land-based plans to stop Japanese progress while Chiang argued that Stilwell's imperialist paternalism and attitude of superiority made him too eager to risk Chinese casualties.[21] An intelligence agreement between the US government and the Chinese central government that was part of the Sino-American Cooperative Organization (SACO) Treaty strictly bound US intelligence officials in China, and a US mission to Yan'an would violate the conditions. However, anecdotal reports of successful CCP guerrilla attacks on the Japanese in north China were irresistible to Stilwell's staff. Even though it was impossible to imagine shifting US allegiance from Chiang to the CCP, Stilwell wanted to know what CCP capabilities were. He was seeking any alternative that might break through the CBI stalemate in China and hurt Japan. Stilwell's frustrated staff wondered if CCP guerrilla fighters along the rear flanks of Japan's occupying troops had the potential to achieve real military progress against Japan.

Based on a seed idea from Davies, a vague plan to send Americans to CCP leaders and determine their capacity to fight Japan began to form in Stilwell's office. In spring 1943, Davies had a conversation with Zhou Enlai, a CCP leader who would eventually become the chief architect of foreign policy for the People's Republic and serve as a colleague of Mao Zedong for decades. Davies and Zhou discussed the possibility of expanding US intelligence in China by including CCP leaders, and Zhou offered space in Yan'an for Americans to observe CCP activities against the Japanese.[22]

In summer 1943, after Service arrived in Chongqing, Davies and Service began to seriously consider Zhou's invitation for a US mission to travel to Yan'an. They got Stelle and the OSS on board. Davies wrote a memo in December 1943 to Stilwell and State Department Headquarters pushing for a Yan'an mission.[23] Recognizing the lack of legitimate US intelligence on the CCP at the time, Davies wrote:

> In Communist China there is: (1) a base of military operations in and near Japan's largest military concentration and second largest industrial base, (2) perhaps the most abundant supply of intelligence on the Japanese enemy available to us anywhere, (3) the most cohesive, disciplined and aggressively anti-Japanese regime in China, (4) the greatest single challenge in China to the Chiang Kai-shek government, (5) the area which Russia will enter if it attacks Japan, and (6) the foundation for a rapprochement between a new China and the Soviet Union.[24]

Mission approval took six months after this memo was received in Washington, DC. President Roosevelt had to be convinced over the objections of Chiang Kai-shek throughout spring 1944. According to Stelle, Roosevelt sent a letter hand delivered by Vice President Henry Wallace to Chiang during the VP's June 1944 trip. The letter requested a mission characterized "in such terms that the Generalissimo found it impolite to refuse."[25] By late July 1944, the first members of the US Army Observers Mission were on their way to Yan'an.[26]

The initial objective of the Dixie Mission was to determine how the CCP leaders were mobilizing guerrillas to attack Japanese troops from behind their lines. To US observers at Yan'an, the CCP guerrillas presented a pathway to progress, fighting the Japanese in China and learning more about how to keep the fight going through intelligence collection. The first Dixie cohort produced nuanced but positive reports about CCP efforts that accurately reflected their observations of CCP capabilities but clashed with reports coming to US war planners in Washington, DC, from the Chinese central government (to the extent that headquarters considered the CCP at all). Dixie Mission members documented unique characteristics of the CCP approach to the fight against the occupying Japanese: the proximity of CCP guerrillas to Japanese front lines, the ability of CCP operatives to mount intelligence and sabotage operations from their rural positions, and the willingness of CCP leaders to cooperate with US officials. Over the summer of 1944, reports to CBI headquarters from Dixie grew more optimistic about developing joint intelligence and sabotage missions with CCP counterparts against Japanese troops in north China.[27] Once fully aired in Chongqing and Washington, DC, these plans faced vehement opposition from higher-ranking State Department, Army, and White House decision-makers who were suspicious of the CCP and feared the effects of such cooperation on the alliance the US had formed with Chiang Kai-shek.

For decades, scholars debated why Dixie Mission members produced a plan at odds with how US policymakers wished to proceed in China. US leaders and scholars alike attempted to come to terms with what happened during World War II, when US officials were aligned with China and providing aid and military training. Had they facilitated China's communist revolution and the establishment in 1949 of the People's Republic of China? In the process, policymakers demanded the declassification of most federal records that pertained to the Dixie Mission, which informed debates and are the primary source base behind this chapter, along with the memoirs and personal correspondence of Dixie Mission members.[28]

Many American observers in the late twentieth century saw China's turn to communism as a product of the failure of US diplomacy during World

War II. As a key location of communication between Chinese Communists and the US government, the Dixie Mission thus became a target of inquiry and critique.[29] Early investigations into Dixie Mission activities revealed a cordiality and level of cooperation between US officials in Yan'an and CCP leaders that made US policymakers in the 1950s deeply suspicious. The controversy put Service, Davies, and several initial Dixie Mission members in the crosshairs of loyalty investigations, with permanent career implications.[30] Historians of China in more recent years have convincingly argued against initial US-centric arguments based on improved access to Chinese sources and new theoretical practices for analyzing postcolonial global history.[31] This development defused the politicized controversy but failed to answer the question of why American officials selected for cultural expertise could yield intelligence and policy recommendations so different from those of their counterparts in rear areas.

Recent scholarship on the behavioral tendencies of mish kids in public service globally during World War II provides new historical context for considering this debate. The activities of the early Dixie Mission members suggest that missionary experiences and values influenced how those US officials viewed the CCP leaders and the actions they took in collaboration with their CCP hosts. Stelle, Service, and Davies approached the CCP leaders with open-mindedness and a willingness to collaborate that may have been encouraged by their missionary childhoods and experience living in China in the 1920s and 1930s. Moreover, these three men were instrumental in hiring the other members of the Dixie crew, and they sought other Americans who shared their attitudes.

Mish kids were used to living autonomously in remote areas, far from quick communications with other Americans. Their childhood experiences were a patchwork of adapting to and enduring unusual conditions, similar to what Second World War deployment to remote areas required of them. Yan'an was a dry and dusty township closer to where Japanese troop lines were than most other Chinese political outposts. Americans deployed on the Dixie Mission lived and worked like the CCP leaders in caves carved into the yellow loess hillsides. Yan'an was beyond the reach of railroads, and regular roads were often too muddy, snowy, or dusty for safe travel. Supply flights came only a few times a month from India over the Himalayas and across central China. In many ways, the Dixie Mission staff were on their own, and they formed a slightly distant community with their CCP hosts— just as the mish kids' parents had done in their missionary communities. Fluency in Chinese made it possible for the US officials to engage in sophisticated conversations with their hosts and learn the details of CCP military and ideological plans. These conversations were some of the very first of their kind between US officials and CCP leaders.

Conversely, the influence of missionary experience may have encouraged Dixie Mission leaders to retain optimism that the CCP leaders could be persuaded to emulate US-style political values and practices associated with democratic liberalism and Protestantism, which was unlikely—or at least quite uncertain—due to the commitment of CCP leaders to Marxist-Leninist ideological values and especially to anti-imperialism. The Dixie Mission case thus is important for understanding the complexity of the production of intelligence about the CCP during World War II, which ultimately shaped outcomes in the CBI theater as well as postwar diplomacy.

Findings of recent studies about mish kids in public service during World War II explain that members of the Dixie Mission may have been predisposed to form more charitable views of the Chinese Communist Party leaders than other Americans serving the US government. They may also have been more willing than American officials in rear areas to cooperate with the CCP on anti-Japanese military operations, even if these views were politically unpalatable in Washington, DC, in the 1940s. Hollinger has demonstrated how missionaries and their family members experienced what he has called "missionary cosmopolitanism," a lived experience of inclusion, exclusion, and identity that contributed to an impulse toward cross-cultural community building and empathy.[32] This cosmopolitanism coupled with the confidence mish kids felt operating with little direction from very remote areas made the cohort attractive to US government recruiters, but the cohort was ultimately misaligned with headquarters' interests. Mish kids brought the missionary cosmopolitanism that Hollinger described into US foreign policy careers, and Davies, Service, and Stelle brought it to Yan'an.

Opposition from Chiang Kai-shek, leader of China's Nationalist Party, US ally in World War II, instantly made the Dixie Mission controversial among American policymakers. The CCP was a Marxist-Leninist political party and revolutionary movement. Nationalist Party leaders considered the CCP to be a rebel group, responsible for challenges that were threatening China's shaky political unity. Under Chiang's leadership, the Nationalists had brutally repressed and isolated the CCP starting in 1927. Nationalist efforts eventually pushed the CCP members on the so-called Long March across China, which ended with the CCP establishing a base area in remote Yan'an. After the Japanese had succeeded with a brutal campaign of invasion of Beijing and Nanjing in 1937, Chiang Kai-shek had relocated the offices of China's central government from Nanjing to the steamy city of Chongqing in China's southwest Sichuan province, about 200 miles through the mountains from Chengdu, where Jack Service grew up. Facing increasing aggression from Japan in 1936, Chiang paused his anti-communist campaign for a grudging agreement to work together to expel the occupying Japanese from China. A tense stalemate between the two parties endured.

The Dixie Mission ran under US Army leadership, but it included officials from various agencies, including a group of OSS officers led by Stelle, who were there to collect intelligence on the capabilities of the CCP with an eye to future covert and unconventional operations. OSS had also encountered many of Stilwell's recruiting challenges for its China mission. President Roosevelt had created OSS to collect and analyze military information and conduct special operations not assigned to other agencies at the behest of its director, General William Donovan, who recognized that the US government lacked the intelligence capabilities the United Kingdom had, and the deficiency was hampering war efforts. OSS was a civilian organization, which Donovan believed necessary to attract new experts into US intelligence work, unlike previous operations which had been the exclusive domain of the US military.[33]

Mish kids also appealed to Donovan as recruits because he believed the US government needed more flexible and imaginative intelligence personnel than the military could provide to meet the expanding strategic intelligence requirements of World War II. Donovan once described the OSS as "an unusual experiment" designed "to determine whether a group of Americans constituting a cross-section of racial origins, abilities, temperaments, and talents could meet and risk an encounter with the long-established and well-trained enemy organizations."[34] One of Donovan's most celebrated ideas was to infuse "new blood" into government work, and he famously raided the Ivy League and top Wall Street firms for staff. In addition to borrowed military officers serving on rotation, Donovan recruited actors, lawyers, professors, and socialites to win the war. Women such as Julia Child and people from racial minority groups such as Ralph Bunche also worked for OSS during the war.[35]

These recruits did bring new ideas, but they did not always blend into remote, foreign areas. Sutton compared early OSS operatives abroad to "tourists who put ketchup on their tacos" instead of helping the new spy service "best exploit and manipulate" foreign cultures.[36] Once Donovan recognized the problem, he sought personnel who could assimilate—and contribute deep expertise on the foreign places about which America most needed information; this naturally led the OSS to hire mish kids, just as Stilwell and the State Department had.[37] Sutton has shown that while Donovan and others in OSS "did not plan or centrally coordinate their recruitment of missionaries," they ended up hiring from missionary families because of the skill set they sought for intelligence work.[38]

Charles Stelle is an example of a mish kid who became one of the OSS China officers, bringing his depth of understanding about China to assist the OSS. In 1943, Stelle applied to work in China. He had been serving in the OSS Far East Division from Washington, working on plans for the Psychological Warfare Subdivision. In a recommendation letter that was part of Stelle's application, supervisor C. F. Remer described the duties Stelle performed in Washington and his qualifications. According to Remer's memo, Stelle worked in a position that "requires a good reading knowledge of the Chinese and Japanese languages, residence in the Far East, and sufficient experience in research to enable the incumbent to plan such research for psychological warfare relating to Free and to occupied China."[39] Stelle's other qualifications included being "a trained historian who is competent to use both Chinese and Japanese sources in research," and that he had "traveled widely" in China and Japan. Stelle was off to Chongqing in May 1943.[40] He initially spent a few months in Chongqing headquarters contributing to OSS plans to assist CBI. Then, starting in July 1944, he served in the initial roster of Dixie Mission members.

Stelle's qualifications developed out of his experience as a mish kid in China. His family on both sides had been in China for decades. His relatives had performed such services as helping to create one of the first Chinese typewriters, establishing a famous school, the Lu He School, with one even serving as English language interpreter to the Qing Empress Dowager Cixi, in addition to the typical service-related functions of American Protestants in China.[41] Stelle's biography made him perfect for the work Donovan wanted OSS to do in China.

Serving under Col. David Barrett at Yan'an, Service and Stelle assumed positions of influence within the Dixie Mission. Service was the chief political officer for the cohort, negotiating directly with CCP Chairman Mao Zedong, Zhou Enlai, and the top leaders of the CCP military forces based nearby.[42] Stelle similarly influenced the other four OSS officials serving in Yan'an. Stelle became a dominant voice and a key interlocutor between the Yan'an mission and OSS China officers in rear areas. Stelle also influenced some of the other non-OSS Dixie crew with technical roles in Army intelligence, such as radio operators.

The Dixie Mission members were among the first US government officials to have face-to-face contact with CCP leaders. Service, Stelle, and Davies all approached this responsibility with the benefit of fluency in Chinese and the experience of years living in China. These men had observed and closely followed the rise of the Guomindang in Republican China and the fate of the CCP in domestic newspapers. They had also been in China during the Japanese invasion. Service, Stelle, and Davies had learned a great deal about CCP leaders through news reports and gossip before they had personal contact with any of them. All three were sophisticated observers of Chinese politics in the Republican era.

With the benefit of the most recent historical scholarship on World War II in China, the influence of missionary worldviews on Dixie Mission reports is apparent. On the one hand, the reports reveal a depth of understanding and personalized experience of Chinese domestic politics that is quite rare in other US government records from the time, including a recognition of CCP capabilities. On the other hand, Dixie Mission reports villainized Chiang Kai-shek as an obstacle to liberal values they sought to establish in China. Recent studies offer a more balanced view of Chiang as well as Nationalist interests and capabilities, recognizing that Chinese leaders from all parties resented Allied attempts to reshape their governments.[43] Stilwell and the Dixie Mission officials may have had good intentions, but they were still outsiders with an agenda, and their objectives warped their understanding.

Through the lens of Sutton's missionary cosmopolitanism, they perceived Chiang Kai-shek and the Nationalist Party as unable to establish a centralized, legitimate government that unified the people of China. This incapacity preceded the Japanese invasion but persisted and worsened through it, they argued. For example, in their government reports, Davies, Service, and Stelle regularly mentioned having observed corruption in the Chinese central government before and during the Japanese occupation. In one report, Davies explained of Chiang Kai-shek: "The Communists are his principal foe, for in the long run it is they and not the Japanese who challenge his supremacy in China. They are the next in line of succession. The Generalissimo realizes that if he accedes to the Communist terms for a coalition government, they will sooner or later dispossess him and his Kuomintang of power."[44] This report proved prescient when the CCP and Guomindang descended into civil war after the Japanese surrender: The Dixie Mission was blinkered, but not wrong.

Service had documented many critiques of Chiang and Guomindang governance in the early 1940s before he was deployed to Yan'an. He observed that urban elites were frustrated with Chiang's policies in 1943 and 1944. One June 1943 report described widespread urban resentment of what Service called "censorship and cultural control by the Kuomintang."[45] Service also met repeatedly with Sun Yat-sen's widow in spring 1944, who critiqued the Guomindang blockade of CCP areas, which prevented food and medicine from reaching people and which she found cruel and inhumane.[46]

When they finally observed CCP operations after the Dixie Mission arrived in Yan'an in summer 1944, Service, Davies, and Stelle all recognized CCP guerrillas' progress against their shared Japanese enemy. The Dixie Mission members shared the CCP dedication to pushing Japan out of China by any means, and they recognized CCP success in sabotage, information warfare, and operations behind enemy lines. As Service noted, "Whether one liked the Communists or not they were doing a better job than the Kuomintang."[47] He separately reported that "the Communists have unquestionably been successful in establishing bases of resistance behind the Japanese lines, especially in north China, and they have in this way prevented large areas from coming under complete enemy domination."[48] He acknowledged some limitations: "Recent Chinese Communist claims of military achievements against Japan seem to have been exaggerated, and it may be that they have exaggerated their military potentialities." The report explained that the CCP avoided direct confrontation with the Japanese and had exacted only minor damage in seven years—despite surprising the American observers with their achievements.

To the Americans at Yan'an, the CCP guerrillas demonstrated serious progress fighting the Japanese in China and in learning more about how to keep the fight going through intelligence collection. Through the end of 1944, Service, Stelle, and Davies produced candid assessments of CCP capabilities and interests. This entailed recognizing CCP shortcomings but also admitting the party's successes when it was unpopular for the US government to do so. In formerly classified correspondence, Stelle argued for increasing American cooperation with CCP guerrillas. "We are completely confident that it will be possible to secure thorough cooperation from the Chinese Communists for OSS operations," Stelle and his OSS colleague John Colling wrote in an internal memo to OSS Headquarters in August 1944. "We cannot too highly stress the potentialities of this center. We are sure that the only limits on the cooperation we can secure from the local Chinese authorities and on the results that can be attained will be the amount of personnel and equipment that we are prepared to invest and able to transport."[49] This assessment was accurate and appropriately documented, but it also reflected naïveté about the audience of the reports from Yan'an, within the theater and in the rest of the US government.

In fact, initial Dixie Mission reports were unconvincing and upsetting to their audience in the rear areas, which included many US officials who were not subject matter experts on China and who were trying to weigh the incongruence of the Dixie Mission reports with the conflicting information coming from China's central government. As Dixie Mission members reported promising interactions with the CCP in the summer of 1944, arguments between Stilwell and Chiang boiled over. President Roosevelt, fearing the discord would sabotage the alliance, replaced Stilwell with General Albert C. Wedemeyer, even though his expertise was on Germany rather than China. Wartime stress and the Stilwell drama had also wearied the long-serving US Ambassador to China Clarence Gauss, who resigned in November 1944. Roosevelt replaced Gauss with Patrick Hurley, a brash Oklahoman who knew little about China. Hurley made a spectacle of himself during his November 1944 tour of Yan'an. He offended Mao Zedong so deeply that, when speaking to Dixie Mission members, Mao referred to Hurley as a "turtle's egg," a serious and vulgar insult in Chinese.[50] Dixie Mission reporting nuance entirely missed Wedemeyer and Hurley, who saw instead disloyalty. Within three months, the general and the ambassador replaced almost all Dixie Mission staff with US officials who had no connection to China and who were not mish kids.

Two problems sourced in missionary experience contributed to the disconnect between headquarters and the Dixie Mission observations: how the Dixie Mission members viewed CCP leaders, influenced by Stelle, Davies, and Service, and the confidence Dixie Mission members had operating autonomously in the foreign and remote location of Yan'an.

The mish kids present in the Dixie Mission contributed a shared set of moral and ethical values, including patriotism, nationalism, rejection of corruption, and a firmly held belief that they could lead the rest of the world to liberalism if they explained and modeled it with sufficient clarity. Sutton and Hollinger documented multiple examples of this attitude among missionaries and their progeny.[51] Stelle, Davies, and Service all respected CCP leadership efforts to improve the lives of Chinese peasants and treat Japanese POWs well. After the war, more evidence emerged of American willingness to engage CCP leaders in the expectation that it would eventually lead to a CCP emulation of US politics. Years after Dixie, the former officials articulated this assumption about American exceptionalism as so ingrained that they rarely even discussed it in Yan'an; they all just saw things that way. A congressional hearing decades after the Dixie Mission itself captures this paternalistic form of missionary cosmopolitanism. On 7–8 February 1972, a few days before President Nixon's historic trip to the People's Republic of China, the US Senate Foreign Relations Committee hosted John Service and Raymond Ludden, another former foreign service officer, to testify in hearings on the state of US relations with China. Service and his former

Foreign Service colleague Ludden had also been detailed to CBI under Stilwell and were part of the initial group of Americans in Yan'an for the Dixie Mission. Committee Chair Senator William J. Fulbright sought the opinions of Service and Ludden, who had deep personal experience in China and were some of the only Americans who had met Mao Zedong and other Chinese Communist Party leaders.

Toward the end of the two-day hearings, Ludden mentioned the problem of Americans trying to "make the world in their own image," which raised a question for Fulbright. He asked Service to explain why Americans are like this. Service said:

> Well, it is partly the puritan ethic. It is our Christian desire to improve and change the world. It is partly our power, our successes, our affluence. It is a conviction that we have the best country and the best society, and therefore, everyone should want to be like us, I suppose. It is the arrogance of power or whatever the phrase is.[52]

This exchange reveals an important irony of the US government's reliance on Americans who developed international expertise through Protestant missionary activity. Although, as Hollinger and Sutton have demonstrated, these children of missionaries did understand China better than anyone else in the United States, their understanding of and interest in China also had a particular agenda. This ultimately hampered their mission to explain the CCP to US diplomats, policymakers, and military leaders who were making short-term plans for the Second World War. Their messages missed their audience. In his 2012 autobiography, Davies took Service's idea a step further. He quoted his own 1943 diary entry:

> We have the weapons, which makes the Chinese willing to string along with us much further than they ordinarily would. We have our ideas of how they should be used and our ideas of command and organization. We want to impose them on the Chinese because we consider the Chinese inefficient and incompetent.[53]

A second aspect of mish kid influence crucial to the failure of the Dixie Mission was, ironically, their willingness to adapt and adjust to all kinds of conditions. The Dixie Mission officials were predisposed to favorable views of CCP leaders and cooperation plans that other Americans found shocking and unacceptable. Dixie Mission members had to cope with a remote duty location plagued with logistical problems and poor living conditions, but mish kids were used to this. Sutton's research documented a willingness for Protestant missionaries in China and Africa, who operated far from assistance, to develop ad hoc solutions to problems. One former missionary who later worked for OSS and became a career intelligence officer, Stanley Lovell, explained that "we had to play it by ear or not at all. . . . Like a pianist, improvising his melodies and rhythms, the chords had to be found and the dissonances corrected or ignored. No one could tell us how to do our job."[54] The first cohort of American officers at Yan'an took the same approach, knowing their overall mission—defeat the Japanese and win the war—and that no assistance was coming. The success of the Dixie Mission in making progress toward fighting Japan would depend on the efforts of the individual officers and their ability to forge ties with their CCP hosts. They did what they felt they should, with little regard for oversight from rear areas.

Not all the Dixie Mission members were mish kids, but the mish kid members (Stelle and Service, with Davies supporting from a distance) set the tone. The other eighteen members of the first cohort were mostly military officers or OSS officers who also previously had endured difficult conditions.[55] Hollinger's research also documented the reaction of missionaries to operating far from home, immersed in a foreign culture. He explained that missionaries, "experienced to a higher degree and within a broader context than most Americans the tension between inclusion and identity, between an impulse to bring everyone together and a need to make a community viable by defining it in some particular set of terms."[56] Hollinger was describing Protestant missionaries in the decades before World War II, but this statement applies to the Dixie Mission officials. They bonded with CCP leaders over the shared commitment to defeating the Japanese by whatever means. They formed a community through this shared commitment while CBI headquarters and its politics were far away.

The 1944 Dixie Mission offers an important example of the ways Americans from missionary families influenced the existence, scope, actions, and outcome of World War II operations, particularly in areas of the world that were foreign to US officials and more broadly of how prewar initiatives and institutions, even ones that seem very distant from military strategy, shaped what was possible for the US government to achieve during the war. The US government desperately needed the skills and cultural understanding of China that the mish kids brought into public service during the war. The Dixie Mission demonstrates that American Protestant missionary characteristics made their adult children appealing hires for the State Department and OSS. Moreover, attitudes about service, morality, and patriotism common to mish kids encouraged their willingness to improvise intelligence tradecraft and cooperate with foreign allies, including the Chinese Communists, for the sake of achieving the war's important ends. But mish kids also brought their own attitudes of cultural and spiritual superiority into their work and a desire to reform the world in an American image, which CCP counterparts found unappealing. CCP leaders experienced their first sustained exposure to US officials during the first months of the Dixie Mission. Mish kids present in this group set a tone for US-CCP relations through the war and for years to come. From this experience, CCP leaders inferred that all US officials sought to bring Chinese people into alignment with the mish kids' Protestant values. Mish kid influence in Yan'an may thus have complicated US diplomatic attempts to resolve the outbreak of civil war in China.

Notes

1. E. J. Kahn, *The China Hands: American Foreign Service Officers and What Befell Them* (New York: Viking Press, 1972), 58–64.

2. Kristin Stapleton, *Fact in Fiction: 1920s China and Ba Jin's Family* (Palo Alto, CA: Stanford University Press, 2016, 123). Di Wang, *The Teahouse: Small Business, Everyday Culture, and Public Politics in Chengdu, 1900–1950* (Palo Alto, CA: Stanford University Press, 2008), 23.

3. Joseph W. Esherick, ed., *Lost Chance in China: The World War II Despatches of John S. Service* (New York: Random House, 1974), xiii–xxiii.

4. A voluminous body of work exists on China's experience in the Second World War. This chapter focuses narrowly on the experience of American mish kids, rather than their Chinese counterparts in the CCP or National Party. For further works on Chinese domestic politics under Chiang Kai-shek, see Jay Taylor, *The Generalissimo: Chiang Kai-shek and the Struggle for Modern China* (Cambridge, MA: Belknap Press/Harvard University Press, 2009); and Grace C. Huang, *Chiang Kai-shek's Politics of Shame: Leadership, Legacy, and National Identity in China* (Cambridge, MA: Harvard University Asia Center, 2021).

5. For a variation of this story in which those of east Asian descent espoused American values for different reasons during the war, see Brian Hayashi's chapter 10 in this volume.

6. Several studies have analyzed the social history and public influence of American Protestant missionaries broadly, including examples from those who served in the Middle East, Africa, and Asia. Of these, three had the greatest influence on this chapter: David A. Hollinger, *Protestants Abroad: How Missionaries Tried to Change the World but Changed America* (Princeton, NJ: Princeton University Press, 2017); Matthew Avery Sutton, *Double Crossed: The Missionaries Who Spied for the United States during the Second World War* (New York: Basic Books, 2019), and Michael Graziano, *Errand into the Wilderness of Mirrors: Religion and the History of the CIA* (Chicago: University

of Chicago Press, 2021). These books refer to examples from China but focus on global trends.

7. See Adrian O'Sullivan's chapter 2 in this volume for a contrasting story of intelligence success where operatives and headquarters shared the same agenda, unlike the mish kids and US Army headquarters.

8. After 1947, full conventional battles between Nationalists and the CCP erupted. The civil war never achieved a formal end, but CCP leaders defeated the Nationalists in battles between 1947 and 1949. They established the People's Republic of China in October 1949.

9. Declassified official records about the Dixie Mission effectively document what the mission was doing, but many of the people who staffed it were of low rank, and little biographical information about them has been preserved to confidently determine their childhood experiences.

10. Yu Maochun, *OSS in China: Prelude to Cold War* (Annapolis, MD: Naval Institute Press, 1996), 107. Ludden was a career diplomat who had learned Chinese through State Department training, and Emmerson had lived in China and Japan as a journalist.

11. Hollinger, *Protestants Abroad*, 13–14.

12. Adam Bernstein, "China Expert John P. Davies Dies, Pushed Out during McCarthy Era," *Washington Post*, December 24, 1999, p. B06.

13. For further information on the 15th Infantry and US troops in China, see Alfred Emile Cornebise, *The United States Army in China, 1900–1938: A History of the 9th, 14th, 15th and 31st Regiments in the East* (Jefferson, NC: McFarland, 2015); and Edward M. Coffman, *The Regulars: The American Army, 1898–1941* (Cambridge, MA: Belknap Press of Harvard University Press, 2004).

14. Barbara Tuchman thoroughly documented Stilwell's career in *Stilwell and the American Experience in China, 1911–45* (New York: Macmillan, 1971), chaps. 5–8.

15. For further work on the social history of China SMEs in World War II, see Sara B. Castro, *Mission to Mao: American Intelligence and the Chinese Communists in World War II* (Washington, DC: Georgetown University Press, 2024).

16. John N. Hart, *The Making of an Army "Old China Hand": A Memoir of Colonel David D. Barrett* (Berkeley: University of California, Berkeley Institute of East Asian Studies, Center for China Studies, 1985), 8.

17. For further information on American traders in China before World War II, see James C. Thomson Jr. et al., *Sentimental Imperialists: The American Experience in East Asia* (New York: Harper & Row, 1981).

18. Sutton, *Double Crossed*, 5.

19. For further information on the work of American Protestant missionaries in China and its results, see, for example, Paul A. Varg, *Missionaries, Chinese, and Diplomats: The American Protestant Missionary Movement in China, 1890–1952* (Princeton, NJ: Princeton University Press, 1958); and Alvyn Austin, *China's*

Millions: The China Inland Mission and Late Qing Society, 1832–1905 (Grand Rapids, MI: William B. Eerdmans, 2007).

20. Letter from John Davies to Harry Hopkins, quoted in Kahn, *The China Hands*, 102.

21. Military and diplomatic historians have used the personal papers of both Stilwell and Chiang as well as the papers of their staff and declassified US government documents from the Army and OSS to describe the volatile relationship between Stilwell and Chiang. Studies in the last decade have found recalcitrant biases on both sides of this relationship that prevented productive cooperation. For further information, see Hans van de Ven, *China at War: Triumph and Tragedy in the Emergence of the New China* (Cambridge, MA: Harvard University Press, 2018); Chi Hsi-sheng, *The Much Troubled Alliance: US-China Military Cooperation during the Pacific War, 1941–1945* (Singapore: World Scientific Press, 2016), and Hans van de Ven et al., eds., *Negotiating China's Destiny in World War II* (Palo Alto, CA: Stanford University Press, 2015).

22. Yu Maochun, *OSS in China*, 107.

23. "Memorandum by the Second Secretary of Embassy in China (Davies) regarding Observers' Mission to North China," *Foreign Relations of the United States [FRUS], Diplomatic Papers, China, 1944*, 305–6. "Yenan" uses an older form of romanization to render the city name 延安, which is rendered "Yan'an" in the pinyin romanization system in official use in mainland China today. Stelle had reported to OSS headquarters on conversations he and Davies had in Chongqing about the need for the Dixie Mission. See "Memo from Spencer to Langer re: Pallisades," June 4, 1944, National Archives and Records Administration, RG 226, entry NM-5453, box 4.

24. Davies memo, *FRUS, China, 1944*, 305–6.

25. "Interim Report on Mission to Yenan" from Charles Stelle to Joseph Spencer, October 27, 1944. US National Archives and Records Administration (NARA) RG226 (OSS Files), entry NM-54 53, box 4 OSS Correspondence with Outposts, 1942–1946.

26. For further information on the decision to create the Dixie Mission, see the official correspondence that the US Department of State released in *FRUS, Diplomatic Papers, China 1944*, 6–7, 299–400. Historian Michael Schaller has also described the negotiations in detail in *The US Crusade in China, 1938–1945* (New York: Columbia University Press, 1979), 147–75.

27. For example, "Interim Report on Mission to Yenan" from Charles Stelle to Joseph Spencer, 27 October 1944. US National Archives and Records Administration (NARA) RG226 (OSS Files), entry NM-54 53, box 4 OSS Correspondence with Outposts, 1942–1946.

28. This chapter focuses on US officials and policymakers, and the primary source base thus is predominately US government documents rather than sources from Chinese archives or anthologies.

29. The first wave of scholars on the Dixie Mission was addressing the question of the so-called "loss of China" by the United States. Important studies in this vein included Herbert Feis, *The China Tangle: The American Effort in China from Pearl Harbor to the Marshall Mission* (Princeton, NJ: Princeton University Press, 1953), which won the Pulitzer Prize, and Charles Romanus and Riley Sunderland, *United States Army in World War II: China, Burma, India Theater* (Washington, DC: Office of Chief of Army, US Defense Department, 1953). In the 1970s, after the declassification of many OSS documents, later historians argued that the United States had lost a chance to engage the Chinese Communist Party and draw it away from the Soviets. An emblematic work in this historiography was Barbara Tuchman, *Stilwell and the American Experience in China, 1911–1945* (New York: Macmillan, 1970).

30. For example, two of the mish kids here faced loyalty hearings. John Service was arrested for allegedly leaking sensitive government files to a liberal publication in 1945. He spent the following decade trying to clear his name (charges were eventually dropped). John Davies, another Foreign Service officer who served General Stilwell and the Dixie Mission, faced nine loyalty investigations between 1948 and 1954.

31. During the 1990s, when historians began combining US records with records from China and a new awareness of decolonization issues, historians successfully argued that the contentious historiography about US-China relations grossly overestimated US agency in Chinese politics. Two studies claiming this include Chen Jian, "The Myth of America's 'Lost Chance' in China: A Chinese Perspective in Light of New Evidence," *Diplomatic History* 21, no. 1 (Winter 1997): 77–86; and Michael M. Sheng, "Chinese Communist Policy toward the United States and the Myth of the 'Lost Chance,'" 1948–1950," *Modern Asian Studies* 28, no. 3 (July 1994): 475–502. These studies settled initial debates, and few scholars have revisited Dixie Mission history since.

32. Hollinger, *Protestants Abroad*, 22–23.

33. However, due to the nature of the work, the foreign deployments, and the skills required, OSS institutionally looked more like an ad hoc paramilitary organization than a typical executive branch civilian agency.

34. Charles Pinck, "Remembering the Work of the OSS," *The Hill* blog, December 16, 2013, accessed on December 1, 2014.

35. See chapter 10 in this volume on Asian Americans recruited by the OSS, and Katrin Paehler's chapter 12 in this volume on the complexities of women's work in wartime intelligence agencies.

36. Sutton, *Double Crossed*, 28.

37. Sutton, *Double Crossed*, 27–29.

38. Sutton, *Double Crossed*, 28–29

39. Memo from C. F. Remer, "Candidates for Commissions—Far East Division, Description of the Position Now Held by Mr. Charles C. Stelle," 19

February 1943, US National Archives and Records Administration (NARA) RG226 (OSS Files), entry 224, box 743, OSS Personnel Files, 1941–1945.

40. Memo from C. F. Remer to Dr. William Langer, 15 May 1943, US National Archives and Records Administration (NARA) RG226 (OSS Files), entry 224, box 743, OSS Personnel Files, 1941–1945. In this memo, Remer was appealing to Langer to adjust Stelle's rank. R&A had mistakenly commissioned Stelle as a First Lieutenant, but his experience and qualifications entitled him to a higher rank with better pay and benefits.

41. Author's personal correspondence with son of Charles Stelle, 2021–2022. For further information on the typewriter designed by Devello Zelotes Sheffield, see Jing Tsu, *Kingdom of Characters: The Language Revolution That Made China Modern* (New York: Riverhead Books, 2022).

42. See Esherick, ed., *Lost Chance in China,* Castro, *Mission to Mao,* and Carolle J. Carter, *Mission to Yenan: American Liaison with the Chinese Communists, 1944–1947* (Lexington: University Press of Kentucky, 1997) for further details. Personal papers of service are preserved at University of California, Berkeley. NARA Record Group 226, OSS Files, preserves the records of OSS members of the Dixie Mission, including Stelle, and their correspondence with headquarters.

43. With limited access to Chinese sources, recent historical studies have revised initial Western views of Chinese experience in World War II. For further information, see, for example, Hans van de Ven, *War and Nationalism in China: 1925–1945* (Abington: Routledge, 2003); and *China at War* (Cambridge, MA: Harvard University Press, 2018); Ch'i Hsi-sheng, *The Much Troubled Alliance* (2015); Zach Fredman, *The Tormented Alliance: American Servicemen and the Occupation of China, 1941–1949* (Chapel Hill: University of North Carolina Press, 2022); and Frederic Wakeman Jr., *Spymaster: Dai Li and the Chinese Secret Service* (Berkeley: University of California Press, 2003).

44. John P. Davies, "The Generalissimo's Dilemmas," December 9, 1944, US National Archives and Records Administration (NARA) RG226 (OSS Files), entry 148, box 7, folder 104.

45. Esherick, ed., *Lost Chance in China,* 104–5.

46. Service, *Lost Chance in China,* 108–11.

47. Kahn, *The China Hands,* 101.

48. John Service report, No. 4, "Kuomintang and Japanese Views of Effectiveness of Communist Forces," September 1944, *FRUS, Diplomatic Reports, China, 1944,* 533–34.

49. Memo to Hall and Peers from Stelle and Colling re: Possible OSS from Yenan as a Base, August 7, 1944, National Archives and Record Administration (NARA), RG226, entry 148, box 7, folder 103.

50. David D. Barrett, *Dixie Mission: The United States Army Observer Group in Yenan* (Berkeley: University of California Center for Chinese Studies, 1970), 74.

51. Hollinger, *Protestants Abroad,* 19–21; and Sutton, *Double Crossed,* 28.

52. John Service, "China Today and the Course of Sino-US Relations over Past Few Decades," Hearings Before the Committee on Foreign Relations: United States Senate, 92nd Congress, February 7–8, 1972 (Washington, DC: US Government Printing Office, 1972), 94.

53. Entry from Davies's diary, February 17, 1943. Quoted in John Paton Davies Jr., *China Hand: An Autobiography* (Philadelphia: University of Pennsylvania Press, 2012), 195.

54. Sutton, *Double Crossed*, 27. Quote of Stanley Lovell.

55. Records lack personal details on the first Dixie Mission cohort. They may have been mish kids, and they may have come to work in China some other way (most likely via military service or journalism).

56. Hollinger, *Protestants Abroad*, 23.

2

The Diversity and Versatility of British Intelligence in Iraq, 1939–1945

Adrian O'Sullivan

These days, the word "Iraq" is like a touch paper guaranteed to set off a barrage of historical interest in, among other things, British involvement in the difficult region formerly known as Mesopotamia and once governed—ever more reluctantly and dysfunctionally—by the Ottoman Turks in the early twentieth century, until ousted by General Edmund Allenby's overwhelming forces in October 1918. Unfortunately, perhaps because generally neglected by intelligence historians, what happened covertly as opposed to manifestly in that region after the First World War and during the Second, has been underreported, over-politicized, and frequently misinterpreted by anticolonial historians and sundry other scholars, none of whom appear to be intelligence historians.[1] Collectively or separately, such critical but nonspecialist observers have failed to perceive certain fundamental truths about the nature of British covert operations in an area known at the time as "the short-cut to India," straddling the essential lines of communication and supply between the United Kingdom and India, the Far East, and Australasia. The most egregious fallacy, often heard anecdotally, is that Iraq was a British colony. It never was. Between 1921 and 1932 Britain merely administered the region on behalf of the League of Nations. Military control was vested largely in Royal Air Force (RAF) Iraq Command, whose "I" Branch was primarily responsible for intelligence operations throughout the Mandate. There was a headquarters at RAF Habbaniya controlling five Area Liaison Officers (ALOs) who handled tribal and political (T&P) intelligence at their stations in Basra, Bahrein, Sulaimaniya, Mosul, and Baghdad. After Iraq gained full independence in 1932, much of the work of the ALOs quickly became the preventive monitoring of the growing tensions among the new central government, the Hashemite monarchy, and the various Shia, Sunni, Assyrian, Yezidi, and Kurdish factions that might have torn the new country apart.[2]

The "True" Middle East

In the face of Axis aggression, the British government faced pressing interwar and wartime needs to consolidate and protect the vital sinews of imperial—not imperialist—power. If we are to ensure that postwar intelligence historiography remains measured and accurate, then unbiased appraisals of the exigencies of Britain's strategic situation in the Middle East, and of the intelligence-and-security decision-making it inherently required, simply must prevail. Beyond the era of RAF air policing during the 1930s, once war broke out in 1939, and Nazi Germany and the Japanese set their sights on nothing less than the disruption of the entire British Empire, Britain's intelligence response was predictable and fundamentally realistic.[3] Highly diversified secret forces were deployed to Cairo and fanned out on the ground east of Suez to control and protect vast regions that were accurately predicted to become targets of essential interest to the Axis. This chapter seeks to explore the extraordinary farsightedness and versatility of British intelligence and security planners and operatives who tackled a range of challenging scenarios and situations in the "true" Middle East—from Sinai to Baluchistan and from the Caspian Sea to the Persian Gulf during the Second World War. Iraq and Persia (Iran) were of immense strategic importance for half a dozen reasons, all to do with global security: (1) the security of Allied oil supply; (2) the security of India; (3) the security of Allied lines of communication and supply east of Suez; (4) the threat of Nazi German invasion of the Middle East through Turkey, Transcaucasia, Transcaspia, and North Africa; (5) the security of the Soviet rear after Operation BARBAROSSA; and (6) after Pearl Harbor, the security of the Lend-Lease supply route from the United States to the USSR via the Persian Gulf.[4]

The planning and initial deployment of Britain's intelligence and security resources to the region was suddenly interrupted in late April 1941 when rebellion broke out in Iraq. Armed with mostly British equipment, the new Iraqi Army laid siege to RAF Habbaniya and the Baghdad embassy. Before long, British and Indian forces of the 10th Indian Division (SABINE FORCE) arrived from Basra, as well as a hastily assembled column of mostly Household Brigade and Arab Legion troops from the Levant and Transjordan (KINGCOL), to assist the beleaguered RAF and ultimately defeat the Iraqi rebels.[5] Immediately after peace was restored on 31 May 1941, to address the post-rebellion situation, a new security-intelligence system was devised and inaugurated, whereby the Combined Intelligence Centre Iraq and Persia (CICI) was rechartered in Baghdad in July 1941 and merged with RAF "I" Branch.[6] Originally constituted under the Middle East Intelligence Centre (MEIC), and subsequently reconstituted as part of the British and Indian

Armies' Persia and Iraq Command (PAIC), the new interservices center was structured functionally as a regional branch of the Security Service (MI5), administered from Cairo by Security Intelligence Middle East (SIME) with local administrative and transport services provided by the RAF.[7]

For the remaining war years, CICI acted as the central clearinghouse for security intelligence throughout the region. Its regular weekly summaries, distributed widely among the intelligence community far beyond the Middle East, covered all conceivable aspects of so-called "nonoperational" (i.e. nonmilitary) intelligence: active espionage; counterintelligence; security intelligence; and finally T&P, economic, and diplomatic intelligence.[8] However, this informative function of CICI was dwarfed by the organization's executive and quasi-police powers which were vested in its two Defence Security Offices (DSOs) in Baghdad and Tehran.[9] Security was defined in this context by SIME as "the safeguarding of the state against attempts to lower the value of its war potential whether by treason, espionage, sabotage, propaganda, carelessness, or political agitation."[10] The nerve-centers of the two independently run DSOs were of course their massive registries, which contained records of tens of thousands of personalities of interest. In addition to the static registries, the records included a dynamic indexing system called Movements of Foreign Agents (MOFA).[11] Agent personality sheets known as "MOFA histories" were constantly updated and shared among DSOs throughout the Middle East and even farther afield. Thus, the movements of enemy agents were tracked, recorded, and distributed globally, greatly facilitating surveillance operations and significantly restricting Axis agents' ability to operate anywhere in the world of war. In his celebrated diary, as a testimony to the wholesale German intelligence failure in the face of such robust British counterintelligence, Guy Liddell of MI5 was able to state conclusively: "The Abwehr have failed to obtain any reliable information of strategic importance."[12] And David Mure, head of "A" Force (strategic deception) in Baghdad, wrote: "In the whole of the Middle East there literally was no genuine Axis espionage network."[13]

When I first started examining in detail the role of British secret intelligence in wartime Iraq—or rather the various clandestine roles of British services and agencies in the region, including the armed forces and other representatives of British India—two things struck me: (1) the diversity of the covert forces assembled there and (2) the sheer versatility demonstrated by the range of operations they undertook. Diversity and versatility are not commonly studied aspects of covert formations and operations. However, in the case of Iraq during the two wars fought in the region between 1939 and 1945—the Second World War and the Anglo-Iraqi War of 1941—so striking were these two organizational and operational aspects (diversity and versatility) that I soon found myself building my entire study of the region around them. The result was my book, *The Baghdad Set*, published in 2019, which uses a social historian's methodology to narrate and analyze the intrinsic element of human agency in covert operations.[14] It was preceded by two books on Persia (Iran) about the failure of German covert operations in the region and the success of the Allied response.[15]

To sustain any narrative or analysis of intelligence organization and operations east of Suez, it is essential to embrace the complexity and dynamism of the region wholeheartedly. One simply cannot characterize British intelligence work in World War II as having been undertaken separately or even competitively by "rival" services, agencies, or formations without any overlaps, cooperation, or coordination among them. There was nothing neat and tidy about rivalry, nor about the Middle East; intelligence work undertaken there was no exception. Consequently, if one restricts one's historical analysis to, say, a "top-down" study of policy and planning at Cairo HQ level, without examining the full spectrum of intelligence formations and their many interrelated functions throughout the region, and without mentioning the vagaries of human behavior, one will have barely scratched the surface of the subject. In other words, a "bottom-up" methodological approach is indispensable.

Seen from the top-down, Middle East intelligence during the Second World War has too often been imagined simplistically as a spider's web with Cairo at its center, from which there supposedly radiated an enormous network of controlled covert formations and activities.[16] In reality, those formations and activities were so heterogeneous and widely dispersed that Cairo was never central to their operational needs and provided little practical leadership. For example, as the official history makes clear, SIME in Cairo received only general directions and policy from London, while passing on directions on policy and methods to regional heads.[17] The same was true of the Special Operations Executive (SOE). Certainly, there was always less central direction of Middle East than of Balkan operations, which SOE controlled mostly from Istanbul, and which the US Office of Strategic Services (OSS) also controlled from Bari (Italy) after the summer of 1943. Also, once PAIC was spun off from Middle East Command (MEC) in September 1942, Baghdad and Tehran effectively replaced Cairo as the headquarters for most regional covert operations east of Suez. Cairo was also generally too unstable an administrative environment to provide any central control or clearinghouse for intelligence operations, as it was perpetually riven by melodramatic dysfunction and intrigue, famously prompting

Bickham Sweet-Escott of SOE to rename the entire region the "Muddle East."[18] One intelligence historian has summarized the disarray concisely: "Cairo revelled in an alphabet soup of secret organisations, each with overlapping responsibilities and minimal co-ordination."[19] Sweet-Escott was quite right about the "muddle" at Grey Pillars, Rustum Buildings, and other headquarters in Cairo. However, there is no evidence to be found of any operational "muddle" in the field east of Suez. Certainly not in Iraq (or Persia), largely because of the highly functional relationship between the head of SIME in Cairo, Raymond "RJ" Maunsell, and the head of CICI in Baghdad, E. K. "Chokra" Wood, supported by his two Defence Security Officers (DSOs) in the field: Hanbury K. Dawson-Shepherd in Baghdad and E. L. "Joe" Spencer in Tehran. These relationships were underpinned by the supportive global reach of the Security Service (MI5) in London, represented by its exceptionally able and prescient Middle East desk head, A. J. "Alex" Kellar, who liaised constantly with all parties.[20]

Partly in response to the inter- and intraservice mayhem in Cairo, what emerged among British operatives in Iraq was a paradigm of versatility, pragmatic cohesion, and self-sufficiency, anchored in shared British sociocultural reference points and a shared perception that the war against Hitler needed to be won at all costs, and was more important than bureaucratic infighting. Such simplistic binary analyses of interservice rivalries as "MI6 ... wanted agents to work undercover to produce intelligence, whereas SOE wanted them to blow things up" contribute nothing to a realistic portrayal of operational conditions in the field.[21] Furthermore, this juxtaposition ignores the fact that at least 50 percent of SOE's global role concerned subversion, not sabotage. Of course, in the crowded covert spaces of European operational theaters there were intense internecine skirmishes over competencies, priorities, or even air transport. However, there was nothing inevitably confrontational about interservice relations specifically in Iraq or generally east of Suez. In the field, secret operations were structurally and functionally polylithic, responsive, and cooperative.

Beyond the Middle East, there were all kinds of British personnel working internationally who were essentially "hybrid operatives" using any kind of cover that could be arranged for them, often in great haste. Take, for instance, the important multiple interservice (SOE/MI5/MI6) roles performed by Walter "Freckles" Wren from 1939 onward.[22] After recruitment as one of the earliest members of Section D of the Secret Intelligence Service (MI6), Wren went on to become an SOE (G Section) military officer. At the same time, Wren performed a pivotal role as MI6 (Section V) Head of Security at British Security Coordination (BSC) headquarters in New York, while also simultaneously functioning as MI5 DSO for the Caribbean, dividing his time between Trinidad, Bermuda, and the United States. And all the while, most of Wren's UK acquaintances thought he was just a kitchen-equipment salesman.[23] SOE, the Foreign Office (FO) (diplomatic and consular), the Ministry of Information (MOI), the Ministry of Economic Warfare (MEW), the Political Warfare Executive (PWE), the British Council, and press organizations like British Overseas Features (BOF) and Britanova, often afforded convenient cover for such operatives.[24] Camouflage of this kind was often associated with "white" propaganda operations (e.g., as FO press attachés), even while some hybrid operatives were actually conducting "black" propaganda operations in their primary covert roles.[25] Operational fluidity seems to have been the name of the game, especially among SOE, MI5, and MI6, where the identity borderline was malleable. So, when examining the subversive roles of any SOE or other personnel, there was always the chance that they might have been simultaneously working for MI6, especially if their provenance included earlier service with Section D, as was the case with some Iraq personnel.[26] Perhaps the ballyhoo about interservice hostility and squabbling, especially in London and Cairo, was to some extent allowed to proliferate in order to conceal the considerable degree of actual liaison and cooperation among the secret services.[27] While using another clandestine service as cover (so-called "cover-within-cover"), as MI6 and SOE officers sometimes did, one's camouflage would be enhanced in terms of density and deniability if the two organizations involved were perceived, especially by the enemy, to be at loggerheads with each other. Perhaps this explains how the black propagandist Christopher Sykes of SOE, already an established author before the war, was granted permission in 1944—even while still in uniform and subject to the Official Secrets Act (OSA)—to publish a satirical *roman à clef* about infighting among secret Cairo bureaucracies.[28]

Even more dense and deniable was the creation of triple cover. The most significant example of the wartime use of FO/SOE/MI6 "cover-within-cover-within-cover" in the region is that of Dr R. C. "Robin" Zaehner, an eminent Oxford Persianist under triple cover in Tehran as a diplomatic press attaché, covering his role as an SOE propaganda officer, which in turn covered his identity as an MI6 intelligence officer operating against the Soviet Union. Together with his deputy Norman Darbyshire (also under similar triple cover), Zaehner played all three parts effectively and courageously, undertaking dangerous deep-cover MI6 espionage missions in the Soviet occupation zone. At the same time, ostensibly as a diplomat, he frequented the imperial court. There, like the OSS Secret Intelligence Branch (OSS-SI) penetration agent (and well-known author) Harold Lamb, Zaehner maintained a close friendship with the Shah and Queen Fawzia. Of course, many British undercover operatives also held military rank, providing them with a kind of extra "quadruple cover." For example, both Zaehner and Darbyshire were also majors in the Intelligence Corps. Consequently, they were covered by an additional superficial layer of service identity. They could, if they wished, identify themselves simply as officers in their particular corps, maybe as field security officers, without any need to elaborate further on their roles.[29]

Diversity

When one isolates Iraq within the overall context of Middle East covert formations and operations, one finds no fewer than at least a dozen formations or agencies deployed, each with its own distinct chain of command and dynamic, responsive regional agenda. After the attack on Pearl Harbor, there was an additional degree of active Anglo-American intelligence liaison and cooperation, especially among Baghdad-based officers of SOE, CICI, and OSS-SI. It needs to be remembered that Persia (Iran) differed from Iraq in many ways, not least because of the Soviet occupation of the northern Caspian provinces and the presence of large numbers of American supply troops in US Persian Gulf Command (PGC). While PGC officially encompassed the entire region (including Iraq) east of the Levant as far as the Indian border, significant numbers of US forces were only ever deployed within Persia (Iran).[30] These circumstances permitted the introduction to Persia (Iran) of three additional secret services not found in Iraq: the Soviet NKVD, the US Counter Intelligence Corps (CIC), and the G2 staff of PGC (military intelligence) under the commanding general of PGC, Donald Connolly. The Soviet presence in northern Persia also precipitated heightened active-espionage activity on the part of the MI6 Tehran station under Robin Zaehner, who personally executed several successful penetration missions within the Soviet occupation zone. At least three OSS-SI undercover agents also conducted similar operations against the Soviet occupiers in 1944. By the end of 1944, Persia (Iran) had become a theater for early Cold War intelligence operations rather than for anti-Nazi warfare.

The transition from Axis-Allied covert conflict to anti-Soviet initiatives was actually set in motion in 1943 by a tacit "heads-up" from the German secret services, which—after the Stalingrad debacle—went on a clandestine offensive in the Middle East, planning and mounting a series of *Ferneinsätze* (long-distance subversion and sabotage initiatives) against Iraq and Persia, all of which were either canceled or failed spectacularly.[31] These pinprick attacks alerted Western Allied intelligence planners to the fact that, with all hope of invading and occupying the Middle East now beyond reach, Nazi Germany was only superficially targeting Allied infrastructure and resources in Iraq and Persia (Iran). The actual, ideologically driven objective, particularly of the SS Foreign Intelligence Service (RSHA VI), was clearly to thwart perceived Soviet (in conflated Nazi parlance, "Jewish-Bolshevik") long-term interests in the region, especially regarding Palestine and oil. Hitler's primary strategic objective was undoubtedly the defeat of Stalinism. Certainly this was the ideological aim of SS covert planning for the Middle East, projected into the postwar era. Why else would Berlin have deployed such futile *Ferneinsätze* as Operation TEL AFAR (targeting Palestinian Jews) in December 1944, Operation REISERNTE (targeting the Persian Gulf) in February–March 1945, and Operation KINO (targeting the Abadan oilfields) as late as April 1945?[32] Once aware of Berlin's changed planning priorities by 1943, the subsequent failure of the regional Nazi threat effectively released British (and US) intelligence and security forces from many of their anti-German obligations, enabling them to turn their attention presciently toward their own premonitions of Stalinist expansionism and the incipient postwar Soviet security threat. By late-1944, apart from sustaining joint cooperation with the NKVD on the KISS radio deception, the British security authorities in the region had more or less withdrawn from fighting the Second World War and had instead adopted an entirely new covert stance that confronted Moscow rather than Berlin.[33]

The diversity of British covert formations deployed in Iraq (and Persia) was astonishing, as may be seen in Figure 2.1. Besides the security-intelligence organization represented by SIME and the DSOs, at least half a dozen definitively "nonoperational" (i.e., nonmilitary) systems operated in the region, covering every conceivable aspect of intelligence, counterintelligence, and other secret functions such as active espionage and counterespionage; T&P intelligence; field security of all kinds (oil, airfield, port, and railway security); border control; passport and visa control; strategic deception; sabotage and countersabotage; propaganda ("black, white, and grey"); subversion and countersubversion; internment and interrogation; and censorship. Additionally, there of course existed numerous "operational" (i.e., naval and military) intelligence systems within the armed forces, represented primarily by the staff of the Senior Naval Officer Persian Gulf (SNOPG), Charles Hammill, in Basra and the G2 staff at Persia and Iraq Force (PAIFORCE) general headquarters (GHQ) in Baghdad. There was significant overlapping between operational and nonoperational intelligence in such areas as sabotage and countersabotage (between SOE and PAIFORCE), and strategic

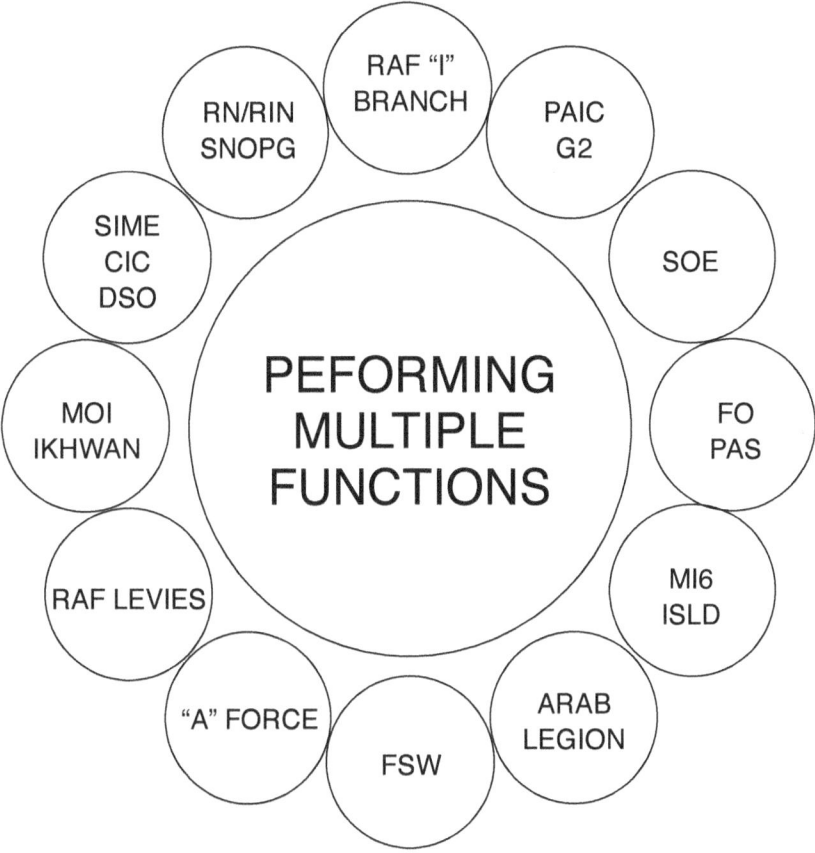

Figure 2.1. Diversity of British covert formations deployed in Iraq

deception (between "A" Force and PAIFORCE), mostly involving operations executed in the field by Royal Engineers (RE) and other PAIFORCE formations that specialized in oil-denial and large-scale camouflage.[34]

The most significant independent covert force in the region was SOE Iraq Command, which was initially organized and led by the brilliant H. F. "Adrian" Bishop until his tragic accidental death in Tehran on 11 October 1942. He tripped and fell from a hotel balcony in full view of his friends in the courtyard below. An Old Etonian and Cambridge intellectual with an exemplary World War I record as an infantry officer, fluent in many languages including German, Russian, and Farsi, Bishop had spent most of the interwar years working capably and courageously in various European political hot spots as a scout on behalf of MI6.[35] Early in the war when

Section D of MI6, to which Bishop then belonged, merged with SOE, he was quickly spotted by the new service as a potential leader in the Middle East, not least because he had spent the years immediately after the First World War and the Russian Civil War as an executive with the Anglo-Persian Oil Company (APOC) and knew the region well. Under Bishop, SOE Baghdad became a highly efficient propaganda and sabotage/countersabotage organization. As the war evolved and any direct threat of German invasion receded, SOE's clandestine activities became less about oil denial or guerrilla resistance to Nazi occupation, and more about subversion and propaganda operations. After his untimely death, Bishop's younger successors, Aidan Philip (formerly with Bishop during the 1920s at APOC in Abadan) and E. C. "Teddy" Hodgkin (a well-known Fleet Street journalist), maintained a high level of propaganda activity that even included administration of the important Sharq-al-Adna (Near East Broadcasting [NEBS]) radio station in Jaffa (Palestine).[36]

The Baghdad station of MI6, known in the Middle and Far East as the Inter-Services Liaison Department (ISLD), cooperated closely with SOE in Baghdad, though it was engaged in very different work. Local personal friendships seem to have alleviated whatever pain might have been caused by bitter rivalry and tension at the Cairo and London headquarters of the two services. Fortunately, Nigel Clive, who was ISLD deputy head-of-station in Baghdad, was close with the SOE officers and spent much of his spare time at South Gate, their Baghdad residential and operational center on the banks of the Tigris. This MI6–SOE connection was only strengthened by Clive's close relationship with the celebrated author Freya Stark (also a former MI6 scout and Section D member), working in the Middle East for MOI, who adored Adrian Bishop and frequented South Gate, largely to savor Bishop's scintillating intellect and witty conversation. It was almost as if Stark sensed instinctively that her charming, brilliant companion was not long for this world.

Relations between MI6/ISLD and SIME/MI5/DSO were also generally cordial and cooperative. As a security precaution during the May 1941 rebellion, ISLD had destroyed most of its Baghdad station records. Consequently, the service was compelled to fall back on those of DSO, most of which had been preserved during the rebellion by RAF "I" Branch. DSO materially assisted ISLD by helping them create a brand-new registry and build fresh records.[37] The quid-pro-quo benefit for DSO consisted primarily in their subsequent ability to rely on ISLD for confirmation purposes.[38]

Another aspect of MI6's intelligence work in the region may be observed in the omnipresence of John Bagot Glubb, commander of the Arab Legion, who, though based in Transjordan, maintained an extensive network of active-espionage agents throughout the Arab world, especially in Iraq and Syria. Many were Bedouin tribesmen with connections across North Africa and as far south as Yemen.[39] Although we know little or nothing of Glubb's formal relationship with "C" (the head of MI6, Sir Stewart Menzies), it is certain that there was one, and that British intelligence in Iraq undoubtedly benefited from Glubb's enormous influence, particularly during the Anglo-Iraqi War and the Syrian campaign that followed. Indeed, the suspicious Gaullist Free French who triumphed in Syria regarded Glubb, who spoke fluent French, disdainfully as nothing more than a British spy working to undermine them in the Levant.[40]

Freya Stark's propagandistic endeavors on behalf of MOI constituted but one of several clandestine information agencies operating out of Baghdad. Originally, when Stark first arrived from Egypt, where she had succeeded in establishing her Ikhwan-al-hurriya (Brotherhood of Freedom) propaganda organization under MOI control, she prevailed upon her old FO (and former MI6) friend Stewart Perowne to provide her with office premises suited to her diplomatic cover as Second Secretary at the Baghdad embassy. Initially, Adrian Bishop of SOE also occupied the same embassy premises, as he, too, was working under diplomatic cover as Services Liaison Officer in Perowne's department. As Press Officer, Perowne appeared to oversee all British propaganda emanating from the embassy. However, in reality, both Stark's MOI "grey" propaganda operations and Bishop's SOE "black" propaganda operations were entirely independent of the FO "white" propaganda operations under Perowne.[41] Nevertheless, these circumstances explain how three close friends, working for three entirely separate British enterprises, became besieged together under the same embassy roof for the whole month of May 1941. Nor did they allow such an opportunity to be squandered. They spent all five weeks of their incarceration jointly developing—together with such other key personalities of the secret world as Pat Domvile (SOE), C. J. Edmonds (FO), Cecil Hope-Gill (SOE), Seton Lloyd (SOE), and the ambassador himself, Sir Kinahan Cornwallis—a master plan for the organization and operation of clandestine activities throughout Iraq, to be implemented as soon as the rebels had been defeated. Adrian Bishop was placed in overall charge of the plan.[42] Thus, while not expressly coordinated, it is highly significant that the covert intelligence and propaganda operations of the FO, SOE, and MOI were regionally harmonized from June 1941 onward.[43]

To implement such an ambitious plan and protect the new Iraqi polity, there was clearly a need for "boots on the ground." First and foremost, the

Iraqi Police were of little use, except perhaps for their Criminal Investigation Department (CID), for they generally could not be trusted, having allied themselves early on with the rebels and other pro-Nazi elements, such as the infamous Shawkat brothers, Saib and Sami, who had to be kept under strict surveillance.[44] Although it was possible to utilize the security resources offered by the thousands of Free Polish troops being assembled and trained in Iraq and Persia prior to the Italian campaign, they were only capable—though extremely willing to provide support—of playing such junior roles as camp guards, prisoner escorts, or general-duty sentries, largely because of linguistic limitations.[45] The only sufficiently talented and suitably trained British personnel to carry out the wide range of security duties involved in maintaining the political and physical integrity of post-rebellion Iraq were the Field Security Sections of the Intelligence Corps (FSS). They were highly mobile, lightly armed units usually equipped with motorcycles and small trucks, though they used horses, mules, or even donkeys in some inaccessible areas. Furthermore, they were under SIME command, which meant that they were already an integral part of the existing security apparatus and, though a British Army formation, could be used without obtaining War Office approval and clearance. Finally, the FSS were disciplined, efficient, multilingual, multicultural, and their morale was generally high. Much of their work called for plain-clothes undercover operations (surveillance, arrest, and detention).[46]

The challenging and varied nature of their assignments, usually involving wide and frequent travel, not without some element of danger, gave these British and Indian troops a shared sense of doing something useful and important in the war. So, although some FSS had been active in Iraq since the armistice, a PAIFORCE FSS contingent was officially established in Baghdad in December 1942. For most of the rest of the war, the regional Field Security Wing (FSW) was under the command of Geoffrey Household, an officer with much experience in covert and semi-covert operations, who later authored spy novels. Although directly answerable as a military unit to PAIFORCE, the Iraq-based FSS effectively continued to be CICI's executive police force, available to the DSO on demand. While individual sections were transferred from time to time, they initially operated in the following four distinct security zones: (1) Basra Port; (2) Shaiba Base; (3) Baghdad; and (4) Iraq Lines of Communication (LOC). Zone 4 mostly involved railway policing. Only one month after their introduction to Iraq, nineteen FSS were already active in the PAIFORCE theater, including Persia. Between 1941 and 1946, a total of fourteen FSS served in Iraq. In fact, the Free Poles became so enthusiastic about the successful performance of the British FSS that they formed at least seven of their own Polish FSS and took them into the Italian campaign. Beforehand, however, they deployed in Iraq, where their knowledge of German proved invaluable to CICI, as they could communicate with German-speaking Arabs of interest to British security.[47]

Supporting the efforts of the FSS to ensure the security of the Iraqi polity were the RAF Assyrian Levies. Though trained along the lines of the RAF Regiment as conventional infantry rather than special forces, they must be considered unconventional troops. They were dedicated to security (rather than military) functions within Iraq, such as the protection of those British assets that had been the prime targets of the rebels during the Anglo-Iraqi War, namely RAF installations (especially the Habbaniya and Shaiba air bases) and the British Embassy. Only their airborne units, which operated outside the Middle East as Royal Marine Commandos, could be considered special forces in the narrowest sense. Additionally, the Levies performed general escort and guard duties in support of the security authorities throughout Iraq and Persia (Iran). Besides ethnic Assyrians, a significant number of Levies companies were composed of Kurds, Yezidis, and in a few cases, Arabs. Another reason for considering the Levies to have been unconventional is that there is at least one instance in which they served as cover for intelligence personnel. While serving in the Levies, an officer named Hugh McNearnie was under triple cover (cover-within-cover-within cover), simultaneously working as an Assistant Political Adviser (APA) for the British Embassy, as an SOE officer, and (probably his real, deep-cover role) as an ISLD (MI6) intelligence officer.

Another unconventional formation was deployed by SIME to investigate rumored Axis submarine landings on the Persian Gulf shores and to ensure that the Axis Powers were unable to supply the pro-German Qashqai and Bakhtiari tribes, or any Iraqi dissidents with war materiel. This was SOE's Force KALPAK, a secret commando unit recruited among mostly Kurdish toughs in Turkey and Syria. These hard men—many of whom were convicted murderers and habitual criminals—were rigorously disciplined and trained by an equally tough SOE sabotage officer named Terence Bruce Mitford, a rugby-playing Scottish academic who had begun the war in Section D of MI6, to become the core of a formidable guerrilla movement ready to resist any putative German invasion of Turkey from Bulgaria.[48] This is yet another example of regional interservice cooperation, in this case between the Baghdad and Tehran DSOs on the one hand, and SOE and SNOPG on the other, with the likely connivance of ISLD, concerned always about the security of oil infrastructure around the Shatt al-Arab. As was customary when working in parallel with SIME, the representatives of ISLD assembled the preparatory intelligence, leaving SIME to execute the appropriate response. It no doubt helped that the British Political Adviser (PA) responsible for overseeing the security of oil infrastructure in Khuzestan, including the Abadan oil refinery, was H. John Underwood, an old friend of the late Adrian Bishop and a former regional SOE field commander with close ties to MI6.[49]

The British were fortunate in having in the person of their ambassador to Iraq, Sir Kinahan Cornwallis, not just an experienced and energetic career diplomat with an encyclopedic knowledge of Middle East affairs, but one with a background in the Political Intelligence Department (PID) of the FO. Consequently, unlike his reactionary ambassadorial colleague Sir Hughe Knatchbull-Hugessen in Ankara, the progressive Cornwallis was convinced of the vital importance of intelligence work and was always positively predisposed toward the efforts of the secret services. However, he went far beyond providing diplomatic cover for key ISLD, SOE, or MOI personnel whenever needed (unlike Hugessen, who loathed doing so).[50] Cornwallis actually created his own intelligence service: the Political Advisory Staff (PAS), whose Political Advisers (PAs), Assistant Political Advisers (APAs), and Deputy Assistant Political Advisors (DAPAs) covered the entire country from their stations in Kirkuk, Baghdad, and Basra, with outstations in Erbil, Kirkuk, Sulaimaniya, Khanaqin, Bakuba, Ramadi, Musayib, Hilla, Kut, Diwariya, Amara, Nasiriya, and even Kuwait and Bahrein.[51] Their regular intelligence reports were automatically sent to Cornwallis, to his senior British adviser at the interior ministry ("CJ" Edmonds), and to CICI. Cannily, to avoid any potential conflict between the civil and military authorities, Cornwallis placed the entire PAS network under CICI control, thereby bridging the gap between the FO, PAIFORCE/G2, SIME, and the provincial authorities. This arrangement also allowed the DSO to post his own ALOs to provincial CICI outstations where they cooperated with PAS advisers.[52]

Versatility

In the context of this chapter, diversity essentially characterizes the wide range of civil or military services or formations employed by the British to implement intelligence or security policy and plans within the "true" Middle East in general, and Iraq (and to a lesser extent Persia [Iran]) in particular. In this sense, diversity is primarily a quantitative factor in any history of intelligence and security success or failure. Versatility, on the other hand, is more about the multiplicity of assigned or assumed intelligence or security functions and thus more about the qualitative assessment of individual roles and activities in the field in terms of success or failure.

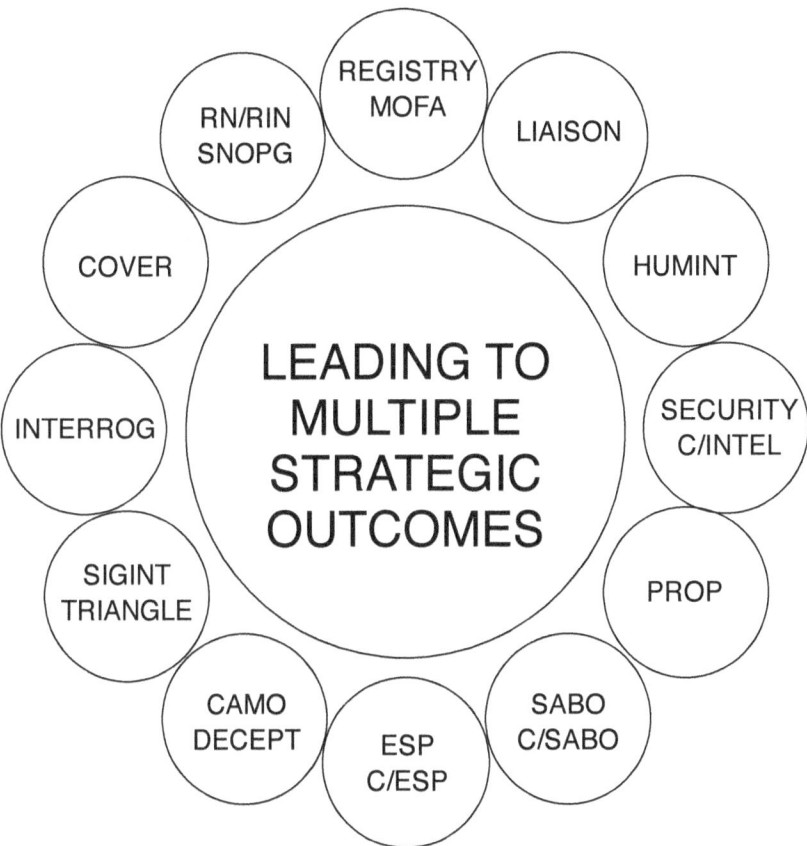

Figure 2.2. Versatility of intelligence and security functions in Iraq

The wide versatility of intelligence and security functions in Iraq is best comprehended when divided into the twelve broad categories illustrated in Figure 2.2. These demonstrate the paramount significance of human intelligence (HUMINT) and human resources in the implementation of regional policy and planning. Only the decrypts of enemy signals that constituted ULTRA, known regionally as TRIANGLE, performed an important SIGINT (signals intelligence) function. The Allies were able to read the Abwehr's ENIGMA code from late 1941 onward, and the SS (RSHA VI) hand cypher even earlier that year.[53] However, this technical element was of less value locally in Iraq and generally in the Middle East than in other war theaters since the Axis had so few agents operating there. Only two categories in Figure 2.2 may be classified as "operational" intelligence in the narrow sense established by the Middle East Defence Council (MEDC) in 1943: SNOPG naval intelligence and PAIFORCE military intelligence. All the remaining categories in the chart may be considered "nonoperational" (nonmilitary) as opposed to "operational"; they were therefore the responsibility of CICI, ISLD, and SOE. The definition of nonoperational intelligence adopted by MEDC was "political and economic intelligence, and security intelligence, in respect of the civil population of the Middle East and the Allied forces located in the Middle East, including counterespionage and countersabotage."[54] This distinction was based on the notion that operational intelligence was rooted in military campaigning, which was geospatially dynamic—always on the move. Conversely, nonoperational intelligence was seen as always rooted in an immobile, constituted polity such as Iraq.[55] In practical terms, formal adoption of this definitive paradigm therefore meant that, even though most of their members had military rank, organizations like CICI, ISLD, and SOE were able to retain exclusive responsibility for such nonoperational functions as active espionage, counterintelligence, security intelligence, countersabotage, and black propaganda. Meanwhile, political, economic, and tribal intelligence remained, as it always had been, firmly under FO (PAS) control.

Within each function of nonoperational intelligence (see Figure 2.2), a plethora of different roles had to be performed, calling for the recruitment of talented, highly trained personnel—mostly but not always commissioned officers—and the development of an astonishing range of skill sets. Feeding into and drawing on their central registries and various specific indexes—numbering perhaps 100,000 carded personalities—all the secret services executed functions that contributed to the accumulation, cross-referencing, and distribution of data or to the maintenance of defense and security throughout the region. In the first instance, data acquisition and maintenance measures included the use of HUMINT, postal and other forms of censorship, and frontier and visa controls, along with real-time surveillance, to monitor latent threats of all kinds. To defend the Iraqi polity and Allied interests, measures included port, railway, and airfield security; regional intelligence acquisition and evaluation, including T&P intelligence; counterintelligence and counterespionage targeting dissident Iraqis and Axis agents and initiatives; and arrest, interrogation, and internment. A dazzling array of professional and occupational skills was required of British and Indian operatives at all executive and administrative levels of the clandestine services in Iraq: records staff, linguists, interrogators, propagandists (including broadcasters), intelligence officers, security officers, sabotage/countersabotage officers, liaison officers, oil-denial officers, field agents, field-security staff, guards and escorts, watchers, drivers, transcribers, clerks and typists of all kinds, telephonists, cipherettes, and so forth. Finally, there was Dudley Clarke's "A" Force, under the command of David Mure in Baghdad, which employed visual-deception experts with extraordinary artistic and engineering talents to create large-scale camouflage projects intended to deceive the enemy as to Allied strategic intentions.[56]

It is deeply ironic that amid the atrocious violence and destruction of war there sometimes occurs a concomitant flowering of creativity and inventive genius that startles the historian who happens to discover its traces. The talented British intelligencers and other operatives who worked clandestinely in the vast covert spaces of the "true" Middle East during the Second World War left behind an important historical legacy that belies the fact that most never had any direct contact with their Axis or pro-Axis enemies and performed purely supportive roles. However, the extraordinary range of skills and strengths that they applied to their daunting challenges greatly advanced the Allied cause and helped protect a distant region of enormous strategic importance. To discover, some eighty years on, this unheralded trove of talent and creativity in the farthermost reaches of the secret world—protected by the sentinels of the "Little Forgotten Army" called PAIFORCE—is as inspiring as it is significant.[57]

Outcomes

The diversity and versatility of British covert organizations, operations, and functions in Iraq are striking. They may be contrasted with the enemy's deployment in very small numbers from 1941 onward of only one significant clandestine formation in the region: the Abwehr's so-called Near East War Organization (KONO), operating not even within Iraq but from the safety of its base in neutral Istanbul.[58] Besides, KONO's main interest was not really in the Middle East, but rather in active espionage and counterespionage operations targeting the European theater (especially the Balkans). Consequently, KONO is known to have mounted only three operations that were perceived as seriously threatening by CICI counterintelligence: the LIBERATORS spy ring (1942–1943), the KHIDIR case (1943), and the NASRET case (1944). Two major cases originally thought to be KONO-inspired (the DODGERS and the SMUDGERS) proved instead to be the work of anti-British Turkish dissidents with no known Nazi connections.[59]

As opposed to their active record in Persia (Iran), the SS Foreign Intelligence Service (RSHA VI)[60] never launched any covert operations against Iraq, nor did the SS run any local agents in the region. RSHA VI had a Berlin desk with responsibility for Iraq but no regional representative in the field. On the other hand, RSHA IV (functionally the Gestapo) had a sole representative in Turkey named Ludwig Moyzisch, who (though part-Jewish) served as SS-and-Police Attaché at the Ankara embassy, and who occasionally dabbled in active espionage, most notably in connection with the infamous CICERO case.[61] There was no official liaison in Turkey between the Abwehr (KONO) and the SS (Moyzisch) concerning Middle East intelligence operations. Otherwise, the execution of two isolated aerial insertions (Operation MAMMUT [June 1943] by the Abwehr and Operation TEL AFAR [November 1944] by the ex-Mufti of Jerusalem's Arab Bureau) can be discounted as total failures.[62] Ultimately, German secret undertakings in the region came to an abrupt halt in February 1944 when three key members of KONO—Erich Vermehren, Wilhelm Hamburger, and Karl Kleczkowski—defected to the Allies, leaving Paul Leverkuehn's entire Istanbul station blown and nonfunctional.[63]

When considering the strategic outcomes of British intelligence operations in Iraq, it must be remembered that the Middle East was never a static theater but evolved as circumstances changed regionally and globally. All British intelligence and security activity in Iraq was conducted in response to numerous rapid chronological and geospatial internal phases like, for example, the rebellion and the atrocious *Farhud* riots of May–June 1941, or to such major external pivots as Operation BARBAROSSA (the German invasion of the Soviet Union); the Japanese attack on Pearl Harbor; and the battles of El-Alamein, Stalingrad, and Kursk. In the context of the global war against the Axis, British intelligence successfully opposed overt and covert enemy threats to the entire region, especially to the Allied oil supply and to the lines of communication and supply between Britain and the furthermost reaches of the British Empire.[64]

After the Armistice that ended the Anglo-Iraqi War was signed on 31 May 1941, there remained in Iraq a substantial dissident element. It was centered mostly on the Iraqi Army and to a lesser extent the Iraqi Police, but also on various prominent figures on the fascist right, many of whom were former adherents of the ex-Mufti of Jerusalem, Mohammed Amin al-Husayni.[65] The ex-Mufti had been a subversive pro-Nazi blight on the security authorities' landscape from October 1939 until his flight to Germany in May 1941. Clearly, as the British DSO saw it, the menace of Iraqi Nazism had to be neutralized and eliminated as quickly as possible. With a combination of various forms of propaganda, including SOE black ops, and relentless vigilance, as well as such security measures as postal censorship and visa controls, this was largely achieved. The inherent maintenance of internal and frontier security ultimately featured arrest, interrogation, detention, and internment, all of which fed into a wider security system that extended via Cairo to the headquarters of MI5 in London. At the same time, much of the stability of the multiethnic, multicultural Iraqi polity was assured by intensive monitoring of tribal and political affairs. This form of surveillance, carried out jointly by civil and military elements of the British security apparatus, covered all the former *vilayets* of the Ottoman colonial administration and all religious or ethnic groups (Shia, Sunni, Kurd, Assyrian, and Yezidi), not just with regard to their interrelations, but also their often-tense differences with the central government in Baghdad.

Finally, with increasing focus on the postwar world order, and on the threat of incipient Soviet expansionism, there was a generally perceived need and effort to promote British democratic values among ordinary Iraqis, especially young men and women who might fall prey to fascist or Stalinist propaganda. In this regard, the curiously apolitical work of Freya Stark and her Ikwhan-al-hurriya persuasion scheme was extraordinarily effective in influencing a whole new class of young, idealistic Iraqi *effendiya*, and in establishing a climate of political freedom that protected the nation from extremism until the bloody overthrow of the Hashemite monarchy in 1958.[66]

To gain a better general understanding of how the counterintelligence and security situation in Iraq evolved between 1941 and 1945, ultimately in readiness for the emerging postwar world order, one could do no better than examine the comprehensive report written (at the request of General Sir Arthur Smith and Sir Kinahan Cornwallis) by the Baghdad DSO, Hanbury Dawson-Shepherd, shortly before his transfer to the civilian intelligence services in the summer of 1945. The DSO's paper provides a penetrating, precise, and prescient history of the role of British intelligence and security in Iraq throughout the war. In his appreciation, Dawson-Shepherd stresses the inherent diversity of the Iraqi polity which had inevitably called for an equally diverse and versatile approach, writing: "There are few countries which ... present more security problems than Iraq. ... The maintenance of security with so many potential causes of conflict would tax the ingenuity of a sophisticated country [which Iraq clearly was not]."[67] The DSO goes on to enumerate some of the issues that gave rise to the challenges then faced by the British secret services in the region: tribal and minority problems (Kurds, Assyrians, and Armenians); religious problems (Shia and Sunni); problems related to Palestine, Zionism, and Jewish settlement; problems associated with the broad question of Arab unity; the spread of Communist propaganda and Soviet influence; the alarming development of Iraqi nationalism into xenophobia; ensuring the continued popularity of the Hashemite monarchy; and finally the history of "difficult" relations with the Iraqi Army. Nevertheless, Dawson-Shepherd's report is a positive and optimistic appreciation that echoes two earlier, equally prescient key papers presented by Alex Kellar of MI5.[68]

Conclusion

When analyzing and evaluating major battles fought in such vast arenas as the Libyan Desert or the Russian steppes, military historians of the Second World War tend to write in both quantitative and qualitative terms of the crucial relationship between space and force.[69] By contrast, intelligence historians of the period, examining covert operations in the immense secret spaces between the Suez Canal and the Indian border, must deal primarily with different quantitative and qualitative factors, such as the sheer diversity of formations or resources and the dynamic versatility of operations or operatives. This difference in analytical styles owes much to the fact that the operational military historian is bound to focus on technical and logistical factors in warfare (manpower, materiel, or movements). The intelligence historian on the other hand must always remain closer to the individual human element in conflict than to the large-scale geospatial aspects of any operational situation. This essay has demonstrated in the case of covert activity in Iraq (and to some extent Persia) how such analytical methodology works in practice, and how it can pinpoint and accentuate the key functions and creative achievements of a diverse array of clandestine services deployed throughout a very large strategic theater—the "true" Middle East.

Notes

1. For a lucid critique of the "lopsided" nonspecialist literature, see the preface to my recent monograph on Iraq: Adrian O'Sullivan, *The Baghdad Set: Iraq through the Eyes of British Intelligence, 1941–45* (London/Chaim: Palgrave Macmillan/Springer Nature, 2019), xi–xvii. Some examples of such "lopsidedness" are Ayad Al-Qazzaz, "The Iraqi-British War of 1941: A Review Article," *International Journal of Middle East Studies* 7 (1976): 591–96; Walid Hamdi, "Iraq in the Aftermath of the Rashid Ali Revolt, 1941," *Arab Researcher/Al-Bahith al-Arabi* 7 (1986): 33–35; Hamdi, *Rashid Ali al-Gaylani and the Nationalist Movement in Iraq, 1939–1941: A Political and Military Study of the British Campaign in Iraq and the National Revolution of May 1941* (London: Darf, 1987); Mohammad A. Tarbush, *The Role of the Military in Politics: A Case Study of Iraq to 1941* (London: Kegan Paul International, 1982). By contrast, for a dependable, though piecemeal, account of regional policy, planning, and operations, see the official histories: F. H. Hinsley et al., *British Intelligence in the Second World War*, vol. 2, *Its Influence on Strategy and Operations* (London: HMSO, 1981), 97, 277–78, 342, 399, 430; F. H. Hinsley and C. A. G. Simkins, *British Intelligence in the Second World War*, vol. 4,

Security and Counter-Intelligence (New York: Cambridge University Press, 1990), 149–53, 162–64, 188–90, 210–15, 231.

2. Anyone in need of general background should perhaps begin by reading the late Bill Cleveland's standard introductory textbook on the Middle East, now in its 6th edition: William L. Cleveland, *History of the Modern Middle East* (Boulder, CO: Routledge, 2018). For a concise, contemporary analysis of forty years of Iraqi history up to 1943, see Freya Stark, "Appendix: Iraq," in *East Is West* (London: John Murray, 1945), 198–213. For an authoritative military history of Iraq (and Persia) during the Second World War, see Ashley Jackson, *Persian Gulf Command: A History of the Second World War in Iran and Iraq* (New Haven, CT: Yale University Press, 2018). For a brand-new synopsis of the political and diplomatic history of the region, see Stefanie Wichhart, *Britain, Egypt, and Iraq during World War II: The Decline of Imperial Power in the Middle East* (London: Bloomsbury, 2023).

3. On the "total reordering of the globe," which was Hitler's intent "from the start," see Gerhard L. Weinberg, *A World at Arms: A Global History of World War II* (Cambridge: Cambridge University Press, 1994), 2–3; on the extent of Japan's disruptive strategy, see Weinberg, *A World at Arms*, 329–30.

4. Throughout the war, Winston Churchill insisted that Iran be referred to as "Persia" or as "Persia (Iran)," to avoid confusion, especially in radio transmission, with Iraq. This is the convention preferred throughout this chapter, not least as it appears in all contemporary British records. See Minute M785/1, 2 August 1941, Prime Minister's printed personal minutes, CHAR 20/36/8, Churchill Archives Centre, Churchill College, Cambridge (CAC).

5. For a vivid eyewitness memoir of the Anglo-Iraqi War, see Somerset de Chair, *The Golden Carpet* (New York: Harcourt, Brace, 1945). For a lively though more detached account, see John Broich, *Blood, Oil, and the Axis: The Allied Resistance against a Fascist State in Iraq and the Levant, 1941* (New York: Abrams Press, 2019). Also of interest is a biographical account, especially of the embassy siege as experienced by Freya Stark, in Jane Fletcher Geniesse, *Passionate Nomad: The Life of Freya Stark* (New York: Modern Library, 2001), 275–86. However, by far the most penetrating account of the siege and of the various British personalities isolated in the embassy, including Stark, Perowne, Bishop, Cornwallis, and others, is Molly Izzard, *Freya Stark: A Biography* (London: Sceptre, 1993), 233–54. As an acute observer of Stark's secret world, Izzard has the rare advantage of having herself served covertly during the war as a propagandist with PWE, while her husband was in naval intelligence.

6. Appendix D, AIR 29/2504, The National Archives (TNA), Kew, Surrey. For a fulsome general account of the Anglo-Iraqi War, see Jackson, *Persian Gulf Command*, 44–130; and in the context of regional intelligence history, see O'Sullivan, *The Baghdad Set*, 31–61.

7. PAIC (including PAIFORCE) was formed under the command of General (later Field Marshal) Patrick Maitland "Jumbo" Wilson in September 1942.

Though remaining in service uniform, CICI's senior officers were formally seconded to MI5. The RAF took care of such routine support services as pay, accommodation, and transport. For more about SIME, see H. O. Dovey, "Maunsell and Mure," *Intelligence and National Security* 8, no. 1 (January 1993): 60–77.

8. The complete series of CICI Weekly Intelligence Summaries is to be found at AIR 29, TNA. The main series of SIME Security Summaries 1–168 is at WO 208/1560, WO 208/1561, and WO 208/1562, TNA. Additional War Office intelligence summaries on Iraq, Persia (Iran), and other Middle East and Eastern Mediterranean regions may be found elsewhere in the WO 208 series, most notably at WO 208/2256–2265, TNA. Central to the compilation and distribution of this intelligence was the Middle East Intelligence Centre (MEIC), which began operation in Cairo in August 1939. In May–July 1943 it merged with the newly established Political Intelligence Centre Middle East (PICME). See H. O. Dovey, "The Middle East Intelligence Centre," *Intelligence and National Security* 4, no. 4 (October 1989): 800–812.

9. About DSOs in general, see Calder Walton, *Empire of Secrets: British Intelligence, the Cold War, and the Twilight of Empire* (New York: Overlook Press, 2013), 24–25.

10. Memorandum on counterintelligence in the Middle East area with special reference to Iraq and Persia, 4 June 1943, KV 4/223, TNA.

11. O'Sullivan, *The Baghdad Set*, 123–25.

12. Diary of Guy Liddell, 22 October 1943, KV 4/192, TNA.

13. David Mure, *Practise to Deceive* (London: William Kimber, 1977), 49. For an alternate example, where no organized network existed, see chapter 1 of this volume.

14. O'Sullivan, *The Baghdad Set*, 2019.

15. Adrian O'Sullivan, *Nazi Secret Warfare in Occupied Persia (Iran): The Failure of the German Intelligence Services, 1939–45* (Basingstoke: Palgrave Macmillan, 2014); *Espionage and Counterintelligence in Occupied Persia (Iran): The Success of the Allied Secret Services, 1941–45* (Basingstoke: Palgrave Macmillan, 2015).

16. See, for example, Max Hastings, *The Secret War: Spies, Code and Guerrillas, 1939–45* (London: William Collins, 2016), 278.

17. Hinsley and Simkins, *British Intelligence*, vol. 4, 189.

18. Bickham Sweet-Escott, *Baker Street Irregular* (London: Methuen, 1965), 73. See also Saul Kelly, "A Succession of Crises: SOE in the Middle East, 1940–45," *Intelligence and National Security* 20, no. 1 (March 2005): 121–46.

19. Nigel West, *Secret War: The Story of SOE, Britain's Wartime Sabotage Organisation* (London: Hodder & Stoughton, 1992), 49–51.

20. On the importance of Kellar's liaison work, see Adrian O'Sullivan, "British Security Intelligence in Occupied Persia, 1942–1944," *Global War Studies* 12, no. 1 (2015): 44; for more about Kellar's influential personality, see Adrian

O'Sullivan, "Joe Spencer's Ratcatchers: British Security Intelligence in Occupied Persia," *Asian Affairs* 48, no. 2 (July 2017): 307.

21. The so-called "hush-hush versus bang-bang" rivalry. Anonymized online contributions to the Special Operations Executive Group, 29 July 2022, https://groups.io/g/specialoperationsexecutive.

22. Malcolm Atkin, "Appendix 2: Officers, Agents and Contacts of Section D of the Secret Intelligence Service," in *Section D for Destruction: Forerunner of SOE* (Barnsley: Pen and Sword, 2017), 79–80.

23. Nigel West, *MI5: British Security Service Operations 1909–45* (London: Triad Granada, 1983), 34, 364; *MI6: British Secret Intelligence Service Operations 1909–45* (London: Grafton, 1987), 311, 343.

24. According to the Foreign Secretary, Anthony Eden, the British Council refused "to allow any employee or person subsidised by it to take part in . . . clandestine activities such as intelligence work." Of course, this authoritative declaration does not preclude the granting of cover by the Council—originally established by the FO in 1934 to fight fascism—to employees or agents of other organizations. See Eden to Knatchbull-Hugessen, Telegram No. 254, 11 February 1942, FO 195/2473/35, TNA.

25. "Black" propaganda is covert propaganda; "white" propaganda is overt propaganda, often synonymous with publicity; "grey" propaganda is unsourced propaganda. "Black operations" or "black ops," which were part of Adrian Bishop's SOE subversion remit, are generally covert, deceptive, deniable operations, such as bribery, blackmail, "sibs" (whispering campaigns), or kidnapping.

26. Notably Adrian Bishop, Pat Domvile, Terence Bruce Mitford, Stewart Perowne, Aidan Philip, and Freya Stark.

27. By "ballyhoo" I mean that, besides the official history of MI6, scarcely a history or memoir of the British secret services exists that does not speak of interservice rivalries. See Keith Jeffery, *The Secret History of MI6* (New York: Penguin, 2010), 352–58. Cf. Gill Bennett (ex-FO), distinguished member of the research team that contributed to Jeffery's official history, who has recently explained that competition for resources, especially in belt-tightening periods, is often the simple reason for conflict and/or rivalry between intelligence services. Gill Bennett, "How the CORBY Spy Case of 1945 Caught Everyone Napping" (presentation, Cambridge Intelligence Seminar, University of Cambridge, 5 February 2021). For informed narratives about rivalries, see David Stafford, *Britain and the European Resistance, 1940–45: A Survey of the Special Operations Executive with Documents* (London: Macmillan, 1980), 38–56; West, *Secret War*, 250–52; Richard J. Aldrich, "Britain's Secret Intelligence Service in Asia during the Second World War," *Modern Asian Studies* 32, no. 1 (1998): 179–217; Kelly, "Succession of Crises," 121–46.

28. Christopher Sykes, *High Minded Murder* (London: Home & Van Thal, 1944).

29. As with most members of MI6, information on Robin Zaehner is difficult to obtain, beyond his scholarly achievements as an eminent Oxford University professor and various references to his postwar role in Operation BOOT/TPAJAX and the overthrow of the Persian prime minister, Mohammed Mossadeq, in 1953. See Wm. Roger Louis, "Britain and the Overthrow of the Mossadeq Government," in *Mohammed Mossadeq and the 1953 Coup in Iran*, ed. Mark J. Gasiorowski and Malcolm Byrne (Syracuse, NY: Syracuse University Press, 2004), 130–35, which reveals something of Zaehner's eccentric personality.

30. Administrative Boundaries-Africa, General Mediterranean and Middle East, World War II Records, folder 158, Record Group 407, National Archives and Records Administration (NARA), College Park, MD. On PGC, see Ashley Jackson, *Persian Gulf Command: A History of the Second World War in Iran and Iraq* (New Haven, CT: Yale University Press, 2018).

31. The failures in Persia (Iran) are all described, analyzed, and documented in O'Sullivan, *Nazi Secret Warfare*, 191–239. The Iraq operations are narrated and examined in O'Sullivan, *The Baghdad Set*, 181–218.

32. For Operation TEL AFAR, see AIR 29/2513, TNA; WO 208/3095. For REISERNTE, all the existing archival and literary sources on REISERNTE are cited in O'Sullivan, *Nazi Secret Warfare*, 209n77. For KINO, see O'Sullivan, *Nazi Secret Warfare*, 210–11.

33. See KV 2/1281–1285, TNA; O'Sullivan, *Espionage and Counterintelligence*, 162–66.

34. The RE macrocamouflage operations will be described in my forthcoming book (co-authored with Claire Hubbard-Hall and due out in 2026) with the working title "The Secret Agent's Wardrobe: Dress, Disguise, and Deception in the Second World War." For another example that illuminates connections between staff organization and operations, see chapter 3 by Jeff Rutherford in this volume.

35. Bishop's life has not been cohesively documented either in the archives or in the literature; his "government" work during his nomadic interwar years, while circumstantially evident, is difficult to trace beyond anecdotes by various friends and acquaintances, some of which are mentioned in O'Sullivan, *The Baghdad Set*, 1–2, 17–18.

36. For further details, see O'Sullivan, *The Baghdad Set*, 93–114.

37. History of Combined Intelligence Centre Iraq and Persia June 1941–December 1944, AIR 29/2504, TNA.

38. Wood to Minister of State, 16 July 1943, WO 201/1404, TNA.

39. Trevor Royle, *Glubb Pasha* (London: Little, Brown, 1992), 238.

40. James Lunt, *The Arab Legion* (London: Constable, 1999), 96.

41. See note 25.

42. Iraq, Mid East, and Balkans Section, 28 April 1941, Survey of Global Activities, War Diary 4, April 1941, HS 7/215, TNA.

43. Consanguinity also doubtless played a part in the success of intelligence relationships in Iraq, for four of these Baghdad-based friends were in fact more

than that: Domvile (SOE), Hodgkin (SOE), Lloyd (SOE), and Perowne (FO) were all cousins. Seton Lloyd, *The Interval: A Life in Near Eastern Archaeology* (Farringdon: Lloyd Collon, 1986), 84–85.

44. O'Sullivan, *The Baghdad Set*, 132–34.

45. Chapter 1 by Sara Castro in this volume describes how foreign language capability affected recruitment of American intelligence officials operating in China.

46. For details of individual sections and the wide range of duties they performed in all theaters, see A. F. Judge, "The Field Security Sections of the Intelligence Corps, 1939 to 1960," unpublished MS, Military Intelligence Museum and Archives, Chicksands, Bedfordshire.

47. For further details, see O'Sullivan, *The Baghdad Set*, 151–68; Geoffrey Household, *Against the Wind* (London: Michael Joseph, 1958).

48. See O'Sullivan, *The Baghdad Set*, 23n10, regarding the ambivalence of Mitford's role as a former Section D officer.

49. See the statement by Sir Dick White, later to become head of MI5 and MI6, in Minutes and notes on the meeting of SIME representatives held at Beirut, 12–13 February 1943, KV 4/240, TNA. For more about Underwood, Mitford, and Force KALPAK, see O'Sullivan, *The Baghdad Set*, 110n8, 161–64, 167n34. Regarding Axis submarine activity in the Gulf, see File 28/15 Submarine menace, IOR/R/15/2/702, India Office Records and Private Papers, British Library (BL).

50. For details of the war-within-a-war waged by Hugessen and the FO against the secret services in their quest for cover, see my forthcoming book *Behind the Veil of Neutrality: Secret Intelligence and Security Operations in Turkey, 1939–45*.

51. Appendix E: Deployment of Area Liaison Officers, Other Security-intelligence Personnel, and Political Advisers in Iraq, ca. early 1944, according to War Establishment (PAIC/1046/I), KV 4/223, TNA, in O'Sullivan, *The Baghdad Set*, 269–70.

52. Cornwallis's entire wartime administration is comprehensively documented in various Baghdad embassy despatches and other FO records published in *Foreign Office Annual Reports from Arabia, 1930–1960*, vol. 3: 1938–1953 (Cambridge: Archive Editions, 1993); Robert Jarman, ed., *Political Diaries of the Arab World: Iraq*, vol. 6: 1932–1947 (Cambridge: Archive Editions, 1998).

53. Hinsley and Simkins, *British Intelligence*, vol. 4, 163.

54. Lascelles to CGS PAIFORCE, 7 July 1943, WO 201/1401, TNA.

55. See O'Sullivan, *The Baghdad Set*, 136–138.

56. See David Mure, *Master of Deception: Tangled Webs in London and the Middle East* (London: William Kimber, 1980); *Practise to Deceive* (London: William Kimber, 1977); Private papers of D.W.A. Mure, 2194, Imperial War Museum (IWM).

57. Private papers of D. Drax, 2164, IWM.

58. KONO = Kriegsorganisation Nahost.

59. History of Combined Intelligence Centre Iraq and Persia June 1941–December 1944, AIR 29/2504, TNA.

60. SS-Auslandsnachrichtendienst. The SS formation was established as RSHA VI (Reichssicherheitshauptamt Amt VI [Branch VI of the Reich Security Directorate]).

61. The Home Office file on Moyzisch is at KV 2/168–169, TNA.

62. For the official CICI reports on both German operations, see AIR 29/2513, TNA; for additional material on TEL AFAR, see WO 208/3095, TNA. The most authoritative secondary source on MAMMUT is Bernd Lemke and Pherset Rosbeiani, eds., *Unternehmen Mammut: Ein Kommandoeinsatz der Wehrmacht im Nordirak 1943* (Bremen: Edition Falkenberg, 2018). For literature on the ex-Mufti, see O'Sullivan, *The Baghdad Set*, 260n26.

63. For a simultaneous story of Soviet defections, including *to* the German side, see Kevin Riehle's chapter 11 in this volume.

64. For more on the strategic success of British intelligence in the region, see O'Sullivan, *The Baghdad Set*, 245–56.

65. See note 44.

66. For more about Freya Stark in Iraq, see O'Sullivan, *The Baghdad Set*, 68–71.

67. An Appreciation of the Security Situation in Iraq in the Near Future and in the Post-war Period, 14 July 1945, KV 4/223, TNA.

68. Note on Future Security Problems in Mid-East, Appendix B, November 1943, KV 4/384, TNA; Report on Visit by Mr A. J. Kellar to SIME and CICI Organizations, 25 April 1944, KV 4/384, TNA.

69. Cf. Basil Liddell-Hart, *History of the Second World War* (London: Pan, 1973), 275. Rutherford makes a similar argument about Operation Barbarossa in chapter 3 of this volume.

3

Prelude to Barbarossa?
The 4th Mountain Division War in Yugoslavia, April–May 1941

Jeff Rutherford

Operation Barbarossa, the code name for the German invasion of the Soviet Union that began on 22 June 1941, has rightly served as the historical focus of Germany's Second World War, as it not only opened the largest, most destructive conflict of the Second World War, but it was also a criminal venture without parallel in modern European history. The invasion demonstrated one logical, if not inevitable, culmination of the Prusso-German "way of war" as it evolved between the wars of unification and the Second World War. This approach to armed conflict can be broken into two related components. On the battlefield, it relied on officers and even NCOs to make quick decisions on their own initiative in the midst of the fray, while emphasizing the use of surprise, speed, and aggression to achieve quick and decisive victories.[1] By marrying this traditional German approach to war with the technology of the combustion engine, the German army defeated a series of opponents in 1939 and 1940 in shockingly swift campaigns.[2] The flip side of the German way of war on the battlefield was the one waged behind the lines. The army viewed modern industrial conflict as no longer consisting of a mere struggle between professional militaries, but rather as one between societies in which the control and mobilization of resources was paramount; in other words, the army believed that the Second World War needed to be waged as a total war in order to avoid a reprise of 1918. Based on its experiences with franc-tireurs in the Franco-Prussian War and the occupation and exploitation of Belgium, the Baltic States, and Romania during the First World War, the German army's institutional approach to total war resulted in sharp and violent policies toward popular resistance, as well as a concerted effort to yoke occupied territories to the larger German war effort.[3]

The culmination of these two approaches—undoubtedly radicalized by the Nazi regime's ideological beliefs—emerged with the invasion of the

Soviet Union. This attack was the first campaign explicitly planned in accordance with the principles of mechanized war, and it demonstrated both the strengths and weaknesses of the German way of war as it developed during the conflict. According to the planning for the Soviet campaign, German armored spearheads would plunge deeply into the Soviet Union, encircling and destroying the bulk of the Red Army in as little as six weeks. Once the invasion was underway, however, various problems hindered the advance of the army as a whole. In particular, the primitive state of the Soviet road network, within a theater dotted with impenetrable forests and large swamps and marshes, not only frustrated troops at the front but ensured that supply was sporadic at best. Battlefield events, however, constituted only one piece of Operation Barbarossa. As a result of viewing war as total, the military campaign was complemented by an ideological and economic program that looked to destroy both the perceived "Judeo-Bolshevik" foundations of the state and any popular resistance it inspired, while simultaneously exploiting the Soviet Union's natural resources—particularly food—for the German war effort. Mass starvation and mass murder, including the beginnings of the destruction of Europe's Jews, thus accompanied the war at the front.

This unprecedented radicalization of total war, however, failed to simply materialize out of thin air and instead fit neatly into the progression of the German conduct of war. Elements of both the military and economic/ideological aspects of the war previously appeared in Poland and the west, but the neglected Yugoslavian campaign proved the closest to that of Operation Barbarossa in merging the operational and occupation practices of the German way of war. For the most part, events in Yugoslavia almost exclusively register in the historiography through a focus on German occupation and the resulting bitterly contested struggle for power between various groups, including the Ustaše, Chetniks, Partisans, Axis collaborators, Italian forces, and the Germans themselves—a struggle that triggered the Holocaust in Serbia.[4] Such attention is clearly warranted, as the insurgency and German responses highlight numerous important issues to understanding German objectives during the war, as well as the history of southeastern Europe. This focus, however, has obscured the importance of the German army's policies and actions from April through early June 1941 in understanding its evolution during the Second World War.

This chapter examines the conduct of the 4th Mountain Division during the neglected, yet breathtakingly quick, eleven-day campaign that subjugated the Yugoslavian state and its brief period of occupation. Initially raised to participate in Operation Barbarossa, the 4th Mountain Division's first experiences of war in Serbia serve as a clear indicator both of the economic and ideological aspects of the German army's war, as well as the strengths and weaknesses of German battlefield practices in 1941. That Yugoslavia was not viewed as a target for German expansion until a mere ten days before the campaign began highlights the importance of the army's approach to modern, industrial war, instead of that of the Nazi state and its ruthless population policies.[5] The interaction between how the army intended to fight the war, the friction resulting from supply problems caused by both terrain and an insufficiently motorized army, and the resulting security and requisitioning policies directed toward the local Serbian population all foreshadowed the invasion of the Soviet Union. In other words, the total war waged by the German army in the eastern theater of war was not sui generis. Instead, the relationship between military and occupation practices that serve as the foundation of our understanding of Operation Barbarossa had already appeared in concert during the Yugoslavian campaign; analysis of the army's practices here shed much light on its evolution during the Second World War.

Preparations for War in 1941:
The Establishment of the 4th Mountain Division

Once the die had been cast for the invasion of the Soviet Union, the German army began a two-tracked planning for the operation. From a battlefield perspective, it was clear that the invasion of the Soviet Union needed to incorporate the lessons learned from the Polish and the western campaigns into operational planning. This meant that speed and mobility needed to be exploited to the utmost to achieve a decisive victory over the Red Army. The panzer group experimentally used in the 1940 French campaign was now institutionalized for the eastern campaign, and four of these mobile groups would be deployed for Operation Barbarossa. While those attached to the northern and southern army groups would drive on Leningrad and Rostov-on-Don, respectively, working in conjunction with the marching infantry armies, the two panzer groups subordinate to Army Group Center were tasked with carrying out massive encirclement operations along the Minsk-Smolensk-Moscow axis, designed to destroy the bulk of the Red Army that the Germans believed would be securing the approaches to the capital. In order to ensure victory, German planners believed that the bulk of Soviet forces needed to be crushed west of the Dvina-Dnieper River line. This meant that the panzer groups would require the necessary amounts of supplies—fuel, ammunition, food, spare parts, and reinforcements—to maintain their momentum. Just as important, the desire for a speedy victory meant that the marching infantry needed to advance as quickly as possible into those areas that the panzer groups had merely darted through. Not only were they essential to secure the rear areas to ensure that the necessary supplies reached the mobile units, but they were also vital to collapse and crush the pockets formed by the panzer groups. Working within the parameters of the traditional German way of war, speed, and aggressive action—from panzer units to those reliant on boot leather for movement—therefore formed the foundation of the army's plan.

Complementing battlefield planning, the army cooperated with other Nazi organizations in planning for the plunder of the Soviet Union, as well as the elimination of any groups it believed ideologically predisposed to lead a popular insurgency. From an economic standpoint, the Soviet Union's agricultural production would be used for the Reich's purposes. Working in conjunction with the economic organization established to exploit Soviet resources for the German war effort, *Wirtschaftsstab Ost,* the army planned to live off Soviet agricultural production to ease the burden on the German home front, with the surplus sent to feed Germans at home. From the ideological standpoint, the army became actively complicit in murder, particularly through its prewar agreement with the SS to support *Einsatzgruppen* activities directed against Communist functionaries and Soviet Jews. The army also directly had its own troops commit murder through the issuing of the Commissar Order, which called for the execution of all Soviet political commissars captured in battle. Finally, the Martial Jurisdiction Order effectively freed German troops from prosecution for mistreating civilians, while simultaneously demanding collective responses to outbreaks of insurgency. In sum, the ideological orders created an atmosphere in which "Judeo-Bolshevism" was seen as animating all resistance and thus needed to be destroyed preemptively.

In order to fulfill this ambitious and murderous plan, the German army took several steps. From the purely military perspective, it needed to grow in size. Most important for the purposes of this chapter, the army needed to expand its forces from the 143 divisions that invaded France to a full 180 divisions.[6] Included in this expansion of the army were the establishment of the 4th and 5th Mountain Divisions on 15 October 1940.[7] Despite the fact that these units would be needed to follow the advancing mobile divisions as quickly as possible, Germany's stunted motorization program made it extremely difficult to outfit these newly raised formations with adequate numbers of vehicles. The 4th Mountain Division complained during its entire mustering and training period of insufficient motorization. Although the division's superior corps recognized 4th Mountain Division's need for vehicles, its response made clear the larger context of German industrial weakness: "As a result of the restructuring of panzer and motorized divisions in conjunction with the strained vehicle situation, it appears that the renewal of your request is pointless at this point in time."[8] One month into its establishment, the division reported that it faced a shortage of 636 vehicles and 547 motorcycles from its authorized strength.[9] The division viewed its reliance on horses for pulling its artillery as a hindrance and requested twelve additional vehicles for this purpose but was once again summarily denied.[10] When it finally received vehicles, many were of foreign manufacture seized in previous campaigns and the unit recognized that once they broke down, their repair would be extremely difficult, if not impossible.[11] From an equipment standpoint, it would be very difficult to characterize the 4th Mountain Division as prepared to move at the pace demanded by the German High Command.

In lieu of vehicles, the 4th Mountain Division's mobility would be based on marching and beasts of burden. According to the German army's table of organization and equipment, a mountain division was originally authorized a total of 6,350 horses and mules.[12] Just as the division found it hard to locate enough vehicles, so it struggled with reaching its authorized strength in animals. With the majority of infantry divisions reliant on horses for their mobility, the scramble for animals assumed a real importance in the mobilization of German units.[13] In late January, it reported a shortage of some five hundred animals, though with the reduction of the authorized strength to 5,658 in February 1941, the division noted that it now reached its full complement.[14] Despite being some 150 vehicles short of its authorized strength when the division deployed for its first combat operations in mid-March, the division commander deemed his unit "completely operational."[15] So even though Operation Barbarossa was conceived of as a blitz campaign based on the necessity for a quick and decisive victory, units such as the 4th Mountain Division fit neatly into Rolf-Dieter Müller's characterization of the German army in early 1941: "The majority of the troops fought and marched as in the time of Napoleon: by foot, with horse and wagon, with rifle and cannon."[16]

Complementing the training and outfitting of units in preparation for Operation Barbarossa was a newfound emphasis on ideological preparation. Each unit's officers served as the conduit for the army's traditional emphasis on spiritual care for its soldiers, but this became increasingly politicized during the Third Reich, reaching a new peak in late 1940 and early 1941.[17] The army high command issued an order on 7 October 1940 that provided the template for ideological instruction.[18] Arguing that what mattered was that "a *uniform* concept of the foundations of National Socialism should exist in the army and become the common property of all soldiers," the directive listed several themes it deemed vital to the "education" of the German soldier, including the "German *Volk*," the "German Empire," "German living space," and "National Socialism as the foundation." During its establishment in 1940, the 4th Mountain Division's troops attended various lectures, ranging from "The Greater European Economy from the Military-Political Perspective" and "Soldiers and *Weltanschauung*" to "Total War" and "The Spiritual War."[19] Such lectures were meant both to place Germany's present war into a longer historical perspective and legitimize German efforts to bring "order" and "stability" to the continent. They also prepared soldiers to view their tasks as more than merely defeating the enemy army; for the German army and the Third Reich, war encompassed more than the battlefield, and this was especially the case for its upcoming clash with the Soviet Union.

Combat and Occupation in Yugoslavia

Developments in southeastern Europe, however, meant that the 4th Mountain Division would see its first action in Yugoslavia instead of the USSR and here it would wage a war that linked the army's previous campaigns in Poland and France with that of the Soviet Union. Italy's precipitate and blundering invasion of Greece in late 1940 destabilized the region and the threat of British troops in southeastern Europe led to Hitler's decision to intervene.[20] Economic thinking drove German policy here; Romanian oil was the most pressing concern for the Germans, but Yugoslavian grain, copper, zinc, and lead, among other raw materials, were vital for the German war effort and needed to be safeguarded from Allied operations.[21] As part of the Twelfth Army, the 4th Mountain Division arrived in Bulgaria in late March for the anticipated invasion of Greece. Following a coup d'état on 27 March that overthrew the pro-Axis Yugoslavian regime, the division and other elements of the Twelfth Army hastily rerouted for an attack on Yugoslavia. The German plan for the destruction of Yugoslavia centered on German forces advancing from the former Austria, Hungary, Romania, and Bulgaria in an attempt to both quickly seize Belgrade and slice Yugoslavia into several pieces, rendering it impossible for its army to mount a coherent defense, and thus allowing the army to refocus on the imminent and far more important invasion of the Soviet Union.

To the north and northeast, the Second Army's commander, Generaloberst Maximilian von Weichs, commanded four corps. XXXXVI Motorized Corps—containing the bulk of his panzer divisions—would attack in two different directions. One wing would advance on Belgrade to the southeast where it was to be met by XXXXI Corps advancing from Romania, while another would drive to the southwest via Zagreb to Karlovac where it would link with the Italian Second Army.[22] Located in the former Austria, XXXXIX Mountain Corps would drive south on the Croatian capital as well, ensuring its quick seizure. The Second Army's attack was to be complemented by that of Generalfeldmarschall Wilhelm List's Twelfth Army. While XXX Corps would directly invade Greece, elements of XVIII Mountain Corps would momentarily cut through Yugoslav territory as a means to outflank the Greek Metaxas line. The Twelfth Army's other two units, however, received much more prominent roles in the invasion of Yugoslavia. Panzer Group One was tasked with pushing north from the border through Niš toward Belgrade where it would meet with Second Army forces advancing on the city, effectively encircling the Yugoslavian capital.[23] XXXX Motorized Corps would drive due west via Skopje to the Albanian border, where it would link with Italian forces.[24] In combination, these two armies' advances would quickly destroy the ability of Yugoslavian forces to successfully resist the invasion, demonstrating the efficacy of the German way of war on the battlefield.

As part of Panzer Group One, the 4th Mountain Division was charged with marching on the Yugoslavian capital located in Serbia. Even before the attack opened, however, redeployment from the Greek to Serbian border was complicated by both the poor state of Bulgarian roads and the weather.[25] This was recognized by the division; its quartermaster noted that the "extremely poor road situation" in the division's area of operations would lead to "considerable difficulties" in supply.[26] Of course, German planning for the invasion of Yugoslavia followed the model set by the campaigns in 1939 and 1940: Speed and decisive attacks were necessary for a quick victory. The division therefore received orders that the invasion of Yugoslavia would be "opened as a surprise" and that while a tenacious and bitter Serbian defense of the mountains was to be expected, German forces needed to reach Belgrade as soon as possible.[27] The tensions between operational objectives and logistic realities that had already appeared in the German way of war during the opening years of the conflict once again reared their heads, and division command foresaw a situation in which combat formations would find themselves increasingly distant from their supply units from the very opening days of the campaign.[28]

The 4th Mountain Division crossed the Bulgarian-Yugoslavian border on 8 April, beginning its own "litmus test" two days after other elements of the Twelfth Army had opened the attack. Spearheading Panzer Group One's assault was the 11th Panzer Division, followed closely by the 5th Panzer

Division, and they made good progress from the opening day of the campaign.[29] Unfortunately, the marching elements of the panzer group struggled to maintain the pace, due in large part to a road network that quickly deteriorated under German use. Since the German way of war demanded quick and decisive attacks, however, the remainder of Panzer Group One trudged behind, trying to close the gap with the onrushing tanks. Despite the abominable terrain, the 4th Mountain Division displayed the verve and aggression demanded by the German army. Its commander, Generalmajor Karl Eglseer, rode in the first vehicle that crossed the Yugoslavian frontier, and while he soon returned to the division's command post to orient himself to the entirety of his front, he still intervened "when necessary" in the fighting.[30] Following the initial breakthrough of the stubborn Yugoslavian defense, the division then trailed in the wake of the panzer units, running into little to no resistance over the next two days.

Despite complaints of exhaustion after four days of forced marches along muddy roads, the division followed the traditional German way of war as expressed by the division commander: "Attack the enemy where you find him." Following his own dictate, Eglseer "determined to give the enemy no time to construct a defense or prepare a counterattack and, instead wanting to attack and destroy him as quickly as possible," on his own initiative ordered his men to push into the Timok-Morava area.[31] Three days later, the division reported the capture of over 17,000 Yugoslavian soldiers and an "unimaginable amount of goods," and it received special recognition from Panzer Group One for its "extremely vigorous attack."[32] In its opening baptism of fire, the 4th Mountain Division fought seamlessly within the German tradition of speedy and independent aggressive attacks.

Of course, to ensure that such vigorous attacks could continue, the division needed to receive necessary supplies from the rear. This, however, proved to be a massive problem during the Yugoslavian campaign. Already on the campaign's second day, terrible road conditions frustrated all attempts to concentrate the unit, resulting in its being strung out for miles. Consequently, supply columns were unable to reach the front, and the troops were forced to purchase their food from the surrounding countryside.[33] The situation only worsened over the coming days, as not only were the mountaineers dependent on a churned-up, muddy track that more closely resembled a quagmire than the paved roads of western Europe, but they shared this solitary supply road with *four* other divisions, ensuring that each unit only received a trickle of supplies at the sharp end. Not only was division's fuel situation "strained," but it also resulted in its most forward units receiving no warm food for over a week. In response to this development, the division ordered that "an extensive living off the land is necessary." All stocks of food discovered by the troops were to be used to cover their immediate needs, and "self-help" became the order of the day. Due to what the army termed the "minimal [stocks] and decentralized" nature of Yugoslavia, the division's supply section could not fulfill this task, and individual soldiers were frequently left to their own devices to feed themselves.[34] Since the invasion occurred during the sowing season, the division requisitioned or simply stole from the depleted stocks needed by peasants to survive until the summer's harvest. The zero-sum nature of food consumption that stamped Operation Barbarossa thus became the rule for the 4th Mountain Division during its two-week campaign in Serbia.

The seizure of Yugoslavian foodstuffs thus figured into the division's daily activities; this, however, was merely the tip of the iceberg of German economic goals. In the days before the opening of hostilities, Panzer Group One issued a detailed summation of the importance of Yugoslavia in the larger context of the "greater German economic area."[35] Declaring any "unauthorized intervention in businesses of any type, especially in the area of agriculture as sabotage," it then detailed the use of *Erfassungkommandos* (collection groups) to secure food and fuel for the unit's advance. The panzer unit also had special staff dedicated to the "takeover and the restarting of Yugoslavian industry and the vital provisioning services." Finally, it tasked its subordinate troops with the securing of industrial concerns when possible. The 4th Mountain Division followed in the panzer group's steps, also establishing its own units to collect captured goods and materials.[36] While there was an emphasis on securing all scattered weapons for reasons of security (a topic discussed further below), other items were immediately pressed into service. The most important items in this respect were Yugoslavian cooking pots and wagons to haul them.[37] These proved invaluable to those units that regular supply failed to reach during the campaign. Other goods and resources were also collected, however, and this process both shed light on the army's attempts to incorporate Yugoslavia into Germany's war economy and the army's appreciation of the links between security and long-term economic exploitation.

Three days into the campaign, the division issued its first order concerning occupation goals. The division's ranking intelligence officer addressed the particular German way of war as it developed during the Second World War and its effects on occupation.[38] The emphasis on speed and mobility resulted in "the temporary use of smaller troop sections which are used tactically in battle, but which are also for the most part on their own regarding supply and administration of territory after the conclusion of combat."

Since German forces overran areas before any administrators from the rear could be deployed, security, administrative, and economic tasks "fall entirely on the troops. Just as the total commitment from every leader and sub-leader is naturally presumed in battle, henceforth so must a complete understanding of the new objectives in the organizational sphere be demanded from everyone."

The order then broke down the division's occupation tasks into two categories. The first was directly related to security. The tasks included the protection of important installations from plundering by German soldiers, as well as the collection and safeguarding of all captured goods. Enemy prisoners were also to be immediately plugged into labor groups to assist with road maintenance; this practice already dated from the second day of the invasion and the division's use of prisoner of war labor remained part of its policy during the remainder of its time in Yugoslavia. Such practices corresponded to German plans for prisoners in the Soviet Union, though the fate of Red Army men in German captivity would soon take a much grimmer and horrific turn. Nonetheless, the utilitarian approach of the army to Yugoslavian prisoners foreshadowed its practices during Operation Barbarossa.

The second half of the order highlighted the economic goals of the division and, by extension, Germany in Yugoslavia. Once the fighting had concluded, the mountaineers needed to both secure vital materials, ranging from food to wood and coal, and to restart the economy. This meant that divisional leaders needed to work with local authorities to restore administrative order. The troops were also charged with supervising the local population and ensuring that they went back to work. Finally, they had to reconnoiter the local area and find all industrial installations. The order's concluding paragraph, however, most fully betrayed the totality of German goals in Yugoslavia:

> In addition to the natural drive of the German soldier "to create order," it is imperative to bring the economic life of the territory temporarily paralyzed by combat back to work through quickly implemented organizational measures. This is because all conquered lands are, in the final analysis, foundations not only for the military's rear area and supply basis or for the Greater German Reich but building blocks for the great economic upsurge after the war.

German goals in Yugoslavia therefore encompassed far more than defeating the enemy army. Economic objectives were viewed as crucial by the Reich and their importance meant that the army needed to secure them immediately for the larger war effort of "the Greater German Reich." Before the complete exploitation of Yugoslavia could take place, however, the campaign needed to be won, and the 4th Mountain Division remained in the field.

Following in the wake of the panzer divisions, the mountaineers' primary task centered on smashing Yugoslavian formations that had scattered into forests and rounding up the survivors.[39] These types of operations allowed for the possibility of popular resistance, and in the age of people's war, German troops feared that Yugoslavian citizens, particularly ethnic Serbs, would actively resist German rule. Such thinking worked its way into the army's orders. At the highest level, the SS Einsatzgruppen accompanied the army into Yugoslavia, where they were initially tasked with eliminating "émigrés, saboteurs, and terrorists." Generaloberst Franz Halder, the Chief of the General Staff, and Generalmajor Eduard Wagner, the General Quartermaster of the Army, however, added "Communists, Jews" to the list on 26 March.[40] The addition of these groups reflected the army's internalization of the Nazi ideological enemy "Judeo-Bolshevism," and fear of this "enemy" directly influenced German policy in Serbia. When the final agreement between the army and SS concerning the employment of Einsatzgruppen in the Soviet Union was signed on 28 April 1941, its provisions were then expanded to both Yugoslavia and Greece. As pointed out by the historian Walter Manoschek, the application of this agreement to the Balkan theater of war, as well as Halder's insertion of communists and Jews as targets, meant that the German military not only viewed the war against the Soviet Union as an "ideological war," but that the Yugoslavian campaign took on similar undertones.[41] The files of the 4th Mountain Division betray no special animus toward either Jews or Communists, indicating that in April and May 1941, these were not viewed as the primary threats to the German army. Serbs, however, were specifically identified in army documentation as the root cause of the region's problems.

Prior to the outbreak of hostilities, the army high command issued the "Guidelines for the Conduct of the Troops in Yugoslavia." Describing Serbian soldiers in particular as "tough, brutish, and callous," it stated that "any leniency—even with prisoners" was out of place.[42] Notions of the Serbs as the instigators of the First World War permeated German and Austrian memories of the earlier conflict and thus influenced behavior in the present war. Generaloberst von Weichs, commander in chief of the Second Army, issued the following order to his troops on the eve of the attack, setting the tone for what eventually developed into a brutal occupation:

> It must be expected that the Serbian population will participate in the struggle against German troops through ambushes (snipers) and sabotage in perfidious ways. The cultural level of the Serbian population is very low. The Serb is

fanatical and is inclined towards atrocities and maliciousness. <u>The sharpest means</u> are to be used to intervene against any act of violence or sabotage. Only a ruthless crackdown at the beginning of the operation makes possible the eradication of these war crimes. I therefore make commanders of all ranks responsible for the nipping in the bud all bandit and malicious acts by all means (the timely and extensive arrests of hostages, especially from the intelligentsia).[43]

In discussion with the XXXXVI (mot.) corps commander before the attack began, Weichs reiterated the need for the "sharpest crackdown against snipers, guerrillas, etc."[44] Divisional leadership shared this general characterization of Serbs, warning its troops to be prepared for "gangs" led by Serbian officers who had fled into the mountains.[45] Serbian officers in particular were deemed both anti-Axis in their outlook and "the instigators of the putsch" and, as such, were separated from Croatian and Slovenian officers and put to work in "difficult and dirty work" such as road maintenance, construction, and cleaning latrines.[46]

In the opening days of the attack, however, the 4th Mountain Division exercised restraint in dealing with popular resistance. Following several of its troops coming under fire, the supply section carried out a sweep of the general area, confiscating numerous weapons and taking five hostages, including a local mayor, to ensure compliance with German demands.[47] Incidents such as this led the division, in accordance with the army's traditional anti-guerrilla practice dating back to the Franco-Prussian war, to order that "hostages are to be arrested anywhere where attacks take place or an unfriendly attitude by the population is spotted as a threat to the troops."[48]

This identification of Serbs as threats to German order in the Balkans was one that German troops could easily absorb and reflect. With the majority of the rank and file having been socialized in the Third Reich, they were conditioned by state and society to both shun and eliminate perceived threats to the *Volksgemeinschaft*, and similar language was used to describe the seemingly "fanatical," "primitive," and "brutish" Serbs.[49] This did not necessarily lead to atrocities or war crimes, though; the files of the 4th Mountain Division reveal no such occurrences. It was, however, an important step in preparing German soldiers for both the campaign against the Soviet Union, one in which various political, ethnic, and religious groups were targeted by the Nazi state, and the subsequent occupation of Serbia.

German operations proceeded relatively quickly, with Zagreb seized on 10 April, Belgrade falling two days later, and Sarajevo occupied on 15 April. Three days later, Yugoslavia capitulated. The 4th Mountain Division was one of the five combat divisions that would initially garrison Serbia, and, as such, the unit remained focused on "pacification and collection of captured goods."⁵⁰ It issued guidelines for occupation on 24 April that demonstrated the mixing of security and economic goals. Believing that "clandestine enemy action" was likely, the division issued several orders to ensure a rapid pacification, including the identification and surveillance of the civilian population in conjunction with local authorities, the conveyance of suspicious individuals and former soldiers to the German authorities, and the seizure of hostages in "unstable" areas. All industrial leaders also needed to be identified and examined, with special emphasis placed on Jewish businesses. The need for *Vetrauensleute*, or local informants, that the Germans could trust to provide them with intelligence and information on the local population was made clear. Here, the fractured ethnic nature of the state gave the division opportunities to exploit. Croats, ethnic Germans, or Slovenes were all suggested for this purpose; Serbs were noticeably absent from the list.⁵¹

Working within this context, the 4th Mountain Division continued its sweeps of the region, collecting men and weapons, before it was sent north to assist the 294th Infantry Division in the destruction of armed bands that had caused significant casualties for German forces in the region.⁵² This operation was also to be carried out according to the German way of war: "The troops are to be deployed for swift, mobile warfare."⁵³ This particular outbreak of insurgency caused XI Corps to issue an order notable for its sharpness. After warning the troops of possible further outbreaks of popular resistance throughout the occupied region, the corps commander stated, "I expect that all resistance will be broken with ruthless severity. Everyone found with a weapon in their hand in resistance or flight is to be shot immediately; those working with them are to be given over to a military or summary court martial for immediate sentencing." After suggesting that hostages be taken and shot in areas of continuing unrest, the order concluded that "all consideration shown by German troops will be construed as weakness and is misguided."⁵⁴

Such security-minded thinking animated the division's policies as it settled into its role as occupier.⁵⁵ The division's 94th Artillery Regiment enacted a strict occupation regime in the town of Požarevac that highlighted the connection between security and economic goals.⁵⁶ Within the region, the unit was responsible for a POW camp, as well as for securing goods captured during the campaign. In the town itself, the regiment worked closely with civilian authorities to identify both former soldiers and refugees; if under forty-five, the former were transferred to the POW camp while the latter were returned to their homes. The threat of terror was also baked into the system. Any Serbs caught sheltering former soldiers or possessing a weapon, as well as anyone who broke the 8 p.m. to 5 a.m. curfew without a pass, should "expect to be shot."

Whereas the ruthless conduct called for in such orders later turned occupied Serbia into a veritable slaughterhouse, the opening stages of German occupation were much calmer. For the 4th Mountain Division, security issues paled in comparison to economic ones. These can be broken into three pieces: resources put to direct use by the division, agricultural concerns, and the restarting of the Yugoslavian economy within the context of the greater German war economy. In early May, the division established two collection points for goods seized by its men.[57] The division had captured a tremendous amount of military equipment during the campaign, including numerous weapons desired by the army: some 10,000 rifles, ten 3.7cm and fifteen 5cm anti-tank guns, ten 7.5cm mountain guns, twenty 10cm field howitzers, and ten 2cm flak guns. Many of these would find use by German military and security forces. The division's rear-area services also received a necessary jolt as thirty captured field kitchens and 230 Serbian cooking pots—described by the division's quartermaster as "lighter and better" versions of the German equivalents—were immediately used by the division.[58] The importance of such collection efforts for the army was made clear in a declaration by Weichs, in which he recognized the troops not only for "their courageous efforts in battle" but also their "tireless work to increase the military strength of the German *Volk*."[59]

Complementing its practices of plundering Yugoslavia for its immediate use, the division also implemented policies designed to link the region's economy to the German war effort. Although food was still needed for the division's "continual supply," now living off the land carried a much different connotation. "Wild" confiscations by the troops were prohibited "in the interests of securing later nourishment and agricultural cultivation."[60] This attempt to limit the disruption of Yugoslavian agriculture fit into Germany's larger economic goals in the region. Fearful of the entire economy simply shutting down, the German army took several steps far outside of its normal remit. First, any firms that had received orders from the army could be paid in advance to maintain their viability. Second, in order to ensure "the preservation of businesses that lay in the interest of the German Wehrmacht and the general economic life," German *Ortskommandanturen* (town or garrison commanders) needed to put pressure on Yugoslavian administrators and banks to issue the necessary lines of credit.[61] Finally, the division also instituted set prices on various goods in its area of responsibility.[62] Reconciling these two competing economic goals—covering the division's immediate needs and a systematic exploitation of Yugoslavia within the larger German war economy—proved difficult. Perhaps the best example of this involved the 4th Mountain Division's reliance on animal power. According to the veterinary officer, the unit had added 657 horses and 913 oxen to its stable by the end of the fighting. When the division shipped out of Yugoslavia in mid-June, these numbers had ballooned to nearly 13,200 horses and over 3,100 oxen, the overwhelming majority of which had simply been taken from the population.[63] Plundering on this scale by the division could only have had catastrophic effects on the population's ability to reap its harvest and feed itself, which in turn would limit what Germany could drain from the country. Competing economic concerns in Yugoslavia thus loomed large during both the invasion itself and the immediate period of occupation for the 4th Mountain Division, and they foreshadowed a much more substantial clash in the Soviet Union.

The Yugoslavian Campaign within the Context of the Second World War

What can a two-week campaign in southeastern Europe tell us about the German experience of war as the conflict neared its zenith with the Reich's invasion of the Soviet Union?[64] From a battlefield perspective, the campaign of the 4th Mountain Division provides a very useful means of evaluating the German way of war before its spectacular successes and then ultimate failure on the steppes and in the forests of the Soviet Union. At the macro level, the German emphasis on speed and initiative proved itself in battle against the Yugoslavian army. Surprise concentric attacks on Yugoslavia staggered its army during the opening days of the campaign, and as noted by the 4th Mountain Division's ranking intelligence officer, constant pressure and bold movements completely unhinged "a morally shaken opponent."[65] This approach also functioned effectively at the micro level. Despite being underequipped with vehicles and utterly reliant on animal power to drag its artillery during the advance, the mountaineers maintained the necessary pace to support Panzer Group One's onrushing panzer divisions. Fulfilling the expectations of a German divisional commander, Eglseer took the initiative and carried out an extremely successful independent operation, destroying the Yugoslavian resistance his troops encountered. Although the "great distances" between the various combat groups "significantly aggravated command," the German emphasis on low-level initiative and commanders leading from the front ensured that "progress in the sense of the entire [operation] was maintained."[66] The troops had also risen to the challenge: "Despite long demanding marches in heat, as well as bad weather ... despite periodic supply difficulties, the attitude, discipline and combat morale was always very high." Therefore, even newly raised units could be expected to perform at high levels of efficiency in combat and this boded well for future German operations in the Soviet Union. On the battlefield, the Yugoslavian campaign built upon the lessons of the Polish and French campaigns and applied them with stunning success.

Numerous problems arose during the Yugoslavian campaign, however, that would prove fatal in the Soviet Union during the second half of 1941. Some of these were specific to the nature of the theater. German advances throughout the fighting in the Balkans were continually frustrated and delayed due to the terrain. The 4th Mountain Division's commander believed that many of the division's difficulties in the Serbian campaign could be boiled down to the "poor road conditions."[67] Unlike the western theater of war, which possessed numerous paved roads that greatly eased both the advance of German mechanized and motorized formations and the supply units so essential to maintaining the momentum of the attack, the Yugoslavian theater of war possessed far fewer decent roads and this continually stymied the 4th Mountain Division's ability to keep its combat units supplied, as well as diminishing its combat efficiency. This was particularly a problem for the reconnaissance section that relied on the use of motorcycles. Noting that the section was "equipped for European road conditions"—a turn of phrase which betrayed the German view of countries east of the Oder and south of the Danube—it reported that the unit's motorcycles became "so full of silt in the shortest time, that they could no longer turn and had to be carried." This decreased the rate of advance to one kilometer per *four* hours. Perhaps the clearest indication of the army's difficulties in adapting to the terrain was the fact that the "practical assistance" for keeping the motorcycles mobile consisted of temporarily loading them on oxen carts to move them across impassable areas. It goes without saying that units dependent on beasts of burden to pull their vehicles could scarcely be expected to maintain a quick pace. Mud, which would prove so debilitating to German fortunes in fall 1941, had already proven in April 1941 to be one of the German way of war's most formidable enemies. Such issues had proved much less debilitating in the western campaign, due to a more robust infrastructure that allowed for faster and denser traffic.

As the division made clear, its inability to maintain a consistent supply of food, ammunition, and other goods to the front was also due in part to its mobility or, more precisely, its lack of mobility. Claiming that its horse-drawn wagons were too heavy for two horses to pull on poor roads or up steep inclines, it requested additional lighter, narrow-gauged wagons. Although the division's motor vehicle stock remained generally undamaged by the campaign, the division emphasized that the only vehicle able to "effortlessly overcome all terrain difficulties was the half-track." As a result of its performance, it was clear that more of these vehicles would improve the division's combat effectiveness. Half-tracks and trucks were also "urgently requested" by one of the division's artillery battalions. Claiming that the III battalion had "completely failed during deployment," the division pointed out that it fell so far behind the fighting troops, that it only caught up with them at the conclusion of the campaign. The strains on the unit's horses were such that they still hadn't recovered by the middle of May, nearly a month after the fighting had ended. Similarly, the division's two engineer battalions required more vehicles that could handle driving cross-country in order to fulfill their numerous tasks.

From an operational standpoint, therefore, the problems that plagued the German army during Operation Barbarossa were already apparent. The disparity in speed between the mechanized and infantry units led to ever growing distances between the armored spearheads and the foot-marching formations to the rear. Compounding this issue was that of terrain. The underdeveloped infrastructure of Yugoslavia far more resembled that of the Soviet Union than it did that of France and Belgium, and as roads continually degenerated under use, German movement became increasingly difficult. In a two-week campaign within a limited operational area against a disjointed and divided enemy, such problems could be overcome. When faced with a determined opponent in an extremely expansive theater of operations, however, such problems proved to be incapacitating.

In order to fit the square peg of a quick and decisive advance into the round hole of inadequately motorized units operating in an environment bereft of solid roads, the 4th Mountain Division was forced to live off the land. Right from the opening days of the campaign, its men scoured the countryside for the nourishment necessary to maintain the attack's momentum. This plundering of Yugoslavian food, however, was merely the most localized piece of German economic plans for the country. In order to maintain its own combat efficiency, the division integrated numerous types of Yugoslavian weapons and equipment into its own ranks, ranging from cooking pots to mountain artillery guns. The fact that a front-line combat unit received orders in late May to locate Yugoslavian army butchering equipment due to shortages in the Reich highlighted the importance of conquered nations to feed Germany's war.[68] The army's experience of living off the land in Yugoslavia also confirmed that such a policy allowed for an attack's momentum to be maintained even when supply from the rear shriveled up to almost nothing. Finally, divisional practices emphasized the contradictions inherent in trying to reconcile meeting the immediate demands of troops on the ground with the broader goals of restarting and exploiting the larger economy for the German war effort. Once again, the 4th Mountain Division's brief stay in Yugoslavia foreshadowed German policy in the Soviet Union.

The security measures that accompanied the Yugoslavian campaign also shared a closer similarity with what came after than with what came before. Certainly, *Einsatzgruppen* activities were bloodier in Poland, as were army responses to popular resistance, real and perceived. Such ruthlessness, however, was generally shelved for the western campaign, with the notable exception of the treatment of French colonial troops. Before and during the invasion of the west, German troops received pointed directives and orders from army leadership that followed the Hague Land War Convention, attempting to avoid another round of the excesses that occurred in 1914.[69] The war against Yugoslavia, however, was viewed by the army as one against a perfidious and savage foe; here Nazi racial superiority toward Slavs complemented German historical memories of Serbian actions during the First World War. These ideas were increasingly hammered home during both the fighting and occupation itself. The targeting of a specific group of individuals—based on historical, cultural, and ethnic reasons—thus first manifested in Yugoslavia, and this carried over into campaign against the Soviet Union, though with much more violence from the very beginnings of the later campaign.

During Operation Barbarossa, the 4th Mountain Division drove from Romania to the Mius River before being forced into winter positions. Its experiences during Operation Barbarossa were typical of German infantry units during that campaign: forced marches in a futile attempt to keep pace with the mechanized and motorized spearheads; crippling supply shortages of fuel and fodder; a reliance on plundered Soviet foodstuffs to feed the troops during the advance; and a brutal response to any popular resistance, which was inevitably chalked up to the influence of "Judeo-Bolshevism." Both elements of the German way of war were on full display in the Soviet Union, as the army sought quick and decisive battlefield decisions, while waging a brutal anti-partisan war in the rear and plundering the countryside for the German war effort. These were clearly foreshadowed in the war in Yugoslavia. Having already secured food on their own and participated in security actions that targeted a specific group of people in Serbia, little mental adjustment would be needed for the men of the 4th Mountain Division to behave in a similar way in late 1941, though, as previously noted, no evidence of any war crimes committed by the division in southeastern

Europe was found in its records. This was not the case for its deployment to southern Ukraine and Russia. So, what caused this shift in behavior?

Certainly, the atmosphere surrounding Operation Barbarossa was significantly influenced by ideology in a way generally absent from the war in southeastern Europe. This partially accounts for the significant uptick in violence. More important, however, the army's ability to wage its desired war faltered in the face of the realities of the Soviet theater. Countless reports, memoranda, and directives from all levels of the army refer to the problem of movement during Operation Barbarossa. The dirt roads that choked soldiers, horses, and engines with dust in the summer, turned into nearly impassable morasses during the fall rains, with soldiers and horses sinking to their waists and wheeled vehicles simply rendered useless. This severely limited the army's ability to advance at the pace demanded by the campaign's planning. Even when no coherent Red Army opposition existed—and this was certainly the case for marching formations for days at a time as they trailed in the wake of the panzer and motorized divisions—units still struggled to carry out any semblance of a quick and decisive campaign. This proved most problematic in regard to supply, as the voracious demands of the front for ammunition, food, and other supplies simply could not be met by the limited vehicles allocated to infantry divisions. This, in turn, only sparked a more systematic looting of the Soviet countryside, which then led to increased resistance by the civilian population. The symbiosis between the two pieces of the German way of war as it developed between 1939 and 1945—the necessity of decisive advances to quickly destroy an enemy army and the mobilization of the enemy state's resources, be they raw materials, food, or manpower, in the face of popular resistance—reached its full fruition in the war against the Soviet Union. As the experiences of the 4th Mountain Division in the Yugoslavian campaign illustrate, however, the seeds for this type of total war were sown by the army before the onset of Operation Barbarossa. In a two-week campaign, they failed to sprout. The failure of the German way of war on the battlefield in the Soviet Union, however, ensured that the army would implement its occupation policies there in a much more violent manner.

Notes

1. Various examinations of the "German way of war" on the battlefield include Robert Citino's seminal *The German Way of War: From the Thirty Years' War to the Third Reich* (Lawrence: University Press of Kansas, 2005); Gerhard Groß, *Mythos und Wirklichkeit: Geschichte des operativen Denkens im deutschen Heer von Moltke d.Ä bis Heusinger* (Paderborn: Ferdinand Schöningh, 2012);

Marco Sigg, *Der Unterführer als Feldherr im Taschenformat: Theorie und Praxis der Auftragstaktik im deutschen Heer 1869–1945* (Paderborn: Ferdinand Schöningh, 2014); Daniel Hughes and Richard DiNardo, *Imperial Germany and War, 1871–1918* (Lawrence: University Press of Kansas, 2018); and Michael Geyer, "German Strategy in the Age of Machine Warfare," in *Makers of Modern Strategy from Machiavelli to the Nuclear Age*, ed. Peter Paret (Princeton, NJ: Princeton University Press, 1986), 527–97.

2. For a look at the problems that plagued French mobilization in 1940, see Cameron Zinsou's essay, chapter 5 in this volume.

3. An explicit link made between operations and occupation is convincingly articulated in Isabel Hull, *Absolute Destruction: Military Culture and the Practices of War in Imperial Germany* (Ithaca, NY: Cornell University Press, 2005). On German occupation practices in the Baltic states and Romania, see Gabriel Liulevicius, *War Land on the Eastern Front: Culture, National Identity, and German Occupation in World War I* (Cambridge: Cambridge University Press, 2000); and David Hamlin, *The German Empire in the East: Germans and Romania in an Era of Globalization and Total War* (Cambridge: Cambridge University Press, 2017), respectively. The Prusso-German army's response to both actual and perceived popular resistance is analyzed in Michael Howard, *The Franco-Prussian War* (London: Routledge, 1991), 249–56; and John Horne and Alan Kramer, *German Atrocities 1914: A History of Denial* (New Haven, CT: Yale University Press, 2001).

4. On the German occupation of Yugoslavia, see, for example, Jozo Tomasevich, *The Chetniks* (Stanford, CA: Stanford University Press, 1975); Jozo Tomasevich, *War and Revolution in Yugoslavia, 1941–1945: Occupation and Collaboration* (Stanford, CA: Stanford University Press, 2001); Stevan K. Pavlowitch, *Hitler's New Disorder: The Second World War in Yugoslavia* (New York: Columbia University Press, 2008); Walter Manoschek, *"Serbien ist judenfrei": Militärische Besatzungspolitik und Judenvernichtung in Serbien 1941/42* (Munich: De Gruyter Oldenbourg, 1995); Ben Shepherd, *Terror in the Balkans: German Armies and Partisan Warfare* (Cambridge, MA: Harvard University Press, 2012); and Klaus Schmider, *Partisanenkrieg in Jugoslawien 1941–1944* (Hamburg: Mittler, 2002).

5. On diplomacy in Southeastern Europe and the late German decision to invade Yugoslavia, see Ernst L. Presseisen, "Prelude to 'Barbarossa': Germany and the Balkans, 1940–1941," *Journal of Modern History* 32, no. 4 (December 1960): 359–70.

6. Bernhard R. Kroener, "The Manpower Resources of the Third Reich in the Area of Conflict between Wehrmacht, Bureaucracy, and War Economy," in Bernhard R. Kroener et al., *Organization and Mobilization of the German Sphere of Power: Wartime Administration, Economy, and Manpower Resources, 1939–1941*, vol. V/IB, *Germany and the Second World War* (Oxford: Oxford University Press, 2015), 949.

7. Oberkommando des Heeres, Chef H Rüst und BdE, Ia (I) Nr. 17 597/40 geh., Betr. Aufstellung von 4.u.5. Geb. Div., 9.10.1940, Bundesarchiv-Militärarchiv, Freiburg im Breisgau (hereafter BA-MA) RH/28/4-2.

8. Generalkommando XVIII. Armeekorps, Abt. Ia Nr.3276/40 geh., Betr. Umgliederung der Radf. Schwadronen der Geb. Aufkl. Abt. zu Kradsch. Schwadronen u. Aufstellung eines Pi. Zuges (mot) bei der Geb. Aufkl. Abt., 18.11.40, BA-MA RH 28/4-2.

9. 4.Gebirgs Division, Zustandsbericht Nov 1940, 25.11.1940, BA-MA RH 28/4-3.

10. Geb. Art. Regt. 94, Abt. Ia 129/40g, Betr.: Tragtierstaffeln f. L.F.H.-Abteilungen, 16.12.40, BA-MA RH 28/4-2.

11. 4. Gebirgs Division, Zusatz zum Zustandsbericht 4. Gebirgs-Division, 20.1.1941, BA-MA RH 28/4-3. The division's vehicle park was about 40 percent foreign manufacture; see Rolf Dieter Müller, "From Economic Alliance to a War of Colonial Exploitation," in Horst Boog et al., *The Attack on the Soviet Union*, vol. 4, *Germany and the Second World War* (Oxford: Oxford University Press, 2015) 222–23.

12. Nigel Askey, *Operation Barbarossa: The Complete Organisational and Statistical Analysis, and Military Simulation, Volume IIA* (Lulu.com, 2013), 487.

13. German infantry divisions were authorized some 4,000 horses on average; see Christian Hartmann, *Wehrmacht im Ostkrieg: Front und militärisches Hinterland 1941/42* (Munich: Oldenbourg, 2009), 32. On the army's efforts to acquire the necessary number of horses in the opening years of the war, see R. L. DiNardo, *Mechanized Juggernaut or Military Anachronism: Horse and the German Army of World War II* (Mechanicsburg: Stackpole, 2008), 25–40.

14. See Zustandsbericht 20.1.1941 and Zustandsbericht 20.2.41, both in BA-MA RH 28-4/3; Tätigkeitsbericht der Abtlg. IVc, 4.Gebirgs-Division, BA-MA RH 28-4/61.

15. 4. Gebirgs Division, Abt. Ia Tätigkeits-Bericht vom 25.10.40—15.3.41, 15.3.41, BA-MA RH 28-4/1.

16. Rolf-Dieter Müller, *Der letzte deutsche Krieg, 1939–1945* (Stuttgart: Klett-Cotta, 2005), 123.

17. Jürgen Förster, "Ideological Warfare in Germany, 1919 to 1945," in *German Wartime Society 1939–1945: Politicization, Disintegration, and the Struggle for Survival*, vol. 9/1, *Germany and the Second World War*, ed. Jörg Echternkamp (Oxford: Oxford University Press, 2015), 531.

18. Anlage 4. zu Ob.d.H./GenstdH/O.Qu.1, Nr. 500/40 g., 7.10.40, reproduced in Jeff Rutherford and Adrian Wettstein, *The German Army on the Eastern Front: An Inner View of the Ostheer's Experiences of War* (Barnsley: Pen & Sword, 2018), 172–73. Emphasis in original.

19. 4. Gebirgs Division, Abteilung Ic Az. 37, Betr.: Geistige und seelische Betreuung, 18.11.1940, BA-MA RH 28-4/63.

20. On the German decision to invade Greece and Yugoslavia, see Detlef Vogel, "German Intervention in the Balkans," in Gerhard Schreiber et al., *The*

Mediterranean, South-east Europe, and North Africa, 1939–1941, vol. 3, *Germany and the Second World War* (Oxford: Oxford University Press, 2015), 451–96.

21. Adam Tooze, *The Wages of Destruction: The Making and Breaking of the German War Economy* (New York: Viking, 2007), 419; Pavlowitch, *Hitler's New Disorder*, 9. For more on German economic interests in Yugoslavia during the late 1930s and early 1940s, see Arnold Suppan, *Hitler—Beneš—Tito: National Conflicts, World Wars, Genocides, Expulsions, and Divided Remembrance in East-Central and Southeastern Europe, 1848–2018* (Vienna: Austrian Academy of Sciences, 2019), 404–5.

22. Generalkommando (mot.) XXXXVI.A.K., Abt. Ia/Ic., 21.4.1941, Gefechtsbericht vom 2.4. bis 20.4.41, 4.6.41, BA-MA RH 24-46/2.

23. Generalkommando XIV.A.K., Abt. Ia Nr. 276/41 geh., 3.4.1941, Korpsbefehl Nr. 9, BA-MA RH 28-4/5.

24. On the German campaign in Yugoslavia, see Vogel, "German Intervention in the Balkans," 516–26; and George E. Blau, *Invasion Balkans! The German Campaign in the Balkans, Spring 1941* (Shippensburg: Burd Street Press, 1997), 48–62.

25. Martin van Creveld, *Hitler's Strategy, 1940–1941: The Balkan Clue* (Cambridge: Cambridge University Press, 1973), 149.

26. 4. Gebirgs Division, KTB Ib, 5.4.41, BA-MA RH 28-4/65.

27. Generalkommando XIV. A.K., Abt. Ia Nr. 276/41 geh., 3.4.1941, Korpsbefehl Nr. 9, BA-MA RH 28-4/5.

28. 4. Gebirgs Division, KTB Ia, 4.4.41, BA-MA RH 28-4/4.

29. Panzergruppe 1, Abt. Ia Nr. 1702/41 geh., Gruppenbefehl Nr. 4, 10.4.1941, BAMA RH 28-4/5.

30. 4. Gebirgs Division, KTB Ia, 4.8.41, BA-MA RH 28-4/4.

31. 4. Gebirgs Division, KTB Ia, 12.4.41, BA-MA RH 28-4/4.

32. 4. Gebirgs Division, KTB Ia, 12.4.41, BA-MA RH 28-4/4, 15.4.41; Generalkommando XI. Armeekorps, Abt. Ia Nr. 534/41 geheim, 15.4.41, Korpsbefehl Nr. 6, BA-MA RH 28-4/5.

33. 4. Gebirgs Division, KTB Ia, 9. and 10.4.41, BA-MA RH 28-4/4.

34. 4. Gebirgs Division, KTB Ib, 14. and 18.4.41, RH 28-4/65; 4. Gebirgs Division, Abt. Ib, 18.4.1941, Bes. Anordnungen für die Versorgung Nr. 17, BA-MA RH 28-4/66; Tätigkeitsbericht Abt IVa 1. IV.1941 bis 15. IV. 1941, 15.4.41, BA-MA RH 28-4/67.

35. Panzergruppe 1, Abt. Qu, Anlage 7 zu Pz.Gr.1 Ia/Op. Nr.142/41 g. Kdos./ Chefs. v.5.4.1941, Besondere Anordnungen für die Versorgung der Panzergruppe 1 und die Versorgungstruppen zum Operationsbefehl v. 5.4.41, BAMA RH 28-4/66.

36. 4. Gebirgs Division, Anlage zum Div. Tagesbefehl v. 12.4.41, BAMA RH 28-4/5.

37. 4. Gebirgs Division, KTB Ib, 18.4.41, RH 28-4/65.

38. 4. Gebirgs Division, Abt. Ic, 15.4.1941, Divisionsbefehl für die wirtschaftlich Erfassung des eroberten Landes und die Verwaltung durch die Truppe, BA-MA RH 28-4/5. The following discussion is based on this document unless otherwise noted.

39. 4. Gebirgs Division KTB Ia, 17.4.41, BA-MA RH 28-4/4.

40. Jürgen Förster, "Operation Barbarossa as a War of Conquest and Annihilation," in Horst Boog et al., *The Attack on the Soviet Union*, vol. 4, *Germany and the Second World War* (Oxford: Oxford University Press, 2015), 492–93.

41. Manoschek, *Militärische Besatzungspolitik und Judenvernichtung*, 41.

42. Vogel, "German Intervention in the Balkans," 526.

43. Generalkommando (mot) XXXVI.A.K., Qu. Nr. 28/41 geh., 9.4.1941, Besondere Anordnungen für die Versorgung Nr.5, BA-MA RH 24-46/150.

44. Generalkommando (mot) XXXVI.A.K., KTB, 5.4.41, BA-MA RH 24-46/2.

45. 4. Gebirgs Division Abt. Ic., Divisionsbefehl für die Säuberung des Bereiches und das Aufschliessen nach Westen, 16.4.41, BAMA RH 28-4/5.

46. 4. Gebirgs Division, Tätigkeitsbericht Ic, BA-MA RH 28-4/44, p. 3; 4. Gebirgs Division Abt. Ib, Bes. Anordnungen für die Versorgung Nr.15, 15.4.1941, BA-MA RH 28-4/66.

47. 4. Gebirgs Division, KTB Ib 15.4.41, BA-MA RH 28-4/65.

48. 4. Gebirgs Division Abt. Ib, 15.4.1941, Bes. Anordnungen für die Versorgung Nr.15, BAMA RH 28-4/66.

49. On the creation of one form of outsider in Nazi Germany, see Christian Gerlach and Mark Edele, "State Violence—Violent Societies," in *Beyond Totalitarianism: Stalinism and Nazism Compared*, ed. Michael Geyer and Sheila Fitzpatrick (Cambridge: Cambridge University Press, 2009), 145–51. For examples of this in Southeastern Europe, see Mark Mazower, "Military Violence and the National Socialist Consensus: The Wehrmacht in Greece, 1941–1944," in *War of Extermination: The German Military in World War II, 1941–1944*, ed. Hannes Heer and Klaus Naumann (New York: Berghahn, 2000), 166–68.

50. Creveld, *Hitler's Strategy, 1940–1941*, 165; 4. Gebirgs Division, KTB Ib, 28.4.41, BA-MA RH 28-4/65.

51. 4. Gebirgs Division, Kommandeur, Nr.167/41 g., Betr.: Abwehrmassnahmen für die Besatzungstruppen, 24.4.1941, BA-MA RH 28-4/44.

52. 4. Gebirgs Division KTB Ia, 27.4.41, BA-MA RH 28-4/4.

53. 4. Gebirgs Division, Abt. Ia, 27.4.41, BA-MA RH 28-4/5.

54. Generalkommando XI. Armeekorps, Abt. Ia Nr. 606/41 geheim, 27.4.41, Korpsbefehl Nr. 9, BA-MA RH 28-4/5.

55. Note in contrast to Cookson-Hills's essay, chapter 8 in this volume, when occupation shifted Canadian soldiers' treatment of German civilians in 1945.

56. The following is based on Geschichte der IV. s. (mot)/Geb. Art. Regt. 94, BA-MA RH 41/1103, 14 unless otherwise noted.

57. 4. Gebirgs Division, KTB Ib 2.5.41, BA-MA RH 28-4/65.

58. On the use of Serbian cooking pots, see 4. Gebirgs Division, KTB Ib 5.2.41, BA-MA RH 28-4/65. On the amount of goods seized by the division, see 4. Gebirgs Division, Ib/WuG. Az. Beute, Betr.: Gesamtbeute der Div., 5.5.41, BA-MA RH 28-4/66. For the items desired by the division, see Anlage 1 zu B.A. Nr. 33 v. 20.5.41, BA-MA RH 28-4/6.

59. 4. Gebirgs Division, Kommandeur, Betr.: Erfassung der Beute, 20.5.1941, BA-MA RH 28-4/66.

60. 4. Gebirgs Division, Abt. Ib, Bes. Anordnungen für die Versorgung Nr. 33, 20.5.1941, BA-MA RH 28-4/66; 4. Gebirgs Division, KTB Ib 7.5.41, BA-MA RH 28-4/6; 4. Gebirgs Division, Abt. Ib, Bes. Anordnungen für die Versorgung Nr. 35, 23.5.1941, BA-MA RH 28-4/66.

61. 4. Gebirgs Division, Tätigkeitsbericht Abt Iva, 27.4.41, BA-MA RH 28-4/67.

62. 4. Gebirgs Division, KTB Ib 2.5.41, BA-MA RH 28-4/65.

63. 4. Gebirgs Division, Tätigkeitsbericht der Vet. Dienste, BA-MA RH 28-4/69, pp. 30, 40.

64. Andreas Hillgruber, *Der Zenit des Zweiten Weltkrieges, Juli 1941* (Mainz: Verlag Phillip von Zabern in Wissenschaftliche Buchgesellschaft, 1977).

65. 4. Gebirgs Division, Tätigkeitsbericht Ic, BA-MA RH 28-4/44.

66. Erfahrungsbericht der 4. Gebirgs Division über den Einsatz in Serbien, 12.5.1941, BA-MA RH 28-4/5. The following discussion is based on this document unless otherwise noted.

67. Erfahrungsbericht der 4. Gebirgs Division über den Einsatz in Serbien, 12.5.1941, BA-MA RH 28-4/5.

68. 4. Gebirgs Division, Abt. Ib, Bes. Anordnungen für die Versorgung Nr. 35, 23.5.1941, BA-MA RH 28-4/66.

69. Hans Umbreit, "The Battle for Hegemony in Western Europe," in Klaus Maier et al., *Germany's Initial Conquests in Europe*, vol. 2, *Germany and the Second World War* (Oxford, 2015), 261.

4

"Believed Reliable"
The "Morale and Opinions" of German Prisoners of War in the United States, February 1944–June 1945

Derek R. Mallett

Lieutenant Colonel Günther Guderian, the grandson of the famed German armor commander Heinz Guderian, served as the *Bundeswehr* liaison to the US Army at Fort Bragg, North Carolina, in the 1990s. He noted, "Sometimes, I get the impression that in the United States Army, even more officers know the name [Guderian] than in the German army." One of the US Army Seventh Corps' ranking officers, Guderian noted, had a large picture of his grandfather hanging on his office wall.[1] Elements of the US military admired the *Wehrmacht* a half century after the Second World War. This admiration had begun much earlier, at least as early as the immediate postwar years. The American military's interest in what it could learn from the German military was reflected in the Hill Project at Camp Ritchie, Maryland, which brought dozens of German general staff officers to the United States in late 1945 and early 1946 for the purpose of studying Wehrmacht performance in the Second World War and gleaning relevant lessons. It could also be seen in the recruitment of hundreds of German general officers to write historical accounts of the Second World War for the US Army Historical Division and in the strong influence of German officers in the rewriting of US Army armor doctrine in the 1950s.[2]

This chapter contends that American admiration for the prowess of the Wehrmacht emerged even earlier, during the US military's interrogation of German prisoners of war at Fort Hunt, Virginia, during the Second World War. This admiration was only one of many reasons for bringing hundreds of German POWs to Fort Hunt. But US infatuation with the Wehrmacht seems to have influenced at least a small portion of the work of the American interrogators at the camp and the larger policies governing the operation. American interest in information to aid Allied governance of postwar

Germany, German soldiers' evaluations of American tactics, weapons, and strategy, Allied propaganda, and the Combined Bomber Offensive also drove the operation. Despite evidence that not all the prisoners were particularly well informed regarding the topics about which the Americans were most interested, American authorities labeled virtually all these prisoners "believed reliable" and took great interest in the information they provided.

The US Military Intelligence Service (MIS) operation at Fort Hunt, Virginia—code-named "PO Box 1142"—served as a secret US interrogation facility for German prisoners of war from 1942 until mid-1945. During this time, the US Army and US Navy housed, interrogated, and eavesdropped on over 3,400 German POWs. American military authorities also amassed an expansive collection of captured German documents at Fort Hunt. Prisoners and American analysts examined these documents in conjunction with the ongoing effort to obtain information directly from the prisoners to form a clearer picture of the German war effort. The MIS Captured Personnel and Material Branch (CPMB) at PO Box 1142 provided reports of information obtained from these prisoners of war to Headquarters (HQ), US Army, European Theater of Operations (ETO), as well as to a variety of other agencies including the US Navy, US Army Service Forces, the Office of Strategic Services (OSS), and the British Combined Services Detailed Interrogation Center (CSDIC).[3]

Broadly speaking, American officials sought "overall strategic intelligence." American policymakers prioritized the following categories of information:

1. All ordnance, signal, and technical intelligence involving theoretical or scientific knowledge of the principles on which armament, signal equipment, or other technical equipment, are contracted or operated.
2. All nonoperational intelligence, including such subjects as the war economy, industrial development, war finance, and civilian morale.
3. Organizational details of enemy high command, military staff organization, espionage and counterespionage, hospital organization, organization of railways and highways for military transportation, the study of objectionable political groups or organizations, or groups and individuals more likely to be considered as friendly to an invading power.
4. All order of battle information pertaining to the German military (*Wehrmacht*), including command structure, recruiting

programs, the nature and employment of special units, hospitalization, and general discipline.
5. Information concerning the methods with which Germany deal[t] with occupied countries, including policing, economic organizations, and the employment of local agents.[4]

Given these stated areas of interest, the parameters used to choose prisoners for transfer to Fort Hunt should not be surprising. American intelligence personnel at the Detailed Interrogation Centers in Western Europe and North Africa, who were the first to interrogate all prisoners captured in the European and Mediterranean theaters of operation, selected prisoners coming from German industrial centers who might provide targeting data or assessments of previous bombing campaigns. Furthermore, American interrogators sought German soldiers with technical expertise, including communications, armor, artillery, ordnance, and gunners, or those with experience in munitions, aviation, or chemical plants. Finally, MIS-Y also found prisoners from the *SS*, *SD*, or *Abwehr* particularly valuable. All of these would have been immediately transferred to Fort Hunt for more comprehensive interrogation.[5]

Once at PO Box 1142, American officials added further details of interest, including questions about the effectiveness of American propaganda. They also provided the interrogators a list of selected topics involving German airplanes, submarines, ships and flotilla commanders, radio devices, economic problems, the German order of battle, and potential bombing targets.[6] Within this framework, of course, much autonomy was bestowed on individual interrogators—largely German and Austrian refugees with the requisite language skills—to determine what information was most valuable. Although authorities offered general categories, the individual interrogators retained the responsibility to determine, within this framework, what the most relevant information would be and what could be discarded or ignored.

To facilitate the collection of useful data, Fort Hunt authorities disseminated "daily bulletins of what information was important and desired." They also held regular staff meetings to clarify what information was needed. Henry Kolm, who worked as an interrogator at Fort Hunt, stated, "Information went back and forth to Europe through official G-2 [military general staff intelligence] channels and air force bases."[7] As was true of other intelligence-gathering endeavors like the Hill Project and the US Army Historical Division's German History Program, specific requests for information from military organizations and commands in the field drove the direction of the interrogation and document analysis effort. These groups would send their requests through the G-2 to facilities like Fort Hunt, where individual interrogators would attempt to obtain the types of information sought. Did American officials find this information valuable? What actionable intelligence did the German POWs at Fort Hunt provide American authorities?

Ultimately, German prisoners of war interrogated at PO Box 1142 provided American authorities with nine distinct categories of intelligence, each of which presented potential significance for shaping various American military courses of action. These categories included: war production and industrial installations; German (and Italian) defensive works; German military and civilian morale and opinions; detailed reports of the situation in individual cities or countries; German assessments of American and British tactics, campaigns, and the Allied war effort in general; German military tactics, training, and the order of battle of various units; German weapons and military technology; German politics and personalities; and the German relationship with Japan. It is important to note that many of the individual reports included multiple categories of information, but the single most discussed topic was war production and industrial installations—eighty-five of the extant 240 reports dealt with this topic in some capacity. Sixty-five reports provided information about German politics and personalities; sixty involved German tactics, training, or the order of battle of one or more military units; and forty-four reports examined German weapons and military technology. The remaining five categories received attention from anywhere from five to twenty-nine reports each.

The CPMB at PO Box 1142 prepared an estimated 1,600–1,700 reports sent from Fort Hunt to HQ, US Army, ETO. Of these, copies of only 240 reports survive in the US National Archives. The reports available are only a small portion of those produced by the MIS during the Second World War and have survived for random, unexplained reasons. Yet the German prisoners of war at Fort Hunt provided American authorities with a great deal of intelligence just in the few reports that remain. Overwhelmingly, the collection provides quantitative intelligence. For example, prisoners offered the locations of potentially valuable military and industrial targets, production estimates, and information about German military technology. This chapter, however, examines a particular subset of sixteen reports that recorded the "morale and opinions" of German POWs at Fort Hunt. This subset affords a fascinating view of the prisoners' personal perspectives on various topics as well as a window into the motivations of the American operation.

The first five reports in this group are titled "Morale Report: Survey of Expressions of German Prisoner of War Opinions" and dated between May and August 1944. The next seven reports are titled "Expressions of Opinion of Recently Captured German PWs on Conditions at the Front and at Home" and dated between November 1944 and April 1945. An additional four reports are also included in this analysis as they offer further expressions of prisoner of war "morale and opinions" on more specific matters. These reports focus on such considerations as "German Impressions of American Weapons and Infantry," "Civilian Morale," and, of particular interest, "Trends in German Morale."

In this series of reports, American interrogators took consistent interest in particular categories of information. These include the prisoners' views of how the war would end (i.e., was German victory still possible?), the ubiquitous question of the prisoners' political loyalties and how they viewed Hitler and his regime, the prisoners' view of the Allied states, their fighting qualities, and weapons, the effectiveness of Allied strategic bombing and its impact on conditions in Germany and civilian morale, their views of the effectiveness of both German and Allied propaganda, and any information the prisoners had about underground movements in Germany or German-occupied areas.

American interest in the German prisoners' views of the Allied nations likely stemmed from American interest in developing a way forward for postwar Germany, the planning for which only began in earnest following the Allied invasion of Normandy in June 1944. The CPMB reports offered the Allies some potentially useful feedback in this regard. American interest in the prisoners' assessments of American soldiers and weapons had a different motivation. One's enemies' views of one's performance serve as an interesting and potentially valuable sort of after-action report. That the German prisoners offered overwhelmingly critical views of American military performance may have heightened American interest in this topic. Yet the time and resources American authorities devoted to gathering these assessments also seem to reflect American admiration for a German military they had been emulating in some measure for decades prior to the Second World War. The prisoners' estimations of the impact of both the Allied strategic bombing campaign and Allied propaganda operations offered the US Army a chance to revise its approach to these types of operations based on information from those who had been targeted by them. Information about any underground movements also offered the Allies potential co-belligerents and collaborators for the end of the war and the postwar occupation. Moreover, in the spring of 1945, at least one prisoner also warned

American interrogators about deception operations and the infiltration of Allied governance of liberated Europe by German military personnel. These appear to be the concerns that motivated American interest in the "morale and opinions" of German prisoners of war at Fort Hunt.

This chapter does not examine the prisoners' expressed views of whether German victory was still possible, the prisoners' political loyalties, or their views of Hitler and the Nazi regime. Theoretically, each of these questions is fascinating. But these reports offer nothing of significant interest in these matters. Not surprisingly, as the war progressed, fewer German POWs thought German victory was possible. Similarly, the longer the war went on and the more Allied victory appeared imminent, the more prisoners seemed to be "anti-Nazi" and less supportive of Hitler and the Nazi Party. In other words, the conclusions the reports draw are exactly what one would expect to find. Consequently, consideration of these questions has been omitted from this study.

One of the key categories of intelligence covered in each of the morale and opinion reports was the German POWs' "Attitude toward the United Nations." (By this is meant how the prisoners viewed each of the major Allied states respectively, not, of course, how they viewed the United Nations organization that had yet to be established.) This category of information seems to have been collected with an eye toward postwar considerations. How might a defeated Germany best be handled by the victorious Allied nations, and what type of reception might Allied occupation receive? The prisoners' perceptions of the Allied nations also spoke to the effectiveness of Allied propaganda and served as a barometer of sorts for Allied actions, such as their treatment of German civilians in occupied areas in western Germany and their treatment of the prisoners of war themselves.

Report 1285: "Trends in German Morale" analyzed the trends observed in the first eight "morale reports," which included the views of the first 433 German prisoners "selected for detailed interrogation." The "Trends" report analyzed roughly six months' worth of intelligence from February 1944 through the first month after the Allied invasion of France in June 1944.[8] Regarding the question of prisoner attitudes toward the United Nations, the "Trends" report states, "The trend in this connection is quite definitely a non-antagonistic attitude toward the United States, noticeably more antagonistic toward the British, and fear and hatred of the Russians [Soviets]. There have been no noteworthy variations from this trend throughout all of the reports."[9] The majority of a group of 130 prisoners (twenty-seven officers, eighty-two non-commissioned officers, twenty enlisted men, and one merchant seaman) interrogated later in July and early August 1944 at Fort

Hunt expressed the same sympathies and offered some explanation for their appreciation of the United States. "Admiration is expressed for the treatment accorded wounded and captive Germans by the Americans. It is stated that the Americans always respect the Red Cross. Most [prisoners of war] feel that they can be assured of fair treatment as prisoners of war only by the Americans." The report then adds, "If occupation of Germany becomes inevitable the US is definitely preferred as the occupying nation. Many [POWs] believe that only from the US will Germany receive humane treatment. The thought of Russian occupation usually elicits the remark 'I would put a bullet through my head.'"[10] The positive view of potential American occupation was consistently supported by later arrivals to Fort Hunt who reported that "the fair and just treatment of the population of Aachen by the Americans" was "more effective than any direct propaganda." The report noted, "Word of this seems to have spread through Germany and has counteracted the attempts of propaganda to make the people believe that American occupation of German cities is accompanied by harsh treatment."[11]

It is not altogether surprising that the German prisoners would express their highest regard for the United States. The Americans and the British had a reputation for treating prisoners of war well during the Second World War. Moreover, as prisoners of the United States being interrogated on American soil, they might well have seen it as being in their best interest to favorably compare their American captors to the British and Soviets. Regardless, prisoner views of the United States, Britain, and the Soviet Union were so consistent that American reports stopped cataloging responses by August 1944. All the "morale reports" that were produced after that date omitted this category from their consideration. It appears as though American interrogators stopped asking the question.

A related category, and one in which American interrogators took even greater interest, comprised German prisoner views of Allied "fighting qualities" and American weapons. The German responses were frequently quite critical of American combat performance, although they held American weapons in high regard. The "Trends" report offers a fascinating summary of the prisoners' views of Allied "fighting qualities" and "American weapons." Each of the morale reports that followed the "Trends" report featured this category of intelligence. Regarding prisoners' assessments of Allied fighting qualities, the "Trends" report states:

> The trend in this connection has been to regard the German and Russian soldiers as the best in the world. The British are considered inferior to both but still of good fighting quality. The Americans are regarded as the poorest

of the four major powers, not because of lack of courage, but through lack of battle knowledge and experience. The leitmotiv of the criticism of American tactics is that [they] tend to rely excessively on superiority of materiel, and that [American] troops do not follow through with sufficient vigor."[12]

The German prisoners, by contrast, valued American weapons. The overwhelming majority of the German prisoners found American artillery and air forces to be exceptionally good, while American machine guns ranked behind the German MG 42. Many of the prisoners also lauded American mortars and grenades. "Most of the [prisoners] regard [American] weapons as quite impressive and many feel that they are outstanding. Only a few feel that they are inferior to the German." Most of the prisoners saw artillery as the US Army's "most effective weapon, with the air force coming second." Most of the prisoners, however, qualified their responses by noting that the German "MG 42 is superior to the American machine gun because of better performance under adverse conditions, superior fire-power, etc."[13] The prisoners' evaluation of American weapons remained steady throughout the morale reports.

Report 1298, dated 28 August 1944, features the perspectives of the 130 prisoners captured in Central and Western Europe and interrogated at Fort Hunt in July and August 1944. These men's views deviate somewhat from previous perceptions about American fighting qualities. Within this group, sixty-two prisoners ranked the American soldiers as "good," while twenty-seven classified the Americans as "fair." The report stated, "For the first time, several [prisoners] felt that the American soldier was as good as the German and in some instances even superior." This assessment, unfortunately, is neither explained nor reflected in the remainder of the report. For example, based on the tally of "votes"—it appears the prisoners were asked to rank each type of soldier, German, American, British, and Soviet, as either "good" or "fair"—this group placed American soldiers ahead of the British and roughly on par with the Soviets. None of the three, however, equaled the German soldier in the prisoners' eyes.[14] Notably, of all the morale reports seeking the prisoners' assessment of American fighting qualities, this report (1298) is the only one in which the prisoners even suggest that American soldiers might be anywhere near as capable as German soldiers. The remaining six reports in the subset that offer substantive comments on the topic offer largely negative estimations of the American soldier like that found in the earlier "Trends" report but with some interesting clarifications. Curiously, comparisons of American, or German, soldiers to those of the British and Soviets do not appear in any of the reports after August 1944. The subsequent reports solely compare German and American soldiers.

One German lieutenant captured in France in June or July 1944 considered American infantry "inferior to the poorest which the German Army has to offer," explaining to his interrogator that Germans and Americans hold a "different conception of warfare." He stated that Americans "spare lives and use materiel, whereas [Germans] do exactly the opposite because we just do not have the materiel."[15] Twelve German officers—ten of whom American interrogators assessed to be Nazis—captured in France between late November and mid-December 1944 offered "the usual stock comments on American reliance on weapons to the detriment of stern fighting qualities, good tactical deployment of troops and aggressiveness." Yet the two highest-ranking prisoners among them—one colonel and one lieutenant colonel—admired the "security consciousness" of American soldiers. The colonel attributed this to good American indoctrination of soldiers and expressed the wish that he could return to Germany and similarly train German soldiers. The lieutenant colonel conveyed that his men had captured four American officers and sixty enlisted men prior to being surrounded and captured by other American troops the following day. "Not one would answer a thing during frontline interrogation, not even perfectly harmless questions," he noted, "and none carried any documents."[16]

Eight prisoners, a captain and seven enlisted men, captured in Belgium and Luxembourg in December 1944 indicated that "the German soldier even though he lacks the tremendous artillery and equipment superiority of the Americans does surpass the latter in fighting ability and training for combat." After offering "the usual comments about [US] forces not being as aggressive as they might," the prisoners suggested that American soldiers had "too great a sense of apprehension as regards the German troops and their MG-42, which they should be taught to overcome."[17] Nine German soldiers captured in late December 1944 and early January 1945, also in Belgium and Luxembourg, compared German and American soldiers similarly. After praising the "effectiveness of American artillery," all nine prisoners felt that "the German infantry soldier, because of his long training and experience, is more effective in battle than the American soldier," and "American success is due chiefly to superiority in arms and equipment."[18]

Two final reports offer German perspectives on the qualities of American soldiers. Nine prisoners (two officers, five NCOs, and two enlisted men) captured in Germany between early February and mid-March 1945, all of whom claimed to be opposed to the Nazi regime, offered two different criticisms of the US Army—aside from the now customary refrains of a lack of aggressiveness and that American success can be attributed largely to superiority of weapons and materiel. One of the NCOs suggested that American soldiers were "careless" with classified papers. He "expressed surprise at the amount of [American] orders and papers marked 'secret' that fell into German hands during the December offensive." This perspective, of course, contrasts with that of the previously mentioned German colonel and lieutenant colonel captured in late 1944 who lauded American security consciousness. But, similarly, another prisoner in this group condemned American security in the field. While on patrol in a village in Luxembourg behind American lines in late January 1945, German soldiers quietly encircled a house with American soldiers inside. The Germans noticed the house because it had only been blacked out on one side, the side facing the German lines across a river. The German soldiers were drawn to the lights coming from the back of the house. They easily overpowered a single guard who was "smoking a cigarette and leaning against the wall with his rifle slung over his shoulder ... while singing was going on inside the house." The German patrol then captured two "sleepy" American officers and sixteen soldiers inside the house.[19]

Finally, report 1517, dated 30 April 1945—the final extant report in this series—provides what may be the most damning commentary on American fighting qualities. Curiously, it begins, "Most of the prisoners have had little occasion to observe and judge the qualities of the American soldier at first hand." Yet the report then chronicles the assessment of an "anti-Nazi" German Army colonel who believed "that in many respects the American soldier is superior to the German ... largely [due] to the fact that the better food and generous amount of equipment given the American soldier give him more confidence in his own abilities." The German colonel then condemned American soldiers, saying "the American is not a real 'soldier' in a military sense but shows many childish sentiments, unlike the German soldier who puts his whole heart into the battle without questioning orders or decisions." The German colonel concluded by declaring that "the American soldier's overconfidence, which he attributes to the repeated successes of the Allied armies, may be detrimental to him in the long run."[20]

The interrogators took great interest in German views of American military performance. Perhaps interrogators found the prisoners' views interesting because they were so critical of US Army performance in the war. The consistency of criticism from different prisoners may also have lent greater weight to the responses. One's enemy's performance critique certainly provides the potential for greater understanding of what needs to improve. Perhaps some of the German prisoners' critiques of American soldiers could be attributed to "sour grapes," so to speak. If so, the Germans would be far from the first defeated army to contend that they were superior to their opponents but had been overwhelmed by better weapons and equipment. Similar comments about the Union Army in the US Civil War, for instance, were made by many a Confederate soldier after that war ended. Yet American interrogators took German prisoner assessments seriously. So much so, in fact, that it almost appears as if the US Army suffered from the need to prove itself to the German Army. As previously mentioned, one group of prisoners at Fort Hunt had indicated that American soldiers had "too great a sense of apprehension as regards the German troops and their MG-42, which they should be taught to overcome."[21] This American interest in what they could learn from German prisoners is akin to their later interest in what they could learn from the German general staff and German general officers after the war, suggesting that the later American infatuation with the German military was already present in the interrogation rooms of Fort Hunt, Virginia.

The American interrogators also devoted considerable attention to the prisoners' views of the effectiveness of the Allied strategic bombing campaign. After all, who would know better the effects of Allied bombing raids than those who had suffered through them? Overall, the prisoners had mixed views of Allied bombing. They consistently indicated that the campaign was doing more to enflame civilian morale than to undermine it. Moreover, their assertions that Allied bombing was hindering German war production were at odds with the conclusions of Allied air forces leadership. Based on the perspectives of German prisoners of war, it seems that Allied bombing and strafing of German rail networks and rolling stock had the most significant impact on the German war effort.

Not surprisingly, when asked about the effects of Allied bombing, over half of the first 433 German prisoners interrogated concurred that the raids "had a very depressing effect." Notably, many prisoners had not actually suffered through a bombing raid on a German urban population. An interesting difference of opinion arose between those prisoners who had been on the receiving end of an Allied bombing raid and those who had not. The "Trends" report in August 1944 stated, "It is interesting to note that from their reactions to the general line of questioning it appears that those [prisoners of war] who have been bombed out are strengthened in their determination to fight on because their only hope of reparation lies in German victory, whereas those who have not suffered are fearful."[22]

This is a fascinating distinction that speaks to the contemporary debate in the decades before and during the Second World War regarding the effects of bombing on civilian morale. Some airpower advocates, like the Italian airpower theorist Giulio Douhet, had argued that bombing alone could demoralize a civilian population and, inevitably, an entire enemy state into submission.[23] This belief, in part, motivated the Allied bombing campaign in the Second World War. Yet by early 1945 the leadership of the Combined Bomber Offensive began to have doubts. And, after the war, Air Chief Marshal Sir Arthur Harris, Commander-in-Chief of the Royal Air Force (RAF) Bomber Command, asserted:

> The idea that the main object of bombing German industrial cities was to break the enemy's morale proved to be wholly unsound; when we had destroyed almost all the larger industrial cities in Germany the civil populace remained apathetic while the Gestapo saw to it that they were docile and in so far as there was work left for them to do—industrious.[24]

Similarly, General Henry "Hap" Arnold, Commanding General of US Army Air Forces, lamented as early as January 1945:

> We have a superiority of at least 5 to 1 now against Germany and yet, in spite of all our hopes, anticipations, dreams and plans, we have as yet not been able to capitalize to the extent which we should. We may not be able to force capitulation of the Germans by air attacks, but on the other hand, with this tremendous striking power, it would seem to me that we should get much better and much more decisive results than we are getting now.[25]

In August 1944, German prisoners of war at Fort Hunt had not only suggested that the bombing campaign might be ineffective but that it was having the opposite effect as intended, indeed steeling the German civilian population to resist. Five months later, in early 1945, British and American leaders of the Allied bombing campaign reached the same conclusion: Strategic bombing was having no impact on German civilian morale and little effect on war production. It cannot be confirmed whether the prisoners' comments made their way directly to the top leadership of either RAF Bomber Command or the US Army Air Forces. However, multiple copies of all six reports detailing the prisoners' perspectives on Allied bombing cited in this essay were sent to US Army Air Forces (Air Intelligence) when they were completed. Consequently, it is possible that the prisoners' assessments influenced American understanding of the effectiveness of air power. It is noteworthy that the impressions the prisoners provided to American interrogators were validated by the later conclusions of the commanders of the Allied strategic bombing campaign.

In addition to attempting to undermine civilian morale, the other target of the Allied bombing campaign was German production. Indeed, American interrogators distinguished these two categories—"Home Morale" and "Production"—when questioning the prisoners about their perspectives of the Allied bombing endeavor. Here too, however, interesting German prisoner perspectives emerged. American interrogators observed, "The number of [POWs] who believed our air raids were playing a definite part in hampering production increased steadily with the corresponding increase in the intensity of the attacks."[26] Indeed, 1944 saw increased numbers of sorties and greater bomb tonnage targeting German industry and military installations, including the so-called "Big Week" in late February in which the US Army Air Forces alone dropped 10,000 tons of bombs in six days.[27] Prisoner assertions that high intensity bombing raids must be damaging German production were at odds with those of Allied air forces leadership, which was reaching the opposite conclusion.

These circumstances expose one of the potential weaknesses of the POW interrogation effort at PO Box 1142: Some of the prisoners may not have had firsthand experience of the matters about which they were being interrogated. As noted in an earlier report, not all the prisoners in American custody had experienced an Allied bombing attack directly. Therefore, at times, it appears the information they provided was based more on conjecture or secondhand information than personal experience. Similarly, this weakness played a role in the prisoners' responses to questions about American, British, and Soviet fighting qualities discussed earlier. Particularly in the earlier reports cited above when American interrogators were asking for comparisons of all four nations' soldiers, it is doubtful that all the prisoners had fought all three opponents. And a later report from April 1945 even stated: "Most of the prisoners have had little occasion to observe and judge the qualities of the American soldier at first hand."[28] So, again, hearsay, reputation, and conjecture may have substituted for firsthand knowledge of the "fighting qualities" of American, British, or Soviet soldiers. Yet, notably, most of the prisoners who provided information for the sixteen reports under consideration by this study had been labeled "believed reliable" by American interrogators.

While many prisoners expressed the view that Allied bombing hampered production, one report said "an overwhelming majority" of the German prisoners doubted that the Allies could ever "succeed in knocking Germany out of the war through air attacks. It is felt that German industry has been too highly decentralized." Many prisoners felt "that the most serious effect of [Allied] air raids on production lies in the loss of manhours."[29] Here, the prisoners seem to be suggesting that work stoppages during raids impacted German production more than damage done to facilities.

Not surprisingly, as bombing intensity increased in 1944 and early 1945, a greater proportion of the German prisoners interrogated expressed the belief that Allied bombing raids were impacting the German home front. Regarding 130 German prisoners interrogated in July and August 1944, American interrogators noted that "the proportion of [prisoners] who feel that [Allied] air raids tend to weaken morale on the home front has increased. The typical reaction can perhaps be said to be one of dull resentment." However, the analysis again belies the data provided later, which states that roughly two-thirds of the 119 respondents indicated that Allied bombing either had no effect or increased popular determination. Indeed, "about a third feel that [the bombings] incite hatred against the Allies for their 'ruthless destruction of German cities,' and increase the spirit of resistance." In contrast, "over three quarters of the [prisoners] responding felt that [Allied bombing raids] do succeed in hampering production, not only through actual destruction to the factories, but through loss of man-hours, stoppages of work, etc., a substantial increase over the last report." But, again, "a slight majority" contended that the Allied bombing campaign would "not be decisive in knocking Germany out of the war."[30]

"Practically all" of the nine German prisoners of war captured in late December 1944 and early January 1945 commented "upon the serious breakdown of transportation and supply. In most cases this is attributed to the effect of air and artillery bombardment. There was a lack of food, a lack of ammunition and, in some cases, even weapons."[31] While this commentary speaks to the impact of Allied bombardment, these prisoners' remarks seem as pertinent to the German tactical situation in late 1944 and early 1945 as they do to the overall impact of Allied bombing. However, the theme of transportation difficulties increasingly emerged among prisoner responses as the war reached its final stages.

Regarding German transportation, all nine German POWs captured at roughly the same time as the previous group were "unanimous in testifying to the havoc that bombing and strafing by Allied planes [was] playing with their supply lines." These prisoners noted that, early in the December 1944 German Ardennes offensive, "supplies of food and ammunition were said to be adequate, ammunition even plentiful.... However, as the Germans advanced supplies kept failing because the means of transporting food, etc., to the advancing troops were lacking." The prisoners emphasized that "the continuous [Allied] bombings of rail centers and railway lines has slowed down and complicated rail transportation to a great degree." Regarding civilian morale, the prisoners "picture conditions at home as being so bad as to have brought the home front to the verge of a breakdown, and a number of them feel that Germany will collapse from within sooner than the troops at the front."[32] This group of prisoners cited the impact of Allied bombing and strafing—highlighting the impact of both strategic bombing and close air support—on German transportation, and, consequently, supply lines. Moreover, they painted a bleak picture of civilian morale on the German home front. However, it is worth reinforcing the speculative nature of some prisoner comments. For example, they stated that early "supplies of food and ammunition were *said* to be adequate . . . ." These prisoners seem to have been replacements sent to support the German offensive and may not have been there in the opening days of the campaign. Furthermore, this report (1461) expresses that the prisoners "*picture* conditions at home as being so bad . . . ." This phrasing too suggests that the prisoners had not experienced the German home front recently and, rather, were offering what they believed to be the case based on rumors among the troops or other secondhand or thirdhand sources of information.

Another ten German Army prisoners captured in January 1945 echoed previous comments. These men lamented the "totally inadequate functioning of the German service of supply at the front caused by the attacks of the [Allied Air Forces]," and the resulting "hunger and insufficient clothing. . . . Many did not have overcoats, blankets or gloves." Although this group assessed German civilian morale as "bad," they, unlike the previous group, believed that the Gestapo was so "completely in control" of German society that the army would break before the civilian population did.[33] Again, the source of their information for these assessments and whether they viewed Gestapo control of the German population as positive or negative, is unknown.

Finally, eleven prisoners captured in Germany in late February and early March 1945—by this point, the Western Front was now in Germany—commented "on the effectiveness of [Allied] bombing of transportation facilities and relate[d] incidents of long delay in movements from one place to another." These prisoners offered multiple examples of troop movements taking ten to twelve days when they should have been concluded in two or three. This was due to "a scarcity of rolling stock, particularly of locomotives, and movements [were] restricted to night travel. During the daytime trains remain[ed] concealed in tunnels."[34]

Questioning the prisoners about the effects of strategic bombing, regardless of the source of the prisoners' information, seems reasonable. Again, the German population could best speak to the impact of Allied bombing even if their perspectives were filtered through the ears and tongues of German prisoners in the United States. But at times American interrogators seemed to be emphasizing the impressions of German prisoners who may not have had the experience necessary to offer informed commentary on these matters.

Publishing, broadcasting, and sometimes dropping information on enemy military forces and civilian populations also constitute a type of military operations: information operations. And, like attempting to assess the impact of the damage wrought by Allied bombs, who would know better the effectiveness of Allied propaganda than the targets themselves? The prisoners' views of German and Allied propaganda over time illustrate some continuities—German soldiers and civilians alike seemed to enjoy and come to trust the news they received from the British Broadcasting Corporation (BBC) above all other radio broadcasts, including German ones.[35] These reports also show some evolution—much skepticism about Allied leaflets in mid- to late 1944 turned to seeing them as positive influences on the German population and even a lifeline for German soldiers needing to surrender. Perhaps unsurprisingly, the reports demonstrate the decreasing effectiveness of German propaganda during the final year of the war. Tales of great victories became less convincing as German soldiers and civilians began to suffer the effects of Allied gains.

Once again, the "Trends" report of August 1944 offers a summary of the first 433 interrogated German POWs' views regarding Allied propaganda. This report offers four basic conclusions. First, while the prisoners believed that some German propaganda was still effective, official German Army communiques for example, most concurred that, overall, its effectiveness had declined since the beginning of the war. Second, "listening to foreign broadcasts seem[ed] to be quite common throughout Germany." According to the prisoners, the most popular foreign broadcast was the BBC. An earlier report, dated 29 June 1944, indicated that over seventy of eighty prisoners admitted to listening to the BBC at some point prior to capture. Considerably fewer prisoners listened to American broadcasts, in large part because of reception difficulties. But, according to the prisoners, American and Soviet broadcasts both suffered from "unskillful handling of propaganda" by ridiculing the Germans, causing resentment.[36] The heavy dose of communist teachings embedded in the Soviet broadcasts also turned off many of the prisoners. Finally, the "Trends" report concluded that "leaflets [were] not too popular with the majority" of German soldiers. The prisoners contended that Allied leaflets were "effective only for those who [were] already amenable to Allied propaganda," and they were "designed so as to appeal only to the uneducated." The prisoners did admit, however, that "the promise of good treatment in case of surrender, contained in front line leaflets, [had] proved effective."[37]

One hundred thirty German prisoners captured between April and July 1944 and interrogated at Fort Hunt between 4 July and 5 August 1944 offered similar views. They too noted the declining effectiveness of German propaganda, although three-quarters of these men still believed it influenced the German people because they had "no other sources of news" and were "forced to believe at least part of the news releases." This group of prisoners again contended that the BBC was the most popular foreign radio broadcast. For example, of seventy-five POW respondents, fifty-four (72 percent) stated that they listened to the BBC, twenty (27 percent) that they did not, and one prisoner had never heard of the BBC. In comparison, of fifty-six prisoner respondents, nineteen prisoners (34 percent) listened to American broadcasts, thirty-five (63 percent) did not, and two had never heard them. And, of fifty POW respondents, fourteen (28 percent) listened to Radio Moscow, thirty-three (66 percent) did not, and three had never heard it. Also like the previous prisoners interrogated, this group suggested that Allied leaflets were largely ineffective. Of 117 prisoner respondents, only twenty-four (20.5 percent) found them effective; the remaining ninety-three prisoners stated that the leaflets were ineffective, or that they had never read or even seen one. Those prisoners who considered the leaflets ineffective felt that they "underestimate[d] German intelligence, and most of [the] leaflets call forth only ridicule" from German soldiers. As one example, some prisoners claimed that the Allies dropped meat ration coupons over Berlin. The coupons were "wrapped around small bundles of hay," and a leaflet was enclosed with the following statement: "If you believe in retribution, eat the hay, if you do not, buy yourself some meat."[38]

This trend only became more pronounced. Report 1464 dated 9 February 1945, states, regarding ten German POWs captured in January 1945, "If these men can be believed, faith in German propaganda is a thing of the past. There is widespread listening to Allied broadcasting stations." One prisoner even claimed that "repeated statements of the good treatment which the German soldier may expect in captivity and emphasis on the simple necessities of life which he can have in captivity are very effective." Only a month later, German prisoners began to laud the influence of Allied leaflets, saying that they were "having a desirable effect by letting the German people and the soldiers know what [was] really going on, as they are kept in virtual ignorance or deliberately misled." And, the prisoners, of course, continued to note the "considerable listening in on Allied broadcasts." One prisoner suggested that the Americans should "drop pictures showing [their] vast massed quantities of tanks, ammunition, stores, etc." Furthermore, "Many German soldiers, in spite of the rigorous penalties prescribed, always carry on their person the so-called 'passes' dropped by Allied planes."[39]

Assessing the impact of both strategic bombing and information operations offered the potential for adjusting the Allied approach, in this war or the next. But assessing the presence of underground movements in German-controlled territory was more about evaluating the domestic political situation under the Nazi regime and finding potential collaborators in the invasion and postwar occupation of Germany. As of May 1944, German POWs at Fort Hunt acknowledged the presence of small, individual underground groups in Germany and "a very large underground . . . in France and other occupied countries." However, the prisoners did not know of any large, organized underground movements in Germany at that time. Although, again, they offered no assessment of whether this was positive or negative or even why they believed this to be the case.[40] The prisoners that came to PO Box 1142 between June 1944 and April 1945 largely echoed these beliefs, although with some interesting qualifications.

Notably, the eighty prisoners interrogated at Fort Hunt in late May and early June 1944 told a completely different tale. This was a varied group, featuring fifty-five NCOs and twenty-five enlisted men. More important, twenty-six of the eighty prisoners were non-German, including nine from Austria, two from Luxembourg, six from Alsace, three from Yugoslavia, two from Czechoslovakia, two from Lorraine, one from Danzig, and one Sudeten German. According to the interrogators' assessment, "Three of the Austrians, the Danziger, and the Sudeten German were Nazi. The remainder of these non-Germans were violently anti-Nazi."[41]

While some of these prisoners insisted that no underground movement existed in Germany, a majority believed that one did, although they did not provide any specific details. The prisoners indicated that there were "three important anti-Nazi groups in Germany" at that point in the war: "the members of the former German Communist Party, ex-members of the NSDAP [Nazi Party], and members of the K.g.F. (Kampfverband gegen Faschismus—Fighters against Fascism)." The prisoners discounted the communists, labeling them "older men and women who cannot be reconciled to any party or government except a communistic one." The former Nazi Party members appear to have been the largest of these groups, according to the POWs, numbering over 300,000. Yet the prisoners portrayed the K.g.F. as having the most potential to resist the Nazi regime effectively. The prisoners did not estimate the size of their group but described them as "former communists and Social Democrats, members of the old Zentrum (Catholic Center Party), and large numbers of persons from the higher economic groups of German working classes who have no political interests." And, perhaps most significantly, the prisoners suggested the K.g.F. was secretly led by Wehrmacht officers and that the members "must be physically able and willing to bear arms against the Nazis." As of June 1944, according to the prisoners, K.g.F. members were biding their time, "gathering arms, spreading propaganda, and enlisting new members."[42]

Notably, three of the eighty prisoners of war in the group claimed to be members of underground organizations in other countries. One prisoner, presumably one of the six Alsatian or two Lorrainer prisoners, identified himself as one of the *Malgré Nous*. The *Malgré Nous*—the term meant "against our will"—were men from Alsace or Lorraine who had been forcibly conscripted into the Wehrmacht or Waffen SS. This prisoner stated that the group composed and distributed underground newspapers clandestinely via railway workers. He assured the American interrogators that the group had "quite a few caches of arms and ammunition stored away by the population in Lorraine ... and the underground should be able to give material aid to the Allies when the time [was] ripe." Two other prisoners claimed to be members of underground movements in Poland and Czechoslovakia. Each lauded the strength of these two movements and the work they were doing to oppose Nazi occupation.[43]

Among a group of nine prisoners captured in Bastogne in late December 1944 and early January 1945, a young prisoner from Hamburg claimed to be "a member of the Hamburg 'Penny Club,' a youth organization of about 1,000 boys and girls who regularly and frequently beat up members of the [Hitler Youth]."[44] Despite the documented existence of underground anti-Nazi youth movements like the "White Rose" in Munich, this author could find no specific information about a "Hamburg Penny Club." This group may have been the prisoner's fanciful creation intended to garner sympathy from his American captors. Yet the activities the prisoner describes—beating up Hitler Youth—sounds very much like another underground collective of German youth: the Edelweiss Pirates. Three of the ten prisoners interrogated at Fort Hunt on 7 February 1945 testified to the existence of the "*Edelweiss Piraten*" [Edelweiss Pirates], describing them as "an anti-Nazi Communist movement ... actively combatting the present regime."[45] The eleven German prisoners interrogated on 14–15 March 1945, while again contending that "there can be no successful effective organized underground" in Germany, also provided "additional confirmation of the existence of the widespread Rhineland group of anti-Nazis known as 'Edelweiss' which combines Communist and strongly Catholic elements."[46] The Edelweiss Pirates, largely teenagers in the Rhineland, were known to beat up members of the Hitler Youth and spread Allied propaganda, among other acts of resistance.

Perhaps the Hamburg Penny Club was part of the Edelweiss Pirates, as they were known to go by different names such as the "Navajos" or the "Roving Dudes," depending on their city of origin. Regardless, American interrogators eagerly sought information about any potential collaborators with their postwar occupation, routinely asking the prisoners at Fort Hunt about underground movements. While the pirates may have been the largest of these groups, the Edelweiss Pirates turned out to be a thorn in the side of Allied occupation authorities. Indeed, shortly after the war, the "pirates" turned their resistance efforts against Allied occupation authorities as they had first done against the Nazis.[47]

The final, albeit brief topic that emerges from these reports is that of potential Nazi infiltration of Allied governance in Western Europe. A German lieutenant interrogated at PO Box 1142 on 14–15 March 1945 testified to two incidents of Nazi infiltration of Allied occupied areas. First, while commanding a company-sized element near the town of Jülich, Germany, about thirty kilometers northeast of Aachen, this prisoner encountered three German civilians asking to speak with him. After apprising them of danger in the area—American troops overran the position the following day—they produced "Gestapo credentials" and stated that their mission was "to get lost behind the Allied lines," which they subsequently did. The prisoner adamantly proclaimed that this sort of thing tied in with the determination of the party diehards to filter into occupied territory and secure positions of trust with the American authorities using forged credentials. The lieutenant also informed his interrogators that sometime earlier, near Namur, Belgium, he encountered other German civilians. This group consisted of adherents of the German Zentrum Party who were being held in a stockade. The men insisted that "SA, Gestapo or similar persons with cleverly forged papers were hoodwinking the American military authorities into placing them in positions of trust, whereupon they report as unreliable any or all Germans they wish out of the way."[48] While this makes for fascinating reading, American interrogators seemed to have taken little interest. In fact, the lieutenant cited in Report 1492, dated 17 March 1945, makes the only reference to Nazi infiltration of Allied-occupied areas to be found in any of these sixteen reports, which suggests that the Americans did not seek this information; rather, the prisoner volunteered it. Given that this is the only report featuring this topic, it appears American interrogators did not see Nazi infiltration as a threat.

Evaluating any intelligence gathering operation is fraught with challenges. Evaluating the reliability and accuracy of opinions expressed by prisoners of war to enemy interrogators is an even more daunting task. That the US Army and US Navy continued to devote resources to gathering this information suggests that they found some value in the intelligence they received. Yet what value, specifically, did it hold for the US military? Prisoner opinions at least offered American authorities a glimpse into the views of their enemy, an after-action report to help revise their approach to war, and some indication of how to plan for the postwar governance of occupied Germany. While not always accurate, American interrogators received information regarding these issues. What the US Army did with these answers once received is another matter. Moreover, American admiration for their German enemy seems to have shaped the conduct of this operation, at least to a limited extent. Otherwise, why would American interrogators repeatedly report the same critical responses to the same questions about American military performance in considerable detail? They stopped asking the prisoners other questions after receiving consistent answers over several months. But they persisted in seeking German evaluations of the US Army. This suggests that the Americans believed the Germans had something to teach them, a belief that remained for decades after the Second World War.

Notes

1. Ronald Smelser and Edward J. Davies II, *The Myth of the Eastern Front: The Nazi-Soviet War in American Popular Culture* (New York: Cambridge University Press, 2008), 125.

2. Regarding the Hill Project and the involvement of German general officers in the work of the US Army Historical Division, see Derek R. Mallett, *Hitler's Generals in America: Nazi Prisoners of War and Allied Military Intelligence* (Lexington: University Press of Kentucky, 2013). For more on the influence of German officers in rewriting US Army armor doctrine, see Kevin Soutor, "To Stem the Red Tide: The German Report Series and Its Effect on American Defense Doctrine, 1948–1954," *Journal of Military History* 57 (October 1993): 653–88. For more on the US Army's "infatuation" with the Wehrmacht, see Ricardo A. Herrera, "History, Mission Command, and the *Auftragstaktik* Infatuation," *Military Review* (July–August 2022): 53–66.

3. For other chapters in this volume considering the work of the OSS and of the importance of foreign language knowledge to wartime work, see Sara B. Castro's chapter 1 and especially Brian Hayashi's chapter 10.

4. Military Intelligence Division, History of the Military Intelligence Division, 7 December 1941–2 September 1945 (Washington, DC, 1946), 102, cited in Steven M. Kleinman, "The History of MIS-Y: US Strategic Interrogation during World War II," master's thesis, Joint Military Intelligence College, August 2002, 85.

5. Kleinman, "The History of MIS-Y," 88–95.

6. Kleinman, "The History of MIS-Y," 87–88.

7. US National Park Service (hereinafter NPS), Fort Hunt Oral History Project, PO Box 1142, "Dr. Henry Kolm," transcript, https://www.nps.gov/museum/exhibits/FOHU_oral_history/index.html (accessed: 12 January 2023).

8. R. A. Osmun, "Report from Captured Personnel and Material Branch: Trends in German Morale," Report 1285, 28 August 1944; container 1367; entry UD 300; RG 498; NACP. The first report in this subset was Report 1168, dated 22 February 1944. "Trends in German Morale" also surveyed reports 1190, 1202, 1228, 1238, 1248, 1261, and 1273; the final report is dated 12 July 1944. The "Trends" report is particularly valuable because only three of the eight reports upon which it is based—1228, 1261, and 1273—are available to researchers. It is worth noting that this author has not exhausted all the approximately 100,000 pages of files in the Fort Hunt collection held at the National Archives in College Park, Maryland. Copies of reports in the CPMB series might be in portions of the collection that the author has yet to examine.

9. R. A. Osmun, "Trends in German Morale," Report 1285, 28 August 1944; container 1367; entry UD 300; RG 498, NACP.

10. R. A. Osmun, "Survey of Expressions of German Ps/W Opinions Taken in the United States 4 July–5 August 1944 Inclusive," Report 1298, 28 August 1944; container 1367; entry UD 300; RG 498; NACP.

11. R. A. Osmun, "Expressions of Opinion of Recently Captured German Ps/W on Conditions at the Front and at Home," Report 1434, 13 January 1945, container 1367, Eentry UD 300, RG 498, NACP.

12. R. A. Osmun, "Trends in German Morale," Report 1285, 28 August 1944, container 1367, RG 498, NACP.

13. Osmun, "Trends in German Morale."

14. R. A. Osmun, "Survey of Expressions of German Ps/W Opinions Taken in the United States 4 July–5 August 1944 inclusive," Report 1298, 28 August 1944, container 1367, entry UD 300, RG 498, NACP. It seems likely that the interrogators' interpretations of the prisoners' responses differed from the data they collected. Perhaps this was based on the tone of the conversations or other intangible factors not captured in a basic tally of votes.

15. R. A. Osmun, "Report from Captured Personnel and Material Branch," Report 1311, 28 August 1944, container 1367; entry UD 300, RG 498, NACP.

16. R. A. Osmun, "Expressions of P/W Opinion on German Military and Civilian Morale, Conditions in the German Armed Forces, and Other Miscellaneous Topics," Report 1420, 2 January 1945, container 1367, entry UD 300, RG 498, NACP.

17. R. A. Osmun, "Expressions of Opinion of Recently Captured German Ps/W on Conditions at the Front and at Home," Report 1426, 6 January 1945, container 1367, entry UD 300, RG 498, NACP.

18. R. A. Osmun, "Expressions of Opinion of Recently Captured German Ps/W on Conditions at the Front and at Home," Report 1434, 13 January 1945, container 1367, entry UD 300, RG 498, NACP.

19. P. E. Peabody, Brigadier General, GSC, Chief, Military Intelligence Service, "Expressions of Opinion of Recently Captured German Ps/W on Conditions at the Front and at Home," Report 1500, 29 March 1945, container 1368, entry UD 300, RG 498, NACP.

20. P. E. Peabody, "Expressions of Opinion of Recently Captured German Ps/W on Conditions at the Front and at Home," Report 1517, 30 April 1945, container 1368, entry UD 300, RG 498, NACP.

21. R. A. Osmun, "Expressions of Opinion of Recently Captured German Ps/W on Conditions at the Front and at Home," Report 1426, 6 January 1945, container 1367, entry UD 300, RG 498, NACP.

22. Osmun, "Trends in German Morale."

23. For Douhet's arguments about the importance of airpower, see Giulio Douhet, *The Command of the Air*, trans. Dino Ferrari (Maxwell Air Force Base, Alabama: Air University Press, 2019).

24. Sir Arthur Harris, *Bomber Offensive* (London: Collins Clear-type Press, 1947), 78, quoted in L. McLean, "Bomber Offensive," *Naval War College Information Service for Officers*, 1:8 (May 1949), 33–34.

25. W. F. Craven and J. L. Cate, *The Army Air Forces in World War II*, vol, 3: *Europe: ARGUMENT to V-E Day, January 1944 to May 1945* (Washington, DC: Office of Air Force History, 1983 [First published: Chicago: University of Chicago Press, 1951]), 716.

26. R. A. Osmun, "Trends in German Morale," Report 1285, 28 August 1944, container 1367, entry UD 300, RG 498, NACP.

27. "'Big Week': February 20–25, 1944," National Museum of the United States Air Force, https://www.nationalmuseum.af.mil/Visit/Museum-Exhibits/Fact-Sheets/Display/Article/1519678/big-week-february-20-25-1944/ (accessed 15 January 2023).

28. P. E. Peabody, "Expressions of Opinion of Recently Captured German Ps/W on Conditions at the Front and at Home," Report 1517, 30 April 1945, container 1368, entry UD 300, RG 498, NACP.

29. R. A. Osmun, "Trends in German Morale," Report 1285, 28 August 1944, container 1367, entry UD 300, RG 498, NACP.

30. R. A. Osmun, "Survey of Expressions of German Ps/W Opinions Taken in the United States 4 July–5 August 1944 Inclusive," Report 1298, 28 August 1944, container 1367, entry UD 300, RG 498, NACP.

31. R. A. Osmun, "Report from Captured Personnel and Material Branch, Military Intelligence Division, US War Department," Report 1434, 13 January 1945, container 1367, entry UD 300, RG 498, NACP.

32. R. A. Osmun, "Report from Captured Personnel and Material Branch, Military Intelligence Division, US War Department," Report 1461, 6 February 1945, container 1367, entry UD 300, RG 498, NACP.

33. R. A. Osmun, "Report from Captured Personnel and Material Branch, Military Intelligence Division, US War Department," Report 1464, 9 February 1945, container 1367, entry UD 300, RG 498, NACP.

34. P. E. Peabody, "Expressions of Opinion of Recently Captured German Ps/W on Conditions at the Front and at Home," Report 1492, 17 March 1945, container 1367, entry UD 300, RG 498, NACP.

35. On American and Canadian troops consuming information and its effects, see Victoria Sotvedt's chapter 7 and Elena Friot's chapter 9 in this volume.

36. For a more complex take on internal Soviet propaganda, see Erina Megowan's chapter 6 in this volume.

37. R. A. Osmun, "Trends in German Morale," Report 1285, 28 August 1944; R. A. Osmun, "Information from Captured Personnel and Material Branch: Morale Report," Report 1261, 29 June 1944; Catesby ap Jones, "Morale Report," Report 1228, 8 May 1944; container 1367, entry UD 300, RG 498, NACP.

38. R. A. Osmun, "Survey of expressions of German Ps/W opinions taken in the United States 4 July–5 August 1944 inclusive," Report 1298, 28 August 1944, container 1367, entry UD 300, RG 498, NACP.

39. P. E. Peabody, "Expressions of Opinion of Recently Captured German Ps/W on Conditions at the Front and at Home," Report 1492, 17 March 1945, container 1367, entry UD 300, RG 498, NACP.

40. Catesby ap Jones, "Morale Report," Report 1228, 8 May 1944, container 1367, entry UD 300, RG 498, NACP.

41. R. A. Osmun, "Information from Captured Personnel and Material Branch: Morale Report," Report 1261, 29 June 1944, container 1367, entry UD 300, RG 498, NACP.

42. Osmun, "Information from Captured Personnel and Material Branch."

43. Osmun, "Information from Captured Personnel and Material Branch."

44. R. A. Osmun, "Report from Captured Personnel and Material Branch, Military Intelligence Division, US War Department," Report 1434, 13 January 1945, container 1367, entry UD 300, RG 498, NACP.

45. R. A. Osmun, "Report from Captured Personnel and Material Branch, Military Intelligence Division, US War Department," Report 1464, 9 February 1945, container 1367, entry UD 300, RG 498, NACP. Essentially these underground members were embracing the reverse politics of Kevin Riehle's Soviet defectors, discussed in chapter 11 in this volume.

46. P. E. Peabody, "Expressions of Opinion of Recently Captured German Ps/W on Conditions at the Front and at Home," Report 1492, 17 March 1945, container 1367, entry UD 300, RG 498, NACP.

47. Perry Biddiscombe, "'The Enemy of Our Enemy': A View of the Edelweiss Piraten from the British and American Archives," *Journal of Contemporary*

History 30, no. 1 (January 1995): 37–63. Current historiography surrounding the Edelweiss Pirates, while scant, struggles to conclude whether they were an underground resistance movement or a large, loosely organized collection of juvenile delinquents.

48. P. E. Peabody, "Expressions of Opinion of Recently Captured German Ps/W on Conditions at the Front and at Home," Report 1492, 17 March 1945, container 1367, entry UD 300, RG 498, NACP.

Part II
Totalization
The Militarization of Civilians

5

Montélimar's Phony War
Requisitions, Mobilization, and French Civilians

Cameron Zinsou

Mr. Peyrouse was a mechanic and reservist who lived in the southeastern French town of Montélimar. As the French neared war with the Germans, France mobilized. Peyrouse's unit activated, and he was called up. On Sunday, 27 August 1939, while Peyrouse was away, 216 French soldiers under the command of a Captain Rouanes billeted at his business without presenting a requisition order. The soldiers stayed at Peyrouse's business until 1 September. When Peyrouse learned what had happened, he filed a complaint with Montélimar Mayor Edouard Tardieu. In his petition, Peyrouse claimed that a rival mechanic shop with whom he was engaged in a legal dispute, Debay & Gisclon, told Captain Rouanes that they could not accept the vehicles and men at their establishment because they had already received a different requisition order. They suggested to Rouanes that he use Peyrouse's garage instead. Peyrouse asserted, "I am ready to do my duty as a citizen, which the present circumstances require, but what I cannot accept is that others have been able to escape this duty and unloaded it onto me."[1] Peyrouse's situation reflected the inherent tension in France between citizenship, patriotism, and private property on the one hand, and national defense requirements and mobilization on the other.

The French army's actions in the Peyrouse case were more characteristic of a foreign occupier than a nation defending its borders. This chapter argues that Montiliens—Montélimar's inhabitants—and the rest of the French population prior to the start of major combat operations in western Europe lived under a state of occupation. From September 1939 through May 1940—a period known as the Phony War due to the inactivity between the German and Allied forces in western Europe—France had more than half a year to prepare to fight Germany. The government's irregular enforcement of requisition policy seemed arbitrary to civilians and threatened to undermine their confidence in the war effort. These views emerged despite other episodes, including those with billeted French colonial soldiers, that included community support for the army. The lack of constructive interaction between local governments and the army reinforced these perceptions. It reveals the limits of state planning and that the consequences of policy introduced French civilians to the everyday life they would experience under occupation after France's defeat in 1940.

As the Peyrouse case shows, however, the requisitions process was not a one-way form of communication. Rather, civilians often contested and questioned state confiscation of their belongings as well as their conscription into the French army. These interactions should be understood as a "politics of requisitions." Civilians used law, perceived notions of fairness, their obligations to France, and public declarations from French politicians to contest requisitions. Throughout France's republican history, French men and women recognized that defeating their adversaries required the possible sacrifice of many of their possessions in service of the nation. What they expected in return, in addition to victory, was fair treatment from the state in distributing these sacrifices. The individuals responsible for facilitating these requisitions—town municipal councils and the military—did so poorly.

Montélimar was one of the 495 mobilization centers throughout France where units would muster in the event of war, making it an ideal site for study. Whereas previous works focus on France's preparations for war and civil/military relations on a national level, assess French army doctrine during the interwar era, or examine French economic preparations, this chapter considers all those facets in Montélimar and analyzes their practical execution and consequences.[2] Montélimar is in southeastern France in the Rhône Valley, a fertile region in France sculpted by the Rhône River. Looking west, one sees the towering heights of the ancient Massif Central across the Rhône in the Ardèche. To the east, one sees the continuation of the Rhône Valley and on the horizon the first mountains that constitute the Alps. It had a wartime population of 15,187, making it the second largest commune in the Drôme department after Valence, a bustling city when war started.[3] It lies along a traditional major highway (National Route 7) that stretches from Paris to the French Riviera. Despite being a provincial backwater for most of its existence, Montélimar has a storied history. The French Third Republic President Emile Loubet was Montélimar's mayor before ascending to the presidency in 1899, and he became the first president of the Third Republic to complete his entire term in office. During his term Loubet brought the city to prominence by giving visiting dignitaries nougat from Montélimar.[4] From 1925 to 1944, Montélimar only had two mayors, which made politics stable. Edouard Tardieu became Montélimar's mayor in 1935 and remained through 1944. This consistency in leadership at the local level differed from the high turnover at the national level.

Overall, however, mayors generally behaved as facilitators, making sure that daily life ran smoothly in their towns. They held prestige as fatherly figures, for their communes and citizens looked to them for leadership even though they had limited ability to influence policy.[5] The prefect—the top state representative in each of France's departments—retained authority over the implementation of the law and the coordination of the department's police and gendarmerie forces. All mayoral decisions required prefect approval.[6] When needed, mayors could appeal to the prefect for additional funds, for adjudication of problems, and other kinds of assistance. As such, the mechanisms of power in the Third Republic remained rigid, with direction flowing from the top down. During the Second World War, mayors received much of the blame for the breakdown of government processes, but their interventions had limited effect.

Formulating Requisition Law during the Interwar Era

France's declaration of war on Germany on 3 September 1939 mobilized the French nation, and 2.7 million Frenchmen joined their units.[7] The manner of rousing France and its resources had roots tracing back to the French Revolution when the *levée en masse* brought the entire French citizenry to bear against its opponents, and this became an important part of the French republican tradition. In 1870–71, during France's defeat in the Franco-Prussian War and the formation of the Third Republic, French politicians recognized that in future wars the entire French nation had to be mustered to face the country's foes.[8] French legislators codified military requisitions with the Law of 3 July 1877 on Military Requisitions. The ruinous experiences of World War I further cemented this view, and in the interwar era France determined it must commit *all* its resources to national defense.[9] The demographic disparity with Germany—France's likely opponent in a future conflict—reinforced the idea of total national mobilization. The military could requisition civilian resources for the safety and security of France. The Law of 3 July 1877 served as the basis for military requisitions in the republic through the end of World War I.

In the aftermath of World War I, a sharp debate arose in the French government about how to organize the nation during war. The government revised the old National Defense Superior Council (Conseil Supérieur de la Défense Nationale, or CSDN) in 1921 to study how to combine civilian and military defense planning. A central issue was how to better mobilize all

French resources, including private property. The government could negotiate with property owners for fixed rates; it would get what it needed through an agreement, although there were restrictions on business profit. If government representatives failed to reach an agreement with a business or individual, then it could requisition.[10]

After Nazi Germany began aggressively rearming in the 1930s, French officials revisited war organization measures. On 11 July 1938, the massive National Wartime Organization Act (Loi sur l'organisation de la nation pour le temps de guerre, or NWOA) outlined in sixty-eight articles how civilian and military responsibilities would operate during wartime. It reflected many of the same conclusions that the CSDN came to over a decade prior. Men over the age of eighteen were required to enlist in some form of national service—from military conscription to serving in the civil defense force— while women were entirely exempt.[11] Government acquisition of civilian property occurred in two steps: In peacetime, the government negotiated with individuals over their possessions; during wartime, resources would be requisitioned with the state paying an indemnity.[12] If the NWOA was the template by which the nation acquired resources, many government personnel and military officers remained ignorant of their duties to facilitate those acquisitions.

During the Munich crisis in September 1938, France partially mobilized and tested the law. Prefects and mayors around France who would perform the day-to-day coordination with the military and collect resources for military use were totally unaware of their responsibilities.[13] This embarrassing reality caused the national government to issue a series of directives that summarized the requisition procedures of prefects and mayors. These efforts resulted in the establishment of an office in every military region (of which there were fourteen in France) known as the Commission on Evaluating Requisitions. The commission consisted of five individuals: two soldiers appointed by the regional commander and three civilians by the prefect. The mayor would forward each reimbursement claim to the commission, which in turn gave its opinion. The region's quartermaster received the committee's recommendation, and he decided within three days whether to accept it. If the quartermaster accepted the decision, he would then notify the mayor, and the mayor would have fifteen days to respond either to accept or decline the offer. If the mayor did not respond, the claim would be considered accepted. If the mayor declined, the case would be deferred to the Justice of the Peace in the department in question, who would adjudicate the situation. After the parties reached a settlement, the Treasury Department would either give cash to the individual or the mayor's office. During war, however, the Treasury Department had the option to issue bonds with interest instead of payment.[14] This new system was a stopgap measure that was unwieldy at best, and ineffective at worst. Originally designed to be transparent and fair, the sheer number of requisitions and disputes quickly overwhelmed the various committees.[15] The new committee system was another layer of administrative tedium that promoted transparency but could not function.

The system of requisitions also differed from how lawmakers outlined it. Montélimar's officials used census data to identify businesses, shops, farms, stables, and homes suitable for the quartering of soldiers and animals. A coordinating officer from a military unit would then supply the barrack's commander (commandant d'armes) in Montélimar, Captain (later Lieutenant Colonel) Piollet with census information.[16] The commander would then contact the mayor informing him of the requisition requirements. The military could use public buildings like theaters and stadiums for the storage of equipment, vehicles, and weapons. Across France, the administrative personnel responsible for organizing these material acquisitions were shockingly understaffed, further complicating efforts to accommodate army units.[17]

Montélimar and the French Army during the Phony War

One of the first units to come through Montélimar on 7 September was the 482nd Régiment Pionniers Infanterie Coloniaux (Colonial Pioneer Infantry Regiment, or RPIC) belonging to the 9th French Army.[18] These units formed in the summer of 1939 in growing anticipation of conflict with Germany. (Pioneer regiments differed from other units of the French army in significant ways: They were composed of old classes of French army units whose primary task was fieldwork. They were often poorly equipped and received less rigorous training than the regular army because they were not expected to fight.) From September to mid-November, 626 soldiers and thirty-five horses from the 482nd—most of them belonging to the regiment's 3rd battalion—arrived in Montélimar.[19] The soldiers began departing on 18 November and had entirely vacated the city by the 23rd. During their stay, most resided in about a dozen residences in a northeast Montélimar neighborhood, the Quartier de Beausseret.

After the unit left, civilians filed numerous reports detailing property damage. Mrs. Nicolas, a widow, owner of Chateau de Milan, tallied an extensive list of damages: Soldiers destroyed twenty windows, two windowed doors, a thirty-meter by fifteen-meter mural, four locks, and twenty electric lamps around the premises. In Nicolas's summary, the officer who made the list noted that there were at least 350 men in Chateau de Milan, which exceeded the building's authorized capacity of 270.[20] There was also a disparity between what the officer listed and the requisition form. The requisition slip provided to Nicolas claimed that there would be 300 soldiers and twelve horses staying at Chateau Milan.[21] The army requisitioned an additional room in Nicolas's personal home for one non-commissioned officer.[22] The number of soldiers at Chateau Milan was between 300 and 350 men, putting the chateau at overcapacity. The damages amounted to an estimated 2,310 francs on top of the 13,925 francs paid to Nicolas for the soldiers' stay.[23]

The 482nd RPIC caused damage in several other places. They billeted at a farm belonging to Mrs. Deloule, a widow, located in the Quartier de Beausseret. Deloule's farm was on the prewar census for soldier billeting in Montélimar.[24] Auguste Audigier, a tenant of Deloule, was preparing to harvest his crops. Deloule and Audigier anticipated receiving forty soldiers and six horses (the requisition slip indicates as much).[25] However, for two months, from 7 September to 19 November, Audigier housed 196 soldiers from the 9th Company, 3rd Battalion of the 482nd RPIC. The company commander delivered a certificate of good standing to Deloule, indicating that they believed they had left the property in good condition.[26]

Deloule and Audigier, however, disagreed. Deloule filed an initial complaint a few weeks into the unit's stay.[27] On 29 November, Deloule wrote Mayor Tardieu again expressing her dismay at the situation. Her first complaint addressed the discrepancy between the requisition slip listing and the actual number of soldiers on the property. Deloule noted that they ended up housing "at least 150 men." The property owner suggested to Tardieu that most of the indemnities be paid to Audigier because he maintained the lodgings.[28] Audigier, for his part, supplemented Deloule's claim with one of his own. He stated that over the course of those two months, the 9th Company slept on and ruined fodder that Audigier intended to sell including: 4,000 kilograms of livestock feed, 150 kilograms of seed, 20 kilograms of chickpeas, 20 kilograms of beans, and 160 kilograms of straw gills.[29] Piollet informed Tardieu that the case had already been sent to other authorities.[30] Audigier summarized his plight, "[I] . . . being a poor farmer, cannot endure such transgressions. As long as the men were there, I could do nothing. It is abominable. . . . Please do not forget me in my sad situation."[31] Audigier sent another letter on 20 May and asked why the mayor had not responded. While he credited the mayor for "doing everything necessary to support my claim," Audigier nevertheless queried why there had been no progress.[32] This letter spurred Tardieu into action, and he wrote the colonel of the military subdivision in Valence.³³ Seven months after the soldiers left, Audigier received 500 francs from the French army.³⁴

There were several reasons why problems arose between the 482nd and Montiliens. First, the unit's substandard training likely contributed to ill-discipline and unruly behavior. Second, overcrowding made incidents more frequent. Third, the discrepancies between requisition orders and the ones Montiliens received led to dismay and confusion. Fourth, the lengthy adjudication process for paying indemnities increased already heavy burdens. Audigier, for instance, could not harvest his crops, and he also could not get other work around the property done. Without the compensatory funds, this period represented a double loss for the farmer.

Soldiers from other units and individual officers also passed through Montélimar during the Phony War. From 25 October to 22 November 1939, soldiers designated as Syrian reinforcements (renfort de Syrie) billeted in Montélimar on Route d'Espeluche, located in the city's south.³⁵ After their departure, Piollet forwarded Tardieu the damages caused by the detachment.³⁶ A Mr. Pinet had the door to his garden broken, several broken tiles inside his home, and drainage pipes broken all over his property.³⁷ A Mrs. Muraour asked that she be allowed to use her laundry room two days a week so she could wash clothes for her large family.³⁸ She also asked to be compensated for 800 kilograms of firewood supplied to the detachment.³⁹ Mr. Michel claimed that a discharged bullet damaged a cast iron kettle and a washing machine. Michel asked for recompense for 500 kilograms of firewood and for 30 fifty-kilogram straw bales the soldiers used.⁴⁰

Another detachment from renfort de Syrie stayed in grounds owned by the city's equestrian society, where the soldiers kept their horses. Mr. Didio, likely a representative of the equestrian society, noticed some of the society's equipment had disappeared and filed a complaint with Tardieu. Didio noted that 600 meters of canvas used to surround the track on race days, 400 meters of rope, and numerous small tools were missing. In his complaint, Didio noted the officer's dismissive response when questioned about the missing equipment. The next day, Tardieu wrote to Piollet—who was apparently unaware of what happened—and expressed "surprise that the officer in charge ... if he did not have time to receive the complaints that various owners might have to make, did not think it necessary to warn you."⁴¹

This situation took months to resolve. On 18 March 1940, Tardieu sent estimates of the damages caused by soldiers staying in the equine center to Piollet.⁴² Tardieu did not understand why it was taking so long for the military to reimburse the equine society. Weeks later there was no resolution. Tardieu wrote Piollet again and asked him if the commander planned to follow up.[43] Piollet responded later in the day, informing Tardieu that an expert from the Damages Commission, Lieutenant Allies, would decide if and how much restitution the equine society would receive.[44] The long times spent resolving claims reflect both the priorities of the army (to get soldiers to the front) and the inefficiencies in French bureaucracy.

Such incidents highlight the politics of requisitions between the army, the mayor, and Montiliens. After initial civilian complaints, the military authorities began a long process of investigation. There were frequent gaps in communication that led to additional loss of civilian revenue. Some businesses and property owners depended on the indemnities to continue their livelihoods. Others lost entire crops due to the soldiers' rough treatment of perishable goods. There was no immediate recompense to ease civilian troubles.

While most enlisted soldiers stayed in civilian homes and businesses, officers billeted in hotels. There were a dozen hotels in Montélimar, and each had to host officers. Hotel Michel housed nine officers during September with an average stay of twenty-two days.[45] A report from 23 October listed forty-four rooms designated for military requisition at any time among the twelve hotels. Captain le Nail warned the hotel owners that "these chambers must be at the disposal of the military authority every day."[46] Requisition slips from the period show officers billeting in hotel rooms across the city from mobilization through the Battle of France.[47] Military considerations superseded civilian ones in almost every circumstance.[48]

The French army needed material goods from civilians in addition to their homes. Civilian and military leaders wanted a thorough accounting of everything deemed strategic under French law. Tardieu wasted no time in tallying up the materials available in Montélimar. In a popular local newspaper, *Journal de Montélimar*, weekly announcements from the mayor's office appeared. In the 23 September edition of the weekly publication, Tardieu announced that all sheep owners had until 25 September to declare the number of sheep and the amount of shorn wool in their possession.[49] Military governor of Lyon, General Jules Hartung, commanded all mayors to count vehicles in their communes.[50]

The French Army also requisitioned a critical civilian item: trucks. The army only had 30,000 trucks, inadequate to motorize.[51] Because the army itself could not furnish the necessary vehicles for its soldiers, it relied on taking them from civilians. This compensatory measure caused problems for civilians who needed trucks for work and transportation. Truck requisitions most affected farmers, bus drivers, and haulers of natural resources across the country.[52] In addition, civilians appealed to the sympathies of soldiers by making declarations about the necessity of their vehicles to complete work.

Civilians who pled with soldiers undermined French government appeals for sacrifice. Often soldiers tasked with requisitioning were themselves civilians a few weeks prior to mobilization. This made civilian pleas more effective because soldiers could empathize with them. As a result, the military would often resort to taking secondhand or lesser trucks and vehicles, decreasing army efficiency.[53] This represents another instance in which the military's reliance on private property created friction with civilians, in addition to degrading military readiness and effectiveness.

Municipal and Civilian Reactions to Requisitions and Mobilization

Occasionally Tardieu would make appeals on behalf of residents to exempt them from requisitions. Tardieu wrote to General Perra, commander of the artillery of the 14th Corps, asking him to exempt Camille Ayme, a mechanic in Montélimar, from requisitions. Tardieu argued that the city needed some mechanics. The mayor added that Ayme should receive special consideration because he "took part in the most deadly business," serving for four years during World War I. Because of his reputation in the city as a skilled mechanic and his status as a World War I veteran, Tardieu believed he could suspend army requisition of Ayme's garage.[54] Tardieu's plea was unsuccessful. In another instance, Mrs. Gaston Taupenas, a widow, wrote to Tardieu on 27 September asking for the return of reservist Roger Faure who worked for her. Since her husband died, Taupenas only had Faure to operate the bus that traveled between Montélimar and Valvignères to the southeast. Failure to return him, Taupenas claimed, would represent "a total loss of my business."[55] Tardieu duly passed on Tauepnas's request to the commandant of arms in Montélimar, Lieutenant Colonel Piollet.[56] He denied the claim and instructed Tardieu to see if there was anyone who could replace Faure.[57] Tardieu's intervention highlights the role mayors played on behalf of civilians. Popular perception viewed mayors as father figures to their communes who guided and defended the population.[58] It also demonstrates the difficult positions that mayors found themselves in: They had to protect the interests of their town's inhabitants while simultaneously following military directives.

If one looks at conscription as another form of requisition, individual petitions to the government for exemptions from military service are also a part of this story of mobilization and its discontents. Historian Eugenia Kiesling noted that exemptions granted to individuals in certain occupations caused resentment in the ranks. The army released some mobilized soldiers, leading more families and soldiers to petition the government for service exemptions.[59] For instance, Edouard Daladier, the prime minister of France, decreed farmers might be eligible to obtain leave.[60] French farmers took this to heart. René Feytel, a Montélimar native who was deployed to Corsica, tried to coordinate with his family to get him an exemption a few weeks after the war began. Over the next three weeks, correspondence between René and his family considered how he might get out of his military obligations. Ultimately, their petitions to Tardieu and the prefect were unsuccessful.[61] There were limits to the ways that "soft" contributions to the war effort could persuade military authorities to release soldiers from their "hard" contributions as warfighters.

While requisition law provisions allowed local governments to pay indemnities to homeowners who hosted soldiers, civilians were still unprepared for the level of disruption to their lives and livelihoods that mobilization brought—a circumstance that would repeat under foreign occupation. Mrs. Tourette, wife of Louis Tourette, detailed her plight in a letter to Tardieu.[62] Louis had been mobilized on 5 September to join his unit. Mrs. Tourette's family lived in half of a property owned by a city council member, Mr. Bertrand.[63] It was an apartment adjacent to the Mille Bodyshop where Louis worked. Since her husband's mobilization, Tourette had been living there with her two children and her parents. On 10 October, Tourette received a visit from the city's architect, Mr. Gilles, Mrs. Bertrand, and two soldiers. Mrs. Bertrand wanted to rent the attic to military personnel. The only access point to the attic, however, was through the garage. Bertrand suggested to them that they make another entry point to the attic through Tourette's apartment.[64] Mrs. Tourette was appalled. The proposed room transformation would destroy Tourette's workspace and make his work impossible. Mrs. Tourette refused the suggestion, and when she did so, Mrs. Bertrand commented, "Since she [Mrs. Tourette] does not want to give up this room, you [the army official] will just have to requisition it." Mrs. Tourette wondered who would pay for the remodeling. Tourette complained that "we'll need to redo everything in the attic: the ceiling, the floor, and the walls. It's easy for you to order this if this is what you want, but at whose expense?" She invoked previous declarations made by Daladier. Tourette asked Tardieu, "Didn't Daladier tell us there would be no war profiteers at the expense of those who are mobilized? There must be some empty attics in Montélimar not belonging to soldiers." She ended her letter by appealing to Tardieu's patriotism, "I am confident, Mr. Tardieu, of your sense of justice and solidarity with the soldier to stop this abuse of authority at the expense of the mobilized."⁶⁵ Tardieu informed Mrs. Tourette the next day that the military would have no need of her room.⁶⁶

The politics of requisitions here show how civilians attempted to use public declarations to their advantage. The Feytels discussed using Daladier's proclamations about farmers to get René leave from his unit. Mrs. Bertrand used her connections through her husband, a council member, to attempt to benefit from a situation in which Mrs. Tourette was made vulnerable. Tourette, in her plea to Tardieu, leveraged the words of Daladier and appealed to Tardieu's sense of patriotism to prevent this requisition. These examples sample civilian requests made to Tardieu and military authorities during the Phony War.⁶⁷ The NWOA placed nothing off limits if military authorities deemed the requisition necessary for the war effort, but civilians could and did still push back against it.

The French Army's movement of soldiers strained Montélimar's ability to accommodate them. Census data showed that 105 private homes, hotels, and businesses were listed as potential lodging for soldiers. Tardieu sent out a memo reminding his administrators that billeting soldiers in civilian homes was mandatory and that anyone who refused would face requisition by force.⁶⁸ Military officials occasionally bypassed Tardieu and the municipal government and soldiers billeted themselves. In late November, Captain le Nail, in charge of billeting soldiers in Montélimar, installed twenty-six airmen in twenty-six different places around the city. He did so without consulting civic authorities because city hall was closed.⁶⁹ Military necessity required occasional circumventing of proper billeting procedure. This expedient action nullified attempts at civilian/military coordination.

By the beginning of 1940 both Tardieu and Montiliens felt the burdens of the army's demands. Tardieu wrote to Piollet on 9 December and informed him that "I am having great difficulty in housing the high number of officers and non-commissioned officers (NCOs) who have been passing through the city since mobilization. I've come to ask you as a favor to me if you could keep all NCOs on military premises."⁷⁰ There was no indication whether Piollet heeded Tardieu's request. The mayor also pushed the army to pay indemnities to Montiliens. He wrote the military commandant in Valence and explained that he was "beset by complaints from Montiliens about the delay of payments made. . . . I've been sending in reports since November. . . . These criticisms [from civilians] seem justified."⁷¹ The commandant replied two weeks later and informed Tardieu that a backlog of claims delayed payments to civilians. The office was also swamped with back-ordered damage reports from all over the department.⁷² Clearly French soldiers had caused damage across wide swaths of the area during mobilization, not just in Montélimar.

With millions of male reservists called up in late August, cities all over France mobilized remaining populations to fill job vacancies. Drôme Prefect Marcel Lanquetin wrote to the mayors and notified them to use "all young people, schoolchildren, and others who will be invoked in the spirit of mutual help."[73] This call to action was reminiscent of the 1793 *levée en masse*'s declaration that "the French people are in permanent requisition for army service." A week later, Lanquetin called on all men in the Drôme to go to city hall and record their address and occupation. He exempted men in the following occupations: baker, miller, butcher, truck driver, bus driver, and metal trades. He also exempted the industry trades of wood and leather-and-hides. Individuals who did not register would automatically become eligible for conscription into the commune's civil defense force, the Défense Passive.[74]

The wartime demands the French government imposed on civilians caused some civilian resistance. They protested and petitioned Tardieu for relief from their obligations. The government attempted to address the hardship by urging mayors to use relocated French civilians to make up for the losses incurred in the communes. Montiliens attempted to secure their own possessions and security, avoiding onerous requisition demands. They also questioned the fairness of the sacrifices asked of them. Still, they wished for French victory.

Efforts to Support the Troops

As France mobilized its military and evacuated civilians from the Franco-German border, the French government generated donation drives to support them. This appeal was critical to the French army's functionality because they lacked so much essential material. For instance, the army lacked 350,000 blankets to keep soldiers warm in the winter.[75] In the Drôme, Prefect Lanquetin urged mayors in a 24 September circular to "gather as many wool and cotton blankets of a neutral color, similar to the military blanket."[76] They would be sent to Lyon, home of the Army's 14th regional headquarters. Anyone who gave a blanket of 120x180 centimeters would receive up to eighty francs and 160 francs for blankets that measured 240x180 centimeters. The mayors had six days to collect them.[77] On 27 September, Mayor Tardieu reached out to civilians, "counting on the devout support and patriotic sentiments of Montiliens so all available blankets are delivered immediately to provide for our soldiers."[78] Only seven Montiliens gave blankets, one of whom was Tardieu's wife, for a total of 337 francs.[79] It is tough to assess why

Montiliens donated so little in this case. Perhaps Montiliens missed the call in the newspaper. After all, they only had three days to respond. In another case, Montélimar's municipal council approved a rearmament donation drive to be held from 15 April to 31 May 1940.[80] Montiliens were not unwilling to give, especially if they felt a special connection to a particular outfit.[81]

Since 1938, the 28th Régiment de Tirailleurs Tunisiens (Tunisian Tiralleur Regiment, or RTT), 1st North African Infantry Division, was stationed in Montélimar. The regiment was one of several North African regiments stationed in France prior to mobilization, and one of two Tunisian regiments stationed in the country.[82] During the regiment's stay, it developed a close relationship with Montiliens. In fall 1938 during the Munich crisis, the army began a partial mobilization that included the 28th RTT, and they left the city. After the crisis had passed, the unit returned. Throngs of Montiliens lined the streets from the train station to welcome the 28th RTT home.[83] This reflected both the relief of Montiliens at averting war and the regard they had for the unit. The regiment's commander, Colonel Arnault de la Mendardiere, stopped at the Monument for the Dead in the city center to lay a wreath to commemorate the regiment's return.[84] There were mutual feelings of fondness between the unit and the townspeople.

Part of this relationship can be attributed to the "addiction," as historian Anthony Clayton called it, that the French army had for conscripting colonial soldiers into the army. After France's horrific losses in World War I, politicians and army planners realized there would need to be a large influx of colonial soldiers if France were to win its next conflict. Consequently, almost 40 percent of France's infantry at the outbreak of World War II were colonial soldiers.[85] The recognition of the need for African soldiers improved conditions for colonial soldiers in the country considerably. The soldiers could use free railway passes for tourism. Towns also organized welcoming committees when these African units were stationed in southern France, helping to make the soldiers feel welcome.[86]

Enthusiastic support for colonial soldiers was also reinforced by racist assumptions that undergirded the French colonial order. French officials adopted paternalistic attitudes toward colonial soldiers and subscribed to prejudiced ideas about African "primitiveness" and baser instincts. These characteristics, French officials believed, made Africans good fighters. French doctrine encouraged close officer ties with enlisted soldiers in colonial units. These attitudes flowed down to the French people. Of course, French civilian fondness for colonial soldiers was also rooted in their genuine appreciation for the men's role in the defense of France. Third

Republic officials strengthened ties between the empire and the metropole after World War I to make colonial subjects feel more French. These efforts seemed to have been effective, as there is much evidence of colonial soldiers' declared pride in fighting for France.[87]

The warm relationship between the soldiers and Montiliens continued into 1939. The 28th RTT mobilized during the last week of August. Between the dates of 10 and 15 September, the unit moved from Grenoble to Cusy, north of Grenoble, and finally to Saint-Offenge. The terrain was mountainous and the temperatures cold. On 10 October, the 28th RTT transferred via rail from Saint-Offenge to Dieppe-sous-Douaumont near Verdun, where the regiment began constructing and improving defensive works along the upper Meuse River.[88] The temperatures continued to drop as fall lengthened. Like the calls for blankets made in September for the army and for evacuees from the Franco-German border, *Le Journal de Montélimar* solicited Montiliens in late October to donate cold weather gear to the 28th RTT.[89] On 2 November, Colonel Mendardiere wrote to Tardieu thanking him for providing soldiers with "woolen socks, slippers, gloves, and clothing that will allow them to resist the cold winter." He also personally thanked Montiliens for their gifts. Mendardiere asked for additional supplies to help the Tunisian soldiers usher in Eid al Fitr, the Muslim holiday that celebrates the end of Ramadan. Requests included items like dominoes, cigarettes, and candy.[90] Tardieu responded on 9 November and informed Mendardiere that the municipal council approved a 500-franc donation to the 28th RTT for them "to use for the festival as you best see fit."[91] In contrast to Tardieu's calls for blankets in September, this targeted drive to supply the 28th RTT found an enthusiastic response. This event, though minor, highlights a fascinating insight into France's cultural diversity and the complex relationship between the French military and Montiliens.

Montiliens supported troops and the war effort in ways besides monetary and material donations. Spiritually, the city coordinated with the military to create a sense of community between soldiers and the citizenry.[92] The Sainte-Croix Catholic Church on Main Street in downtown Montélimar had been one of the city's marquee attractions since the twelfth century. It maintained significance as a place for Roman Catholic worship and Montilien pride. This dual meaning to citizens of Montélimar came to the fore when the 146th Infantry Regiment billeted in the city. On 12 November the church held a mass attended by retired military veterans, the commandant of arms, Lt. Col. Piollet, Mayor Tardieu, several city councilmen, sixty soldiers from the 146th regiment, and parishioners. The presiding priest led a prayer for the dead and had the entire congregation turn to face the list of Catholic Montiliens killed during World War I. The priest beckoned everyone present to "live in full duty of the present day, and to unite our efforts and our prayers to them [the mobilized soldiers]."[93]

The church's bimonthly publication, *l'Echo Montilien*, denounced Hitler. The "Portrait of Hitler by Bossuet" noted Hitler's megalomania, his belief that he had a right to everything, and that he infringed on the rights of free people. According to Bousset, Hitler's worst trait was that "he knows neither God nor man."[94] This outpouring of patriotic sentiment and anti-Hitler literature was consistent with the positions of the French Catholic Church during the war.[95] Because Pope Pius XII remained a staunch neutral at the outbreak of war, bishops in dioceses across France and other parts of Europe exhibited more independence in addressing the war than they otherwise might have. Left to their own devices, French bishops relied on their strong sense of patriotism. To many French Catholics, engaging in the fight against Nazi Germany was acceptable because it fell under the "just war" position articulated by St. Thomas Aquinas.[96]

The ceremony at Sainte-Croix tied the spiritual and the material together through the community's children. The "Valiant Hearts" was a church organization that enlisted girls between the ages of four and seven.[97] A similar group for small boys, the Cub Scouts (*louveteaux*), sent gifts to the soldiers. These organizations sent small parcels containing desserts, including the famous Montilien nougat, to the 28th RTT during the Christmas season. For New Year's, the children wrote letters to the regiment.[98] A sergeant from the 28th RTT responded. His letter, published in *l'Echo Montilien*, thanked the children for their touching gesture, which meant a lot to his fellow soldiers who knew that "there is a small town where generous souls think of us." The sergeant ended the letter by asking the children to pray for the dead, the wounded, living soldiers, and that "your big brothers will watch over you and defend your property, your home, and your life to the end."[99] This display of cross-cultural patriotic sentiment mediated through the church tied the attendees of Sainte-Croix closer together to the soldiers.

Outward displays of patriotism demonstrated the duality of Phony War France. On one hand, demands for total national mobilization caused great consternation among Montiliens. On the other, the French proudly rallied to their fighting soldiers when called upon. Voluntary contributions to the war effort were much easier for them to manage and embrace than forced requisitions.

Conclusion

France faced a daunting problem at the beginning of the Second World War. It had to mobilize the entire nation—and its empire—to fight Nazi Germany. The mechanism to enforce this mobilization, the National Wartime Organization Act (NWOA), placed enormous strain on France's civilians. They understood, however, that as part of the French republican tradition that they would have to make sacrifices for the war effort. What they asked from the state in return was fair and consistent treatment, which they believed they did not receive, and may have been impossible to grant them during wartime.

Officials implemented the NWOA inconsistently, which contributed to civilian pushback. The dialogue between civilians and government officials—the politics of requisition—contrasted civilian concerns with state imperatives. In Montélimar, its denizens used the declarations of politicians, the law, and personal appeal to reduce or negate requisitions orders, or to personally benefit from them. The French army received what they wanted most of the time, leaving local administrators to deal with the fallout from aggrieved civilians. These circumstances threatened to undermine already fragile support for the war effort.[100] Local leaders and officers compensated for this by holding rallies of different kinds. They collected monetary, clothing, and other material donations for the army. Civilians aided the war effort on the condition that it was voluntary and that they believed that their sacrifice was worthwhile. Increased material deprivation and the stalemate during the Phony War—the lack of real fighting—severely tested civilian support.

The story of mobilization in Montélimar hints at what was to come. In May 1940 German forces attacked the Allies, beginning the Battle of France, which Germany won in an astounding six weeks. After France's defeat, governing authority in Montélimar changed multiple times: Vichy, Italian, German, and eventually the provisional French government supplemented by Allied forces ruled there. These changes, however, did not alter the fundamental realities of city requisitioning. Requisitions became worse by degree, but not in kind. Any effort to understand French life under occupation during the Second World War, the period that dominates the current literature, cannot be undertaken without analysis of France's initial movements at the conflict's outbreak, before its invasion and defeat by a foreign power. Returning to the Phony War sheds light on the agency of the French national state, the municipal government, and that of soldiers and civilians in this crucial period. The relationships and conflicts established then set the tone for the rest of the war. This first situation resembled that of many civilians under more sinister governing authorities elsewhere and later on. Crucially, the first months of the war—the Phony War—constituted France's first occupation.

Notes

1. Peyrouse to Tardieu, 1 September 1939, box 18, series 5H, "Affaires Militaire," Archives Municipal de Montélimar (AMM), Montélimar, Drôme, France. Peyrouse's and Rouanes's full names are unavailable. Local archives are indispensable for understanding how civilians navigated the first months of the war in France. Municipal governments received requisitions slips from military authorities and had the responsibility for executing them. This gives us the other side of mobilization, those of the civilians and their property. Analysis of national defense usually stays at the federal governmental level and with the military. Showing how those policies affected locals produces a holistic picture of how citizens and the state envisioned civilian direct participation in the war effort absent military service. Unless otherwise noted, the author made all translations.

2. The three mainstays of French army doctrine in World War II in English are Douglas Porch, *Defeat and Division: France at War, 1939–1942* (New York: Cambridge University Press, 2022), 5–123; Robert A. Doughty, *The Seeds of Disaster: The Development of French Army Doctrine, 1919–1939* (Mechanicsburg, PA: Stackpole Books, 1985); and Eugenia Kiesling, *Arming against Hitler: France and the Limits of Military Planning* (Lawrence: University Press of Kansas, 1996). Other works on French preparation include Talbot Imlay, *Facing the Second World War: Strategy, Politics, and Economics in Britain and France, 1938–1940* (New York: Oxford University Press, 2003); Julian Jackson, *The Fall of France: The Nazi Invasion of 1940* (New York: Oxford University Press, 2004); Philip Nord, *France 1940: Defending the Republic* (New Haven, CT: Yale University Press, 2015); Philip Nord, *France's New Deal: From the Thirties to the Postwar Era* (Princeton, NJ: Princeton University Press, 2010).

3. Report, "Recherche des crimes de guerre ennemis" (Research of Enemy War Crimes), Montélimar Police Commissioner May 2, 1945, box 67, series 2286W (Commissariat de Montélimar), Archives départementales de la Drôme (ADD), Valence, Drôme, France.

4. City of Montélimar, "Histoire de la ville" (History of the City), https://www.montelimar.fr/montelimar-et-son-histoire/histoire-de-la-ville (accessed December 13, 2023).

5. Further centralization occurred under the Vichy regime. For an exploration of how mayoral duties changed under Vichy, see Robert Gildea, *Marianne in Chains: Daily Life in the Heart of France during the German Occupation* (New York: Picador, 2002), 158–90.

6. Stéphane Beaumont, *Histoire de Montélimar* (Toulouse: Privat, 1992), 273–74.

7. Jackson, *The Fall of France*, 80.

8. Scott Lytle, "Robespierre, Danton, and the Levée en Masse," *Journal of Modern History* 30, no. 4 (December 1958): 325–37.
9. Doughty, *Seeds of Disaster*, 15–17.
10. Kiesling, *Arming against Hitler*, 14–17.
11. Kiesling, *Arming against Hitler*, 26–27, 34.
12. Kiesling, *Arming against Hitler*, 36.
13. Kiesling, *Arming against Hitler*, 37.
14. A. Malizard to Tardieu, 15 September 1939, box 16, 5H, AMM. Malizard attached "Regles Generales concernant le Reglement des Requisitions" (Guidelines concerning Requisitions Regulations) to the letter.
15. For instance, the Military Commandant of Valence wrote to Tardieu of the backlog, "As of 25 February [1940], I am still receiving reports from the Mayor of Montélimar of billeting reports dating back to last October, November, and December." Box 18, 5H, AMM.
16. Piollet's full name is unavailable.
17. Porch, *Defeat and Division*, 72.
18. Order, "Cantonnement des Troupes" (Soldier Billeting), 26 October 1939, box 18, 5H, AMM.
19. Report, "3rd Battalion, 482nd Regiment de Pionniers Coloniaux, état des Cantonnements" (Billeting Report, 3rd Battalion, 482nd RPIC), 19 November 1939, box 18, 5H, AMM.
20. Report, "État des Degats commis au Château Milan" (Château Milan Damage Reports), 19 November 1939, box 18, 5H, AMM.
21. Order, "Soldier Billeting," 28 October 1939, box 18, 5H, AMM.
22. Order, "Soldier Billeting," 16 November 1939, box 18, 5H, AMM.
23. Report, "Château Milan Damage Reports," 19 November 1939, box 18, 5H, AMM; Report, "Etat des cantonnements occupés à partir du 7 Septembre 1939 et diverses autres dates" (Status of Billeting: Occupied from 7 September 1939 and Various other Dates), 19 November 1939, box 18, 5H, AMM. For comparison, the average price of a kilogram of bread in 1939 was about 3,15 francs. André Piatier, "Les prix de detail en France depuis 1914," *Revue économique* 1, no. 2 (1950): 227–31.
24. Schall to Tardieu, 26 August 1939, box 18, 5H, AMM.
25. Order, "Billeting of Soldiers," 28 October 1939, box 18, 5H, AMM.
26. Deloule to Tardieu, 29 November 1939, box 18, 5H, AMM.
27. This information comes from a letter Tardieu addressed to Piollet concerning the matter, Tardieu to Piollet, 27 September 1939, box 18, 5H, AMM.
28. Deloule to Tardieu, 29 November 1939, box 18, 5H, AMM. Deloule claims that in her personal home she had to house five soldiers but that there were no damages to it.
29. Audigier to Tardieu, 3 April 1940, box 18, 5H, AMM.
30. Piollet to Tardieu, 6 December 1939, box 18, 5H, AMM.
31. Audigier to Tardieu, 3 April 1940, box 18, 5H, AMM.
32. Audigier to Tardieu, 20 May 1940, box 18, 5H, AMM.

33. Tardieu to Colonel of Subdivision of Valence, 28 May 1940, box 18, 5H, AMM.

34. Note, 8 June 1940, box 18, 5H, AMM. The full note reads, "Eight June 1940, in the presence of Mr. and Mrs. Audigier, renters of the Deloule property on the Quartier de Beausseret, Lieutenant Allies and Mr. Gilles, Architect of the City, have come to the following agreement: The money [to be given] to Mr. Audigier from the damages of the billeting and occupation caused by 3rd battalion of the 482nd RPIC estimated to be 500 francs has been accepted by all parties." 8 June 1940, box 18, 5H, AMM.

35. Memo, "État des Reclamations des Proprietaires ayant Cantonne le Renfort sur la Route d'Espeluche" (Claims Report from the Property Owners on Route d'Espeluche), box 18, 5H, AMM.

36. Piollet to Tardieu, 4 January 1940, box 18, 5H, AMM.

37. Piollet to Tardieu, 4 January 1940, box 18, 5H, AMM. Full name of Pinet is unavailable.

38. Full name of Muraour is unavailable.

39. Piollet to Tardieu, 4 January 1940, box 18, 5H, AMM.

40. Piollet to Tardieu, 4 January 1940, box 18, 5H, AMM.

41. Didio to Tardieu, 22 November 1939, box 18, 5H, AMM; Tardieu to Piollet, 23 November 1939, box 18, 5H, AMM. Full name of Didio is unavailable.

42. Tardieu mentions the March 18 letter in Tardieu to Piollet, 6 April 1940, box 18, 5H, AMM.

43. Tardieu to Piollet, 10 April 1940, box 18, 5H, AMM.

44. Piollet to Tardieu, 10 April 1940, box 18, 5H, AMM.

45. Calculations made by the author. The list of officers and the duration of their stay is found in box 16, 5H, AMM.

46. Captain le Nail to Lt. Col Piollet, 23 October 1939, box 18, 5H, AMM.

47. List of numerous receipts from officer billeting found in folder "Logement des Officiers 1939–1940," box 18, 5H, AMM.

48. Compare this to the military-civilian divide (or its absence) in the mobilization of the Soviet Union in Erina Megowan's essay, chapter 6 in this volume.

49. "Ordre de Requisition des Laines" (Wool Requisition Order), *Journal de Montélimar*, 23 September 1939, ADD, series 236/27, "Journal de Montélimar"; box 16, 5H, AMM.

50. Hartung to Tardieu, 17 September 1939, box 16, 5H, AMM.

51. Kiesling, *Arming against Hitler*, 75.

52. Compare to US civilian protests on vehicle requisitions and other rubber rationing in 1942 in Tracy Campbell, *The Year of Peril: America in 1942* (New Haven, CT: Yale University Press, 2020).

53. Kiesling, *Arming against Hitler*, 75–76.

54. Tardieu to Pera, 12 September 1939; box 16, 5H, AMM.

55. Taupenas to Tardieu, 27 September 1939, box 16, 5H, AMM.

56. Tardieu to Piollet, 27 September 1939, box 16, 5H, AMM.
57. Piollet to Tardieu, 28 September 1939, box 16, 5H, AMM.
58. Nico Wouters, *Mayoral Collaboration under Nazi Occupation in Belgium, the Netherlands, and France, 1938–1946* (New York: Palgrave Macmillan, 2016), 304.
59. Kiesling, *Arming against Hitler*, 36–37.
60. Feytel to all, 18 September 1939, series 44S "Feytel Family Letters," number (no.) 1, AMM.
61. Marius Feytel to René Feytel, 9 October 1939, 44S, no. 5, AMM.
62. Full name of Mrs. Tourette unknown.
63. Full name of Bertrand unknown.
64. Tourette to Tardieu, 10 October 1939, box 18, 5H, AMM.
65. Tourette to Tardieu, 10 October 1939, box 18, 5H, AMM.
66. Tardieu to Tourette, 13 October 1939, box 18, 5H, AMM.
67. Additional documentation for requests located in box 18, 5H, AMM.
68. "Logement des Officiers" (Officers' accommodations), *État civil de Montélimar du 1er au 8 Novembre 1939*, 8 November 1939, box 18, 5H, AMM.
69. Le Nail to Tardieu, 26 November 1939, box 18, 5H, AMM.
70. Tardieu to Piollet, 9 December 1939, box 18, 5H, AMM.
71. Tardieu to Commandant l'Intendant a Valence, 22 February 1940, box 18, 5H, AMM.
72. Commandant l'Intendant a Valence to Tardieu, 4 March 1940, box 18, 5H, AMM.
73. Lanquetin to Mayors, 27 August 1939, box 16, 5H, AMM.
74. Lanquetin to Mayors, 3 September 1939, box 16, 5H, AMM.
75. François Couchet, *Les soldats de la drôle de guerre, Septembre 1939–Mai 1940* (Paris: Hachette littératures, 2004), 44; Porch, *Defeat and Division*, 73–74. The army also lacked 150,000 pairs of pants and 600,000 pairs of boots, meaning that there were widespread instances of soldiers marching in their civilian attire for months.
76. Lanquetin to Mayors, 24 September 1939, box 11, 5H, AMM.
77. Lanquetin to Mayors, 24 September 1939, box 11, 5H, AMM.
78. Announcement, "Demande de couvertures" (Request for blankets), *État Civil de Montélimar du 20 au 27 Septembre 1939*, box 11, 5H, AMM.
79. List, "État des sommes dues à divers pour Fourniture de Couvertures à l'Armée" (Donated Blankets to the Army), 18 October 1939, box 11, 5H, AMM; Tardieu to l'Officier Gestionnaire du Magasin Militaire d'Habillement de Lyon, 14 November 1939, box 11, 5H, AMM.
80. "Extrait du Registre des Délibérations du Conseil Municipal" (Extract from Municipal Council deliberations), 21 March 1940, box 12, 5H, AMM.
81. Compare to the attachment of US. civilians to "their" soldiers fighting at Bataan in chapter 9 in this volume.
82. Anthony Clayton, *France, Soldiers and Africa* (London: Brassey's Defence Publishers, 1988), 254–55. For more on how the French viewed the

implementation of colonial soldiers in France's defense, see Martin Thomas, "At the Heart of Things? French Imperial Defense Planning in the Late 1930s," *French Historical Studies* 21, no. 2 (Spring 1998), 325–61.

83. Kader Ferchiche, *Un siècle à Montélimar* (Montélimar: Kader Ferchiche, 1999), 192–93.

84. Ferchiche, *Un siècle à Montélimar*, 192–93.

85. Clayton, *France, Soldiers and Africa*, 38.

86. Myron Echenberg, "'Morts pour la France': The African Soldiers in France during World War II," *Journal of African History* 26, no. 4 (1985): 363–80.

87. Sarah Ann Frank, *Hostages of Empire: Colonial Prisoners of War in Vichy France* (Lincoln: University of Nebraska Press, 2021), 25–50.

88. État-Major de l'Armée de Terre, Service Historique, *Les Grandes Unités Françaises: Guerre 1939–1945*, vol. 2 (Paris: Imprimerie Nationale, 1967), 853–57.

89. Mendardiere to Tardieu, 2 November 1939, box 16, 5H, AMM.

90. Mendardiere to Tardieu, 2 November 1939, box 16, 5H, AMM.

91. Tardieu to Mendardiere, 9 November 1939, box 16, 5H, AMM.

92. For another chapter indicating the complex role of religion in wartime behavior, see Castro's chapter 1 in this volume.

93. "Chronique Paroissiale" (Parish Chronicle), *l'Echo Montilien* 30, no. 11 and 12 (November–December 1939), AP 345/3, ADD.

94. "Portrait de Hitler par Bossuet" (Bossuet's Portrait of Hitler), *l'Echo Montilien* 30, no. 11 and 12 (November–December 1939), AP 345/3, ADD.

95. W. D. Halls, *Politics, Society and Christianity in Vichy France* (Providence: Berg, 1995), 15–45.

96. Halls, *Christianity in Vichy France*, 34.

97. "Les Coeurs vaillants et Patronage Ste. Croix" (Valiant Hearts patronage of St. Croix), *l'Echo Montilien* 31, no. 1 and 2 (January–February 1940), AP 345/3, ADD.

98. "Regards vers le front" (Looking toward the Front), *l'Echo Montilien* 31 no. 1 and 2 (January–February 1940), AP 345/3, ADD.

99. "Un joli document" (A Happy Letter), *l'Echo Montilien* 31 no. 1 and 2 (January–February 1940), AP 345/3, ADD.

100. This complex and not unlimited support for the war effort then had ramifications under occupation in the ways that French civilians cooperated and collaborated with the German occupation. See Robert O. Paxton, *Vichy France: Old Guard and New Order, 1940–1944* (New York: Alfred A. Knopf, 1972); Philip Morgan, *Hitler's Collaborators: Choosing between Bad and Worse in Nazi-Occupied Western Europe* (Oxford: Oxford University Press, 2018); Sandra Ott, *Living with the Enemy: German Occupation, Collaboration and Justice in the Western Pyrenees, 1940–1948* (New York: Cambridge University Press, 2017); Megan Koreman, *The Expectation of Justice: France, 1944–1946* (Durham, NC: Duke University Press, 1999).

Red Army Divisions' Growing Demand for Artistic Service
Entertainment at the Front, 1941–1945

Erina Megowan

Within a few weeks after the German invasion of the Soviet Union in June 1941, the first Soviet concert brigades had left for the front lines. Over the course of the war, the Soviet Union dispatched thousands of artists of all types to the front in close to 4,000 brigades. Performers ranging from the nation's top classical musicians to acrobats gave more than 400,000 concerts, sometimes only a few kilometers behind the Soviet artillery. Including those at recruiting points for reserve divisions, and in barracks and hospitals, the total number of performances reached 1,290,700.[1] The scale of this program represented a massive expenditure of money, human capital, and logistical effort in a country devoting up to 60 percent of its GDP to defense and suffering from vast territorial, industrial, and agricultural losses.[2] By comparison, the United Service Organizations (USO), responsible for the entertainment of US soldiers, put on around 400,000 shows from 1941 to 1947, though only some of these went abroad in the "Foxhole Circuit."[3] US concerts were disproportionately performed in 1944–1945.[4] The Third Reich managed total performance numbers closer to the Soviet Union's, with 24,000 performers providing 836,000 troop entertainment events for an audience of upward of 275 million soldiers, though Germany did not focus on the Eastern Front until 1943.[5]

By 1942, "mixed brigades" were finding their way to each of the numerous Soviet fronts, where they performed in all imaginable conditions. Their audiences varied from a handful of viewers in an underground dugout to thousands in an open field. While open truck beds were a common stage, concerts also took place in the middle of fields and forests (sometimes on makeshift stages built for the purpose), inside barns and other outbuildings, in dugouts, atop tanks or plane wings, on ships, and even on submarines. Mixed brigades consisted on average of ten to twelve members with different talents, with a program that consisted of declamation, singing, skits or one-act plays, jokes, and sometimes dance or instrumental numbers.[6] Depending on the background of the brigade members, the repertoire might lean toward drama, classical music and dance, or *estrada* (Soviet variety theater). A master of ceremonies tied the numbers together. An undated program for the "Iskra" front theater consisted of an introduction by the master of ceremonies; a declamation piece; a nineteenth-century vaudeville act titled "Fiancé by Proxy"; "character songs" (Soviet and folk songs); a dance number; a skit based on a Zoshchenko story; "partisan jokes"; and Soviet vaudeville; the show concluded with a "drinking song" performed by the entire ensemble.[7] By contrast, a program led by Aleksandr Tomskii from the Nemirovich-Danchenko theater on the Voronezh front in 1943 consisted of Russian folk songs performed on the accordion; recent Soviet songs; opera arias and romances by Soviet composers; a one-act skit titled "At the Tenth Bench"; Russian folk songs and lyric arias; a Russian dance; oratory; operetta duets; another dance; more duets; and *chastushki* (simple, humorous rhyming ditties).[8]

Concerts at the front were not a new phenomenon in the Soviet Union, which had experimented during the Civil War with "agittrains," "living newspapers," and other performances with overt political ends.[9] The tradition of military patronage had existed since the Civil War (1918–1922), and many theaters had long-standing connections to the army.[10] Despite these traditions, the first few months of front concerts showed that cultural institutions and the military were surprisingly unprepared to collaborate in time of war. No one, it turned out in 1941, understood what distinguished the Red Army combatant as a viewer, or what sort of entertainment and cultural (or political) enrichment he required. Vladimir Filippov was deputy director of the Central House of the Actor, which was crucial to the wartime formation and management of performance brigades. He conceded somewhat ruefully in 1948 that the "problems of serving the front with artistic performances had not been developed theoretically and had not even been raised."[11] While the Committee for Artistic Affairs (KPDI) had issued a circular immediately after the war's start instructing performers to prioritize serving the Red Army and "raise its fighting spirits," it provided little concrete advice on how to do this.[12] Although the state clearly expected the support of the creative intelligentsia, when it came to front-line concerts, they did not identify a clear and specific objective. Instead, central authorities were preoccupied with overseeing defense and the preservation and evacuation of cultural institutions as national valuables. The exodus of administrative workers from the House of the Red Army (DKA), Committee for Artistic Affairs (KPDI), and other institutions into the armed forces threw their work into chaos.

This overall ambiguity meant that fundamental questions about the goal and purpose of the concerts plagued early events. Many writers and artists had initially assumed that wartime cultural production should be about war and that their primary task in 1941 was agitation, writing and performing exclusively "antifascist" or "defense" materials.[13] In the context of performing at recruitment centers, this was a solid assumption. Could the performing arts best assist the war effort by acting as agitators, with performers working to stir up hatred toward the Germans and incite soldiers to fight harder? Agitation was the sibling strategy to propaganda in the Soviet Union. Whereas Soviet propagandists tended to rely on texts to provide ideological training or promote complex ideas, agitators employed visual aids and aimed at emotions.[14] Agitational work during the war combined news and political interpretation. Its general topics ranged from the "current state of the war, the party line in international affairs, Nazi activities in occupied territories, Nazi ideology towards the Soviet people, allied activities in the Pacific, etc."[15] Calls for "agitational" performance material during World War II meant a repertoire that directly addressed the current situation and sought to shape responses to it in ways that aided the Soviet war effort.

This was itself a wide-ranging proposition. For example, much early wartime journalism, like that by Ilya Ehrenburg, aimed to incite or deepen hatred toward the Germans, to strengthen the Soviet will to fight.[16] It might also work to drum up loyalty to the Soviet Union, provide hope and encouragement that the war could be won, and demonstrate how the home front was working to support them. Dramatic repertoire could theatricalize desired behaviors such as courage, selflessness, watchfulness, confidence in victory, and attentiveness to work, while criticizing laziness, cowardice, or avarice. Performances offered an extra level of potential emotional response when compared to lectures, reports, political meetings, or even reading newspapers. Ultimately, agitational repertoire at the front sought to manipulate soldiers' emotions in a variety of ways that would lead to positive military results. Ideally, agitational performances inspired promises to fight harder and kill more Germans. For example, after a performance by Konstantin Iartsev's brigade on the Kalinin front in fall 1942 the night before an attack, one soldier gave a speech thanking the artists for coming to support them at the front and in return promising "to beat the damned fascists even harder!"[17] By the same token, though, poorly selected repertoire could convey the wrong message and potentially harm morale or "fighting readiness."

However, artists debated about other objectives as well and developed a range of opinions on what it meant to best serve the Red Army. Perhaps soldiers would best be served by concerts that provided entertainment, rest, and relaxation, or that simply demonstrated unity with the troops. Should content focus on the patriotic, heroic, and sacred? Were satire, humor, and comedy appropriate for wartime? In the absence of clear central guidance, many of the concerts in the summer and fall of 1941 were essentially spontaneous, the initiative of individuals and troupes. Artists, rather than being confident in the value of their performances, openly questioned whether they were appropriate at all.[18] The question of whether or not to prioritize agitation had serious implications for repertoire, complicated by a paucity of appropriate material in the early months of the war; artists compiled their initial programs using material that they had on hand.

For its part, despite earlier precedents, the military does not appear to have counted on extensive front-line cultural service at the war's start. However, once authorities realized that soldiers on active duty enjoyed such performances and that they constituted a rare "carrot" to encourage behavior, they sought to harness the performances for their own purposes. GlavPUR-KKA's (Main Political Directorate of the Red Army) control of the concert program inevitably raised the question of concerts as propaganda, given its responsibility for political education in the Red Army.[19] This in turn meant that concert brigade repertoire emerged as a primary point of contention among performers, commanders, and political officers, and the central authorities.

Brigade Purposes: Agitation or Entertainment?

The origins of the front concert program embedded competing objectives in it from the start, vacillating between entertainment and catering to soldiers' tastes and agitation or political education. Additionally, since they were spared both the draft and industrial labor, artists needed a visible, politically accepted way to participate in the war effort.[20] No individual artist was ever required to join a brigade, nor was brigade participation a substitute for military service. Rather, it became a kind of privilege that artists vied for. Being present at the front and sharing in the attendant hardships of front-line life were a way of staking out a claim to a meaningful contribution to the war, but this only worked if soldiers enjoyed the concerts. Insecure over whether or not their concerts actually did "help" soldiers, artists' primary objective was to ensure that audiences enjoyed and appreciated them. As they accumulated more experience on the front, they developed strong feelings about the benefits of entertainment. Such views predisposed them to prioritize humor, comedy, and romantic drama.

The concert programs' origins as a spontaneous revival of earlier practices seeking to include the intelligentsia in the war meant they were not formally state or military propaganda. These performances were always on the margins of political and propaganda efforts in the armed forces, usually relegated to leisure time.[21] However, care for their material needs was thought to influence soldiers' political and moral condition and enhance command authority.[22] In performances, political officers and military authorities sensed the enticing possibility of conveying agitational content in a more palatable and emotionally powerful form than the usual lecture, discussion, or meeting. GlavPURKKA representatives had long been responsible for morale and the organization of soldiers' free time, celebrations, and holidays, not dissimilar to the American USO or German KdF.[23] Unlike the Americans, GlavPURKKA representatives had very few "carrots" they could offer soldiers and few ways to improve soldiers' welfare. In 1941 and 1942, "comfort" foods were out of the question, as was short-term leave.[24] Films, though wildly popular, were always in short supply and required infrastructure to be shown, complicating showings at the front. Live performances were a rare perk that could be obtained and provided to soldiers. The fact that the state was trying to provide *something* for its soldiers was not trivial, as Brandon Schechter has shown.[25] Even here, though, interests were not perfectly aligned. Concerned with the moral and political education of soldiers, GlavPURKKA in Moscow preferred concerts with a mobilizing or educational effect. Political officers at the front and military commanders were more often concerned with morale. They regarded concerts as a chance to distract soldiers, help them relax, and reassure them of civilian support. Although sensitive to repertoire they felt might negatively impact soldiers' moods, they were some of the most vocal supporters of the entertainment model.

All parties involved were deeply invested in the success of front concerts, in the sense of desiring to assist the armed forces. Consensus even emerged rapidly over the three key areas determining brigade success: content and repertoire, performance quality, and the behavior of the brigade members. Reflecting their competing incentives, however, each group defined success differently. These definitions of success could overlap, but at other times they were at odds, and disagreement frequently hinged on repertoire. Central authorities and GlavPURKKA, military and political officers in the field, and performing artists all had their own opinions on what soldiers should get out of front-line concerts. Political officers fixated on the repertoire—the text or lyrics, the subject matter, who the heroes are and how they were depicted—and excluded things they considered "harmful," replacing them with more appropriate content. Artists took a different approach, worrying less about content and more about presentation. They excluded pieces that were poorly received by soldiers, not what Party authorities in Moscow objected to (unless pieces were banned outright). Instead, they sought to find ways to maximize appeal and emotional impact. Using the information they had gained via surveys and personal experience, these strategies included maintaining performance quality, tailoring each concert to local circumstances, and maximizing interaction with the audience. These were all audience-centric strategies that had little to do with ideology but facilitated the creation of "emotional bridges," and they indicate the degree to which audience preference drove the concert brigade program. Although the repertoire debates were never formally resolved, in other areas artists and political officers collaborated to highlight artists' presence as a form of agitation.

Expanding Provision

Throughout the summer and fall of 1941, spontaneous concerts proliferated in the western USSR. As these concert brigades completed their first tours, commander complaints began pouring into the Moscow city directorate for art. They reported boring, repetitive performances of only one genre (all music or all readings); incoherent programs; a lack of humorous content; brigades consisting only of "second rate" performers with little talent; and the use of a single program for all audiences, whether for hospitals, the small propaganda centers or corners that were a regular feature of all Soviet public buildings, recent draftees or trained specialists—thereby failing to please any of them.[26] An August report by one administrator criticized the meaningless nature of a single, universal concert program for all audiences. In his view, a program that did not reflect the particular concerns of its audience "loses all meaning."[27] The spontaneous and haphazard nature of the early concerts raised the question of who would screen repertoire and vouch for performance quality to ensure that the concerts actually helped rather than did damage.

The Soviet state did not appear to have foreseen the military's wartime demand for entertainment, having already evacuated most artists to the Urals, Siberia, and Central Asia away from the front. Aside from concerts at garrisons and recruitment centers, there were few preexisting organizations that were easy to immediately scale up during the war. However, to the surprise of artists remaining in Moscow after the evacuations, the armed services proved to be eager consumers of Soviet culture. On 19 October 1941, remaining artists from the Nemirovich-Danchenko theater were hanging up posters for *Kornevil'skie koloki* (*Les cloches de Corneville*), the nineteenth-century French comic opera with which they reopened their season. These were seen by an NKVD combat division sergeant who arrived to request a concert to commemorate the anniversary of the October Revolution on 20 October.[28] Given the unsuitable conditions for a performance—no stage, no heat, and no musical instruments with which to accompany them—the theater turned him down. Not to be denied, the disappointed sergeant returned several days later with a "beaming face" to announce they had built a stage, put in a stove, and acquired a piano, and they were expecting the artists for the holidays.[29]

The sergeant's behavior is representative of a general shift toward fulfilling military needs that grew more pronounced as the front stabilized in late 1941. Even if initially caught off-guard by the demand, providing the armed forces with front-line entertainment brigades was a service central authorities could plausibly provide. Doing so, however, necessitated improved organization, clearer logistics, and a greater degree of central control, to preclude performances that might inadvertently do harm. In November 1941 the Committee for Artistic Affairs (KPDI) created the Headquarters for the Artistic Service of the Red Army and Working Front. The headquarters functioned as a centralized clearinghouse for processing military requests. It was staffed by representatives of the VTO (All-Union Theatrical Organization), VGKO (All-Union Guestrole-Concert Organization), Central House of Workers of Art, and the Moscow Administration for Artistic Affairs.[30] In 1941, its staff resorted to auditioning individual artists, forming them into "combined brigades," and sanctioning their repertoire and concert programs. By 1942, the KPDI had asserted central control over the provision of entertainment to the front, taking the initiative out of the hands of individual actors and theaters; at this point staffing brigades became a group obligation for the Soviet intelligentsia. The KPDI began requiring cultural institutions (theater groups, symphonies, etc.) to form brigades according to a central schedule and send them to Moscow, where they would be dispatched on front tours. Thus, in May 1943, the Azeri, Tadzhik, and Uzbek republics, the Cheliabinsk and Sverdlovsk theaters, the Leningrad youth theater and Pushkin theater (all evacuated to Novosibirsk), and the merged Stanislavsky and Nemirovich-Danchenko theaters, all formed new cultural brigades.[31] To prevent brigades from either becoming a refuge for underqualified performers or from performing inappropriate material, all gave a trial performance of their repertoire in Moscow before leaving for the front. The audiences included representatives of the KPDI, VTO, DKA, GlavPURKKA, and occasionally the NKVD.[32] These screenings could and did result in demands for changes in repertoire or the rejection of individual performers or entire brigades.

The KPDI managed brigade formation and closely monitored their repertoire, but their authority ended after they signed off on a brigade's composition and concert program. GlavPURKKA was responsible for submitting requests for the number and type of brigades they wanted to the DKA.[33] After their programs were confirmed in Moscow, ready-to-go brigades became the administrative responsibility of the House of the Red Army and GlavPURKKA until they returned from the front. GlavPURKKA determined in Moscow which divisions on which fronts would receive performances and established brigade travel routes.[34] When artists arrived at the front, political officers met them, made lodging and transportation arrangements, and chaperoned the brigade for the duration of their time there. As arriving artists had no way of knowing where exactly to go for their performances, for example, this was critical logistical assistance. Since no commander wanted the embarrassment of artists being killed or injured on their watch, chaperones helped ensure an extra level of safety, advising artists on what to do during bombardments. They also policed artists' behavior while at the front. Instances of "panicking" or cowardice in case of an air raid, for example, generated serious reprimands from political officers.[35] "Demanding" brigades that were unprepared to deal with front-line hardships and share the same conditions as soldiers—for example, protesting over available housing conditions—were scandalous and came in for criticism and complaints sent directly by commissars to the KPDI.[36] Complaints of "opportunism," excessive demands, and irresponsible behavior by actors occasionally made it all the way up to the Central Committee.[37] Because of this, artists rarely found themselves outside Party supervision.

Trying to Ensure Success
All parties involved agreed on the need to ensure the positive reception of the concerts. This entailed first establishing where audience dissatisfaction came from. During the brigades' pre-departure screenings, the KPDI surveyed their trial audiences and documented their impressions. These included conversations with military members of all ranks in Moscow, surveys taken in military hospitals, written reviews that performers brought back from their trips, and the personal impressions of performers themselves. They found that soldiers and commanders were almost universally enthusiastic about the prospect of front-line entertainment. However, the surveys

also confirmed that a concert was not a universal good in and of itself; reception and impact varied dramatically. Cultural administrators discovered to their surprise that comparatively minor logistical details in a concert program's format, length, and "management" vastly outweighed factors such as how well the concert was performed or the kind of repertoire. At the most basic level, to "reach" viewers, a good concert program required artistic coherence with a carefully thought-through program and a competent MC to tie it together. Programs needed to be "accessible" to soldiers. Based on post-concert conversations, one brigade member concluded that for Red Army soldiers, "the most essential . . . is immediacy, sincerity, and the skill to bring both ends together, give a complete image."[38] Circumstances such as whether or not the soldiers had recently taken losses; whether they were on the offensive, retreating, defensive, or in the hospital; the length of the program; the size of the audience and the venue for the performance (an open field versus a small dugout) all influenced how audiences perceived programs.

In addition to logistics, artists were quite sensitive to the different cultural and educational levels of rank-and-file soldiers and officers. Concerts required time limits, with soldiers losing interest in anything longer than one and a half hours or with an intermission. Concerts for the command, on the other hand, could go for two and a half or even three hours.[39] Commanders were assumed to have the cultural sophistication to appreciate, and even expected, longer and more complex programs. Dinner and extended socialization with the command after the performance became a routine part of a performance brigade's activities, with declined invitations causing serious offense. Akiva Diner's brigade performed a concert for the 80th Division on the Stalingrad front in April 1943 as it received its Guards designation (signifying elite status after distinguishing itself in combat). However, the brigade departed immediately after the performance in order to arrive on time for their next concert for the Voroshilov artillery regiment, thereby causing "great offense" to the commanders who had pressured them to stay for the celebratory banquet.[40] Finally, programs needed to be diverse and contain a mix of genres to "get through."[41] Boris Filippov, who later directed the VTO's First Front Theater, formed one of the earliest front brigades in Moscow (including Lidiia Ruslanova, one of the Soviet Union's most famous performers of popular songs) and spent August 1941 touring the western front around Viazma. In his diary entry for 1 September, he reflected that repertoires had been poorly chosen for the front; each front group needed to offer at least heroism, lyricism, and political satire. He likewise considered that readers should have specific pieces prepared for pilots, tankists, artillerists, the cavalry, sailors, and the infantry.[42] At the same time, surveys did not consider differences in gender, national origin, or native language. Women's military divisions received the same brigades and concerts as their male counterparts. With the exception of a few national brigades, the repertoire was overwhelmingly Slavic. ("National" influences appeared primarily in the form of folk dances, or occasionally at the initiative of individual performers.)

Even if a clear decision had been made to pack brigade repertoire with agitational material, it would have been difficult to acquire enough of it to suit immediate needs, as the military situation changed constantly between summer 1941 and 1945. An audience of retreating soldiers suffering enormous casualties in the fall of 1941 was very different from the advancing army of 1944, on track to defeat Nazi Germany.[43] Therefore, efforts to "know" the audience and determine what would be most beneficial to them continued. If artists and authorities sparred over repertoire until the war's end, these surveys nevertheless suggested other strategies for influencing their audiences by highlighting the importance of external factors in performance reception and pointing to other concert benefits. With these in mind, performers developed techniques for morale-boosting impact. These included keeping performance quality high and maximizing interactions between audiences and performers; the dedication of individual performances to honor specific individuals in attendance; and on-the-spot composition and performance of new works based on local material and ideally, local heroes—soldiers from the division where the artists were who had recently distinguished themselves in battle.[44]

Repertoire Conflicts

Perceptions of what military audiences needed changed once artists began traveling to the front in large numbers. Even as the brigade structure moved from voluntary in 1941 to KPDI scheduled in 1942, the obligation to entertain the front was shared equally among all cultural institutions.[45] These ranged from variety theaters (*estrada*) to dramatic theaters and opera companies.[46] Performers were simply expected to bring the best of the genre they normally worked in and to find a way to make that repertoire relevant. The most obvious choice for concert repertoire would have been the *estrada* genre, which was highly politicized. The most "agitational" material tended to come in the form of small-form dramatic repertoire, *estrada* numbers, and one-act plays or sketches. Since these forms were shorter and faster to write, they could be frequently updated to reflect changing conditions at the front. They often dealt with the image of Germans and Nazi ideology and could be very successful. As one political officer commented in late 1941, a performance of the skit "'Nose with a Hump' in its expressiveness and intelligibility . . . is worth a two-hour political lecture on that topic."[47] Written in 1935, the skit satirized Nazi racial theory.

Based on feedback provided to individual brigades and the KPDI as well as articles in military and government newspapers, one can trace a very broad evolution in the repertoire debates that coincides with the course of the war itself.[48] In fall 1941, when the Red Army was retreating and it was not clear the Soviet Union could hold out, the demand for openly political repertoire was highest. The need for "agitational" material was discussed, as political officers tried to bolster hopes that the Germans could be halted and shore up soldiers' will to fight.

Political officers never officially "stopped" wanting agitational material, but several things changed in 1942. First, the military situation stabilized, and growing awareness of German atrocities alleviated the need for performers to create separate fighting motivation. Central authorities began to emphasize that treating culture only as propaganda and performing exclusively antifascist or "defense" material was a mistake. Central pressure for full-length plays meant that more playwrights turned away from one-acts toward longer scripts that were difficult to produce or modify fast enough to reflect real-time conditions. Much of the material produced in 1941 became outdated. As more brigades returned with reviews from the front, the reviews emphasized the relaxation and "cultured rest" the soldiers needed, and requested light-hearted, happy material.[49] Artists confirmed this in their debriefings. Many commanders had rejected the idea of purely defensive repertoire from the beginning. They insisted on the inclusion of "as merry as possible a program, the more it arouses laughter from the soldiers the more it is necessary to them."[50] In this view, concerts were a source of distraction and relaxation, which in turn improved morale. Lt. Gen. Pavel Rotmistrov, who commanded armored troops in most major battles throughout the war and later became the first Soviet Marshal of Armored Troops, explained that soldiers wanted to "relax and laugh," and emphasized the need to be distracted.[51] In February 1943, the head of the DKA of the Central Front wrote to Moscow to complain that some brigades' repertoires reminded soldiers too much of the difficulties of wartime life, and aroused serious worries.[52] Gen. Shatilov informed Tatiana Kutasova and Aleksandr Tomskii in 1943 that there was no need to "agitate" soldiers to battle the Germans. They understood how to do that perfectly well on their own.[53] Instead, artistic performances reassured soldiers that the home front was behind them. These interactions could have the secondary impact of improving fighting performance, but it was not the concerts' main objective. Rather, the artists sought to fill what they perceived as a gap, something that was missing at the front.

The belief that entertainment did, in fact, assist soldiers had circulated among artists since fall 1941, and their accumulating experience at the front only confirmed it. At a KPDI debriefing session in October 1941, one of the earliest participants emphasized that while sending brigades to the front was critical, it was senseless to "agitate" the soldiers. However, the chance for them to relax and laugh was a big deal.[54] Such sentiments from commanders only gave artists more incentive to focus on entertainment. Performers encountered very few requests from soldiers for more antifascist or "defense" plays or skits. Soldiers preferred not to watch material "about the front," since they had enough of it. Moreover, war depicted on stage inevitably paled in comparison to the reality of the war surrounding them. Instead, soldiers needed "life-affirming works" that were humorous and that reminded them of home or depicted how their families were living on the home front.[55] This did not entirely preclude agitational material. All concerts included declamation pieces drawn from current Soviet newspapers, such as the poems of Konstantin Simonov and Aleksandr Tvardovsky or the incendiary essays of Ilya Ehrenburg and Aleksei Tolstoy. Singers benefited from the fact that group singing was the most productive Soviet performing art, and composers flooded the market with wartime songs.[56] These were popular and frequently requested by soldiers, via notes sent up to the stage. However, this focus ensured the continued place of jokes, folk songs and dances, and classical music. For dramatic performers, it also heavily predisposed them toward "lighter" repertoire.

Consensus about the focus on entertainment (although it was never formally declared) meant that dramatic repertoire continued to draw heavily on prewar comedy, satire, vaudeville acts, and Russian classics. By 1942 its previous success meant that brigades were required to have dramatic, story-driven repertoire.[57] Dramatic repertoire, far more than music or dance, brought performers into conflict with Party authorities. Skits, vaudevilles, one-act plays and the rarer but highly desirable full-length plays, however, rarely dealt with the war. Vladimir Filippov left behind a list of the works performed by his brigade in 1941 and 1942. Out of seventy-three works in total (plays, sketches, etc.), twenty-nine were classics, primarily Russian, and thirty-seven were Soviet. Only six of these were "defense" works and another six "antifascist," while fifteen dealt with the "heroic past of the Russian people."[58] The Iskra theater's first concert program in September 1941 relied heavily on agitational material such as Ehrenburg's "Hitler's lackies," "Red

Army *chastushki*," poems by front-line soldiers, and Maxim Gorky's "Song of the Falcon." By early 1942 they had moved to include lyrical songs, folk songs, and dances as well as agitational sketches such as Kvasnitskii or Erdman's "The Elixir of Courage," satirizing the Wehrmacht as semiliterate and incompetent.[59] But by August 1942, they had expanded to include a vaudeville play and excerpts from Ostrovsky; they also diversified their song and dance offerings. These continued to expand throughout the war, and by 1944 they had two vaudevilles, as well as the Spanish comedy "The Phantom Lady."[60]

Artists' focus on entertainment raised new questions for political officers. As the war progressed and Soviet victory became more certain, political officers became increasingly concerned with the ideological content of the repertoire rather than its agitational nature. This is to say, political officers worried less about justifying or explaining the war to their men and became more invested in a generally correct Soviet worldview. The continued reliance on vaudeville and comedy drew ire from central Party authorities, who would have preferred that soldiers enjoy a more "wholesome" diet of either Russian classics such as Ostrovsky or high-quality Soviet dramaturgy. In 1944 and later, reports called for eliminating "low-quality" or artistically and politically "weak" repertoire.[61] In 1944, Georgii Aleksandrov, head of the Propaganda and Agitation Department, reviewed the work of the Soviet Union's twenty front theaters. In his report to Aleksandr Shcherbakov, head of the Political Directorate of the Red Army, Aleksandrov criticized the "low ideological-artistic quality of the theaters' repertoire" and the theaters' tendencies to stage too many "weak, second-sort" plays. Political officers complained that artists performed "vulgar" skits and or "*poshlo*," which they claimed the audiences did not enjoy, an unlikely claim.[62] Such concerns manifested themselves primarily at the end of the war, as the Red Army was fighting on foreign territory. Political officers may have been confident in soldiers' understanding of the war in 1944, but they wanted to ensure that concerts upheld Soviet perspectives abroad. Vaudevilles and prewar romantic comedies, all very popular, did not.

Enhancing Impact

Although brigades' travel routes and performance schedules were set in Moscow by GlavPURKKA, when brigades arrived at the front artists found themselves the objects of competition amongst officers and hindered by local circumstances. When Anastasia Zueva and Alla Tarasova arrived in Smolensk in 1942 with an MXAT (Moscow Art Academic Theater) brigade, the fact of their arrival made "an enormous impression. . . . [Neighboring divisions] sent representatives and discussions began: 'Comrades, surely you won't pass over us?'"[63] Commanders would insist artists disrupt set schedules by claiming that their company deserved a performance more, for example, on the eve of a fight. Olga Beiul with the Leningrad Children's Theater wrote of her trip to the Volkhov front in 1943 that just as soon as Lieutenant Zaks had managed to secure their performance for his troops, a senior lieutenant appeared demanding a concert the same day for his guards division, insisting that he "needed it more."[64] Ballet dancer Akiva Diner noted in 1943 outside Stalingrad that the biggest tensions at the front arose when the brigade was scheduled to move to a different division. Their current hosts would work to convince the brigade to stay, arguing that there were still many "wonderful heroes [who had not seen their performances yet], who had the right to a performance."[65] Occasionally commanders took matters into their own hands. Upon finishing a concert outside Moscow in January 1942, Garen Zhukovskaia's brigade was invited to get into a waiting car that they assumed would transport them to their next scheduled concert. After a lengthy trip including a river crossing, the artists arrived at a recently constructed stage made from pine trees and decorated with wildflowers and discovered that they had actually been "stolen" by a tank detachment scheduled to go into battle the next morning. The tankists had not been scheduled for any concerts but decided to rectify the situation themselves.[66] They did not even insist on a concert (though the actors insisted themselves) but had just wanted to enjoy the artists' company.

Artists' roles as representatives of both the state and the home front meant that their behavior at the front, living among soldiers, took on new significance. Commanders also recognized, perhaps more than GlavPUR-KKA, artists' value as a link between the front and those at home. As General Shatilov explained to Kutasova and Tomskii's brigade, "no political lecture, not agitators, not movies—nothing can substitute for the actors who have come to us. Live people, the live word—they prize this above everything else."[67] For this reason, military commanders paid attention to the quality of the brigade's performance and their behavior at the front, as well as how concert repertoire was calibrated to particular audiences. The mere presence of artists at the front was highly political, and the presence of civilians (including women) was also a major change. Artistic brigades thus became an important way of demonstrating the unity of front and rear areas. Artists' behavior (especially those from elite theaters) at the front was intensely scrutinized, and their interactions with soldiers influenced a concert's overall success. This was one matter where artists and political officers were in accord.

The more famous the artists performing, the greater the cachet for a military unit of obtaining a performance, and the greater the sense that the concert was a "reward" or privilege that distinguished its recipients. This was heightened by attempts to assign concerts to soldiers receiving honors or distinctions, such as those receiving the Guards designation.[68] Singers Lidiia Ruslanova and Klavdiia Shul'zhenko were enormously popular, but few could hope to see them even once, let alone regularly. The same applied to the more prestigious brigades from the Vakhtangov, Bolshoi, Kirov, Nemirovich-Danchenko theaters, and others. Aleksandr Reziapkin, an officer posted on the Kalinin front, enjoyed many concerts by professional artists. He nevertheless explicitly noted the arrival of Moscow artists.[69] In one of their early trips in August 1942, Nikolai Dorokhin's brigade's departure to forward positions was delayed by the head of the House of the Red Army. He explained to the disconcerted artists that all the political officers had gathered for a meeting and that "they would kill me, if I don't show them MXAT. . . . So you'll spend the night here and depart tomorrow."[70] Culture occupied a particular place in the Soviet mind, having been the object of extended campaigns in the 1930s. Hosting prestigious brigades indicated a certain status. This also suggests that the concerts' importance lay not just in their repertoire but in the fact and symbolism of their provisioning by the state.

Artists themselves understood that what their concerts achieved was reminding soldiers about the life they had left behind and reassure them it still existed—providing an "emotional bridge" to the prewar period, to quote Klavdiia Shul'zhenko.[71] Virtually all brigades were a mix of women and men, often in their twenties and thirties. Appearing in costume freshly ironed and made-up, no matter what the conditions were, was a point of pride for artists. In contrast to lavish US and German programs, Soviet concert brigades were modest in their costumes, appearance, and performance content. Even the dancers' costumes often resembled national costumes with short sleeves and knee-length skirts or tutus. Nevertheless, the appearance of civilians in areas where soldiers had seen none for up to a year generated excitement. A brigade of musicians in the Far North in November 1942 reported that "the mere fact of the performance of honored artists in evening costumes and lacquered shoes close to the line of fire, in difficult conditions, aroused enormous enthusiasm amongst the soldiers and commanders. The concerts turned into passionate meetings and took on great agitational-political meaning."[72]

Artists' arrival also meant a chance to hear firsthand about life in Moscow and elsewhere. Soldiers' access to information was comparatively limited, and being at the front isolated them intensely from prewar and civilian life. Both performers and authorities noted soldiers' strong interest in "home front thematics," persisting until as late as 1944.[73] Such interests placed performers in an awkward position, as they had the smallest repertoire on home front matters, perennially unpopular topics with writers and playwrights. Performers reported with some chagrin that audience members always wanted to ask about Moscow after the concerts—while performers themselves wanted to hear more about life at the front. To enhance the sense of unity, artists' activities at the front were not limited to concerts. They were expected to interact with the soldiers formally and informally. After each concert interactions with soldiers would occur, ranging from spontaneous "meetings" requested by political officers to more casual interactions. Occasionally this also entailed exchanging information about what was happening in Moscow for tales of stories about battles between actors and soldiers.

One area of frequent collaboration between artists and political authorities was the development or performance of "local material" and individual dedications. This corresponded to a general policy shift away from collectivism: Central authorities and GlavPURKKA decided to deliberately highlight individual heroism and the "best people of the front" as examples for everyone else to emulate.[74] Poets and composers accompanying brigades to active divisions would draw on military newspapers and interviews with commanders to compose skits, *chastushki*, and songs about the division itself. Although soldiers were not eager for military material, "local material" was an exception. Such unit-specific repertoire modifications were declared to "entirely answer the demands of the front" and enjoyed enormous success.[75] This tactic was risky, as life at the front was deadly and did not make for lighthearted fare. When Sara Magdesian hesitated to recite a poem about the Panfilov tank division given the poem's somber ending, the commanding officer assured her that the tankists would be far more flattered by the fact that someone was composing and singing songs about them than they would be upset by the tragic ending.[76]

In consultation with local political officers, performers frequently dedicated individual numbers to men who had recently distinguished themselves in battle.[77] After the number, the soldier in question often stood up or came on stage to meet the performers and respond, usually with a promise to fight harder. Georgii Orlov led a cultural brigade from the Mariinsky theater to the Kalinin front in summer 1942, to make up for a poor previous brigade, both in terms of its repertoire and behavior at the front.[78] He later concluded that "at least 50% of our success [can be attributed] . . . to the fact that 100% of our brigade interacted quite socially with the soldiers, in addition to performances on stage."[79] He later wrote in the Mariinsky newspaper that "artists should enter [into] close contact with soldiers, and the result of this should be friendly personal ties. Only then will military patronage work be successful."[80] The front left little room for "neutral" behavior. In a review of the Vakhtangov theater, Shilov concluded that "the actors were brave and happy, and this transferred itself to the soldiers and commanders."[81]

Artists' willingness to adapt to primitive front-line conditions and the lack of "amenities" demonstrated their "courage under fire" and resulted in warm feelings from the military. Accusations of "opportunism," "self-enrichment," or irresponsible behavior by actors drew critiques that were discussed at high levels.[82] Officers took particular offense at demanding artists. In February 1945, a brigade that arrived in East Prussia was offered an entire house that the political officers considered to be one of the best in the village. When one performer complained that it was "impossible to live in such a shed [*sarai*]," the commander refused to show their concert to his troops.[83] In light of such behavior, the commanding officer promptly rejected the brigade's scheduled performances.

Conclusion

Front brigade program evolution was surprisingly contingent. Although it drew on earlier Soviet experiences in the Civil War and the prominent role culture occupied in the 1930s, the evolving program confirms the disagreement about the wartime role of culture in 1941 and unpreparedness generally—front brigades only became a fixture once it was clear that the military and political officers really wanted them and that there were artists who needed to be employed. The program evolved through improvisation. Especially early on, the program expanded thanks to the existence of a cultural bureaucracy that could package Soviet artists and offer them to the military essentially "ready to go." Concerts were more important to the artists performing than to political officers, who had an array of tools at their disposal. Artists' early initiative also ensured their influence on repertoire, since Party officials were preoccupied with matters such as distributing the brigades at the front.

Despite their revolutionary antecedents, the cultural brigades of World War II were in some ways traditional and conservative. On the whole, they mainly sought to achieve impact not by experimenting with format or content, but by managing the concert's approach and appeal to its audience. Notwithstanding the dissatisfaction of central authorities, "light" repertoire remained a staple throughout the war. Some brigades did eventually present full-length plays, which included Soviet dramaturgy, but such front theaters were limited in number and always continued to offer lighter fare as well.

The brigades confirm how audience-oriented the concerts were, and how invested authorities and artists were in their positive reception. If artists insisted on working in "their specialty," they had to figure out how to extract the maximum impact from their particular genre. Performing artists seem to have disregarded the central authorities' repertoire preferences as much as they could (since vaudeville and "light" pieces remained fixtures of concert brigades up until the end); the artistic intelligentsia was incentivized to figure out how to apply their particular skills and specialties to what was demanded of them and rose to the occasion. Most artists were aware of the potential political fault lines. While accusing others of disingenuousness, they emphasized their own deep moral and emotional commitment to serving soldiers as their equals.[84]

The debates and incentive structure operating here nevertheless point to an underlying question unresolved during the war: Should art and propaganda perform the same function? Performers and political officers agreed on the sorts of things that would make or break a brigade's success, but they never fully agreed on the overall goal. This was complicated by military input, which sided more with performers and opted for entertainment and human interaction over propaganda.

Concerts, in commanders' eyes, when done well and especially when humorous, could temporarily provide soldiers with complete and total distraction from the front, which is what was most beneficial. Even political officers' goals changed with the course of the war. Maintaining morale outside Moscow in 1941 required a different approach than in Poland in 1945, when complaints about vulgarity and unseriousness in the repertoire became much more common. The military didn't want to damage morale, but even the greatest enthusiasts of performance brigades were unable to rely on them exclusively for serious political agitation, given the mismatch between the small numbers of brigades and the huge size of the army. At their best, concerts represented a one-off boost before an offensive or a reward after battle: At the front, officers were much concerned with the morale of their soldiers and less concerned with agitational or propaganda content.

Notes

1. GARF f. 5508 op. 3 d. 3 l. 48. Audience numbers are difficult to determine but could frequently be large; a report by the group Iskra claimed they served more than 500,000 soldiers with 1,000 concerts.

2. See Mark Harrison, "Industry and the Economy," in *The Soviet Union at War, 1941–1945*, ed. David R. Stone (Barnsley: Pen and Sword Military Press, 2010), 3. For an overview of Soviet losses, see Mark Harrison, "Barbarossa: The Soviet Response, 1941," in *From Peace to War: Germany, Soviet Russia and the World, 1939–1941*, ed. Bernd Wegner (Providence, RI: Berghahn Books, 1997), 431–48; and Alec Nove, *An Economic History of the USSR, 1917–1991* (London: Penguin Books, 1992), 271.

3. See https://www.uso.org/stories/2368-uso-camp-shows-d-day-and-entertaining-troops-on-the-european-front-lines-in-wwii, last accessed 22 October 2022.

4. James Cooke, *American Girls, Beer, and Glenn Miller: GI Morale in World War II* (Columbia, MO: University of Missouri Press, 2014), 128.

5. Julia Timpe, *Nazi Organized Recreation and Entertainment in the Third Reich* (London: Palgrave Macmillan, 2017), 124.

6. Most brigades averaged around ten people but were occasionally smaller. As the war progressed, there were a growing number of larger "front theaters." The makeup of the Vakhtangov front theater on the First Ukrainian Front in November 1943 consisted of twenty-six people, including a stage manager, electrician, costumer, and makeup artist, as well as two musical accompanists. Estimates of the total number of artists who performed at the front vary. *Krasnaia Zvezda* put the number at over 32,000 in September 1944. See *Krasnaia Zvezda*, 23 September 1944, 3. Komskii and Podobed claim over 42,000. See I. M. Podobed and B. G. Komskii, *Kogda gremeli boi: Kul'turno-prosvetitel'naia rabota na fronte v gody Velikoi Otechestvennoi voiny* (Moscow: Voennoe izdatel'stvo, 1983), 204.

7. RGALI f. 962 op. 7 d. 1303 l. 22.

8. RGALI f. 3012 op. 1. d. 27 l. 70.

9. On agitbrigades, see Robert Argenbright, "The Soviet Agitational Vehicle: State Power on the Social Frontier," *Political Geography* 17, no. 3 (1998); Lynn Mally, "Shock Workers on the Cultural Front: Agitprop Brigades in the First Five-Year Plan," *Russian History* 23, no. 14 (1996); Lynn Mally, "The Americanization of the Living Newspaper," Carl Beck Papers no. 1903 (2008).

10. "Voenno-shefskaia rabota v eto vremia stala osnovoi," *Otechestvennye arkhivy*, no. 3 (2005). GARF f. 5508 op. 3 d.1 l. 6.

11. V. A. Filippov, *Ochen' tochno, ochen' srochno!* (Moscow: Artist. Rezhisser. Teatr, 2020), 22.

12. *Muzy v shineliakh: Sovetskaia intelligentsia v gody Velikoi Otechestvennoi voiny* (Moscow: Rosspen, 2006), 20.

13. RGALI f. 962 op. 3 d. 1082 l. 5.

14. Karel C. Berkhoff, *Motherland in Danger: Soviet Propaganda during World War II* (Cambridge, MA: Harvard University Press, 2012), 3.

15. Richard J. Brody, "Ideology and Political Mobilization: The Soviet Home Front in World War II," *Carl Beck Papers in Russian and East European Studies*, no. 1104 (October 1994), 3.

16. For other work on manipulating and understanding soldiers' picture of their enemies, see Derek Mallett's essay, chapter 4 in this volume.

17. Konstantin Iartsev, *Aktery i boitsy* (Moskva: VTO, 1959), 87.

18. See Erina Megowan, chapter 5, "Artists at the Front," in unfinished book manuscript.

19. As scholars have noted, propaganda in the army often consisted of promoting the current Party policies rather than complex ideological education. Roger Reese, *Why Stalin's Soldiers Fought: The Red Army's Military Effectiveness in World War II* (Lawrence: University Press of Kansas, 2011), 190.

20. Exceptions include the military's own theaters and ensembles and a handful of performers who formally enlisted, such as jazz singer Klavdiia Shul'zhenko on the Leningrad front. Most artists at the front were civilians who either were not subject to the draft or who had received a deferral or exemption by virtue of their age or health, educational status, or professional qualifications. Most top-tier cultural institutions were able to obtain exemptions for their best-qualified performers, though they frequently had to release chorus members and assorted personnel. The Kirov theater, for example, submitted lists of "absolutely necessary" workers that it wanted to remain on the deferral list in 1941. See TsGAIPD f. 2245 1 6 78 l. 117. Because deferrals rested on status, the cadres of regional theaters were decimated by the draft, as they were less distinguished by qualifications or honors. See, for example, the Tobolsk Dramatic Theater, which lost well over half its performers to the draft in the first days of the war. T. O. Adrianova, "Tobolskii dramaticheskii teatr v gody VOV," in *Sotsium, Ku'ltural, Nravstvennost', Dosug: Materialy mezhdunarodnyoi konferentsii 15 aprelia 2010*, l, 86.

21. See, for example, *Partiino-politicheskaia rabota v Sovetskoi armii i flote* (Moscow: Voennoe izd-vo Ministerstva oborony SSSR, 1953).

22. *Partiino-politicheskaia rabota v Sovetskikh Vooruzhennykh silakh v gody Velikoi Otechestvennoi Voiny, 1941–1945* (Moscow: Voennoe izd-vo ministerstva oborony SSSR, 1968), 81.

23. Reese, *Why Stalin's Soldiers Fought*, chap. 8; All major combatants provided entertainment to their troops. On the USO, see Cooke, *American Girls, Beer, and Glenn Miller*; Lowell Matson, "Theatre for the Armed Forces in World War II," *Educational Theatre Journal* 6, no. 1 (1954); Gary Bloomfield, *Duty, Honor and Applause: America's Entertainers in World War II* (Guilford, CT: Lyon's Press, 2004). On German front entertainment, which also emphasized "light entertainment," see Julia Timpe, *Nazi Organized Recreation and Entertainment in the Third Reich* (London: Palgrave Macmillan, 2017), chap. 4; Geerte Murmann, *Komödianten für den Krieg: Deutsches und alliiertes Fronttheater* (Düsseldorf: Droste, 1992). On the British institution, ENSA, see Andy Merriman, *Greasepaint and Cordite: The Story of ENSA and Concert Party Entertainment during the Second World War* (London: Aurum Press, 2013).

24. Reese, *Why Stalin's Soldiers Fought*, 212.

25. Brandon Schechter, "*Khoziaistvo* and *Khoziaeva*: The Properties and Proprietors of the Red Army, 1941–1945," *Kritika: Explorations in Russian and Eurasian History* 18, no. 3 (2017).

26. TSGAM 2007 1 26 l. 144; *Muzy v shineliakh*, 23. "Propaganda centers" refer to "agitational points" or "agitpunkty." These were propaganda and mass political work centers established in train stations and other public buildings. They might be no more than a designated corner, cabinet, or small room in a larger institution but were decorated and visually distinguishable and provided a venue for agitational work.

27. See also TSGAM f. 2007 op. 1 d. 26 l. 144.

28. For an overview of Operation Typhoon and the Battle for Moscow, see David Glantz and Jonathan House, *When Titans Clashed: How the Red Army Stopped Hitler* (Lawrence: University Press of Kansas, 2015); David Stahel, *Operation Typhoon: Hitler's March on Moscow* (New York: Cambridge University Press, 2013).

29. IRI RAN f. 2 razdel VIII op. 2 d. 7 l. 8.

30. Filippov, *Ochen' tochno, ochen' srochno!* 17.

31. GAPK f. 629 op. 1 d. 2 l. 15. The brigades could be ordered either from an oblast, in which case it was up to local authorities and local branches of the Committee for Artistic Affairs to select artists (usually from more than one theater), or from a specific theater (usually larger theaters from Moscow or Leningrad).

32. Gosudarstvennyi teatral'nyi muzei im. Bakhrushchina f. 546 op. 1 d. 204 l. 1.

33. For example, see a 1945 Navy concert request, specifying a "high quality" brigade for the Danube flotilla and another for the Dnepr flotilla. RGALI f. 962 op. 5 d. 872 l. 65.

34. RGALI op. 962 op. 5 d. 616 l. 36-67.

35. Konstantin Iartsev, *Aktery i boitsy*, 77; *Malyi teatr na frontakh Velikoi Otechestevennoi voiny* (Moscow: Iskusstvo, 1948), 35.

36. See, for example, RGALI f. 962 op. 5 d. 872 l. 48; f. 962 op. 5 d. 616 l. 156.

37. GARF f. 5446 op. 44 d. 1105 l. 276.

38. IRI RAN f. 2 razdel VIII op. 2 d. 5a l. 26.

39. IRI RAN f. 2 razdel VIII op. 2 d. 5a l. 42.

40. A. E. Diner, "Frontovye zametki," in *Teatry Moskvy v gody Velikoi Otechestvennoi voiny : Arkhivnye dokumenty i materialy*, ed. Ia. A. Ononenko (Moscow: Glavarkhiv Moskvy, 2019), 116.

41. RGALI f. 962 op. 5 d. 987 l. 140.

42. B. M. Filippov, *Muzy na fronte: Ocherki, dnevniki, pis'ma* (Moscow: Sovetskaia Rossiia, 1975), 65.

43. For how these different moments in the war affected Soviet soldiers who defected, see Kevin Riehle's essay, chapter 11 in this volume.

44. This tactic was not limited to the front; highlighting and distinguishing the "best people" from factories and collective farms was in widespread use. At the front, this highlighted Red Army heroism.

45. The military had its own theatrical groups and performance ensembles, staffed by active members of the military. For those arriving in brigades sent by the KPDI, they were either not eligible for military service (often due to age or health issues) or had already received an exemption. Brigade work was not a substitute for military service. Artists who were drafted might find themselves assigned to forms of cultural work during the war, but through separate military channels.

46. *Estrada* refers to a particular genre in Russian culture that had roots in the pre-revolutionary period, referring generally to any performance outside the "big," or classical, stage. In the 1930s and '40s, *estrada* tended to rely on "verbal comedy routines embellished with popular music and dance." For an overview of its evolution, see Richard Stites, *Russian Popular Culture: Entertainment and Society since 1900* (Cambridge: Cambridge University Press, 1992). As David MacFayden points out, forms of *estrada* expression were adaptable and short-lived, encompassing light comic theater, satirical and mass songs, folk music, parody, feuilletons, comic stories or literary readings, puppetry, and even circus acts. See David MacFayden, *Red Stars: Personality and the Soviet Popular Song, 1955–1991* (Toronto: McGill-Queen's University Press, 2001), 16–18. In the second half of the twentieth century, it became associated with Soviet pop music.

47. IRI RAN f. 2 razdel VIII op. 2 d. 5A l. 28. "Nos s gorbinkoi" was an *estrada* one-act play written by Lev Kvasnitskii in 1935 that satirized Nazi racial theory. Kvasnitskii volunteered for the *opolchenie* in 1941 and went missing in action outside Viazma in September 1941. His vaudeville piece, "Ticket to Eisk," was performed very frequently during the war.

48. Compare this to the media narrative of the US loss at Bataan in Elena Friot's chapter 9 in this volume.

49. See, for example, RGALI f. 962 op. 5 d. 653 l. 41; RGALI f. 962 op. 7 d. 1193 l. 23.

50. IRI RAN f. 2 razdel VIII op. 2 d. 5a Filippov l. 39. "Serious" in this case refers to high art.

51. I. M. Podobed and B. G. Komskii, *Kogda gremeli boi: kul'turno-prosvetitel'naia rabota na fronte v gody Velikoi Otechestvennoi voiny* (Moscow: Voennoe izdatel'stvo, 1983), 202.

52. Podobed and Komskii, *Kogda gremeli boi*, 202.

53. RGALI f. 3012 op. 1 d. 27 l. 91.

54. "Doklady brigadirov o rabote kontsertnykh frontovykh brigadakh na soveshchanii v KPDI," *Muzy v shineliakh*, 29.

55. RGALI f. 962 op. 3 d. 641 l.

56. On the wartime production of songs, see Suzanne Ament, *Sing to Victory: Song in Soviet Society during World War II* (Boston: Academic Studies Press, 2019), chap. 1.

57. On the excitement over dramatic repertoire, see Olga Beiul, "Frontovoi dnevnik artistki Leningradskogo Novogo TIUZa Ol'gi Beiul," https://theatre

museum.ru/naukpubl/olga_beyul, last accessed 4/18/2025; *Malyi teatr na frontakh*, 141; RGALI f. 962 op. 7 d. 1193 l. 69.

58. V. A. Filippov, *Ochen' tochno, ochen' srochno! Frontovye brigady vserossiiskogo teatral'nogo obshchevsta* (Moscow: Artist. Rezhisser. Teatr, 2020), 46.

59. See the scene's text in *Literaturnaia Gazeta* no. 7 (20 February 2008).

60. D. V. Rodionov, A. M. Vorob'eva, N. Katonova, eds., *Dnevnik Frontovogo Teatra* (M: Gosudarstvennyi tsentral'nyi teatral'nyi muzei im. A.A. Bakhrushina: Moskovskii teatr Masterskaia P. Fomenko, 2015), 220.

61. *Muzy v shineliakh*, 66.

62. RGALI f. 962 op. 5 d. 987 l. 27.

63. RGALI f. 962 op. 5 d. 653 l. 41.

64. Olga Beiul, "Frontovoi dnevnik artistki Leningradskogo Novogo TIUZa: prodolzhenie," https://theatremuseum.ru/naukpubl/olga_beyul_2, last accessed 4 April 2023.

65. Diner, "Frontovye zametki," 120.

66. RGALI f. 3215 op. 1 d. 43 l. 3.

67. RGALI f. 3012 op. 1 d. 27 l. 91.

68. Diner, "Frontovye zametki," l. 116; Bakhrushin f. 546 op. 1 d. 105 l. 1; IRI RAN f. 2 razdel VII op. 2 d. 6 l. 8.

69. Aleksandr Reziapkin, *Dnevnik Velikoi Otechestvennoi Voiny* (M: Novosti, 2009). See entries from 25 August 1942; 25 December 1942; 8 June 1943; 9 May 1945.

70. Nikolai Dorokhin, *Po Dorogam Voiny* (M: Iskusstvo, 1950), 9.

71. Podobed and Komskii, *Kogda gremeli boi*, 204.

72. RGALI f. 962 11 570 l. 71.

73. RGALI f. 962 op. 3 d. 641 l. 6.

74. See David Glantz, *Colossus Reborn: The Red Army at War* (Lawrence: University Press of Kansas, 2005), 584.

75. RGALI f. 962 op. 3 d. 1037 l. 42.

76. S. A. Magdesian, "Chetyre goda," in *Teatry*, 403, 461.

77. The idea of highlighting the "best people" in a division was quite popular, especially among military officials. See IRI RAN f. 2 razdel I op. 27a d. 11 l. 141-142; and RGALI f. 3065 op. 1 d. 31, on perceived importance of works devoted to local conditions.

78. Teatral'nyi Muzei im. Bakhrushina f. 546 op. 1 d. 681 l. 1.

79. Teatral'nyi Muzei im. Bakhrushina f. 546 op. 1, d. 681, l. 1.

80. *Za Sovetskoe Iskusstvo* (20 October 1942), 2, G. Orlov, "God voenno-shefskoi raboty".

81. Teatral'nyi Muzei im. Bakhrushchina f. 546 op. 1 d. 227 l. 4.

82. GARF f. 5446 op. 44 d. 1105 l. 276. In a letter addressing these complaints to Yakov Chadaev, chief of administration of the Council of People's Commissars,

Shikin conceded the KPDI was not conducting the necessary "character building" work with its performers; but he also recommended that official payrates for front performers be increased.

83. RGALI f. 962 op. 5 d. 872 l. 48.
84. RGALI f. 3012 op. 1 d. 27 l. 90.

7
From Covert Reports to Front-Page News
How North American Newspaper Reports Contributed to Views of Reconnaissance Actions in Northwest Europe

Victoria Sotvedt

During the Second World War, both Allied and Axis forces utilized battalion-sized armored reconnaissance units that provided invaluable battlefield information and filled the significant gap between foot patrols and aerial reconnaissance. Reconnaissance units operated on or beyond the front, and the information they gleaned was thus a key part of battle planning. These units engaged in more than just scouting, however, and were frequent participants in combat, both directly and indirectly, and sometimes without support from other units. As a result of their forward position, actions involving armored reconnaissance were secret, and reconnaissance regiments received less attention in the newspaper and radio reports on which the public depended for information. When reports on reconnaissance units were done—something impossible to avoid given the number of troops who served in them—both Canadian and American newspapers used similar journalistic practices, despite writing for very different audiences.

First and foremost, articles were delayed; most reports with any level of significant detail were published at least four weeks after the events they described and could be delayed up to twelve weeks. Second, reports tended to focus on an individual or a single vehicle crew, minimizing combat and emphasizing emotions, personalities, and personal victories to create feelings of familiarity while obscuring details of the larger action, and often using the less formal "recce" in place of "reconnaissance." The tone was generally optimistic and downplayed the danger of being at the front, to help reassure audiences at home and abroad. Even reports on exceptional actions that resulted in the Victoria Cross or Medal of Honor—the highest awards for valor for Canadians and Americans, respectively—rarely dealt with reconnaissance forces in combat in detail.

These reporting strategies were designed to balance informing the public with the need for wartime secrecy to protect troops on the front, and they were remarkably successful. Although democratic nations were obliged to provide some level of information to the public, secrecy was a tactical and strategic advantage and thus was always prioritized. However, partly because of the obligation to maintain secrecy and the low level of reporting on reconnaissance units in general, the actual role and impact of reconnaissance units in the war has been grossly underestimated. Sources such as newspapers, instead of the typical war diaries and after-action reports, can offer new insight on why previous works have tended to push supporting regiments to the sidelines. These sources can also help address the resulting gap in assessing the overall effectiveness of armies in the Second World War. Then-contemporary emphasis on the more "exciting" combat operations overemphasized infantry and tank exploits while minimizing the role of battlefield support. Because newspapers framed reconnaissance units as scouting ahead but never in any real danger, and by releasing reports so long after the (usually victorious) conclusion of an operation when public attention was already focused elsewhere, they helped develop the narrative that reconnaissance contributed only by gathering information and was relatively easy—light work.[1] By examining these newspaper articles, we can see how the public was led to believe that armored reconnaissance—in addition to other combat support units—did not contribute significantly to ground combat, which was instead presented as occurring primarily via infantry and tank units. This public perception of combat became the general narrative of the war, which in turn has hindered the development of a robust historiography on combat support units. This narrative has only recently begun to be challenged, but it is already apparent that reconnaissance units played a much larger role in Canadian and American military successes in the Second World War than previously thought.

Both the Canadian and American armies maintained armored reconnaissance units. In the Canadian military, each of the divisions had an attached reconnaissance regiment; of these, the 7th Canadian Reconnaissance Regiment (17th Duke of York Royal Canadian Hussars) and the 8th Canadian Reconnaissance Regiment (14th Canadian Hussars) saw the most action and were the most followed by the press—particularly the 7th, as it was based in Montreal where several daily papers enjoyed large circulations. In the American army—which, it should be noted, mobilized ninety-one divisions compared to Canada's five—only armored divisions maintained divisional armored reconnaissance battalions. Infantry divisions had the much smaller armored reconnaissance squadrons or even smaller troops, usually pulled from cavalry divisions, and sometimes also called mechanized-horse units. Of the full-sized American formations, the 82nd Armored Reconnaissance Battalion was by far the most covered in the press, in part because of its attachment to Patton's 2nd Armored Division and in part because they repeatedly distinguished themselves in the North African Campaign, the Invasion of Sicily, the landings on Omaha Beach, and other major engagements. Most sources used in this chapter are newspaper articles published throughout the war that specifically discuss reconnaissance actions. Additionally, war diaries (and their appendices), after-action reports, and administrative orders are used to verify newspaper information and provide important context to the historical articles. Although these sources are not new, they previously have not been used in conjunction with each other to assess either combat efficiency or the home front. Both newspaper articles and sources produced by reconnaissance units have been overlooked in the many popular histories that address the Canadian or American experience in the war, in large part because these histories tend to emphasize the role of infantry and tanks in ground combat. This overemphasis on infantry and tanks is at least partly rooted in *how* combat was transmitted to civilians via newsreels, radio, and most important, by newspapers.

Public demand for information from the front was strong. Although letters from soldiers were an important source of information for families, they were limited in scope and censored. Censorship was not always black bars over sensitive content; it was in many ways built into the system. Soldiers rarely knew where they were beyond a vague generalization, and they did not usually have access to other information from the front. They could not give away key information as they themselves did not possess it, and when combined with official censorship in the mail stream, it meant troop letters tended to contain more opinions than facts regarding the overall state or success of the army.[2] To get more detailed information, the public turned to official sources. Of these official sources, "the newspaper was king."[3] Unlike the contemporary era, it was difficult to view images from the front: Journalists had only limited clearance, and what footage was shown was often not an authentic representation of combat. Footage reels were shown in theaters before films but were generally unavailable in the home as television ownership was limited, with only a few thousand personal sets across North America. Still, footage from the war had its widest distribution in North America. Both American and Canadian film crews had more access to the battlefield than their British and Commonwealth counterparts, and both America and Canada created special units for filming and transmitting the war to civilians.

However, even with the greater rate of access, newsreels were supplementary at best, especially as they were heavily edited and usually featured only a small portion of a battle. Longer films, such as the 1944 documentary and propaganda film, *The Memphis Belle: A Story of a Flying Fortress*, were also heavily edited. In the case of *The Memphis Belle*, the story addresses only one crew of one bomber (albeit a famous one, being the first B-17 of the 8th Air Force to survive twenty-five bombing runs) and did not actually feature a single raid, as it purported.[4] Footage for the film was stitched together from several bombing runs, not all of which were even aboard the same aircraft.[5] *The Memphis Belle* was certainly a draw to the theater, but even though it had a longer runtime than most of the newsreels, it did little to elucidate the whole war picture—something done intentionally, as films like *The Memphis Belle* were produced for entertainment and civilian engagement with the war effort and were not meant to accurately portray the front. Although such films were produced frequently and at least offered a theatrical glimpse into the war if not an entirely honest one, none were produced that focused on reconnaissance troops. To compound this lack of visualization, shorter newsreels almost never dealt with reconnaissance troops, in part because of their extreme forward positions. Therefore, most Canadians and Americans relied on radio reports and newspaper articles for information on recce actions, since they were virtually never captured on film.

Radio reports tended to be the most dramatic. BBC's *War Report* was a syndicated report series from the front that began with the invasion of Normandy in summer 1944 and concluded just under a year later with the collapse of German forces in spring 1945. Reporters were at or just behind the front—and therefore behind reconnaissance units, which operated well beyond the front—and interviewed numerous soldiers fresh from action or reported their own observations.[6] Howard Marshall, a British journalist reporting on the Normandy landings on 6 June 1944, began by saying, "I'm sitting in my soaked-through clothes with no notes at all; all my notes are sodden—they're at the bottom of the sea."[7] The landing craft he had been on hit a mine and sank in five feet of water; Marshall waded ashore amid the ongoing assault. Such proximity to the front meant that it was not uncommon to hear artillery or aircraft in the background while interviews were ongoing. These reports and others like them were listened to eagerly by individuals around the globe. However, although more informative than most letters could be, these front-line reports were subject to many of the same official restrictions. Locations were vague or went unstated, and details of the larger action were often unclear. They also focused on individual experience, limiting the scope of each report, and therefore limiting each report's possible use as enemy intelligence. German intelligence staff listened to broadcasts, watched films, and read whatever they could get their hands on, desperate for information about Allied plans. It was therefore critical to minimize possible contextual details for each report, radio or otherwise. Additionally, *War Report* featured a reconnaissance regiment only once, the British 6th Airborne Armoured Reconnaissance Regiment. Other radio programs were similarly lacking in their reconnaissance coverage, in part because they could be up to thirty miles ahead of the main army.[8] This left newspaper reports as the best source for detailed information.

Newspaper reports were usually delayed two to eight weeks to avoid giving hints of planned actions, though most reports on reconnaissance were delayed by at least four weeks since large-scale operations were often at least partially planned based on reconnaissance actions and observations. Less in-depth reports did not have the same level of delay but had more of the same vague or completely omitted details. Material for reports also underwent review by official censors who removed anything considered secret. Military censors reviewed anything produced in the field before it was wired home and removed specific details of operations still in progress or marked if the report could be published after delay, and civilian government censors re-reviewed articles before they were published to remove any remaining sensitive content. In short, civilians at home had to be content with an information gap that could never be fully filled to maintain wartime secrecy and thus soldier safety—both for the reconnaissance troops and for the soldiers committed to operations based on the intelligence reconnaissance troops brought back. Civilians occasionally expressed displeasure with this strategy, such as when the front page of *The Claresholm Local Press* noted it was "unfortunate that our [Canadian] censorship made it necessary for direct news of Canadians to come through German sources."[9] Although civilians were aware of the gaps in reporting, they could do little to gain more information in the face of government censorship.

Information manipulation was not restricted to the omission of contextual details and a general vagueness. Most photographs that accompanied newspaper articles and appeared to depict the war were staged outright, a practice dating back to the First World War. The famous VJ-Day photograph taken by Alfred Eisenstaedt of an "uninhibited sailor" kissing a nurse in celebration of victory has been seen around the world and remains one of the most enduring images of the war. In 1996, the sailor in the photograph, Signalman Second Class Jim Reynolds, admitted that the photo was from

VE-Day, more than three months earlier, and Eisenstaedt had asked him to pose with the young woman, assuring him he would remain anonymous when he protested that he was engaged. Eisenstaedt then "posed the two of them carefully, even positioning their hands, the angle of their bodies, the position of their lips, the clutching of the purse and skirt."[10]

Purported pictures of the front were similarly artificial. Troops such as those pictured fording a flooded road in Bren-gun carriers in an article from late 1944 were usually moving behind the front line, and usually beyond the range of German artillery or counterattack. Frequently, they were in rest areas several miles from the front.[11] Many articles included portraits of soldiers taken before their deployment, rather than candid shots of troopers that might give away important background details that could be used to identify their location. Most candid photos from the Second World War were taken by soldiers themselves, usually without prior sanction and in fact breaking some of the most basic security rules. These candid photos have largely only just begun to enter the public eye, as they are often donated after the death of veterans. For obvious reasons, these candid photos did not appear in newspapers.

It should be noted that the rules regarding combat photographs, particularly in newspapers, were often challenged. War correspondents and photojournalists argued it was important for the public to see what was really happening, while governments contested this by saying it was more important to prevent the enemy from seeing as much as possible, in addition to other domestic concerns such as maintaining civilian morale and thus support for the war.[12] For example, the Australian government aggressively attempted to keep newspaper photographers from taking photos of combat in the Pacific theater, both for security reasons and because they were concerned about potentially antagonizing American troops whom they had been fighting alongside since early 1942 by inadvertently minimizing their accomplishments or creating security risks that would affect American positions. These policies were contested by independent journalists, news organizations, unions, and citizens who wanted more information about their troops.[13] Similar disputes existed between Canadian and American journalists and their governments, despite the comparatively high level of access they had to troops. Nevertheless, war images continued to reach civilians, but they were limited and highly selective about what was depicted in their carefully curated content and could misrepresent the outcome of battles or operations. Although it is likely that soldiers could occasionally spot fake photographs as they had in the First World War when the images didn't match their lived experiences, there is minimal evidence to suggest that audiences at home were aware that most images they saw were not an accurate depiction of the war.

As early as the First World War, civilian governments had recognized that images were necessary to convey the war to civilians thousands of miles away: "It is hard enough for the civilian ... to realise conditions at the front; without photography it would be practically impossible. ... Photography has about it the convincing atmosphere of naked reality."[14] The *Canadian Army Newsreel*, a short film program released monthly to Canadian forces both at home and abroad, routinely captured live combat footage, but after filming it was immediately sent to London for "censorship and editing."[15] Footage was carefully selected to limit the spread of potentially sensitive information and to maintain both troop and civilian morale; keeping the home front invested in the war effort was critical for maintaining war production and support for the war generally, and significant personnel losses or major defeats unsettled troops and endangered the "keep calm and carry on" attitude adopted by most democratic governments. After the failed raid on Dieppe on 19 August 1942, so disastrous that it effectively destroyed the 2nd Canadian Infantry Division, the *Newsreel* program focused heavily on surviving veterans receiving awards at Buckingham Palace and made virtually no mention of the actual raid.[16] Some troops training in England who saw only this short film assumed that Dieppe had actually been successful.[17] Audiences at home and in the field only rarely saw images depicting reconnaissance troops, given their forward positions (which were often off limits for photographers for both security reasons and their own personal safety) and the higher level of general secrecy reconnaissance work required. Staging photos of reconnaissance actions was also more difficult than staging infantry or tank battles, given the secret nature of reconnaissance (particularly the way wireless equipment was used in the cars) and the fact that recce troops were typically so far ahead of the photographers that they were unavailable as subjects. Simply put, there was no opportunity for civilians to truly visualize reconnaissance operations on the front. In combination with the widely available (but staged) photos of infantry and tank regiments, this has shaped the public's perception of combat as almost exclusively occurring between massed forces of infantry and tanks, with only a vague idea about the role other types of units played in large battles.

In addition to these limitations, reporters had difficulty in accessing reconnaissance troops, both before and after they were deployed in active combat. Canadian and American troops were repeatedly reminded in administrative orders, standing orders, lectures, and training programs that speaking to journalists was strictly forbidden without direct clearance from army command. A routine daily order from October 1943 for the 8th Canadian Reconnaissance Regiment reminded troops that "no officer or soldier will dispatch or submit directly or indirectly for publication in any newspaper, book, pamphlet, magazine, or other periodical either in Canada or elsewhere ... [on any] matter whatsoever without special permission" from Canadian Military Headquarters (CMHQ).[18] If, despite this, troops had a story, poem, or other potential publication they wanted considered, they were to submit the written piece in triplicate to their commanding officer, who would in turn submit it to the Military Intelligence branch of CMHQ, where it would be "classified as 'Secret'" and "safeguarded as such."[19] After review, unless there were exceptional circumstances, the work would only be released for publication if it was of a "professional, technical or military nature" that would appear in a relevant trade or professional publication, or if it was a "general article" that was "of a noncontroversial nature."[20]

Noncontroversial general articles were typically poems or essays that were submitted to local publications, newspapers, or periodicals back at home; in many cases, these addressed the war only tangentially and certainly did not give any impression of the actual fighting situation of Allied forces. The necessity for secrecy was constantly reiterated. A different order reminded troops that "experience has shown that newspaper stories, radio broadcasts and loose talk" from former Allied captives who had escaped made their way back to German forces.[21] This caused the Germans to "tighten their security measures thereby prejudicing the chances of escape of other Prisoners of War and jeopardizing the lives of those assisting in these escapes."[22] Troops were therefore "forbidden to publish" escape accounts "in any form whatsoever or to communicate with the press, either directly or indirectly."[23] It is interesting to note that these very specific instructions were separate from those that governed the actual activities of reporters during the war. They also were only partly applicable to the regimental newsletters that some units produced and circulated among their own troops, mostly because these publications were typically concerned with noncombat intra-unit activities, such as sports scores, promotions, marriage announcements, and other "trivial" matters that were nevertheless important for troop morale. Although this did not necessarily limit the access of war reporters who were attached to troops, it certainly limited the ability of troops to engage with newspapers on their own terms, something critical for security but also detrimental for all reports on operations where a journalist had not been present. Journalists were rarely attached to reconnaissance regiments, in part because the front-line nature of reconnaissance made it both riskier for noncombatant civilians to tag along and because of the heightened demand for secrecy in reconnaissance operations. As 1944 approached—and with it, the start of combat operations for most Canadian and American troops—these stringent security rules became even more strict. Newspapers with reporters or services in Britain received notice early in January about the need for "utmost care" when reporting even on noncombat circumstances: It was generally known by troops (or at the very least, generally guessed) that the great Allied invasion of the continent would occur sometime that spring or summer, but this information had not yet been released to civilians, and would not be released to civilians until the invasion had actually occurred. The British government and newspapers were "assured" that the American Press Censor would enforce similar reporting restrictions, even going so far as to prevent reports on the continuing arrival of American troops in Britain.[24]

Despite the barriers that impeded the use of authentic photographs and limited access to firsthand informants, official reports from the war's front line were frequent occurrences in the daily papers and served as the main source of information for civilians and soldiers alike (or what had been the front line at the time the article was written). The use of bylines like "somewhere in France" was common, but most North American civilians did not have a sufficiently precise grasp of European geography to note discrepancies between the location of described actions and the then-current location of troops. However, official reports were not immune to errors. For example, the front page of the *New York Times* on 6 June 1944 announced the landing of Allied troops in France, replacing stories about the fall of Rome two days earlier. Despite the landings being the largest amphibious assault ever and the importance of opening a second front (really a third front, considering the ongoing battles in Italy) the article was sparse in detail and contained several significant errors. Most notably the article stated that troops had gone ashore at La Havre and fighting "raged at Caen."[25] Le Havre was almost one hundred kilometers from the actual landing site, and Allied forces would not reach Caen for a month. The *New York Times*, like many newspapers were obliged to do, was quoting "German reports" as the top-secret nature of the invasion meant no details were released until they had already become known to German intelligence.[26] According to Britain's *Evening Despatch*, even Eisenhower's very brief confirmation of the landings did not occur until "German radio stations had been reporting 'the invasion' for upwards of three hours" and German High Command released an official statement "admitting that "the long prepared and expected attack on Western Europe by the enemy began last night." [27] This ensured that no information could be revealed that the German forces did not already have, though it could and did lead to errors in reporting. Errors were sometimes corrected in future releases, especially if they involved a large action such as the landings. The detailed but delayed reports were often the most accurate and could help correct the narrative created by the more error-prone early articles, but not all limited articles were expanded upon in future pieces, meaning small errors and oversights could proliferate in the public zeitgeist. Still, these reports were the best source of information available to the public, and they continue to be critical historical sources, which can lead to the compounding of errors, especially when used without comparing them to official documentation.

In addition to these errors, there were problems of bias, and particularly in the sense of attempting to appeal to a wide audience. Articles tended to focus on large-scale operations, dramatic battles, and famous or infamous individuals and units. Before their deployment in combat, for example, the American 82nd Armored Reconnaissance Battalion had numerous articles written about them because they were assigned to Patton's famous 2nd Armored Division, the so-called "Hell on Wheels" that could "wage [a] small war alone."[28] Further, the 82nd distinguished themselves in early training exercises under Patton's command, leading to coverage of their organization, training, and overall role in gathering information.[29] When the demand for protecting valuable reconnaissance information and personnel finally superseded their rockstar status after deployment, these reports dried up. However, broader reports on the 2nd Division continued through to the end of the war, as a division was often the smallest unit that could be effectively followed through major operations. This meant that although the American public might recall there was an armored recce unit with 2nd Division, that unit was not typically specified in reports on 2nd Division and had not been initially described as a combat unit in the same way infantry and tank units were. Civilians could thus incorrectly assume that reconnaissance troops were not participating significantly in combat activities and were limited to the scouting roles that had been described in 1941 and 1942.

Appealing to the public extended beyond writing about famous units and actions. In general, the public sought reassurance from newspaper reports. Loved ones were thousands of miles away and delays in communication—the result of both limited technology and a drastically overburdened mail system—meant they could be effectively missing for weeks or even months. Without direct communication, families at home relied heavily on official reports for hints about the welfare of their loved ones. Additionally, maintaining morale at home was critical for maintaining support for the war. Newspapers therefore tended to adopt optimistic or reassuring tones and focused heavily on personal valor or calmness in the face of battle (especially when it led to military success) rather than dwelling on difficult conditions. Even delayed reports, with their higher levels of detail, were carefully phrased to minimize reader concerns. This was especially true of articles about reconnaissance units, as leaning into the cheerful tone and the narrative of troops "soldiering on" helped obscure critical details regarding location, equipment, and tactics. A report that appeared in the Montreal paper *The Standard* on 22 July 1944 was emblematic of this practice. Titled "Hussars Probe German Lines: Montreal Recce Regiment Plays Big Role at Caen" and written by Gerald Clark, a war correspondent with *The Standard*, the article was published unusually close to the events it described.[30] The article followed a car from the 7th Canadian Reconnaissance Regiment and covered a series of events that took place between the 7 and 9 July, only two weeks before the article appeared instead of the usual four to six. Several factors contributed to the shortened delay period. The liberation of Caen was a critical success in the Battle of Normandy and included what Clark called "some of the bloodiest fighting since the invasion."[31] It was also a target that had eluded Allied forces for more than a month—initial plans for D-Day included the capture of the town by day's end. And finally, there was no risk in exposing the Canadian positions in the article, as the Germans had been definitively pushed south and east and were no longer in a position that enabled them to make a counterattack on the town. These unique circumstances allowed *The Standard* to reduce the usual delay from four weeks down to two.

Despite alluding to the difficulty of the battle for Caen and the airfield at nearby Carpiquet, Clark did not dwell much on the danger. In fact, the article started by remarking not on the dangers of combat, but on the risk of troopers getting drunk after liberated civilians "climbed all over their armoured car and brought them wine."[32] The article was narrow, following only the four-man crew of a single car lovingly nicknamed "Annabelle." Throughout the article, personal feelings were highlighted, and the dangers of combat were downplayed. "Annabelle had seen quite a bit of the Caen fight and so had the men in her," Clark wrote, "but so far as they were concerned the fighting . . . was a sideshow."[33] While it is true that reconnaissance troops were primarily focused on intelligence gathering, they were heavily involved in combat situations throughout the war, and at times, operational plans explicitly placed reconnaissance in a combat role—a far cry from the "sideshow" that Clark made combat out to be. There was some combat described in the article, but this was again downplayed. Clark reported that Lt. Douglas Johnson "stood up in full view of the German infantrymen" in a machine gun nest as he was attempting to survey the area and then unloaded his Sten gun at them. Johnson "just kept on firing, not feeling any emotion about the Germans who fell from his bullets."[34] Slightly later in the article, Clark described how the carrier driver was wounded in the head by a grenade and "covered with blood" but "as cool as though he'd just been stung by a bee."[35] His emotional state aside, the driver was seriously wounded and later evacuated to England, where he remained in the hospital for several weeks; the real severity of his injury was unmentioned in the article.[36] Clark further downplayed the regiment's role in combat in a section subtitled "Safest Job," in which he quoted one of the troopers as saying, "All we come against is the odd bit of machine-gun fire. . . . Mortars leave us alone. They go for the infantry further back."[37] Although it was true that during the reconnoitering of Carpiquet they encountered mostly machine gun nests, it was incorrect to suggest reconnaissance only experienced limited machine gun or small arms fire—troop accounts, war diaries, and internal reports all make frequent reference to mortars and artillery fire, and particularly emphasized the damage 88mm guns inflicted on armored cars and their crews. One sergeant recalled vividly that an 88mm shell would go "right through a Humber from the front through the driver, the turret through the motor, and out through the back."[38] Recce troops faced more than just the occasional trifling bit of machine-gun fire, but even German machine-gun nests caused Allied reconnaissance casualties. For example, 7th Canadian Reconnaissance Regiment suffered 117 fatal casualties in their eleven months of active service and had approximately four times as many wounded, meaning that roughly 85 percent of the regiment's full-strength War Establishment of seven hundred men became casualties.[39] Similarly, the 29th Armoured Reconnaissance Regiment (The South Alberta Regiment) was slightly smaller and suffered 316 casualties during action.[40] This was a lower casualty rate than many infantry units (infantry regiments frequently had more than 100 percent casualties by the end of the war), but reconnaissance was clearly not as "safe" as Clark presented it.

Clark's article, like many others, was sure to highlight the victorious outcome of the battle. Clark ended with a triumphant description of how the crew were the first Canadians (and potentially first troops overall—it was almost certainly either the 7th or the British Inns of Court Regiment) to reach the center of Caen, "just a few minutes after the Germans had withdrawn."[41] This was corroborated by a delayed article in the *Globe and*

Mail, which reported that "armoured cars of the 17th Duke of York's Canadian Hussars [7th Canadian Reconnaissance Regiment] also shared in the advance on Caen, moving into the city alongside a famous British cavalry regiment."[42] Despite the detail in these reports (especially Clark's, which neatly listed the names and addresses of Annabelle's crew along with the [downplayed] description of their actions), there were still omissions. The commanding officer of the regiment, Lt. Col. T. C. Lewis, was identified only as "a 35-year old Montrealer whose name can't be mentioned for security reasons."[43] There were other more subtle omissions, such as vehicle types and particular tactics—while the article suggests only the single car recce'd Carpiquet and returned with valuable information, the war diary indicates that "one sec[tion] of carriers, one [armored] car patrol and one sec[tion] of assault troops" were involved and covered multiple sectors for the approach.[44] By downplaying the role of the regiment, the danger they were in, and the effort required to actually perform reconnaissance, articles by Clark and other correspondents further reinforced misconceptions about what was required for a successful armored recce patrol. They suggested that strength and combat ability were less than it really was.

At times, the stripped-down reports necessary for maintaining this level of secrecy barely addressed anything beyond a unit's existence, even when that unit was known to the public. One report from September 1944 in the *Lewiston Evening Journal* on the 82nd Armored Reconnaissance Battalion described in clipped tones what the unit had done after the conclusion of the Battle of Normandy. Troops were on patrol "perhaps 25 or 30 miles ahead of the main front."[45] This distance allowed them to cross the "Reich frontier" and assess the state of German forces following their collapse and withdrawal from French territory. These patrols "ranged about in German territory, and then withdrew to the main American position . . . their reconnaissance mission accomplished."[46] Those who wished to know what exactly the reconnaissance mission had been were disappointed. However, it should be noted that this group was largely limited to those with personal connections to reconnaissance regiments, rather than a broad public demand for more detailed reports on armored recce—in part because of the public perception that infantry and tanks conducted the "real" actions that were more exciting to read about. Thus, there was no further description of the patrols or what their mission was; their encounters or engagements with German forces were not mentioned, although it is certain that elements of the 82nd engaged German troops during these and other patrols. Armored reconnaissance, while stealthy to some degree, was simply not as subtle as foot patrols.

Furthermore, standard armored reconnaissance doctrine required troops to test enemy positions by firing directly at their positions. This was not necessarily with the intention of destroying or pushing back an enemy position, but rather for testing the enemy's resolve under fire. Troops that offered strong resistance to a few well-placed test shots from a recce car were much more likely to aggressively hold a position than troops who surrendered, attempted to withdraw, moved into cover, or made only perfunctory responses. This information was key for the allocation of infantry resources in Allied planning.[47] Given the importance of this battle testing, and the amount of territory an armored reconnaissance patrol covered, virtually all patrols ahead of the front experienced combat. There was no way for the *Lewiston Evening Journal* (or other papers) to explain this for their readers—both for reasons of secrecy and because reporters themselves did not understand unless they rode along on specific patrols, like Clark did. Therefore, despite the frequency of combat encounters on armored recce patrols, articles that touched on reconnaissance units rarely addressed combat or even specific objectives at all, limiting the public perception of how much combat they saw.

If we compare reports on reconnaissance actions to those of infantry, the disparity in coverage becomes more apparent. An article written by war correspondent Drew Middleton and published in the *New York Times* on 31 July 1943, titled "Americans and Canadians Gain on a Wide Front in Sicilian Drive," described the situation after the first three weeks of the Sicilian Campaign. The article took pains to situate both the Americans and Canadians in their geographical context, while also explaining why that geography was important. American troops had "driven the northern flank of the German line in Sicily back into the mountains northwest of Troina" as part of "one of the most astonishing sustained advances of the war."[48] This pushed the Germans "back onto the main Axis lines of communication" while the Canadians were "striking toward the towns and supply bases that feed the stubborn German lines in front of Catania."[49] It was easy to infer what the infantry was trying to do—collapse communications and supply lines and reduce opposition at Catania—unlike reconnaissance, which merely "ranged about . . . and then withdrew" when their unknown objectives were completed.[50] During the advance, "little groups of infantry stole out to harass the enemy and smash up advance positions in dozens of encounters."[51] These skirmishes were very similar to those experienced by the 7th Recce when they reconnoitered Carpiquet and by recce units generally when on patrol, but Middleton acknowledged that they were occurring constantly out ahead of the front for the infantry, while Clark did not—despite reconnaissance being, by its nature, ahead of the front. The article also clearly explained infantry operations and objectives: The Germans who had been driven from Nicosia were falling back to an "extremely strong defensive position in the mountains" under pressure from the Americans, but this mountain position was threatened by a "general breakup in the center of their line, which was pierced yesterday by the Canadians when they captured Agira."[52] The article then went on to describe the series of objectives for totally breaking the line and pushing the Germans off Sicily. Perhaps the biggest difference between articles on the infantry as opposed to reconnaissance was the tone. Middleton's article leaves the overriding sense that combat was occurring constantly or near constantly and was achieving objectives, whereas articles on reconnaissance went out of their way to minimize combat. The American infantry was described as "fighting for the high ground with the support of their deadly 'Long Tom cannon'" and had "scored gains on a forty-mile front."[53] The Germans withdrew under pressure from infantry and "under the lash of American shellfire and Allied bombers and fighter-bombers."[54] Meanwhile, the Canadian infantry "directly menace[d] Regalbuto" but were "meeting with the sternest kind of opposition. . . . The Germans [were] fighting and dying with great bravery."[55] Reading Middleton's article, it is easy to visualize combat. While that visualization may have been inaccurate, it was at least present—unlike in reconnaissance articles, despite reconnaissance participating in both small- and large-scale combat operations.

It was not just reports on big battles that minimized reconnaissance actions. The disparity between the lived experiences of reconnaissance troops and what was reported is perhaps nowhere more evident than in the articles discussing the 8th Canadian Reconnaissance Regiment's Major David Vivian Currie. Currie became the seventh Canadian of the war to win the Victoria Cross and was the only Canadian in an armored unit to win one during the war. Currie received the award for his leadership during seventy-two hours of intense fighting to help close the Falaise Gap and cut off a critical escape route for German troops. *The Times* ran a small article on 27 November 1944 titled "Canadian Major Wins V.C." with two subheadings to highlight the critical points: "Gallant Leadership in Normandy" and "Troops Inspired."[56] The article, published more than three months after the actions that won Currie the Victoria Cross, was still brief (only six paragraphs) and lacked context, while also omitting details found in the after-action report and the citation for the award. The much longer article that ran the same day in the *Sun Times*, published in Currie's hometown of Owen Sound, Ontario, devoted two paragraphs to describing Currie's actions. The rest of the article discussed his education and peacetime work ("automobile mechanic and welder"), the two other Owen Sounders to win the Victoria Cross (including First World War flying ace William "Billy" Bishop), and how Currie's wife was "thrilled" by the news of his award.[57] American news reports on Currie were succinct. The *New York Times* article was similar to the Canadian reports, although without the background material on Currie's home life.[58] The only newspaper to carry a fuller summation of Currie's actions was the *Manchester Guardian*, which was not likely to make it into the hands of Canadian and American civilians at home.[59] When King George VI presented the award, newspapers also neglected to describe Currie's actions. They were far more interested in the fact that he arrived in "tankman's overalls over his battledress" as he had been rushed by "motor torpedo-boat and express train" from the battlefields of Holland for the ceremony.[60] One article also noted he was "three-quarters of an hour late" and arrived partway through the awards ceremony.[61] Much more ink was spent musing about Currie's race to the ceremony and his informal dress than his time in combat. Despite the interest Currie generated because of his combat capabilities, very little about his combat experience could be gleaned.

Nor was this attitude limited to Canadian reconnaissance troops. American 2nd Lt. Gerry H. Kisters won the Medal of Honor while serving with the 91st Reconnaissance Squadron in Sicily. Kisters single-handedly captured a machine gun post, despite "suffering five wounds" in the attempt.[62] Despite the fact that Kisters was the holder of both a Medal of Honor and a Distinguished Service Cross—the first American, in fact, to achieve this, according to the *New York Times*—there was no more space devoted to his actions than in the articles about Currie. Kisters's actions were summarized in a paragraph, half of which was devoted to his previous DSC award. When he returned home to Indiana, articles appeared about how he was received by thousands "despite the 12-above-zero weather" and the gifts he and his wife were given (including a "pre-war smoked ham"), in addition to his honorary acceptance by several prominent clubs.[63] Almost as an afterthought, it was mentioned he had earned a Medal of Honor and a DSC, with no other details about his combat service. An article on fellow Medal of Honor winner Lieutenant David C. Waybur similarly failed to explain recce combat. Waybur also won his Medal of Honor in Sicily, while serving with the 3rd Reconnaissance Troop. A picture of Waybur receiving his medal was accompanied by a few sentences on his "brilliant heroism" when he "held off three enemy tanks attacking his reconnaissance platoon and destroyed a fourth while seriously wounded."[64]

All articles about reconnaissance troop awardees were equally succinct, offering only a brief overview of the actions that won the award and not situating them in the broader war context. Readers again had little access to real representations of reconnaissance forces in combat; none of the articles on recce troops who had distinguished themselves presented readers with an understanding of the work recce forces engaged in, creating a gap in public perceptions of combat, but they were not meant to explain combat to civilians.[65] They were meant only to highlight exceptional individuals in a titanic struggle and give a face to valor and heroism, not to explain the actual inner workings of war, and the brief articles served their purpose well. The descriptions of reconnaissance troops in combat were tiny compared to representations of infantry and tank combat—the reports detailing large actions often provided some detailed description of operations, easier to do when following large units such as brigades and divisions, as opposed to single regiments or even smaller reconnaissance Squadrons—further stymieing the public perception of reconnaissance troops as a combat force.

Ultimately, a combination of factors prevented the public at home from critically engaging with the lived experience of armored reconnaissance operations. Limited technology prevented the transmission of video footage of the front. The alternatives, newsreels and newspaper photographs, were edited or staged, minimizing danger and emphasizing the optimism and superiority of Allied troops. Lacking any real visualization of North African and European battlefields, citizens turned to the written word.[66] Letters offered personal insights, but they were limited in scope and information. That left newspapers, which were prone to errors, censorship, and security laws. To balance information and secrecy, newspapers held back detail, which meant more timely reports had few specifics on combat operations and included errors. Reconnaissance suffered most strongly from this as they were by the nature of their role most likely to be engaged in forward operations that had to maintain strict secrecy. As a result of these factors, the public was rarely exposed to narratives of reconnaissance regiments engaging in combat, and even more rarely exposed to images thereof. The public was informed of general combat operations in detail, but these were much larger in scope, such as the liberation of Caen or the routing of enemy formations in Sicily. These operations, although often the result of information gathered by reconnaissance units, featured mostly infantry and tank regiments, and omitted the reconnaissance men's role. Even reconnaissance troops who engaged in exceptional actions and won awards for gallantry received little attention, further minimizing their role in combat. By the end of the war, therefore, citizens had a good grasp of combat scenarios but lacked an understanding of the role of reconnaissance. This has contributed to a narrative of the limited role of reconnaissance units in the Second World War.[67] The prevailing understanding of reconnaissance remains one limited to scouting. Reconnaissance is not the only branch of the armed forces to have experienced this—many supporting units, such as artillery, signals, and sappers, have also been chronically overlooked despite their vital roles in the field, in no small part due to their limited exposure to the public. It is critical we continue to seek more information about these roles and the individuals in them, as we cannot truly assess the efficiency of armies in the field unless we understand all the units that contributed to their overall successes—or failures. Virtually all the large land operations of the Second World War involved reconnaissance troops in some way, and their participation was vital to Allied successes, but until we address their role, we cannot truly understand why the war unfolded as it did. Although classic infantry and armored units have dominated understandings of combat in the public zeitgeist, new data can introduce new narratives and expand understanding about the importance of supporting units in the ultimate Allied victory.

Notes

1. Chapter 9 in this volume by Elena Friot also considers the way that newspaper articles shaped public perceptions of the war, focusing on examples of newspaper coverage of American experiences in Bataan and Corregidor.

2. Claire Cookson-Hills documents similar issues with letters sent home from the front in chapter 8 of this volume .

3. Brian P. D. Hannon, "Creating the Correspondent: How the BBC Reached the Front Line in the Second World War," *Historical Journal of Film, Radio, and Television* 28, no. 2 (June 2008): 176.

4. Robert Morgan and Ron Powers, *The Man Who Flew the Memphis Belle: Memoir of a WWII Pilot* (New York: Dutton Caliber, 2001), 375.

5. Morgan and Powers, *The Man Who Flew the Memphis Belle*, 177–80.

6. *War Report* and other programs/publications did not typically use embedded reporters (reporters attached to specific military units). Most recce actions were reported by general war correspondents, and although these war correspondents were sometimes temporarily embedded for ride-alongs, none were permanently attached to recce.

7. Desmond Hawkins, ed., *BBC War Report: From D-Day to Berlin as It Happened*, 3rd ed. (London: BBC Books, 2019), 83.

8. Hawkins, *BBC War Report*, 384.

9. "Invasion Started Tuesday," *Claresholm Local Press*, 8 June 1944.

10. George Byron Koch, "An Old Sailor Confesses," *Wall Street Journal*, 14 August 1996.

11. "Road to Holland," *The Standard*, n.d., October 1944.

12. Prue Torney-Parlicki, "'Grave Security Obligations': The Australian Government's Refusal to Accredit Newspaper Photographers to Combat Areas during the Second World War," *War and Society* 16, no. 1 (May 1998): 105–6.

13. Torney-Parlicki, "Grave Security Obligations," 107–8.

14. Martyn Jolly, "Composite Propaganda Photographs during the First World War," *History of Photography* 27, no. 2 (2003): 155.

15. Sarah Klotz, "Shooting the War: The Canadian Army Film Unit in the Second World War," *Canadian Military History* 14, no. 3 (2005): 26.

16. The raid occurred in 1942; the 2nd CID did not reenter combat until July 1944, having lost approximately half its operational strength and requiring over eighteen months of rebuilding before it could even resume training.

17. Klotz, "Shooting the War," 25.

18. Lt.-Col. F. A. Vokes, *Part I Orders*, 28 October 1943, RG24-C-3, volume 14224, file 501, reel T-12687, Department of National Defence Fonds, LAC.

19. Vokes, *Part I Orders*.

20. Vokes, *Part I Orders*.

21. Major M. H. Wright, *29 Canadian Armoured Regiment (S.ALTA.R.) DAILY ORDERS PART I*, 29 July 1942, RG24-C-#, volume 14292, file 933, reel T-12766, Department of National Defence Fonds, LAC.

22. Wright, *DAILY ORDERS PART I*.

23. Wright, *DAILY ORDERS PART I*.

24. Siân Nicholas, "The British Press and D-Day: Reporting the Launch of the Second Front, 6 June 1944," *Media History* 23, no. 3–4 (September 2017): 493.

25. "Allied Armies Land in France in the Havre-Cherbourg Area; Great Invasion Is Under Way," *New York Times*, 6 June 1944, in *The New York Times Front Pages: 1851–2013* (New York: Black Dog & Leventhal, 2013), 187.

26. "Allied Armies Land in France in the Havre-Cherbourg Area," *New York Times*.

27. The confirmation message read only "Under the command of Gen. Eisenhower, Allied naval forces, supported by strong air forces, began landing Allied armies this morning on the northern coast of France." "Invasion Going Well: Tanks Ashore; Allies Have Foothold: Slashing Inland All to Plan—and What a Plan," *Evening Despatch*, 6 June 1944.

28. "Panzer Unit 'Little Army' Is Complete: 2nd Armored Division Can Wage Small War Alone," *Town Talk*, 25 July 1941.

29. During the Carolina Maneuvers, the 82nd identified the "enemy" commander and captured him in the opening ninety minutes of an exercise meant to last up to a week. This remarkable success directly contributed to the

commander in question, Lt. Gen. Hugh A. Drum, being passed over for field command.

30. Gerald Clark, "Hussars Probe German Lines: Montreal Recce Regiment Plays Big Role at Caen," *The Standard*, 22 July 1944.

31. Clark, "Hussars Probe German Lines."

32. Clark, "Hussars Probe German Lines."

33. Clark, "Hussars Probe German Lines."

34. Clark, "Hussars Probe German Lines."

35. Clark, "Hussars Probe German Lines."

36. "July Troop Return," *War Diary of 7 Canadian Reconnaissance Regiment (17 D.Y.R.C.H.), June–September 1944,* Textual Records, RG 24-C-3, volume 14217, microfilm reel T-12660, The Department of National Defence Fonds, LAC: 12–22.

37. Clark, "Hussars Probe German Lines."

38. Sergeant John F. McGowan, interviewed by author, London, ON, June 2012. Transcript.

39. Capt. Walter G. Pavey, *An Historical Account of the 7th Canadian Reconnaissance Regiment (17th Duke of York's Royal Canadian Hussars) in the World War 1939–1945* (Montreal: Harpell's Press, 1948), 138–39.

40. Donald E. Graves, *South Albertas: A Canadian Regiment at War,* 2nd ed. (Toronto: Robin Brass Studio, 2004), 11.

41. Clark, "Hussars Probe German Lines."

42. "Eisenhower Says Canadians Broke Strongest Lines," *Globe and Mail*, 31 August 1944.

43. Clark, "Hussars Probe German Lines."

44. *Cdn Inf Div report on employment & equipment of 7 Cdn Recce Regt*, Textual Records, vol. 235C3.043 (D1), file 17 D.Y.R.C.H., The Department of National Defence Fonds, LAC: 1.

45. "France, Cont. from Pg. 1," London – (AP), *Lewiston Evening Journal*, 6 September 1944.

46. "France, Cont. from Pg. 1."

47. According to the *Cdn Inf Div report on employment & equipment of 7 Cdn Recce Regt*, for example, the reconnoitering of Carpiquet and testing the enemy in this way resulted in adding an additional infantry regiment to the attack on the airfields, as the Germans were highly aggressive in response to Canadian test-shooting. Even with the additional infantry regiment, troops had a difficult time clearing the airfield and would have been much harder pressed if the original plan had been used, an example of successfully adapting a plan based on reconnaissance patrols.

48. Drew Middleton, "Americans and Canadians Gain on a Wide Front in Sicilian Drive," *New York Times*, 31 July 1943.

49. Middleton, "Americans and Canadians Gain on a Wide Front in Sicilian Drive."

50. "France, Cont. from Pg. 1."

51. Middleton, "Americans and Canadians Gain on a Wide Front in Sicilian Drive."

52. Middleton, "Americans and Canadians Gain on a Wide Front in Sicilian Drive."

53. Middleton, "Americans and Canadians Gain on a Wide Front in Sicilian Drive."

54. Middleton, "Americans and Canadians Gain on a Wide Front in Sicilian Drive."

55. Middleton, "Americans and Canadians Gain on a Wide Front in Sicilian Drive."

56. "Canadian Major Wins V.C.," *The Times*, 27 November 1944.

57. "Major Wins V.C.," *Sun Times*, 27 November 1944.

58. "CANADIAN HERO HONORED: Major Currie Gets Victoria Cross for Stand in France," *New York Times*, 27 November 1944.

59. "CANADIAN MAJOR'S V.C.: 'Inspired Leadership,'" *Manchester Guardian*, 27 November 1944.

60. "VC's Race to the Palace," *London Times*, 20 December 1944.

61. "Currie Arrives at Buckingham in Overalls," *Globe and Mail*, 20 December 1944.

62. "PRESIDENT HONORS 2 COMBAT HEROES: He Awards the Congressional Medal of Honor for Munda and Mediterranean Feat," *New York Times*, 9 February 1944.

63. "INDIANA HOME TOWN WELCOMES WAR HERO: Bloomington Turns Out to Honor Lieut. G. H. Kisters," *New York Times*, 13 February 1944.

64. "HARD FIGHTING BRINGS HIGH HONOR," *New York Times*, 3 December 1943.

65. In chapter 8 in this volume, Claire Cookson-Hills documents another example of how unreported actions that would have harmed the image of Canadian soldiers contributed to the heroization of soldiers.

66. Americans seeking to learn about battles and make sense of defeat in the Pacific also turned to newspapers and magazines, according to Elena Friot in chapter 9 in this volume.

67. For example, Mark Zuehlke's *Breakout from Juno: First Canadian Army in the Normandy Campaign* (Vancouver: Douglas & McIntyre, 2012) typically only notes when reconnaissance forces were attached to larger Canadian formations and does not address their actual role in combat despite their key role in the liberation of Caen and in closing the Falaise Pocket; additionally, it ascribes a report on a series of difficulties involving running out of ammunition at the front to an infantry regiment, rather than 7th Reconnaissance Regiment, despite the report being exclusively about reconnaissance actions.

8

"Everything We Can Lay Hands On"
Canadian Soldiers and Sexual Violence in Germany in 1945

Claire Cookson-Hills

Private Ambrose Abbott was a "quiet and unassuming" soldier in the Lorne Scottish Regiment of the Second World War Canadian Army.[1] At the time of his arrest for rape he had been in minimal disciplinary trouble with the Canadian Army: breaking out of barracks twice and absent without leave twice.[2] In May 1945 when his regiment was billeted in Oldenburg, Germany, Abbott was thirty-one, sober, and married with a wife and young child. Yet on the nights of 4 and 10 May 1945, Abbott raped three German women. He then stood guard while his comrade Signalman Jack McGill raped the same women and a fourth.

This chapter aims to interpret the sexual violence enacted by these two Canadian soldiers in May 1945. Abbott and McGill were bit players in the military actions of the Canadian army at the very end of the war, and the sexual violence they perpetrated was also part of a larger wave of violence that targeted German civilians and their possessions. The trials that resulted from their actions were similarly part of a wider crackdown on sexual violence by the Canadian military. Overall, their trial transcripts demonstrate that their violence was representative of the types of humiliation and pain that some German women endured at the hands of Canadian soldiers. As such, this chapter is both a critical exploration of the actions of two men, and an attempt to understand how they came to take those actions. The motivations offered by Abbott and McGill are interrogated and placed in the wider contexts of their situation and the war.

The primary sources for this chapter are Second World War Canadian Army documents, which must be treated with suspicion and read against the grain. The details of Abbott's and McGill's crimes are derived from the transcripts of their trials. The soldiers and civilians provided distinct but complementary narratives of these crimes. Although the Canadian soldiers and German civilians told their stories (in the trial transcripts and the censorship reports, specifically), the trial transcripts represented heavily self-edited accounts of their actions. Aware of the possibilities of severe military consequences and operating within the legal confines of examination and cross-examination, the soldiers presented their actions in terms most favorable to their interests.[3] Similarly, the military justice system was not kind to the German civilians who reported the rapes, and their motivations for coming forward must remain shrouded. Indeed, historian Miriam Gebhardt has stressed that Germans who admitted to being raped by Western Allied soldiers could suffer social isolation for "fraternizing" with the enemy.[4] However, Gebhardt emphasizes that German women reported rapes to Western Allied police because they were afraid of being branded either a traitor or a prostitute otherwise.[5] Civilian testimonies before the courts were heard in translation, but their written statements in German were recorded and included in the court transcripts. This chapter also relies on courts martial abstracts, censorship reports, regimental war diaries, and orders to fill in the wider context of the Canadian army in early 1945. Although the soldiers were more open in their personal letters, they knew that those letters would be opened and read by military censors.[6] Furthermore, as Alison Twells and other scholars have convincingly argued, the process of letter writing emphasized some aspects of the author and de-emphasized others (such as a son's desire to not worry his mother).[7]

Canadian military data reveal about sixty-five courts martial for sexual violence against German women in 1945, although that number is an estimate, and an underestimate, of the number of crimes that actually occurred.[8] Most incidents of sexual violence were never reported to military police, and in every other country including France, most reported incidents did not result in a court martial. However, in Germany, a nonfraternization policy mandated that all the reported incidents of sexual violence should go to trial. Due to the Covid-19 pandemic restrictions (2020–2022), the undigitized provost (military police) war diaries were inaccessible for this research, and without access to the provost war diaries (the provosts may not have been recording sexual violence) there is no way to check this statistic. However, in a similar time frame in the Italian island province of Sicily, the official historian reported at least seven rapes, but none of these were prosecuted; all this chapter can say is that the actual incidence of sexual violence was probably much higher than reported.

In this chapter, the term sexual violence is defined broadly as the *charges* brought against soldiers for rape, attempted rape, indecent assault, and sexual misconduct in formal Field General Courts Martial—these were hastily assembled courts (often within weeks of the date of offense). Overall, sixty-five courts martial are insignificant, especially when compared to the estimates that from 1.4 to 1.9 million civilians were raped during the conquest of Germany, mostly by Soviet soldiers pushing westward.[9] However, the fact that *Canadian* soldiers perpetrated sexual violence during the Second World War is still very rarely discussed in the Canadian historiography.[10] As Atina Grossman wrote almost thirty years ago, the question of silence is still "that of the historian trying to tell the story."[11] Canadian historians, especially Matthew Barrett, have discussed aspects of Canada's Second World War military legal history, including execution and desertion of soldiers, and courts martial for officers, but only one published book chapter (written by this author) has focused on sexual violence committed by Canadian soldiers.[12] Discussing the war from a wider perspective, excellent scholarship is now emerging about the widespread sexual violence perpetrated by German soldiers in conquered territories in Eastern Europe, as well as the sexual violence perpetrated during the Holocaust.[13] Critically, these histories reveal "typical pattern[s]" within the violence, to borrow a phrase from J. Robert Lilly's pioneering work on the sexual violence of American GIs in the Second World War.[14] Discussing how sexual violence was policy in the *Wehrmacht*, Regina Mühlhäuser has argued that the German military created a liminal space for "sexual violence by not prosecuting offenders."[15] Mühlhäuser is echoed by other historians who highlight the public and vengeful nature of the German army's sexual violence and their attempts to induce population-wide terror through sexual violence against Soviet and Eastern European civilians.[16]

The Canadians in Germany, although a small part of the 21st Army Group (just 50,000 soldiers), created their own "patterns" of violence, although those patterns were roughly in common with other Allied soldiers in Germany. Operating under a strict nonfraternization order, the Canadians were subject to severe military punishment if their sexual transgressions were discovered or reported. Military courts were often highly successful in prosecuting the soldiers because sexual misconduct could usually be proven even if the court was skeptical of the exact nature of the sexual interactions. Broadly speaking, Canadian soldiers gained access to German homes using the pretense of searching for weapons, and they usually carried out the sexual violence in private rooms with another soldier or soldiers standing guard nearby. Canadian soldiers were rarely sober when they conducted these searches, or they became drunk while performing them, and they often stole or left small items.[17] American soldiers seem to have enacted similar types of violent behavior. For instance, Lilly documented drunken American soldiers brandishing weapons and then gang-raping German women.[18] Within this historiography, focusing on a single case facilitates analysis of the aforementioned patterns of sexual violence, and highlights the ways in which Abbott and McGill acted individually even as part of a larger group perpetrating similar behavior.

This chapter focuses on Pte Ambrose Abbott, placing Abbott's actions in their historical context. This allows for a detailed explanation of the tactical and environmental conditions, the legal situation in which Abbott found himself, the details of Abbott's actions, and the implications surrounding the presence of his comrade McGill. Overall, these individual instances of sexual violence are broadly consistent with the motivations for other acts of sexual violence by Allied soldiers in the weeks before the end of the war, especially 24 April to 5 May 1945.[19] Canadian soldiers opportunistically plundered, humiliated, and exacted revenge on their enemy's civilian population, while their officers and high command seemed reluctant to punish these transgressions.[20] Indeed, the title of this article is borrowed from a censorship report highlighting the plunder and vengeance that Canadian soldiers exacted and their excitement at being able to do so. However, as with every case study, Abbott's actions and testimony both reinforced and undercut such generalized motivations; he was looking to rape German women and had the means and the opportunity to forcibly do so. To examine these acts of sexual violence, this chapter first reconstructs the details of Abbott's crimes, then analyzes the overlapping contexts (environmental, legal, personal, camaraderie) of Canadian soldiers in Germany in 1945.

Abbott's Case: Details

On Friday, 4 May 1945, at 9:30pm, two Canadian soldiers came to the house of E.K. (victim identities anonymous) where she lived with her mother and father in Oldenburg.[21] That evening, her aunt and young cousin were visiting, and all the family was herded into their kitchen. Although the whole family agreed that the Canadians had come to search for guns and German soldiers, E.K.'s mother remembered that they were specifically "looking for German soldiers who had shot their comrade."[22] E.K. testified that the family was very worried that the Canadians would shoot them all because the soldiers found a picture of E.K.'s brother in his uniform. In the words of Abbott himself, when he and McGill entered the house, they saw "a tall good-looking girl."[23] After searching the house for weapons, Abbott took her into the living room, indicated that she should take off her clothing, forced her down on a couch, and raped her. Afterward, he said in German, "Kamerad auch!"

(Comrade also), and although she pleaded against it, he forced her back into the kitchen, put a gun to her father's head, and handed her to McGill.[24] In a written statement taken before the trial, Abbott testified that although he had communicated to her that he would ask McGill not to rape her, he did not appeal to McGill, because, "it would not have stopped him."[25] McGill then raped her in the living room while Abbott held the family at gunpoint.[26] Abbott may have watched the family to prevent them from trying to help E.K., or to stop someone from getting aid (not from the police but possibly other Canadian soldiers or the provosts), or possibly just to leave a terrible situation—these motivations were not explained during the trial, but the other Germans did try to stop the Canadian soldiers.[27] Before and after the rapes, Abbott and McGill offered cigarettes to the family and stole a pair of silk stockings.[28] When they left the house, Abbott and McGill left a bar of chocolate on the kitchen table.[29]

On Thursday, 10 May 1945, Abbott and McGill again searched German homes, ostensibly for guns and soldiers. Calling out in German, "Polizei," they entered a house with multiple apartments and herded two of the women they found there into Frau M.D.'s kitchen. The soldiers, when going through the apartment building, ordered an elderly couple to stay in their beds, the parents of a young widow, E.S.[30] E.S. was then taken into the neighbor's bedroom and raped first by Abbott and then by McGill. E.S. was terrified of Abbott's pistol but struggled to the point of bruising and cried throughout.[31] She was then locked into her apartment. Abbott next raped another woman in the house, Frau M.D. However, by his admission, he thought she was a "whore" because she did not resist his instructions as soon as he had placed the pistol beside him in the bed and his knife on the bedside table.[32] His characterization of M.D. as a prostitute may explain why he raped her four times, including oral rape. Afterward Abbott felt comfortable enough to sit on her bed and, according to M.D.'s testimony, he "took a picture of his wife in Canada out of his pocket and showed it to me. He asked me where my husband was."[33] McGill then went to M.D. and raped her orally as well as vaginally. Once M.D. had left her bedroom and freed E.S., she went back into the kitchen and discovered that a family pocket watch had been exchanged for a cheaper one, two items were missing, and E.S.'s father's bicycle was missing.[34] McGill was later convicted of the theft of the bicycle.[35] The soldiers offered the women cigarettes, left behind a box with a "cheap brooch," and wished them goodnight before leaving.[36] Abbot and McGill then went to another house, where McGill raped a fourth woman, A.H., while Abbott guarded the other occupants.

Analysis

The court martial files of Abbott and McGill demonstrate similarities with other Canadian courts martial for rape in Germany and some key differences. To clarify these differences, this section has been broken into four parts: environmental and tactical analysis, legal and procedural analysis, individual analysis, and an analysis of the function of camaraderie. The environmental and tactical analysis focuses on the locations and days of the rape, and knowledge of the presence of a harsh nonfraternization order. Abbott's case has commonalities with other courts martial with respect to how the courts martial dealt with sexual violence (the charges brought against Abbott, the evidence they prioritized, and the execution of military justice). Some specifics of Abbott's offenses are similar to those of other Canadian soldiers who were court martialed for sexual violence in Germany: offering trinkets, conversing with the women, stealing household goods. Finally, the supporting and co-criminal presence of his "buddy" McGill indicates (and is representative of) the kinds of camaraderie that the Canadian soldiers were building among themselves.

Environmental and Tactical Analysis

This brief section will focus on Privates Abbott's and McGill's actions in the environmental context of the way they experienced the end of the war. Abbott was a non-commissioned member (NCM) of the Lorne Scottish Regiment, part of the 2nd Canadian Infantry Division, itself part of the First Canadian Army in Northwest Europe. McGill was a signalman in the same Division. Canada's 2nd Division ended its war in Lower Saxony in the northwest of Germany, with the Dutch border to the southwest, and Hamburg to the northeast. Abbott's and McGill's actions, as mentioned above, took place on two different days (Friday 4 May and Thursday 10 May). However, the fact that Abbott and McGill raped German women on 4 May was part of a larger wave of attacks and crimes: of the sixty-five soldiers court martialed for sexual contact with German women in 1945, nineteen were for acts committed on either 4 or 5 May 1945. On that weekend, the last weekend of the war, Canadian troops ended up in a series of towns that were relatively unscathed by combat but that provided poor billeting conditions, were not off-limits to them, and were full of internally displaced German civilians and other Europeans.

Oldenburg was a town that had not felt much of the war directly. About 1 percent of the civilian infrastructure had been bombed, although nearby barracks and factories were destroyed. As a region, Lower Saxony was predominantly rural, with comparatively low levels of industry and high unemployment, although nearby industrial towns such as Wilhelmshaven were badly bombed during the war.[37] Oldenburg appeared in only one potential list of targets for Allied aerial bombardment during the Second World War: as a specifically non-strategic target in retribution for the V-1 rocket attacks on London.[38] The town was therefore a hub for refugees and internally displaced persons (IDPs), but also one where conquering soldiers were billeted with civilians. On 4–5 May, soldiers from the 2nd Division were billeted in German homes within the city limits.[39] They were, therefore, in very close physical proximity to the civilians with whom they were technically still at war. Private Charles Gladue, for instance, was court martialed for sexual misconduct on 5 May with a woman called M.P., an IDP with four children. Gladue had been billeted in the same house as M.P., although his commanding officer testified that the soldier hated Germans, had requested to be billeted elsewhere, and the officer had requested that some of his troops (including Gladue) be moved because the house was overcrowded.[40] In the case of Abbott and McGill, McGill testified that they "looked through [one] house, more or less to see how the people lived."[41] They could enter homes on the pretense or with the legitimate purpose of searching for weapons; at least one other soldier also raped civilians while allegedly searching for weapons.[42] McGill and Abbott seem to have targeted the Germans in such homes, and in this, they were not alone. When Privates Paul Patterson and Malcolm Leonard went into a German home in March 1945, they raped the German women there, *not* the eleven non-German refugees who were also living in the house.[43]

Other environmental factors were at play when Abbott and McGill were pillaging. First, 4 and 5 May were a Friday and Saturday and the last weekend of the war in Europe. Soldiers may have suspected that the war was ending and may have suspected that any command (or perceived) leniency would end with the end of hostilities.[44] The weather in Oldenburg was, in the words of the Calgary Highlanders' War Diarist "unsettled with heavy rain at night."[45] However, soldiers are not usually granted the luxury of taking weekends off while on campaign, and it appears that three different things happened to the Canadian soldiers in the First Canadian Army on 4–5 May. First, the 3rd Division had ended its drive into Germany by 2 May, and its soldiers were billeted around Leer, west of Oldenburg. At the end of a long, hard-fought campaign, nine soldiers from the 3rd Division were charged with offenses committed during the weekend of 4–5 May. Second, on 4 May, the 4th Canadian (Armored) Division ended its drive in Bad Zwischenahn (23 April–4 May 1945), a final offensive which cost the Canadian 10th Brigade hundreds of casualties; the town was almost twelve and a half miles away from Oldenburg. Upon arriving at Bad Zwischenahn's outskirts on 30 April, Divisional Commander Christopher Vokes declared the town off-limits. On 4 May, it was designated the 4th Division's headquarters—the "cooling-off" period had ended.[46] There, only Gunner MacKenzie from 4th Division was court martialed for sexual violence, and that on 4 May; no other soldiers from 4th Division were charged with sexual violence between 30 April and 5 May. In contrast to Vokes's order, Oldenburg, where the 2nd Canadian Infantry Division ended their drive on 5 May, was never declared off-limits. The remaining nine courts martial from 4–5 May were from 2nd Division in Oldenburg, including, of course, those for Abbott and McGill.

Abbott's and McGill's second acts of rape took place on May 10, notably during their first free period after the German surrender. As the Lorne Scots War diary reported laconically, the weather on 10 May was "clear and warm."[47] Only three other soldiers were court martialed for sexual violence between 6 and 10 May 1945. Multiple potential reasons could contribute to this stark difference, including poorer weather, more work as the units were integrated into the Army of Occupation, more appropriate billeting conditions, more command oversight, and a better sense of the consequences of sexual violence for soldiers who committed it. Alternatively, the soldiers might have been less inclined toward violence against a population that had surrendered. Although speculation, this fits the lack of courts martial into the cognitive reframing and subsequent narrative shift from Germans as villains to Germans as victims, as documented by Petra Goedde.[48] The German women may also have been less inclined to report rape at the hands of occupiers who might be part of their lives and in authority over them for the long term (Canadian troops occupied Lower Saxony until mid-1946). Pillaging Canadians on May 4–5 might also have been part of a crackdown on sexual violence, and provosts might have been unwilling to prosecute sexual violence as aggressively after the official end of hostilities on 5 May. As outlined by Andrew Ritchie, the provosts' historian, the provosts themselves felt that their most important tasks in Germany were handling traffic (especially during battle in March and April) and dealing with former Eastern European forced laborers and German prisoners of war.[49]

Procedural and Legal Analysis

The purpose of military justice is the maintenance of good order and discipline, and the emphasis of that justice was different in Germany than the other campaigns in Northwestern Europe. In contrast to the other Northwest European campaigns from 1944 to 1945, when the Canadian troops occupied northern Germany, they were under strict nonfraternization orders. The order is worth quoting at some length to indicate the strong language used:

> Non-fraternization means having nothing whatever to do with German people except the minimum contact required for the execution of military duty. . . . Sexual intercourse with German women is a flagrant breach of the "non-fraternization" directive *and will always be dealt with by courts martial*. Due to propaganda, German women may be in fear of Allied soldiers and may consent to intercourse through fear of the consequences of refusal. Where consent to intercourse results from fear the crime of rape is committed.[50]

The purpose of this order was to stop troops in the British army from sympathizing with German civilians and to keep interaction to a minimum. The harsh nonfraternization policy was enacted by the Supreme Headquarters Allied Expeditionary Force (SHAEF)—both the American and French zones of occupation used similar nonfraternization policies (i.e., policies that prevented informal contact with German civilians) until at least July 1945.[51] When German women reported rape at the hands of Canadian soldiers, the JAG officers were always compelled to take sexual contact to court martial, rather than allowing the discipline to be handled by the unit. Internal unit discipline meant a variety of field punishments, and a line on the soldier's individual file; for most Second World War Canadian soldiers, these files are not yet publicly available. As a side effect, the nonfraternization order made rape an issue of military *discipline* and allows the historian to observe the only instance of widespread prosecution of sexual violence in the war. After a German woman reported her rape, the JAG had very high probability of successfully prosecuting rape, or at least a breach of the fraternization orders. In Germany all fifty-two soldiers who were charged with rape (Army Act 41, hereafter referred to as AA41) were also charged with breaching the nonfraternization orders (Army Act 40, hereafter referred to as AA40). Of the sixty-five known trials for reported sexual contact in Germany in 1945, 86 percent ended in conviction (fifty-six out of sixty-five).[52] To put these statistics into perspective, Karen Dubinsky's analysis of Canadian civilian sexual violence placed rates of conviction from 28 percent (assaults on first dates) to 68 percent (assaults by strangers). British civil law, from which Canadian civilian law was drawn, placed a heavy burden of proof on women accusers, who had to prove that they were not falsely accusing their rapists.[53]

The charges that were brought against Abbott were also similar to those in other Canadian soldiers' trials. Abbott was charged with rape, specifically, "carnal knowledge of a woman without her consent" and "conduct to the prejudice of good order and discipline, that is to say fraternized with M.D. not his wife." The charge specifying "M.D. [was] not his wife" does not indicate adultery, but nods to the fact that sexual violence within marriage was not recognized in the legal system, and that Canadian soldiers could not marry German women. Key to his successful prosecution was the fact that Abbott was charged six times—under two different British military legal codes (AA41 and AA40). Abbot was charged for both rape (AA41) against M.D., E.S., and E.F., and "conduct to the prejudice" (hereafter referred to as sexual misconduct) for breaching the nonfraternization orders. The existence of AA41 in a code of military law was a recognition that sometimes soldiers committed acts that were also crimes in civil legal codes. British military codes for AA41 included a wide range of so-called "civil crimes" including traffic violations, forgery, robbery, common assault, rape and attempted rape, sexual contact with children, and even manslaughter and murder. During the Second World War, AA41 was a relatively uncommon accusation: of the approximately 13,400 courts martial brought against soldiers between 1943 and 1945, only approximately 600 were for any "civil crime." AA40, by contrast, was a catchall military law—"conduct to the prejudice of good order and discipline"—that indicated that the *soldier* had misbehaved, including disobedience to standing orders and misappropriating a military vehicle for their own private uses. Of the 13,400 courts martial from 1943 to 1945, AA40 was brought 3,800 times.[54] By charging the accused soldier with both rape *and* violation of a fraternization ban, the soldier was tried twice for the same crime, under two different legal statutes.

The nonfraternization order meant that all reported sexual contact would be dealt with by courts martial but did not mean that all charges or that all convictions were for *rape*. The provosts had some leniency about which charges were brought against individual soldiers—sexual misconduct (AA40), indecent assault (AA41), and rape or attempted rape (AA41)—and they did prosecute the full range of charges. Reporting a rape or sexual contact with Canadian soldiers did not mean that the army was beholden to court martial a soldier for rape, although their testimony was relevant to the charges. The testimonies of women (and their families) were only part of the evidence gathered, which included the testimonies of other Canadian soldiers, an identification parade of soldiers drawn from the regiment, and a medical exam of the woman (or women). Breach of the nonfraternization order (those charges under AA40) was easier to prove: Did the officers of the court believe that the soldier had been in contact with German civilians? Rape was more difficult to convict, as in the 1940s army, officers of the court determined if completion of vaginal sexual intercourse had occurred *and* that there was an absence of consent *and* presumed the innocence of the soldier. At McGill's court martial, the judicial advocate (or JA, a military officer with expert legal knowledge) went into details about the differences between attempted rape and indecent assault:

> On a charge of rape, the accused may be found not guilty of rape but guilty of attempted rape, or alternatively, not guilty of rape but guilty of indecent assault. The ingredient of attempted rape is the intent. You would have to ask yourself this question: "Is it a fact that the accused tried to commit rape and was frustrated?" Indecent assault is common assault (which would be complete with the mere touching of the person of the aggrieved person) accompanied by indecent acts.[55]

Rape, attempted rape, and indecent assault were all options that the officers of the court martial could and did convict soldiers of during this crackdown in 1945. Historian Hugh Gordon provided a partial analysis of the findings of the German courts martial for rape and attempted rape, and his findings were: seven acquittals, three attempted rape convictions, four indecent assault convictions, nineteen convictions for sexual misconduct, seventeen convictions for rape, with one conviction of both rape and indecent assault (one Gunner Lefebvre) and one conviction of rape and sexual misconduct (Abbott).[56]

Abbott's trial ended in conviction for both rape and sexual misconduct. Abbott's JA indicated that the court should give the accused the benefit of reasonable doubt on these cases, but he also indicated that the Standing Order for any "consent to intercourse result[ing] from fear" to be treated as rape needed to be factored into their decision. Abbott admitted that he had had sexual intercourse with E.K. and E.S., but not M.D. Because he had brought out his pistol, he was therefore convicted of rape of E.K. and E.S., and sexual misconduct with M.D. Abbott was sentenced to five years penal servitude and discharge with ignominy.[57]

Although Abbott's conviction represented a successful prosecution of military justice, the overarching purpose of this system affected the length of his sentence. As mentioned earlier, military justice was and remained primarily about the maintenance of good order and discipline, and the tenor of military justice changed after combat ended. After mid-1945, the overwhelmingly volunteer Canadian army was expected to return to civilian life. Having many military personnel in prison prevented soldiers from returning to civilian life and did not serve military justice.[58] For the crime of raping

German civilians, the execution of military justice became about *sentencing* soldiers, not about requiring them to serve their full sentence. Signalman Jack McGill, convicted on 11 June 1945, was released from prison in Canada on 22 July 1946.[59] Furthermore, by the late 1940s, the Canadian government was under increasing pressure to give all Second World War soldiers benefits, even criminals like Abbott and McGill. By 1948, Abbott had not only been released but had his sentence altered from "discharge with ignominy" to discharge, making him eligible to collect his wartime pension.[60]

Individualized Analysis of Abbott's Actions

To attempt an understanding of the actions of Pvt. Abbott, this section provides a detailed analysis of the contradictory and unsettling actions on the nights of 4 and 10 May 1945. First discussing the importance of revenge narratives and then plundering German homes, this section incorporates censorship reports to provide context. However, after discussing plunder, this historian is left, awkwardly, with the acknowledgment that Abbott and McGill left trinkets for their German victims; the final part of this section discusses why they might have done so.

Canadian soldiers were generally angry at the German army and German civilians, and this anger may have manifested through sexual violence. Revenge against the German people as a potential motivation for sexual violence also fits into the narratives that surround the courts martial for rape, even though the soldiers who were being court martialed shied away from that rationale in the trials, as it meant an admission of guilt.[61] Historians Hugh Gordon and Miriam Gebhardt both attribute the high number of rapes in Germany to the desire for revenge. Gordon states that the rapes in Germany were a mix of attempting to humiliate the enemy and a "victory ritual" in which "Germans were the enemy and the soldiers were acting out their conquest in a more personal manner than simple territorial occupation."[62] Gebhardt attributes the increase in the number of rapes in April and May to the discovery of German war crimes and the horror at the concentration camps.[63] German women were explicitly blamed for falsely claiming rape in both Abbott's trial and the trials of others. At their trials, Abbott's and McGill's defending officers outlined the conspiracy theory that German women were out to "win the peace" by sabotaging the good name of the British army by going werewolf.[64] "Going werewolf" in this context meant "crying rape" to besmirch and lower the morale of British Army soldiers, including Canadians. In fact, American Lt.-General E. L. Clarke investigated rumors that there was a conspiracy by German women to falsely accuse American troops of rape and thereby lower morale; in June 1945 Clarke reported that there was no planned sabotage.⁶⁵ Still the rumors demonstrate the ugly mood of Canadian and American troops toward German civilians. The persistence of such rumors imply that vengeance was being taken and revisited by both sides, and German women's bodies bore the brunt of such inflammatory perceptions.⁶⁶

For Abbott and McGill, revenge was enacted on the women's bodies and through their discussions with the German civilians. Their conversations could be interpreted in at least three ways: as signs of discomfort, perfunctory courtesy, or (most compellingly) a way to remind themselves that these women were the enemy. Specifically, Abbott asked questions about each of his victim's marital status and her husband's location on three occasions either immediately before or after the rapes: once to E.K. on 4 May, once to M.D. on 10 May, and once to F.E., another neighbor of M.D.'s, on 10 May. Asking these questions in at least rudimentary German could mean that Abbott was discomfited by his act and trying to make his actions seem less damning to himself and to the Germans. This explanation seems unsatisfactory, given the continued presence of McGill and the pistol. It might have been a perfunctory conversational gambit exacerbated by Abbott's limited knowledge of German. However, if the soldier was discomfited, or being courteous, he could have asked about more innocuous topics or simply kept quiet. Abbott chose to ask the questions that would reinforce his perception of these women as his enemies, or at least the wives of his enemies. He did rape the wives of German soldiers; both E.K. and M.D. said that their husbands were in Norway. According to the neighbor, Abbott "asked after my husband who is in Norvegia. [He expressed his belief that] they should all be made prisoners of war and came [sic] to France for one or two years."⁶⁷ This recollection of the neighbor seems to reinforce the ill will of Abbott and Canadian soldiers toward the German army. Keeping all the German army as prisoners of war for a year or two was not something that was going to happen.

The soldiers may have seen their ability to take loot and rape German civilians as a form of informal reward. As Anthony Kellett has discussed, plunder was historically a common system of reward for soldiers.⁶⁸ In the Second World War, plunder could be what soldiers felt entitled to take from a conquered enemy population. A sense of entitlement is described in the statement of one infantryman: "We [occupied] a new farmhouse every night or so, enjoying commandeered cattle, pigs, preserves out of cellar, and fresh milk."⁶⁹ Another Canadian soldier was quoted by the censors in a letter home saying: "I tried to send your parcel and my officer wouldn't pass it, as it was all loot. Anyway, I'll hold onto it until I get leave."⁷⁰ The officer in this letter is permissive of the looting: Although he did not allow the parcel to be sent, he did not take the treasure away. Another letter included in the censorship reports read, "The Germans have lots and *whatever they have belongs to us now and we mean to take everything that we can lay hands on and leave nothing behind*. . . . The boys are helping themselves to everything they see."[71] The soldiers in these letters seem almost giddy with their ability to procure exclusive souvenirs. Particularly when the Canadians first entered Germany in February and March of 1945, the military authorities were disinclined to enforce limits on their soldiers. A Canadian soldier quoted in the March 1945 censorship report said that "they haven't told us not to loot yet, and everybody is lifting everything in sight."[72] Officers were not stopping the theft of German material possessions, and explicit orders condemning looting were not issued until 28 March 1945.[73]

The court martial records also make frequent reference to the soldiers demanding alcohol and sex, and sometimes stealing personal items from German civilians. Gunner P. J. Claus was charged with two counts of robbery with aggravation for stealing a radio and ring from a farmhouse and for violating the nonfraternizing order by laying in a bed with Fraulein G.H. (aged thirteen).[74] Claus was acquitted on all charges, but the adult German victims told a story of being held hostage by four soldiers, having their possessions stolen, and being forcibly separated from G.H. and her younger sister. Including McGill's bicycle theft, five soldiers were charged with rape *and* theft. These actions on the part of Canadian soldiers indicate a few points of analysis. First, making up almost 10 percent of the courts martial for rape in Germany, soldiers' theft was obviously a point of some concern for the army, and all the prosecutions for rape and theft came *after* the order banning looting. Second, the theft of stockings, other personal items, food, or alcohol was rarely prosecuted; only valuable stolen items came before the courts, and most of those items were jewelry.[75] In at least one other German trial, the court heard that the first thing two soldiers demanded was alcohol, then watches, then cigarettes, then a German woman alone. They took all except the alcohol because the civilians did not have any. Although that soldier was brought up on charges of rape and sexual misconduct, he was not charged with stealing.[76]

Abbott and McGill stole from their victims. Stealing was widely reported in the occupation of Germany, both associated with rape and not. Abbott and McGill took a pair of silk stockings from E.K.'s home, a pocket watch, and a bicycle from E.S.'s and M.D.'s apartments. McGill tried to explain away the bicycle theft by saying that he "traded" bicycles, but he was convicted of the theft anyway; his statement about trading was in direct contradiction of an earlier statement that he had gone to the first home "looking for loot."[77] The loss of the small items could be meant as gifts for soldiers' family, for resale, or personal souvenir-taking. The theft of the silk stockings raises the ugly image that Abbott planned to send them to Canada as a present for his wife. However, as they were not new stockings, the prospect of them being gifts or items for resale is unlikely. The most likely explanation is that the stockings became personal souvenirs. Instances of soldiers taking personal souvenirs was widespread in the Allied armies. The stockings and other small items were not recovered by military police, and Abbott was not charged with any theft. Instead, Abbott and McGill were notable for what they did not steal: alcohol. According to witnesses on both nights, Abbott and McGill appeared sober; Abbott agreed that he had only imbibed his rum ration. In this way, Abbott is an anomaly; most of the Canadian soldiers prosecuted for rape were reportedly drunk.[78]

However, and paradoxically, Abbott and McGill offered goods and food to the women they had just raped. Offering chocolate, cigarettes, a cheap brooch, and "goodnight" after having raped and traumatized E.K., E.S., and M.D. could suggest a level of discomfort with their own actions. Alternatively, Abbott and McGill could have been acting out scripts about how to behave around women—even women that they had just raped. One of those scripts would have been how to conduct sexual relations with European women. In her article, British historian Alison Twells shows that British soldiers and sailors regularly wrote flirtatious letters to women, even women they did not know. In their thank-you letters for knitted garments (socks, sweaters, mittens, etc.), many soldiers offered dinner dates, even though the woolens were knitted and distributed through charitable societies like the Red Cross.[79] Sharing cigarettes with the women and leaving small tokens made the rape transactional; it allowed the rapist-soldier to reframe his actions as prostitution. Trading sex for goods and food meant that (to the Canadian military in Europe) the women were acting like prostitutes, who rarely had claim to legal protections against sexual violence.[80]

In his written testimony, McGill attempted to provide another explanation for leaving trinkets: trying to put the German civilians at ease. Of his activities on 4 May, McGill wrote, "I gave the man and other women cigarettes and chocolate explaining that I was not going to harm them."[81] Incredibly, McGill was holding a pistol while he was explaining this, leaving this reader to wonder if he was desensitized to violence or if his words were a hollow attempt to placate the Germans—or both. About his visit to E.S. and M.D.'s house on 10 May, he testified, "the man who was up was quite civil, so I gave him a cigar and cigarette *as I usually do.*" These offers of cigarettes, cigars, and chocolate happened while he was guarding the other inhabitants of the houses while Abbott was raping a woman. McGill also argued that he got E.S. a chair and a drink of water to stop her from crying "while I was guarding [her]"—she had just been raped by first Abbott and then McGill. His actions may have been motivated by consideration, remorse, or (more probably) an attempt to divert E.S.'s attention and that of her family away from what had just happened.[82] McGill, therefore, looks less like a considerate fellow, than a rapist redirecting attention from what was happening in the other room and rewarding the "civil" behavior of the Germans who did not fight the man with the pistol. In this context, such "rewards" were still transactional.

Camaraderie Analysis

Abbott did not act alone, and the presence of McGill as a co-conspirator was crucial to understanding camaraderie in the Canadian army. McGill enabled Abbott and Abbott enabled McGill in turn. Without McGill, it is unlikely that Abbott could have subdued E.K.'s family. Abbott's threat to her father's life ensured that she would go with McGill and ensured his continued compliance. However, the fact that they raped the same women did not extend to a shared intimacy: on both nights the men were pointedly not in the same room. Whether this was from their perceived need to keep the rest of the household hostage or to ensure privacy or allow for voyeurism is unclear from the testimonies. At least one successful defense against the Canadians did happen in May 1945: a mother stopped two drunken Canadian soldiers from coming near her daughter even though they put a gun to her chest. The daughter ran away during the confusion and the soldiers could not find her.[83] From his own testimony, Jack McGill was a twenty-year-old bachelor Torontonian, who had joined in 1943 and gone overseas in 1944.[84] In his written testimony, McGill painted himself as an accomplice who did not himself hurt the German women but used Abbott's threats of violence to have sexual intercourse. McGill testified that he had acquiesced to Abbott's suggestion that they pillage and "go into the houses looking for loot and to find some women to have sexual intercourse with if they were willing more or less."[85] The use of "sexual intercourse" probably reflects the fact that McGill was aware of his audience (the court), but McGill's phrasing "more or less" is unclear. Probably "more or less" reflects his own attempt to summarize a conversation without incriminating himself, but in this context strongly implies that the women may have been less willing. The assistance of another soldier meant that both were able to get what they wanted.

In Germany, J. Robert Lilly has termed the camaraderie of at least two soldiers raping the same woman or women "buddy rape."[86] This practice was so common that it became what the American JAG called a "typical pattern." The JAG included in the "typical pattern" the entrance into "a home at night in a somewhat isolated section of a town."[87] McGill and Abbot certainly fit this "pattern," as both times they entered German houses in a town at night. The fact that they conducted their attacks inside the relative privacy of a house (after using a pretense to get entrance) indicates that the rape was supposed to remain a secret, not a source of intimidation of civilian society in general. However, as Maris Rowe-McCulloch has argued about Germans in the Soviet city of Rostov-on-Don, while the rape was supposed to be secret in one respect (kept from the Canadian authorities), it was still a display of power and dominance in another, vis-à-vis the German population.[88] Entering a private dwelling, searching the home, and stealing from, and raping the inhabitants signaled to the Germans that Canadians were in command.

Fewer German women were named in the courts martial than Canadian soldiers; multiple Canadian soldiers raped the same women. Unsurprisingly, their comrades had many reactions: Some privately cheered, and some seem to have been horrified. In the trial of Acting-Sergeant Frederick Gaspich, his fellow soldier testified against Gaspich and provided clear evidence that Gaspich had isolated a woman in order to rape her. Although he was personally horrified, the soldier did not report the rape himself; even if they disapproved, the soldiers' loyalty was to their comrades.[89] Lilly wondered if "buddy rapes" were adopted strategically by rapists "to ensure a successful assault [or] to ward off interference and competition."[90] Given the aggressive prosecution for breach of the nonfraternization laws, the strategy to ensure a successful assault seems the more likely explanation for the high rate of buddy rape in the Canadian army's files. Among the Canadian soldiers brought to trial for sexual violence in Germany, buddy rapes were frequent. Seventeen women, including E.K., E.S., and M.D., reported being raped by two or three attackers. They named thirty soldiers (58 percent of the courts martial for rape). On two other occasions, charges were brought against a pair of soldiers who raped women in the same family; one other woman was raped by five soldiers. If we take these other cases into account, 75 percent of Canadian soldiers were working with at least one other soldier to commit sexual violence against civilians.

Throughout the war in Europe, Canadian soldiers often worked together to commit many different types of crime. One such joint trial occurred in Germany in 1945, when Craftsmen McKay and Smith of the Workshop corps broke in and stole clothing from a private residence. McKay and Smith were also charged with sexual misconduct, although they were acquitted on that charge.[91] However, buddy rape had been a part of the Canadian war experience since the beginning of combat in 1943; in late 1944, for instance, Privates Brown and Parker of the North Nova Scotia Highlanders were convicted of the rape of L.B., a French woman, and sentenced to five years penal servitude. In France, the Canadians were generally welcomed as liberators, and the JAG was unwilling to prosecute for rape. When they did convict, sentences were long.[92] Brown and Parker were still in prison after the war, having been sent back to Canada for detention.[93] Of the non-German courts martial for sexual violence, over half (59 percent) were for buddy rapes or rapes with more than two soldiers participating in a single crime.[94] Furthermore, unlike Abbott and McGill, many of the Canadian buddy rapists were from the same unit. Ten buddy rapes in Germany (naming twenty-three soldiers) were from at least two soldiers within the same units.[95] Lacking an in-depth study of the regimental cultures, this chapter can only hazard that command neglect or permissive attitudes toward sexual violence played a role in buddy rapes (as seen by the comparative lack of soldiers from the 4th Division being charged with sexual violence). However, it is possible too that buddy rapes occurred because of male bonding within the regiment, and a need to prove heterosexual masculinity.

Although Lilly referred to the buddy rapes as "social events," he did not explore the social aspects in detail.[96] The possibility of rapes as "social events" is reinforced in some aspects of the courts martial of Abbot and McGill. For instance, Abbott and McGill were not in the same units (Abbott was infantry and McGill signals) but they went out together on two separate nights. There is no other known connection between them, although McGill admitted that they knew each other at least by 4 May if not before. Certainly emboldened after the first encounter with E.K., these two seem to have been titillated by and enthused about their crimes and planned a second evening. Second, the Germans believed that Abbott and McGill were both sober, and although many similar rapes ended evenings of stolen alcohol consumption, Abbott and McGill (especially on the second night) isolated their victims immediately after confirming that there were no weapons in the house. The singular purpose and the planning to reunite indicates that Abbott and McGill enjoyed and found social acceptance in their sexual violence. In thinking about "buddy rapes," this analysis has been heavily influenced by Elissa Mailänder's "Making Sense of a Rape Photograph" from 2017, which analyzes a photograph taken of a group of laughing Wehrmacht soldiers as they gather around a woman and (possibly pretend to) rape her. This photo is a "rape-joke," as Mailänder understands it, and the joke reinforced soldiers' camaraderie and their heterosexuality, through their cruel fun.[97] Furthermore, as she writes, it is within "situations of violent male bonding—with the acceptance of a man's comrades—that violence demonstrates social power."[98] Mailänder's insight complements the plunder and vengeance narratives discussed above: Abbott and McGill were not only taking their anger and frustrations out on German women, they were bonding by doing it together. "Buddy" violence demonstrated heterosexual masculinity to male companions and claimed power over conquered populations.

Conclusion

This chapter has placed one court martial for sexual violence into a wider framework of Canadian soldiers' behavior and thereby provided context for one soldier's behavior. On one hand, this story is of a criminal conviction for sexual violence in wartime: Abbott was acting on his own initiative when he raped E.K., E.S., and M.D. in early May 1945 and was then prosecuted for his actions. Furthermore, the actions of individual Canadian soldiers are not on the scale of the mass rapes of the German, Soviet, or Japanese militaries, but the increase of courts martial for sexual violence represented a drastic intervention by the Canadian military justice system at a particular moment and with particular effects.

Deciphering a single case gets the military historian uncomfortably close to an ordinary soldier, his friendships, and his actions in the course of his duties. Abbott's threats of violence, his commission of the buddy rape, the thefts, his presents to the women, and even his conversations are like the actions of other Canadian soldiers and indicative of the lives that these soldiers lived in Europe at the end of the war.[99] The single best explanation for Abbott's actions comes from McGill who simply stated they "[went] into the houses looking for loot and to find some women to have sexual intercourse with if they were willing more or less."[100] From this case study, it appears that Canadian soldiers exacted vengeance against the wives of German soldiers, and some soldiers pillaged German property and women by opportunistically raping civilians and looting their possessions. Abbott and McGill may have been personally interested in looting and sexual violence for the thrill of domination and cruelty. Not all soldiers were afforded the chance—4th Canadian (Armored) Division declared the town of Bad Zwischenahn off-limits—to prevent fraternization and crime against German civilians. As Western Allied soldiers with guns (the only people with legal weapons), and the authority to search German homes, the Canadian army empowered Abbott and McGill to act on their vengeance, anger, and greed toward German civilians and their possessions. Abbott and McGill raped three German women at gunpoint, stole, and cooperated to intimidate the other people in their households.

While the Canadian Army never accepted or promoted sexual violence by its troops, and never adopted a policy where rape was used as an instrument of subjugation, the army turned a blind eye to sexual violence when prosecution did not serve military interests. Evidence from the Canadians in Sicily and other Allied occupations indicate that not all reported instances of sexual violence were prosecuted.[101] Such organizational behavior is consistent with the behavior of other Allied armies' military justice apparatuses in the Second World War and raises intriguing questions about the actions of the British Army within which the Canadians were operating. Prosecutions for rape in Germany are visible because the Canadian Army finally used the instruments of military justice to crack down on sexual violence when they had not before.

Notes

1. According to his commanding officer, Lt. Pateman at the time of his trial in June 1945. Court Martial reel T-15550, image 60, "Court Martial of Pte Abbott." In this instance, "images" are a substitution for pagination within the microfilm reel.

2. T-15550, image 68, "Abbott."

3. Matthew Barrett, *Scandalous Conduct: Canadian Officer Courts Martial, 1914–1945* (Vancouver: UBC Press, 2022), 14–15.

4. Miriam Gebhardt, *Crimes Unspoken: The Rape of German Women at the end of the Second World War*, trans. Nick Somers (Cambridge: Polity Press, 2017), 117–18.

5. Gebhardt, *Crimes Unspoken*, 119–20.

6. An officer was designated the censor in every army company, and their task was to read all the letters, and submit reports of what the soldiers were talking about to the official censors. These reports would themselves be abbreviated. The other task of censors was to determine what constituted illegal discussions of the war. Soldiers could be court martialed for compromising the "recruiting, training, discipline or administration" of the military. Jeffrey Keshen, *Saints, Sinners and Soldiers: Canada's Second World War* (Vancouver: UBC Press, 2004), 229.

7. Alison Twells, "Sex, Gender, and Romantic Intimacy in Servicemen's Letters during the Second World War," *Historical Journal* 63, no. 3 (2020): 735. Victoria Sotvedt describes similar challenges working with letters home in chapter 7 in this volume.

8. The number of courts martial in the courts martial index files from the military's Directorate of History and Heritage (DHH) is less than the total

number found by combing through full-text transcripts (held at Library and Archives Canada, or LAC). The only other historian to treat this material in depth, Hugh Gordon, found fifty-two courts martial, using both the index files and the transcripts, but he stated that he could not find at least one of the files. Between the two source bases, and with the assistance of fellow military legal historian Matthew Barrett, sixty-five courts martial transcripts were identified as sexual offenses committed against German civilians in 1945. The difference is partially explained in the records for the two types of courts martial: field-general courts martial (FGCM) and general courts martial (GCM). Almost all the trials for sexual violence were FGCM, but at least two were GCM, and the GCM index cards were incomplete at DHH. Without the index cards, searching through the courts martial transcripts becomes the proverbial "needle in a haystack" as they were filed by the soldiers' surnames. Although this chapter mostly uses the more complete sixty-five as my base, when I do use Hugh Gordon's work, I identify it as such. Similarly, it is possible that some courts martial for sexual violence have not been recovered, and until the digital courts martial transcripts are keyword searchable, the historian cannot know. Hugh Gordon, "Cheers and Tears: Relations between Canadian Soldiers and German Civilians, 1944–1946" (PhD diss., University of Victoria, 2010), 202.

9. Philipp Kuwert and Harald Jürgen Freyberger, "The Unspoken Secret: Sexual Violence in World War II," *International Psychogeriatrics* 19, no. 4 (April 2007): 783. Estimates of the number of rapes vary widely, but the Soviet armies are always assumed to have committed the most and most frequent rapes, as many as two million according to some estimates, without factoring in other armies. For a breakdown of how these numbers are derived, see Gebhardt, *Crimes Unspoken*, 17–22.

10. Robert Engen, *Strangers in Arms: Combat Motivation in the Canadian Army, 1943–1945* (Montreal: McGill-Queen's University Press, 2016); and Barrett, *Scandalous Conduct* are two recent notable exceptions. The marginalization of sexual violence scholarship in the historiography of the Second World War is also the theme of Annette Timm's "The Challenges of Including Sexual Violence and Transgressive Love in Historical Writing of World War II and the Holocaust," *Journal of the History of Sexuality* 26, no. 3 (September 2017): 351–65. Other chapters in this volume have similarly complicated the history of wartime narratives, documenting how details that get told or omitted shape how the home front viewed soldiers. Victoria Sotvedt described how mass media warped American and Canadian narratives of the war, and Elena Friot in chapter 9 challenges the heroization of American soldiers through the curation of stories in mass media.

11. Atina Grossman, "A Question of Silence: The Rape of German Women by Occupation Soldiers," *October* 72 (Spring 1995): 45.

12. Andrew Clark, *A Keen Soldier: The Execution of Second World War Private John Pringle* (Toronto: Knopf, 2002); Matthew Barrett, "'He would be

expected to crack': Battle Exhaustion, Desertion, and the Court Martial of Lieutenant R. J. Woods," *Canadian Military History* 30, no. 1 (2021): 1–50; Barrett, *Scandalous Conduct* (2022). In *Scandalous Conduct*, Barrett does discuss the court martial of an officer for sexual violence. Similarly, in his thesis, Hugh Gordon discusses the German courts martial for sexual violence. Aside from "Cheers and Tears," I have published a book chapter about combat motivation and sexual violence. See Claire Cookson-Hills, "Sexual Violence and Combat Motivation," in *Why We Fight: New Approaches to the Human Dimension of Warfare*, ed. Robert C. Engen, H. Christian Brede, and Allan D. English (Kingston: McGill-Queen's University Press, 2020), 72–118.

13. S. Hedgepeth and R. Saidel, *Sexual Violence against Jewish Women during the Holocaust* (Hanover, NH: University Press of New England, 2010).

14. J. Robert Lilly, *Taken by Force: Rape and American GIs in Europe during World War II* (New York: Palgrave Macmillan, 2007), 119.

15. Regina Mühlhäuser, "Reframing Sexual Violence as a Weapon and Strategy of War: The Case of the German Wehrmacht during the War and Genocide in the Soviet Union, 1941–1944," *Journal of the History of Sexuality* 26, no. 3 (September 2017): 395.

16. Maris Rowe-McCullogh, "Sexual Violence under Occupation during World War II: Soviet Women's Experiences Inside a German Military Brothel and Beyond," *Journal of the History of Sexuality* 31, no. 1 (January 2022): 20–26. For a discussion of the public aspects of sexual violence in the Eastern Front, see Elissa Mailänder, "Making Sense of a Rape Photograph: Sexual Violence as Social Performance on the Eastern Front, 1939–1944," *Journal of the History of Sexuality* 26, no. 3 (September 2017): 489–520.

17. Edward Westermann has documented the connections between drunkenness, drinking rituals, and male bonding and acts of violence and genocide in the context of the Third Reich. See Westermann, "Drinking Rituals, Masculinity, and Mass Murder in Nazi Germany," *Central European History* 51, no. 3 (September 2018): 367–89.

18. Lilly, *Taken by Force*, 119–20.

19. Grossman, "A Question of Silence," 46. Grossman was discussing the week of mass rapes committed by Soviet soldiers in Berlin, but that fits remarkably well with the peak of Canadian prosecuted sexual violence between 20 April and 10 May. Cookson-Hills, "Sexual Violence and Combat Motivation," 63.

20. Cookson-Hills, "Sexual Violence and Combat Motivation," 69–74.

21. Although referred to by their full names in the transcripts and the index files, the German women are here referred to by their initials to avoid naming and shaming. It is also worth noting that there were no courts martial for sexual violence against German men and boys. This absence may be partially explained because the nonfraternization order explicitly discussed German women and girls. The Canadian government has allowed the courts martial of all Second

World War soldiers to be online at the government-affiliated website Canadiana Héritage (https://heritage.canadiana.ca). As this is a publicly and freely available set of documents, these soldiers have no anonymity. I have not granted them any.

22. T-15550, image 87, "Abbott."
23. T-15550, image 63, "Abbott."
24. T-15550, image 86, "Abbott."
25. T-15550, image 63, "Abbott."
26. T-15550, image 86, "Abbott."
27. Gordon, "Cheers and Tears," 218–22.
28. T-15550, image 87, "Abbott."
29. T-15550, image 86, "Abbott."
30. T-15550, image 79, "Abbott."
31. According to the medical examiner's testimony. T-15550, image 101, "Abbott."
32. T-15550, image 51, "Abbott." In his words, she "seemed to understand immediately what was expected of her. She undressed herself, laid down on the bed, pulled up legs, and spread them for me to have sexual intercourse" (T-15550, image 51, "Abbott"). In her words, "Then he threw me onto the bed and inspected my whole body with his torch. The pistol was lying on the bed. Then he raped me, and I was afraid of the pistol that was lying next to me so I did not resist" (T-15550, image 75, "Abbott").
33. T-15550, images 44, 46, "Abbott."
34. T-15550, image 79, "Abbott."
35. Courts Martial Indices, 1943–1947 (111.6 (D3)) box 11, book 5P, pg. 34.
36. T-15550, image 79, 95, "Abbott."
37. Tamás Vonyó, "The Bombing of Germany: The Economic Geography of War-Induced Dislocation in West Germany," *European Review of Economic History* 16, no. 1 (2012): 100, 108.
38. Randall Hansen, *Fire and Fury: The Allied Bombing of Germany, 1942–1945* (Toronto: Doubleday Canada, 2008), 189–90.
39. Court Martial reel T-15809, image 225, "Court Martial of Pte C. Gladue."
40. Court Martial reel T-15809, images 224–25, "Gladue."
41. Court Martial reel T-15704, image 4029, "Court Martial of Sgn J. McGill."
42. For example, Acting Sergeant F. Gaspich demanded a young woman accompany him into a bedroom while he searched for weapons. Court Martial reel T-15807, image 3527, "Court Martial of A/Sgt F. Gaspich."
43. Court Martial reel T-15837, image 3852, "Court Martial of Pte P. Patterson."
44. Engen, *Strangers in Arms*, 185–86.
45. I was assuming that rain would dampen soldiers' enthusiasm for going out, but this was an incorrect assumption. The Calgary Highlanders were part of the 2 Canadian Infantry Division. RG24-C-3, Calgary Highlanders War Diary, May 1945, vol. T-15021, file 192, 4 May 1945.

46. "Bad Zwischenahn," Canadian Soldiers.com https://www.canadiansoldiers.com/history/battlehonours/northwesteurope/badzwischenahn.htm (accessed 27 July 2020).

47. Lorne Scots War Diary, May 1945, RG24-C-3, Vol. T-15310, File 503; 10 May 1945.

48. Petra Goedde, "From Villains to Victims: The Feminization of Germany, 1945–1947," *Diplomatic History* 23, no. 1 (1999): 1–20.

49. Andrew R. Ritchie, *Watchdog: A History of the Canadian Provost Corps* (Burlington, ON: Canadian Provost Corps Association, 1995), 100. Ritchie has written the only dedicated history of Canada' provost corps, and although he used a wide array of sources, it is not the work of a professional historian.

50. Courts Martial reel T-15809, image 759, "Order 443, 23 February 1945." My emphasis.

51. Goedde, "From Villains to Victims," 2–3. The French zone of occupation was administratively messy; at first, they used the American handbook for Germany, and only in July 1945 was a uniquely French occupation policy rolled out. Jessica Reinisch, "Chapter 8: The Forgotten Zone: Public Health work in the French Occupation Zone," in *The Perils of Peace: The Public Health Crisis in Occupied Germany* (Oxford: Oxford University Press, 2013), 10.

52. Compiled Courts Martial Data, from Directorate of History and Heritage, Courts Martial 1943–1947 (111.6(D3)), box 5, book AA—box 12, book GCM-A. This is a very high percentage for successful prosecution of crimes of sexual violence. For a modern comparison of the Canadian military's attempts to prosecute sexual violence, see Elaine Craig, "An Examination of How the Canadian Military's Legal System Responds to Sexual Assault," *Dalhousie Law Journal* 43, no. 1 (2020): 1–39.

53. Karen Dubinsky, *Improper Advances: Rape and Heterosexual Conflict in Ontario, 1800–1929* (Chicago: University of Chicago Press, 1993), 23. For a more detailed discussion of British civil law, see Elizabeth Kolsky, "'The Body Evidencing the Crime': Rape on Trial in Colonial India, 1860–1947," *Gender & History* 22, no. 1 (March 2010): 110–11, 116.

54. Compiled Courts Martial Data.

55. Reel T-15704, image 4037, "McGill."

56. Gordon, "Cheers and Tears," 209–10.

57. Compiled Courts Martial Data.

58. For an American comparative study, see Susan L. Carruthers, *The Good Occupation: American Soldiers and the Hazards of Peace* (Cambridge, MA: Harvard University Press, 2016).

59. T-15704, image 3981, "McGill."

60. Matthew Barrett, "'A bad soldier seldom makes a good citizen': Canadian Veterans and Dishonourable Records, 1945–1948" (presentation, 30th Canadian Military History Colloquium, Waterloo, ON, 3–4 May 2019).

61. Joanna Bourke, *Rape: A History from 1860 to the Present* (London: Virago Press, 2007), 359–60. Bourke is generally skeptical of the conflation of rape as a part of total war but points out that scholarship on rape as vengeance needs to include the British, American, and Australian militaries as well as (for instance) the Soviet army in Germany.

62. Gordon, "Cheers and Tears," 200, 203.

63. Gebhardt, *Crimes Unspoken*, 113.

64. Defending officers were army officers who had been railroaded to serve as defense advocates in these trials. Such officers were rarely legal experts, although accused could request defense lawyers. See, for instance, Court Martial reel T-15837, image 3851, "Court Martial of Pte Patterson." Patterson requested a lawyer because of the complexity of his case, and possibility of a long sentence if convicted. T-15704, image 4032, "McGill"; T-15550, image 55–57, "Pte Abbott."

65. Gebhardt, *Crimes Unspoken*, 93.

66. In his work, Nicholas Stargardt discusses rumors among German civilians that they were being punished by the Allied armies for their own atrocities. See Nicholas Stargardt, *The German War: A Nation under Arms, 1939–45* (London: Bodley Head, 2015).

67. T-15550, image 95, "Abbott."

68. Anthony Kellett, *Combat Motivation: The Behaviour of Soldiers in Battle* (Boston: Springer Science, 1982), 202.

69. Quoted in Tim Cook, *Fight to the Finish: Canadians in the Second World War*, vol. 2, *1944–1945* (Toronto: Allan Lane, 2015), 398.

70. Censorship Reports, Canadian Army Overseas, 21 Army Group, for period 16–30 April 1945, LAC microfilm reel T-17925.

71. Censorship Reports, Canadian Army Overseas, 21 Army Group, for period 16–30 April 1945, LAC microfilm reel T-17925. My emphasis.

72. Censorship reports, Canadian Army Overseas, 21 Army Group, for period 1–15 March 1945, LAC microfilm reel T-17925.

73. "Food Stolen in Germany, 28 March 1945," page 2 in Discipline—Own Forces, File 219C1.009 (D245) RG 24 10739, Library and Archives Canada, Ottawa, ON.

74. Courts Martial reel T-15792, images 1258–1307, "Court Martial of Gunner P. J. Claus."

75. The exception that proves the rule was when Pvt. Russell was brought up on charges of stealing "a brilliant diamond collar, 2 diamond rings, one gold watch chain, one magnifying glass, one pocket watch and one pencil" from E.D. and raping her. Court Martial Index File, box 10, book 5K, 150.

76. Courts Martial reel T-15820, images 4890, 4893, "Court Martial of Pte Krauchi."

77. Court Martial reel T-15704, images 4028, 4027, "McGill."

78. See Gordon for examples of drunken Canadian soldiers sexually assaulting Germans. Gordon, "Cheers and Tears," 217–19.

79. Twells, "Sex, Gender, and Romantic Intimacy," 741–42.

80. Keshen, *Saints, Sinners, and Soldiers*, 246.

81. T-15704, image 4027, "McGill."

82. T-15704, image 4028. "McGill." My emphasis.

83. Gordon, "Cheers and Tears," 218. The soldiers, Privates Gallagher and Goodwin, were charged with sexual misconduct rather than indecent assault, or attempted rape.

84. McGill chose to take the witness stand himself, so he answered questions about his relationships with women. Tellingly, he stated that until his deployment overseas, he had not been discomfited by the fact that he had never had sexual intercourse with a woman. Reel T-15704, image 4024–4026, "McGill."

85. T-15704, image 4030, "McGill."

86. Lilly, *Taken by Force,* 127–32.

87. Lilly, *Taken by Force*, 119.

88. Rowe-McCulloch, "Sexual Violence under Occupation," 21–22.

89. Cookson-Hills, "Sexual Violence as Combat Motivation," 70, 72.

90. Lilly, *Taken by Force*, 63.

91. Cfn. Smith and Cfn. MacKay, box 11, book 5N, pages 146 and 147, Courts Martial Index Files.

92. Compiled Courts Martial Data. Five Canadian soldiers were prosecuted for rape of French women, of whom four were convicted. These were actually two buddy rapes, and each soldier was sentenced to five years penal servitude.

93. Court Martial reel T-15659, image 636, "12 February 1946."

94. The total number was twenty of thirty-four soldiers involved in non-German courts martial between 1943–1945. Compiled Courts Martial Data.

95. This figure was based on a partial list of forty-nine sexual violence courts martial in Germany. Compiled Courts Martial Data.

96. Lilly put the term "social event" in quotation marks. See Lilly, *Taken by Force*, 63.

97. Mailänder, "Making Sense of a Rape Photograph," 489.

98. Mailänder, "Making Sense of a Rape Photograph," 497.

99. Mary Louise Roberts has recently turned her attention to the physical conditions of American soldiers during the Second World War. Her overall conclusion was encapsulated by the book's title: sheer misery. Mary Louise Roberts, *Sheer Misery: Soldiers in Battle in World War II* (Chicago: University of Chicago Press, 2021).

100. T-15704, image 4030, "McGill."

101. Cookson-Hills, "Sexual Violence and Combat Motivation," 72–118.

Part III
Cultural Transformation

9

"The Men of Bataan Lived Up to the Best American Tradition"
Journalists, Civilians, Politicians, and the Meaning of Surrender during World War II

Elena M. Friot

In late March 1943, almost one year after Bataan surrendered to Japanese forces, Clark Lee visited New Mexico. Lee was an Associated Press (AP) correspondent and happened to be in the Philippines when the Japanese attacked Pearl Harbor. His visit fulfilled a promise he had made to the soldiers that when he got out of the Philippines he would "come to New Mexico and tell their families about it." The *Gallup Independent* reminded its readers, "Lee lived and talked with these men from New Mexico in their fox holes on Bataan. His stories ... often bore the names of the boys with whom he talked.... It was through Lee's stories that parents and friends received the only word from the soldiers after the outbreak of the war."[1] Lee and other correspondents who found themselves in the Philippines when war broke out in late 1941 mediated Americans' knowledge of the defense of Bataan and wielded significant power in shaping contemporaneous and later narratives of the campaign.[2] These stories helped Americans on the home front make sense of and ascribe meaning to the surrenders of Bataan and Corregidor.

Using newspaper articles, personal letters, official government and military communications, congressional records, editorial cartoons, and cultural products such as films and museum exhibits, I argue that Americans on the home front repudiated the stigma of surrender and developed a rhetoric that helped them recast the defeat in the Philippines as an essential part of final Allied victory over Japan.[3] First, I detail the ways war correspondents shaped home front American imagination about the course of events in the Pacific, and how their stories contributed to the formation of a vocabulary of surrender. I examine how writers, photographers, and editorial cartoonists visually rendered the defense of Bataan for domestic consumption and gave civilians fodder for their conversations about the causes and consequences of the surrender. Next, I explain how journalists, politicians, and civic leaders drew analogies between past military defeats and the loss of the Philippines to fit defeat during World War II into a narrative of the nation's triumphalist martial heritage. Finally, I explore debates over Senate Bill 1374, legislation introduced by one of New Mexico's Democratic senators, Dennis Chávez, that called for the promotion of American prisoners of war who were stationed in the US territories of Wake, Guam, and the Philippines when the war against Japan began. Support for and opposition to the bill's passage revealed an undercurrent of uncertainty over how to manage some of the consequences of surrender. Reckoning with the legacies of the Bataan defeat helps fill the historiographical gap in the literature on America's experience of World War II. The surrender was a defining moment of the war for many Americans, and we need to better understand how home front Americans imagined and managed its causes and consequences.

Numerous losses in the Pacific at the end of 1941 and the first few months of 1942 forced Americans to come to terms with what surrender and defeat meant for its combat soldiers, the likelihood of Allied victory in the war, and long-held convictions about the nation's martial superiority. While Gen. Douglas MacArthur readied his retreat into the Bataan Peninsula, the small American garrison at Wake Island surrendered to the Japanese after a two-week battle on 23 December 1941: a first, clear defeat. The public's response forecast how the nation would grapple with the feeling of military failure. Newspaper headlines regaled readers with tales of valor in the face of overwhelming odds, and few stories referred to surrender. Instead, they said the island was "invaded," "lost," "taken," "captured," or "fallen." Americans were uncomfortable with surrender; to overcome that anxiety they looked for ways to reframe and repurpose military defeats.[4] An editorial in *The Oregonian* even proclaimed that Wake Island was really a victory for the United States. It had "not fallen, but has risen," because "Remember Wake Island" was a "vow of vengeance on barbarian treachery."[5] This framing of the defeat at Wake Island was a useful strategy to help incorporate the surrenders of Bataan and Corregidor into a victorious war narrative, and the same type of language would dominate the stories reporters managed to get out of the Philippines before the islands fell in April and May 1942.

President Roosevelt's administration had done its best to prepare the public for defeat in the Pacific. Indeed, the War Department's top-secret war plans, known as RAINBOW 5, made limited provisions for the defense of the Philippines and prioritized offensive operations in the European theater.

Despite a short-lived alteration of these plans after Gen. Douglas MacArthur assumed command of United States Army Forces in the Far East (USAFFE) in late July 1941, Roosevelt and his administration thought increasing the Philippine garrison would do little more than stall Japanese aggression in the Pacific while the United States built up its military arsenal.[6] On 23 February 1942, Roosevelt put an end to any further speculation about the likelihood of reinforcements reaching the Philippines. The islands were completely encircled by the Japanese, and no enforcements could reach them. "For forty years," he counseled, "it has always been our strategy . . . [to] fight a delaying action." Furthermore, "we knew all along . . . to obtain our objective . . . operations would be necessary in areas other than the Philippines," and "nothing . . . in the last two months has caused us to revise this basic strategy of necessity." MacArthur and his men, he concluded, "are gaining eternal glory" and "making Japan pay an increasingly terrible price."[7] Officials couched this doomed defense as a temporary sacrifice essential to permanent victory, and both war correspondents and journalists writing on the home front made this position an important part of the stories they told about the fighting in the Philippines.

Transmission difficulties, battlefield perils, robust censorship, and relative apathy on the part of stateside superiors who were more interested in events in Europe hampered correspondents' efforts to relay timely and candid front-line reports. Yet MacArthur had promised a "ringside seat" to the reporters who found themselves in the Philippines when the Japanese attacked if they were "willing to risk being killed."[8] Along with Clark Lee, several other correspondents were in the Philippines at the time of the Japanese attack. They and their families met a variety of fates: Some were wounded, others taken prisoner, and a few killed. Frank Hewlett was Manila's United Press bureau chief and accompanied the retreating forces to Bataan; he and Nat Floyd of the *New York Times* left Corregidor in April 1942. Hewlett's wife, Virginia, worked for Frank Sayre, the High Commissioner of the Philippines. She stayed in Manila when he left for Bataan and was imprisoned at Santo Tomas until it was liberated in February 1945. Carl Mydans, a *Life* magazine photographer, and his wife, Shelley, a researcher for the magazine, also remained in the city. They were both captured and held prisoner for almost two years by the Japanese, only repatriated during a prisoner exchange in 1943. Melville and Annalee Jacoby arrived in Manila in late November after fleeing China. He was a correspondent for *Time* and *Life* magazines, and she wrote for *Liberty*. They left the Philippines with Lee in February 1942; Mel was later killed in Australia when a pilot lost control while landing his P-40 Warhawk at Batchelor Field. Despite the limitations imposed by government censors, these reporters and photographers, along with the analysts, editors, and illustrators working on the home front, produced the words and imagery Americans unaccustomed to defeat used to make sense of what was transpiring in the Philippines.[9]

War Department regulations guided dispatches from the front: Articles had to be "accurate"; they could "not supply military information to the enemy" or "injure the morale of our forces, the people at home, or our allies," and could not "embarrass the United States, its allies, or neutral countries."[10] Folks at home consequently read mostly "anodyne" stories about the Pacific theater that emphasized the "heroes and goats of the war," but it was precisely these stories that armed the public with a vocabulary of heroism, courage, and gallantry. Although they were unable to share most of the "bitter truths" of the doomed campaign, correspondents did their part to ensure folks on the home front knew that the men fighting in the Philippines were heroes, who, but for lack of supplies and reinforcements, poor nutrition, and a slew of debilitating tropical diseases, would have successfully fended off the Japanese invasion.[11]

Newspapers published the War Department's daily communiqués, but they offered little context for people on the home front. For example, the communiqué for 24 December 1941, the day MacArthur's forces began their withdrawal into Bataan, reported additional Japanese landings on Luzon. It read that "though American and Philippine troops are greatly outnumbered they are offering stiff resistance ... in a series of delaying actions." Frank Hewlett's article on the landings, however, embellished the details. MacArthur had "assumed personal command," he wrote, and suggested to readers the ensuing battle might decide "the immediate fate of the Philippines." Lee described the sounds of war, telling readers how in Manila "the scream of air raid sirens mingled with the tolling of the church bells."[12] The public appreciated even more the stories that told them about the fighting men themselves. The Japanese invasion interrupted mail service, and for the duration of the defensive campaign those back home received little mail from the front lines. Short of this intimate contact, stories from men who had seen their loved ones—like Lee's—were the next best thing.[13]

These stories and photographs—of ordinary men at war—gave a "hero-hungry nation" what it needed during the darkest and most uncertain days of the war and fostered a connection between civilians and the young men engaged in the Bataan campaign.[14] MacArthur's biographers have chronicled the overwhelming attention he received (and sought) as the indefatigable leader of US forces in the Pacific, but the press also paid attention to average

GIs and personalized them for Americans back home. A couple of days after the attack on Clark Field, for example, Lee filed a story about the antiaircraft artillery unit responsible for shooting down the first Japanese plane during the air assault. He had spent the night with "American youngsters," who after just "one day of war" had become "tough, determined soldiers" and were no longer "kids in soldiers' uniforms." The Office of Censorship's press guidelines prevented him from identifying the unit by name, but Lee's careful remark that they spoke with "the drawling accent of a Southwestern State" convinced editors at the *Albuquerque Journal* he was talking about the 200th Coast Artillery, and they printed the story with the headline "Southwest Gunners Knock Down Five Jap Planes."[15] Other papers across the nation, however, emphasized the universal message of the story—that war had made the boys tough, grizzled fighters. *Life* later printed firsthand accounts of Clark Field written by Joe Smith and Paul Womack, both sergeants from Carlsbad. Their tales confirmed both the *Journal*'s deduction and Lee's assessment of the soldiers' overnight transformation. "We were just a bunch of little kids out there when we started," Womack wrote, but "we know now we've got what they can't take."[16]

The feature in *Life* introduced the nation to Smith, Womack, and Battery F. In April 1942 they became hometown heroes when Lee wrote a story about Carlsbad's "First in Spite of Hell" just before the surrender. Lee did not identify the unit, but the details did.[17] He reassured families that their boys were alive and reported statistics about their battlefield successes. He named several of the young men—Smith, Gene and Dwayne Davis, and a Sergeant Hall—and remarked they had "Bataan faces" that were "lined, strained, and streaked with dust." Despite the harsh battlefield conditions "none of them was grumbling." When the next day's headlines reported Bataan had fallen, the people of Carlsbad clung to Lee's assurances "the boys were all alive and well."[18] Ken Dixon captured the town's mood when he penned a letter to Lee as his daily editorial. The AP picked it up, and papers across the country reprinted the editorial, commenting, "Wherever people read it they were proud of their fighting men." Dixon shared with Lee "how much that story . . . pepped up" the families back home. "Things are plenty bad on Bataan," he wrote, "and those boys' parents here in this little Pecos river valley city know it." But, he continued, "You said 'I talked to them' and 'I heard them say,' and . . . it was as good as hearing direct. . . . These folks have come to regard you as a personal friend who brings them daily messages from their boys." In fact, "if we took a vote among all the families of the . . . boys as to their favorite hero, they'd pick MacArthur first—but we believe you'd be second."[19]

Advertisements for John Hersey's first book, *Men on Bataan*, published in June 1942, reflected this infatuation with MacArthur. Many people remember Hersey for his account of the devastating destruction of the atomic bomb from *Hiroshima*, but in this lesser-known work he paid attention to the everyday heroism of America's earliest combatants. Some reviewers carefully pointed out half of the book was filled with "stories of individuals ... of privates, corporals and sergeants and commissioned officers" and their "acts of heroism that became commonplace in Bataan." Hersey relied on dispatches filed by the Jacobys and Mydans, but he did some of his own research: He contacted families for information about the men, asking for intimate details like nicknames, hobbies, talents, idiosyncrasies, girlfriends, wives, and children so that the "heroes [were] made human." He wanted Americans to appreciate "the good young men who loved their mothers."[20] And so he told them how tough Smith was. He "grew up muscular" and broke his nose when he "played soldier" with his brother. He was a strong swimmer and liked to box. Womack loved to make people laugh, and he collected Indian artifacts and wanted to be a doctor like his father. Hersey filled the "crying vacuum" of American morale by helping readers humanize the "Bataan defenders," portraying them as "reluctant warriors ... average, clean-living young men from small towns whose patriotism led them to fight a war in tropical jungles."[21] One biographer noted the patriotic impulse behind *Men on Bataan*, written largely "for the sake of morale and truth in this year of American defeat," and the hero-hungry public lapped it up. It sold more than seven thousand copies in six months and spent twenty-six weeks on the *New York Times* best-seller list.[22]

Lee, Hersey, and the Jacobys gave the public stories of boys who became men overnight, of sons who wrote letters home and carried them in their uniform pockets, and of battle-weary soldiers who did their duty despite immense fatigue. They ensured that the GIs on Bataan were not anonymous. They were brothers, sons, fathers, husbands. Their families and communities missed them, felt their sacrifices deeply, and mourned them when they died. Americans were compelled to identify with the soldiers, imagine them as the boys next door, and admire their skill and courage in the heat of battle. The point was this: Families with men in the Philippines need not be embarrassed that they had surrendered, because the boys were "like you and your sons and your sisters and your friends. They have reacted as you will react when your crisis comes, splendidly and worthily."[23] Editorial cartoonist Henry Barrow emphasized that the soldiers on Bataan embodied the qualities of martial masculinity with his drawing, "Eternal Fire," published around the country a week after the surrender. Barrow's cartoon featured a flame comprised of soldiers ready for battle rising out of one of the deep black "foxholes of Bataan," each soldier labeled with one of the qualities to which every fighting man should aspire: patriotism, courage, valor, heroism, spirit, and fortitude.[24]

The surrender, the media narrative asserted, was not a reflection of the men themselves and could not be blamed on weakness of character, body, or will but was instead militarily necessary. It was an outcome the soldiers neither desired nor welcomed, and most probably resisted. To underscore this point, the *Coast Artillery Journal* recommended *Men on Bataan* as a must-read for officers, soldiers, and civilians. Its excerpt featured Smith and his fellow artillerymen and ran with the title, "Better Than the Enemy," a less-than-subtle insistence on the American fighting man's combat superiority.[25] Radioman Irving Strobing's last message out of Corregidor before the "enemy snatched his fingers" away from the telegraph machine was also reprinted in the issue, and the accompanying introduction—"He was only one of several thousand Americans who did what they could" in the Philippines and "stuck to his post to the very end"—reinforced this sentiment.[26]

Frank Hewlett's front-line reporting proved to readers that the men on Bataan bore none of the blame for the surrender. One of his first dispatches detailed how, according to a *Daily Herald* correspondent who interviewed US troops involved in the fighting at Lingayen Beach, a US Army colonel in command of troops at Lingayen Beach voiced "the sentiments of men of all ranks" when he "promised to fight to the last man." "Spirits were high in these beleaguered islands," he reassured readers, and there were few American casualties. Hewlett's reporting was so associated with the campaign that when, in December 1942 he reported on MacArthur's first offensive at Buna, the United Press editors inserted a lead-in to his story describing him as "heretofore a reporter of American defeats." Most of his reports from Bataan had little to do with the overall course of the defensive action and instead offered vignettes to give readers a more personalized account of the battle. His first dispatch off the peninsula described the makeshift prison holding captive Japanese soldiers. He hinted at Japanese attitudes toward surrender, and the likelihood US troops would soon face a similar choice: "The impression here is that ... if the tide of battle turns, there will be no Luzon counterpart of Dunkirk; rather, the men must fight or die." His first transmission out of Corregidor reported that the Rock "still stands, a great headache to the Japanese warlords." The "Stars and Stripes still wave," and "the garrison shows not the least sign of faltering." American artillerymen had managed to shoot down enough Japanese planes to discourage Japanese air raids, and one of those downed planes "cost United States taxpayers a total of $15 for 260 rounds of ammunition." This commentary was a clever reminder of the comparatively meager financial sacrifices civilians were being asked to make to equip the army. Hewlett made much of the morale of men fighting on the island and told civilians that MacArthur's escape to the Philippines "renewed hope that a way will be found to send them reinforcements." Men on Corregidor, he wrote, "were sticking gamely to their posts against the most tremendous odds." With only antiaircraft guns to deter Japanese bombers because "the defending forces are without air strength" the task was a formidable one.[27] He exaggerated soldiers' morale, but his stories gave folks on the home front a useful rhetorical framework for imagining and describing the soldiers and the conditions under which they fought.

Clark Lee tempered Hewlett's overzealous description of the soldiers' mood when he shared the satirical conversations a few "hard-bitten soldiers" had about rumors that help was coming—a million-man convoy was on its way, and a quarter mile of a new bridge between San Francisco and Manila was already finished. The story was meant to be entertaining, but the fanciful banter belied their sense of despair and isolation, made clear in a private's melancholy comment: "I bet my mammy and pappy done forgot they had a son. They probably sawed my corner off the dinner table," bemoaned Pvt. Williams.[28] Hewlett highlighted the gloomy satire of these exchanges when he penned the ditty that has since come to epitomize the sense of abandonment the men on Bataan felt. *Time* used the first two lines of Hewlett's tune in a story in its 9 March 1942 issue, and Americans wasted no time incorporating them into their letters urging the Roosevelt administration to speed relief to the Philippines. Upon his return to the United States in 1945, Wainwright included the entirety of "the little tune" in his autobiographical account of the war, which ran in newspapers across the country:

> We're the battling bastards of Bataan,
> No momma, no poppa, no Uncle Sam
> No aunts, no uncles, no nephews, no nieces,
> No rifles, no guns or artillery pieces
> And nobody gives a damn.[29]

The rhyme reinforced Americans' faith in the soldiers' courage and resourcefulness but also forced them to recognize nothing was going to be done for the islands. After news of MacArthur's departure from Corregidor to the relative safety of Australia in early February 1942, Robert Noble and Ellis Jones, who led the antiwar organization Friends of Progress, co-opted the couplet from *Time* to criticize the general for running "out in the dead of night" and leaving his men behind. They were subsequently arrested on charges of sedition and accused of libel for "impeach[ing] MacArthur's] honesty and integrity" and "expos[ing] him to public contempt and ridicule."[30] Their arrest shows how sensitive US leadership, and the public, was to any suggestion that the men in the Philippines—especially MacArthur—were anything less than heroes. Any interpretation of events in the Philippines that threatened to undermine the carefully crafted image of MacArthur as the islands' savior—an image made more powerful by his well-publicized assurances that his priority in Australia was to organize relief for the Philippine garrison—was unacceptable. Though the men doing the fighting felt less than charitable toward "Dugout Doug," news of his daring escape to Australia thrilled stateside admirers, for whom his surrender "would be a symbolic and psychological shock," and further convinced them he was the only one who cared about the boys in the Philippines.[31]

If Hewlett's "battling bastards" hinted at the deteriorating conditions on Bataan, his dispatches post-surrender confirmed them and rendered the reputation of the men on Bataan unassailable. "Courage seemed too weak a word to describe the conduct" of men who were "hard as nails from the rugged outdoor life" and from "fighting the Japanese." They were "tough," and "suffered the tortures of hell" during the campaign and ultimately were felled not by lack of spirit, courage, or will, but by "fever, hunger, and fatigue."[32] Medical personnel estimated that 80 percent of soldiers on the peninsula were unfit for duty due to disease, and reported that giving

> an accurate word-picture of conditions . . . at the time immediately preceding the surrender of our forces on Bataan would tax the descriptive powers of a rhetorical genius, but . . . almost every man in Bataan was suffering, not only from the effects of prolonged starvation, but also from . . . dysentery and malaria. . . . Of the supposedly well men . . . all were thin and weak from starvation. Many were swollen with nutritional anemia.[33]

Hewlett reported, it was malaria and dysentery, not the Japanese, who were "the deadliest of our enemies." *Life* published a series of photographs taken by the Jacobys in two issues that offered further proof of the soldiers' bravery and the toll illness, disease, and a lack of supplies extracted. Doctors, lacking proper medicine and equipment, resorted to treating gangrene by slicing open festering wounds and exposing them to air.[34] Readers could see severed skin, shredded muscles, and hints of bone. Wallace Perry, editor of the *Las Cruces Sun Times* in New Mexico, contended that "parents and other kin of soldiers at the front" felt "resentment . . . doubt and foreboding" when they read these stories. For them, he alleged, the terrible conditions on the front lines pointed to "unpreparedness or suspected mismanagement of the American war effort." Another reflection on the impact of insufficient medical supplies suggested the outcome of the battle was less important than the will of the men who fought it. The loss of Bataan surely brought "bitter grief," but people should take comfort in the "spiritual compensation" that Hewlett's story provided, that "the fighting edge of the troops was never dulled" and "remained keen in spite of everything."[35]

Two cultural projects born out of these attempts to manage the consequences of defeat disguise the more complicated and problematic impact surrender had on the men and their families back home. Metro-Goldwyn-Mayer's 1943 film *Bataan*, for example, suggested that most heroic soldiers on Bataan fought to the death rather than surrender or be taken prisoner. The Museum of Modern Art's exhibit *Road to Victory* opened to the public on 21 May 1942. A photographic collage of America's early days at war, the exhibit made room for the defeat in its otherwise triumphal parade of American military, industrial, and economic successes—but recognized the dead, not the living. Beneath a life-size photograph of general infantrymen (GIs) with guns at the ready, an ode penned by Carl Sandburg paid tribute to the defenders. Both projects ignored the reality that when Bataan and Corregidor surrendered, approximately 78,000 soldiers—66,000 Filipinos and 12,000 Americans—became prisoners of the Japanese. Folks on the home front had limited knowledge about what happened after the surrender. Some families received occasional formulaic postcards while others never heard a word. A joint report released in January 1944 detailing Japanese atrocities against US personnel captured on Bataan and Corregidor, colloquially known as the Dyess Story, put an end to those nagging questions with its horrifying detail.[36]

These stories of boy-next-door heroism and "last stand" imagery made it easy for home front Americans to recall similarly inspiring tales from the nation's past, in particular the heavily mythologized and symbolically powerful "epics of defeat" like the Battle of Bunker Hill and the Alamo.[37] Comparing the defeats at Bataan and Corregidor to these formative moments in the nation's military heritage helped Americans reframe the defeat as both a practical and a figurative victory: practical because the loss was deemed essential to the final conquest of Japan and figurative because it demonstrated the proficiency, spirit, and devotion of America's fighting men. Casting the men who surrendered on Bataan as descendants of the nation's earliest troops and soldiers who continued fighting against hopeless odds reconfigured constructions of martial masculinity to make room for suffering male bodies by emphasizing their self-sufficiency, discipline, obedience, and sacrifice. Collectively, this helped Americans give meaning to the sacrifices made by the men on Bataan. If men died at Bunker Hill and the Alamo to forge the American republic, men died—and surrendered—at Bataan to preserve it.

Newspaper editors, public officials, and even Roosevelt were quick to give readers history "lessons" that provided context for the Bataan surrender. One applauded Clark Lee's reporting, particularly his stories about the gunners, and claimed his dispatches did "more than 50 home-front rallies to stir patriotism." He reminded readers that what marksmen "did at Bunker Hill . . . is being repeated on Bataan Peninsula where a new generation of Americans is taking careful aim when it sees 'the whites of their eyes.'" History was repeating itself, argued another: Gen. MacArthur was "giving to Bataan the immortality that Capt. Prescott gave to Bunker Hill." Speaking to Nebraska businessmen, Nebraska Supreme Court Justice Bayard H. Paine acknowledged America has always made "a slow start in war," like losing the "battle of Bunker Hill in 1775," but American spirit and production would soon "turn the tide our way." A widely circulated commentary on Rudyard Kipling's *White Man's Burden* professed the bard had been wrong; Filipinos thirsted for freedom and instead of a liability were "the white man's boast." The "brown legion of Bataan, MacArthur's stubborn fox-hole fighters," were the "heirs of Bunker Hill [and] the Alamo." When Roosevelt issued the annual proclamation recognizing 6 April as "Army Day," he highlighted the contributions of citizen-soldiers to the cause of liberty, like "Israel Putnam, who left his plow in a New England furrow to take up a gun and fight at Bunker Hill." Harry Saylor of New Jersey's *Courier-Post* remarked Bataan was the "Bunker Hill of the 20th Century," and comforted citizens by reminding them that "Americans ever have drawn their most inspiring battle cries not from the glories of victory, but from the challenge given by temporary defeats." America had lost the battle, he continued, "but we will win the war."

An editorial in *The Express*, the local paper for Clinton County, Pennsylvania, which had sent a number of young men to the Philippines, declared, "Hero is an inadequate word for those men whose feats of arms have been military miracles. . . . [They] fought a battle which ranks with Bunker Hill. . . . For heroism has nothing to do with defeat or victory; its spiritual triumph rises above the military outcome of a courageous fight against overwhelming odds." The men who defended Bataan possessed "heroism, dauntless courage, unconquerable spirit," and the surrender would only become a defeat if home front civilians "let disappointment weaken our efforts" and "betrayed the heroes of Bataan by lukewarm and gloomy attitudes." Indeed, "Bataan was another Bunker's Hill, important merely as a milepost in the war." These "hard-fighting grim veterans ... [made] a stand for freedom" and because they "refused to break faith, sealed Japan's doom." Bataan was a "victorious defeat" because "they accomplished exactly what they set out to accomplish." Americans should remember its "soldiers have been beaten before" at the Alamo and Bunker Hill, but "the Stars and Stripes still wave over Massachusetts and over Texas," and "Old Glory again will wave over the Philippines." Dr. Edgar Jones, a clergyman, wrote that Bataan would "go down in storied page alongside Bunker Hill" and "evoke encomiums, inspire poetry, and give magic to the painter's brush," and was, like Valley Forge, a "synonym for suffering and sacrifice." And when Corregidor, too, fell, people still found the metaphor useful and reiterated it was "materiel, not manhood" that failed. "American blood had soaked the battlefields of defeat" like Bunker Hill and the Alamo, but Bataan and Corregidor were not "conquered" but "occupied," and in time the American flag would "run up on every flagpole in Manila."[38]

People found the Alamo an especially appealing trope for the heroism of the men on Bataan. Unlike Bunker Hill, which largely functioned as an allegory for martial tradition, courage, patriotism, and freedom from tyranny, the Alamo recalled an "apocalyptic" clash between "civilization" and "barbarism." It was consequently a more tempting analogy for the first prolonged war between the United States and Japan.[39] One editorial, for example, scoffed at the surrender and charged the "little brown ... barbarians" won only victories of "overwhelming numbers ... and treachery," not of "superior soldiery" nor "braver hearts." In her syndicated column, Elsa Maxwell asserted that when historians wrote about Bataan and Corregidor "500 years from now," their accounts would "outrival the Odyssey of Homer and the battle of Thermopylae, where a handful of Spartans (like our peerless Filipinos), led by Leonidas (like our General Wainwright), held the pass of Thermopylae against the barbaric hordes ... to the last man." A Texas newspaper gave readers a brief lesson on the significance of the Alamo for the present day: The defeat at the Alamo "might well have ended the great adventure" of winning freedom for Texas, "but not for stout men who knew what they wanted and were willing to pay whatever the cost to get it." Americans had failed to recognize the threat Axis nations posed to their liberties and were "paying dearly due to our lack of preparation," but America would ultimately "preserve its own freedom ... and make all men free." Another compared MacArthur to Davy Crockett and claimed his "stand" was being made by "the kind of soldiers that exemplify American manhood." In a *Los Angeles Times* piece on the Alamo, the fort's defenders "peered from the Valhalla of America's valiant" onto "MacArthur and his men" who "would without question ... go to their deaths fighting." A month before the surrender, the *Lansing State Journal* remarked that a lesson of the Alamo was that "no matter how brave ... the soldiers of one side may be, they cannot win if vastly outnumbered," and the United States was approaching a similar juncture "this coming spring." Richard Morehead, a reporter for the United Press, pointed to other similarities between Bataan and the Alamo. In both instances, the beleaguered garrisons requested help that never came, and kept the enemy busy long enough to give the country "time to prepare for later victory." Like the Alamo, Bataan should "be remembered as one of the great feats of courage that make freedom and democracy possible." Furthermore, Japanese commanders had asked US forces to surrender—a demand well-publicized (and extensively mocked) in the American press—and they refused, another parallel that did not go unnoticed. Like their frontier ancestors, the men on Bataan "ignored the demand" and fought "against overwhelming odds with ... courageous hardihood."[40] California Bank printed an ad for defense bonds that claimed Bataan would "live forever in memory with Bunker Hill [and] the Alamo" as "a story of American courage, initiative, self-sacrifice and heroism."

Drawing upon these powerful precedents gave Americans a way to make the surrender more palatable. It furthermore helped them explain it as a cultural and political problem and not just a military one. Indeed, if American "lethargy" bore some of the blame for the defeat, then "Remember Bataan!" could be an effective clarion call for meeting the demands of the warfare state. No sacrifice on the home front could come anywhere close to matching those made on Bataan, and so citizens should do their duty cheerfully; to do otherwise would certainly hamper the war effort but would also dilute the hard-won spirit of Bataan and betray the men who fought. An editorial in the *Asheville Citizen-Times* crystallized the ways Bataan became a benchmark for wartime sacrifice:

> The loss of Bataan is bitter medicine for the American people ... all the more unpleasant because our nation with its tremendous military potential had to leave the men to their fate ... but ... it may enrage us so that we will begin now to throw our whole effort into the desperate job of winning this war. ... If the loss of Bataan has such an effect on all of us, then it may prove to be the turning point in the war. For America aroused, unified and busy is invincible. ... To all of them, we the American people owe much. They fought prodigiously and suffered greatly. They have furnished a new yardstick by

which patriotism is to be measured in these testing times. May all of us . . . emulate in our several duties the sacrificial spirit which they have shown!"[41]

In the House and Senate, frustrated congressmen rebuked their colleagues for all manner of behaviors they asserted broke faith with the men on Bataan and made those at home unworthy of their sacrifice. They furthermore used Bataan as a symbol of the consequences of inaction. For example, Sheridan Downey, a Democrat from California, railed that the "wounded, captured, and even dead men of Bataan . . . stand invisibly at our elbows" and reminded Americans of "some bitter truths" (most importantly for his fellow senators) that Bataan fell "because of our lack of foresight, our slothfulness, our incapacity to make up our minds and act." Representative James O'Connor shrewdly pulled out the Bataan yardstick when he advocated improved living conditions in Washington, DC. The chaos in the city prevented officials from getting about the business of war. "The starving boys of Bataan scanned the skies and seas for planes and ships that never came," he griped, and when they looked to Washington, they found a "city overflowing with pleasure seekers, grafters, chiselers, and other parasites."[42]

These senators and representatives believed—like many of their constituents—that the Bataan defenders' sacrifices demanded accountability. For some, however, the guilty rhetoric was not enough. To that end, with almost two thousand of his own constituents in the Philippines, Senator Dennis Chávez, a Democrat from New Mexico, became an important spokesperson for soldiers and their families and proposed legislation to reward their sacrifice.[43] In September 1943, he introduced Senate Bill 1374, "A Bill to Provide for the Promotion of Certain American Prisoners of War," and by doing so provided citizens a way to further articulate the significance of the Bataan surrender. Chávez's introduction of the bill was largely a response to the suffering of families throughout New Mexico who had men in the Philippines, but the legislation found an eager audience among other Americans who believed the men deserved recognition from the government that let them down. Letters of support poured into the senator's office.

Promotion, they argued, was "one of the few ways to repay our men for their sacrifices." While "it was true we could not help them on Bataan," we "have a chance to help them now in Washington," because "our men in the Philippines knocked a home run even though many of them will never reach the homeland again." Families at home "haven't forgotten" about the men on Bataan, but "sort of felt that everyone else had." If the legislation passes, "they will know that they were remembered by the country for which they fought." The "fine brave men deserve this promotion as much as some men

... who will never see actual overseas service," especially since they "had the misfortune to be sent to the Philippines when we were so patently unprepared to defend the islands."[44] Proponents of the bill made it clear that they believed the men did not choose to surrender but were forced to do so.

The word "surrender" is noticeably absent from most of their letters. This tendency hints that they sensed the implicit awkwardness of rewarding defeat. They instead chose to describe soldiers' resistance *up to the point* of surrender, and comment upon their suffering as captives *after* the surrender. They overcame this hesitancy, however, when Secretary of War Henry Stimson sent a letter to Senator Robert Reynolds, chairman of the Committee on Military Affairs, opposing the legislation. His response antagonized the families of the surrendered men, and they took it as a personal attack on the heroism of the Bataan defenders:

> The War Department recognizes the spirit that prompted the introduction of the proposed bill but believes that granting of additional benefits or pay to captured personnel should not be accomplished by means of promotions. The prime consideration in the making of wartime promotions is to give [personnel] the rank appropriate to the duties and responsibilities they are discharging.... Other circumstances besides capture, such as prolonged illness or hospitalization for wounds, may hinder or prevent a soldier's promotion. In the case of captured personnel there is no way to distinguish between those men who, by virtue of having fought to the last, might be deserving of a reward in the form of promotion and those who surrendered in circumstances under which they might reasonably have been expected to continue to resist. The general effect of promoting such personnel would be to establish a reward for becoming a prisoner.[45]

For Stimson, rejecting the bill was a matter of policy. Passage of the bill would be a slippery slope to the wholesale promotion of POWs, regardless of the circumstances of their capture.

To the mothers and fathers whose sons were prisoners, however, his coldhearted response was a rejection of the men and the sacrifices they made for an ungrateful nation. The Navy, too, opposed the bill, but Secretary of the Navy Ralph A. Bard avoided the surrender question and argued that the bill discriminated against men missing in action. Stimson's rejection horrified Chávez:

> How in God's green earth would he expect the boys in the Philippines ... to continue to resist. I think the implication ... is that those boys, who are now

going through the agony of the damned because they were captured ... quit of their own volition. ... To come around here and say that there might have been an American boy in the Philippine Islands, Guam, or Wake that dared to quit because he didn't want to fight is beyond comprehension. ... Why is it up to someone behind the lines to judge as to why those boys are prisoners ... ? Now I know why, and everybody else knows why. They didn't have the wherewithal with which to fight. It was not their fault; it was probably the fault of someone who could write such a letter.[46]

The day after the hearing, Chávez went before his colleagues in the Senate to express his indignation at Stimson's insinuations. He took the opportunity to emphasize New Mexico's significant sacrifices in the Philippines. "I have in my hand a list of every boy from New Mexico who was in the Philippine Islands," he offered. "The list comprises 38 pages of closely typewritten names," and "I resent the intimation ... even one of [those boys] would surrender when he might still be able to continue to resist."[47] His fellow senators were sympathetic, and news agencies quickly picked up the story. They branded Stimson's rejection of the bill as a "'sneer' at Yanks," and repeated Chávez's charge that he had accused the soldiers of "cowardice" and suggested they were "yellow-bellies." These epithets angered families across the country and drew attention to Chávez's bill, prompting another spate of letter-writing.

Citizens' angry responses to Stimson's rejection of the bill drew on the rhetoric they had stockpiled in the early months of the war and reinforced that there was nothing shameful in the soldiers' surrender. Their insistence the men on Bataan deserved promotion despite their current state of captivity shaped a hierarchy of sacrifice, with Bataan defenders occupying one of the highest positions. At the bottom were "chair warmers" and officials like Stimson, who was not "even half the man he was supposed to be," and "sitting on velvet in Washington" had the gall "to "call someone who was fighting, dead, wounded and rotting in a prison camp ... yellow bellies." Not too far from those officials were workers who were too busy striking instead of "being Americans," like "our boys in the Japanese prison camps." In the middle were other servicemen, who spent the war "doing nothing but sitting behind desks and taking it easy" yet were "promoted over nite and make stripes and bars." Alfredo Trujillo, from Taos, complained it was unfair there were "thousands of men in this country who never have seen a single day of active warfare, are being well fed, are enjoying every luxury our government affords them, and are being promoted every few months." Even soldiers serving in other combat areas could not match the suffering of the Bataan defenders, because they "have weapons to fight with, full stomachs to build up their strength. If sick or wounded they have medicine, blood plasma and hospitals."[48] These arguments for promoting the men on Bataan eroded much of the stigma attached to surrender. If the soldiers lacked the materiel and medicine to wage a proper war, they could hardly be blamed for the defeat.

To people at home, the deprivation of the Philippine campaign amplified the martial masculinity of the Bataan defenders because they had to fight with less: "Unless the public has been badly misinformed, our men . . . surrendered only after taking physical, mental and moral beatings beyond the capacity of human nature to absorb."[49] They had to rely on things no quartermaster could provide to endure privation, hunger, and illness—a state of affairs that regrettably continued after the surrender, when attempts to send relief and aid to prisoners in the camps were repeatedly squashed. They pushed their bodies and minds to the edge of human endurance, and thus could lay claim to an unimpeachable masculinity that dwarfed that of men who had the luck not to have been assigned to the Philippines. Furthermore, some recognized that if the soldiers returned home, the physical and psychological consequences of combat and captivity would persist—thus their time on Bataan imposed a lifelong burden. The Buckners from Hope, New Mexico, argued that we "sit in luxury, enjoying more than ever before," "and every dime is stained with the lifeblood of our poor boys that gave their all." Even if the boys returned home, they predicted, "their lives are wrecked, their ideals shattered, they can never forget."[50] Despite being reintroduced several times, Chávez's legislation never passed. Its language excluded far more men than it included. Nevertheless, the proposed law called attention to the fact that many Americans believed the sacrifices and suffering of men who were in the Pacific between 8 December 1941 and 6 May 1942 deserved recognition, especially from the government that had so callously sent them to the Philippines and then abandoned them.

After Army Rangers, Alamo Scouts, and Filipino guerrillas liberated Camp Cabanatuan in January 1945, an editorial in the *Charlotte Observer* reflected on the sacrifices of the Bataan defenders and summarized how many grieving, but proud, families viewed the surrender and its ghastly cost, and the relative impossibility of adequately honoring them:

> When rescue came at last, those who could still walk marched proudly out with heads high like the American soldiers they were. . . . At that moment the saga of American courage rose to new heights and reached the sublime.

... Surely their devotion has gone above and beyond the call of duty. But what medal ever struck could be a fit emblem of their sacrifice? What sculptor could fashion a symbol worthy of their ordeal? Their decorations are the scars of wounds and torture that can never be erased from their bodies. . . . Let them all have the Medal of Honor. It is the highest we can give them, but tawdry in comparison with the deeds it recognizes. We at home cannot face these men.[51]

The language that Americans used to describe the service, sacrifice, and suffering of their men in the Philippines shows they did their best to strip surrender of its negative connotations. Rather than repudiate the surrender as weak, unmanly, or cowardly, armed with the vocabulary and imagery provided by war correspondents, reporters, and cartoonists writing from the front lines and on the home front, civilians positioned the Bataan defenders' willingness to continue to fight against impossible odds as the epitome of what it meant to be an American soldier. Civilians grabbed onto both the good (heroics, morale, patriotism) and the bad (abandonment, starvation, disease) to make sense of their significant losses, to inspire home front sacrifice, to demand accountability from the federal government, and to transform the surrender from a story of defeat to one of ultimate victory.

Notes

1. "Lee to Tell of Bataan in Talk Tonight," *Gallup Independent*, 29 March 1943; "Clark Lee in High Tribute to 200th," *Clovis News-Journal*, 29 March 1943.

2. For further on wartime narratives and the involvement of the press in shaping the public imagination of the war, see chapter 7 by Victoria Sotvedt in this volume.

3. The "stigma of surrender" refers to the "social pressures that compelled soldiers to view surrender as shameful." Writing about German prisoners of war during World War I, Brian Feltman notes "soldiers and civilians alike revered sacrificial death as the highest expression of national devotion," and so "society often relegated prisoners of war to the commemorative emptiness between victory and death." See Brian K. Feltman, *The Stigma of Surrender: German Prisoners, British Captors, and Manhood in the Great War and Beyond* (Chapel Hill: University of North Carolina Press, 2015), 3.

4. Chapter 12 by Katrin Paehler in this volume also discusses ways that individuals redefined wartime experiences.

5. "Remember Wake Island Also!" *Oregonian* (Portland, OR), 26 December 1941; Lowell Limpus, "Hitler Learns What It's Like to Catch a Few on the Chin," *New York Daily News*, 18 December 1941.

"The Men of Bataan Lived Up to the Best American Tradition" | 225

6. Louis Morton, *Fall of the Philippines: The War in the Pacific* (Washington, DC: Center of Military History, 1993), 31–32; In late 1940 and early 1941, slow progress was made in modernizing and enhancing Filipino defenses, but this process accelerated in late summer of 1941. General George Grunert was responsible for the defensive buildup in the Philippines, which he suggested would check the "defeatist attitude" in the Philippines that the US cared little. Functional, financial, and philosophical limitations stifled a robust amplification of the island's defensive capabilities. See Mark Skinner Watson, *Chief of Staff: Prewar Plans and Preparations* (Washington, DC: Historical Division, Department of the Army, 1950), 411–52; Douglas MacArthur, *Reminiscences* (Annapolis, MD: Naval Institute Press, 1964), esp. part 4, "In Defense of Peace"; Christopher L. Kolakowski, *Last Stand on Bataan: The Defense of the Philippines, December 1941–May 1942* (Jefferson, NC: McFarland, 2016); Glen M. Williford, *Racing the Sunrise: Reinforcing America's Pacific Outposts, 1941–1942* (Annapolis, MD: Naval Institute Press, 2010).

7. Franklin D. Roosevelt, "Fireside Chat on Progress of the War," 23 February 1942, *Public Papers and Addresses of Franklin D. Roosevelt, 1942* (New York: Harper & Brothers Publishers, 1950), 105–16.

8. Steven Casey, *The War Beat, Pacific: The American Media at War against Japan* (New York: Oxford University Press, 2021), 4–8; "War Orders," *Time* 38, no. 24 (15 December 1941): 56.

9. For a similar look at how a few individuals in a cohort played important roles in the cultural and social history of the war, see chapter 10 by Brian Hayashi in this volume.

10. War Department, *Regulations for Correspondents Accompanying US Army Forces in the Field*, 21 January 1942.

11. Steven Casey argues that much of the Pacific War was "shrouded." MacArthur exercised heavy-handed control over press releases, and civilians on the home front received few battlefield details. Between December 1941 and May 1942, the "veil over the Philippines campaign had been partial," but the stories that made it out were far more cheerful and optimistic than the combat reality. Casey, *The War Beat, Pacific*, 4–8, 36–37, 42.

12. War Department, "War Department Communique No. 27," 24 December 1941; Frank Hewlett, "MacArthur, Manila's Own Forces Rush to 'All Out' War Front, Face Foe of Superior Numbers," *Salt Lake Telegram*, 24 December 1941; Clark Lee, "Island Defenders More Than Holding Own," *Casper Star-Tribune* (Casper, WY), 25 December 1941.

13. For a discussion of the relationship between mail and morale, see Judy Barrett Litoff and David C. Smith, "'Will He Get My Letter?' Popular Portrayals of Mail and Morale during World War II," *Journal of Popular Culture* 23, no. 4 (Spring 1990): 21–43.

14. "Hero-Hungry Nation Goes for MacArthur in Big Way," *Life* 12, no. 13 (30 March 1942): 43.

15. Clark Lee, "Southwest Gunners Knock Down Five Jap Planes," *Albuquerque Journal*, 11 December 1941.

16. Joe Smith and Paul Womack, "We Shoot Down the First Japs," *Life* 11, no. 25 (22 December 1941): 29–30.

17. Both the War Department's field manual for war correspondents and the Office of Censorship's *Code of Wartime Practices for the American Press* asked reporters not to publish details that revealed the identities of troops or their units. See Office of Censorship, *Code of Wartime Practices for the American Press*, edition of 15 June 1942 (Washington, DC: United States Government Printing Office, 1942).

18. Clark Lee, "All Alive, Carlsbad Boys Keep 'em Falling on Bataan," *Daily Current-Argus*, 8 April 1942; "Small Ray of Hope Seen for Carlsbad Boys," *Daily Current-Argus*, 9 April 1942.

19. Kenneth Dixon, "Letter to Lee," *Daily Current-Argus*, 9 April 1942.

20. John Hersey, *Men on Bataan* (New York: Alfred A. Knopf, 1942); Review of *Men on Bataan*, by John Hersey, *Kirkus Reviews*, 1 June 1942; S. T. Williamson, "The Heroic Defense of Bataan," *New York Times*, 7 June 1942. Despite his open acknowledgment that much of his writing came from the dispatches filed by the war journalists Melville and Annalee Whitmore Jacoby and Carl Mydans, some have accused Hersey of plagiarism. See Anne Fadiman, *Ex Libris: Confessions of a Common Reader* (New York: Farrar, Straus and Giroux, 1998); Jeremy Treglown, *Mr. Straight Arrow: The Career of John Hersey, Author of* Hiroshima (New York: Farrar, Straus and Giroux, 2019), 63–69; "Jacoby, Melville," in Mitchel P. Roth, *Historical Dictionary of War Journalism* (Westport, CT: Greenwood Press, 1997), 155–56; and Nicholas Lemann, "John Hersey and the Art of Fact," *New Yorker*, 22 April 2019, https://www.newyorker.com/magazine/2019/04/29/john-hersey-and-the-art-of-fact.

21. The phrase "crying vacuum" is drawn from Alfred Knopf's letter to Hersey just after Pearl Harbor asking him to write something about the war with Japan. Quoted in Treglown, *Mr. Straight Arrow*, 63. Gary R. Hess, *The United States at War, 1941–1945* (Wheeling, IL: Harlan Davidson, 2011), 63.

22. David Sanders, *John Hersey* (New Haven, CT: Twayne, 1967), 23–25; Treglown, *Mr. Straight* Arrow, 67; Sheila K. Johnson, *The Japanese through American Eyes* (Stanford, CA: Stanford University Press, 1988), 14.

23. Williamson, "The Heroic Defense of Bataan."

24. Henry Barrow, "Eternal Fire," *New York Daily News*, 16 April 1942.

25. John Hersey, "Better Than the Enemy," excerpt from *Men on Bataan*, reprinted in *Coast Artillery Journal* 85, no. 4 (July–August 1942), 8–11.

26. Private Irving Strobing, "Corregidor's Last Breath," *Coast Artillery Journal* 85, no. 4 (July–August 1942), 2–3.

27. Frank Hewlett, "Not a Jap Lands Alive In 3-Day Luzon Battle," *New York Daily News*, 16 December 1941; Frank Hewlett, "US Infantry Chases Japs in First Clash," *New York Daily News*, 19 December 1941; Frank Hewlett, "'Buna Busted!'

All-American Cheer," *New York Daily News*, 17 December 1942; Frank Hewlett, "Jap Captives Revel in Good Yank Food," *New York Daily News*, 4 February 1942; Frank Hewlett, "Lone Filipino Sticks to Gun, Kills 11 Japanese," *New York Daily News*, 21 February 1942; Frank Hewlett, "1,500 Bombs—But Corregidor Flag Is Still Flying," *New York Daily News*, 13 March 1942; Frank Hewlett, "Bataan Awaits MacArthur," *New York Daily News*, 27 March 1942; Frank Hewlett, "Corregidor Guns Down 9 Jap Planes," *New York Daily News*, 28 March 1942.

28. Clark Lee, "Hard-Bitten Soldiers in the Philippines Know How to Evaluate All the Rumors," *Clovis News-Journal*, 4 February 1942.

29. "No Mama, No Papa," *Time* 39, no. 10 (9 March 1942): 22; Jonathan Wainwright, "This Is My Story," *San Francisco Examiner*, 15 October 1945. Wainwright's story was published in a series of installments in newspapers and published as a book. See Jonathan Wainwright, *General Wainwright's Story: The Account of Four Years of Humiliating Defeat, Surrender, and Captivity* (Garden City, NJ: Doubleday,1946), 54. The interior title page of the book identifies Wainwright as the man "who paid the price of his country's unpreparedness," offering him as a victim rather than an agent of the defeat, thereby absolving him of any blame or guilt for surrendering his men.

30. "Accused of Libel on Gen. M'Arthur," *New York Times*, 1 April 1942.

31. "Nab 3 for 'Criminal Libeling' M'Arthur!" *Santa Rosa Republican*, 31 March 1942; Ray Tucker, "National Whirligig—Help," *Albuquerque Journal*, 26 January 1942.

32. Frank Hewlett, "Our Boys on Bataan Now Tanned, Bearded, Hard as Nails," *Spokane Chronicle*, 3 April 1942; Frank Hewlett, "Bataan's Brave Defenders Suffered Tortures of Hell, Says Hewlett," *Knoxville News-Sentinel*, 11 April 1942.

33. Wibb E. Cooper, *Medical Department Activities in the Philippines from 1941 to 6 May 1942, Including Medical Activities in Japanese Prisoner of War Camps* (Washington, DC: United States Army Medical Department, 1946), 44–45, available at https://collections.nlm.nih.gov.

34. Notably, most of the wounded pictured were Filipino, either military personnel or civilians. Most of the Americans in the images were shown in hospital beds or sitting outside convalescing. "Philippine Epic," *Life* 12, no. 15 (13 April 1942): 25–37; "Bataan Wounded Live with Pain," *Life* 12, no. 16 (20 April 1942): 32–35.

35. Frank Hewlett, "Remaining Americans on Bataan Surrendered to Japs," *Bakersfield Californian*, 11 April 1942; Wallace Perry, "Chaparral," *Las Cruces Sun-News*, 19 April 1942; "Enemy Malaria," *Billings Gazette*, 26 April 1942.

36. When Congress approved release of the report, newspapers immediately published the story in full. The details in the report came from prisoners who escaped from the Japanese in the spring of 1943, most notably William Dyess, an officer in the Army Air Forces. He was barred from sharing information about the defense of Bataan and what happened afterward. He was killed in action before its release. People criticized the government for holding onto the story for

so long without releasing it. Newspapers had carried occasional stories about Japanese mistreatment of American prisoners (and in fact, James Young mentioned "the death march of the Corregidor captives" in a serial story that ran in the *Shreveport Journal* in August 1943, and the lack of robust responses to those stories is surprising). See James R. Young, "Author Tells of Horrible Torture Japs Inflict on Their Prisoners," *Shreveport Journal*, 31 August 1943.

37. See, for example, Paul Lockhard, "'Remember Bunker Hill!'?" *Quarterly Journal of Military* History 23, no. 4 (Summer 2011): 72–77; Nathaniel Philbrick, *Bunker Hill: A City, a Siege, a Revolution* (New York: Penguin Books, 2013); Holly Beachley Brear, *Alamo: Myth and Ritual at an American Shrine* (Austin: University of Texas Press, 1995); Richard R. Flores, *Remembering the Alamo: Memory, Modernity, and the Master Symbol* (Austin: University of Texas Press, 2002); Phillip Thomas Tucker, *Exodus from the Alamo: The Anatomy of the Last Stand Myth* (Philadelphia: Casemate, 2010).

38. "Marksmanship," *St. Louis Globe-Democrat*, February 5, 1942. Historians dispute whether the exact phrase "don't fire until you see the whites of their eyes" was uttered during the battle at Bunker Hill, but that it or a similar phrase was said is part of the battle's lore. "General MacArthur," *Elizabethton Star* (Elizabethton, TN), 19 February 1942; "Justice Paine Advises Business Men to 'Win the War First,'" *Lincoln Star*, 22 February 1942; "Where Kipling Was Wrong," *St. Louis Post-Dispatch*, 7 March 1942; Franklin D. Roosevelt, "Proclamation 2542—Proclaiming April 6 as Army Day," 20 March 1942, https://www.presidency.ucsb.edu/documents/proclamation-2542-proclaiming-april-6-army-day; "Bataan: Bunker Hill of the 20th Century," *Courier-Post* (Camden, NJ), April 10, 1942; "Clinton County Heroes on Bataan," *The Express* (Lock Haven, PA), 10 April 1942; "Wartime Alexandria," *Alexandria Daily Town Talk* (Alexandria, LA), 11 April 1942; "A Victorious Defeat," *Times Herald* (Port Huron, MI), 10 April 1942; Dr. Edgar Dewitt Jones, "Bataan—A New Symbol," *The Pantagraph* (Bloomington, IL), 20 April 1942; "Corregidor Like Bunker Hill," *Times Recorder* (Zanesville, OH) 12 May 1942; "Corregidor Isn't Conquered," *Wilmington Press Daily Journal*, 13 May 1942.

39. Randy Roberts and James S. Olson, *A Line in the Sand: The Alamo in Blood and Memory* (New York: Free Press, 2001), 170–73; John Dower, *War without Mercy: Race and Power in the Pacific War* (New York: Pantheon Books, 198).

40. "Cheer, Barbarians, While You May," *Spokane Chronicle*, 9 April 1942; Elsa Maxwell, "Daily Particles of Patter," *Salt Lake Telegram*, 17 April 1942; "Today Is April 21 . . . " *Valley Morning Star*, 21 April 1942; "An Inspiration," *Reno Gazette-Journal*, 16 February 1942; V.R.W., "Alamo Recalled in Bataan Conflict," *Los Angeles Times*, 7 March 1942; "Getting Ready to Commence," *Lansing State Journal*, 16 March 1942; Richard M. Morehead, "Bataan Stand Stirs Memory of the Alamo," *The Times* (Munster, IN), 3 April 1942; "Remember Bataan," *Hartford Courant*, 10 April 1942; "New Glory for 'Old Glory'!" *Los Angeles Times*, 25 March 1942.

41. "Alamo, 1942 Model," *Asheville Citizen*, 10 April 1942.

42. Senator Downey, 77th Cong., 2nd sess., *Congressional Record* 88 pt. 3:3439; Representative O'Connor, 77th Cong., 2nd sess., *Congressional Record* 88 pt. 3:3462–63.

43. Roy Lujan, "Dennis Chávez and the National Agenda, 1933–1946," *New Mexico Historical Review* 74, no. 1 (1 January 1999): 61–66.

44. US Congress, Senate, Committee on Military Affairs, *Promotion of Certain American Prisoners of War: Hearings Before the Committee on Military Affairs*, 78th Cong., 1st sess., 1943, 5–9, hereafter *Promotion Hearings*.

45. Stimson to Reynolds, reprinted in *Promotion Hearings*, 11–12.

46. *Promotion Hearings*, 15.

47. Senator Chávez, 78th Cong., 1st sess., *Congressional Record* 89, pt. 8:10207–13.

48. Eugene Hooker to Chávez, 4 December 1943; Riley Edwards to Chávez, 5 December 1943; Marie Malosek to Stimson, 7 December 1943; Ida Drake to Chávez, 10 December 1943; R. E. Aldrich to Chávez, 29 December 1943; H. R. Hopper to Chávez, 3 December 1943; Alfredo Trujillo to Robert Reynolds, 30 January 1944.

49. "Prisoners from Bataan," *Portage Daily Register* (Portage, WI), 10 December 1943.

50. Mr. and Mrs. J. C. Buckner to Chávez, 5 February 1944, box 92, folder 52, Chávez Papers. University of New Mexico Center for Southwest Research and Special Collections, Albuquerque, New Mexico.

51. "Men of Bataan," *Charlotte Observer*, 7 February 1945.

10

Who Do You Believe?
Loyalty and Asian Americans in the OSS during World War II

Brian Masaru Hayashi

Central to any intelligence organization is the reliability of its personnel who gather and submit strategic and tactical information. An agent's reporting, if accurate, could conceivably lead to victory; inaccuracy, whether deliberate or unintentional, may result in needless casualties, death, and battlefield defeat. In a global war such as World War II, these rewards and the risks related to reliability are magnified, as intelligence agencies must extract, collate, and assess information from diverse linguistic and cultural groups with varying degrees of accessibility. Some European American individuals with the necessary linguistic and cultural expertise on Asia were recruited by the Office of Strategic Services (OSS), America's first centralized intelligence agency, but their numbers fell short of the demand for translators, interpreters, analysts, propaganda production writers, artists, and field agents with the correct "racial uniform," the physical features normally associated with Northeast Asians to allow them to operate safely behind enemy lines. Asian Americans thus became the target of OSS recruitment, but the problem of reliability cropped up when the OSS realized they lacked background knowledge of these potential recruits. For their part, with few exceptions the recruits had no proven record of loyalty to the United States, such as service in the US Armed Forces, to vouch for their reliability. Linguistic and cultural skills primarily and racial appearance secondarily became factors for consideration in the search for qualified, loyal Asian Americans to reliably serve in the OSS.[1]

For historians, however, no such studies of Asian Americans in the OSS exist.[2] While much has been written on OSS operations in Europe, the few studies that include brief accounts of Asian Americans highlight racial discrimination they faced or simply place them (undistinguished from other Asians) in the agency's China or India-Burma theaters of operation. Such an oversight is hardly justified, given their immense linguistic and cultural importance to OSS operations in these two theaters. Moreover, the National Archives has made available to the public well over 5,000 cubic feet of OSS records for a quarter of a century. Given the increased availability of records related to agency and others related to Asian American communities from which these agents hailed, it is now an opportune moment to examine Asian Americans in America's first centralized intelligence agency.[3]

To that end, this chapter presents two Asian American recruits whose participation in the OSS raised the possibility of a Trojan Horse inside America's first centralized intelligence agency. Were Joe Koide (1903–1976) and Kunsung Rie (1911–1991) working for Imperial Japan even though they were employed by America's first centralized intelligence agency? The OSS wrestled with this problem in the summer of 1945 as American forces prepared for an assault on the home islands of Japan. Despite assurances to the contrary from their immediate superiors, others within and without the intelligence agency believed Koide and Rie to be agents for Imperial Japan. Some within Morale Operations questioned the loyalty of Koide and those of his team members, particularly his unwillingness to smear the Japanese emperor, which his European American superiors believed was the best way to demoralize Imperial Japan's military and civilian defense prior to an invasion of the main islands of Japan. A couple of them scrutinized Koide's propaganda radio broadcasts for hidden messages to Japanese authorities. Rie, too, faced similar skepticism, with some believing he would sell out his Special Operations team members of "Napko" to Japanese authorities once they landed in Occupied Korea. Even if Rie proved not to be a traitor, Operation Napko, with the aim to establish a spy network to eventually infiltrate the Japanese home islands and to set up guerrilla warfare inside Occupied Korea, was deemed too risky and not likely to succeed. Even Rie's immediate superior, Colonel Carl Eifler, later admitted after the end of the war that he, too, thought all Napko team members would die during the mission.[4]

The expressed doubts seem uncharitable now given the situation in which the OSS found itself in spring 1945. The defeat of Nazi Germany was only weeks away and Imperial Japan's surrender in mid-August barely more than four months into the future. However, when understood from within the context of projections regarding the war's end, concern about Asian American agents' continued loyalty to the Allied cause was understandable. The war, as many military planners saw it, was going to continue into 1946 with an amphibious assault and landing of ground forces on to Japanese territory proper, a necessity to secure unconditional surrender. That invasion of the main island of Japan, they believed, would be particularly costly, requiring over a million American casualties until Japanese leaders were compelled to surrender. Even if the Japanese capitulated, there remained the question of whether the Imperial Japanese forces in Manchuria, numbering 700,000 in 1945, and another 5.2 million troops still occupying various parts of China, would lay down their arms. Faced with this formidable force, the United States Army in April 1945 had only eighty-nine divisions in all theaters of operation or about 1.2 million soldiers. That numerical inadequacy, in turn, meant American commanders had to rely exclusively on the Chinese Nationalist forces and the forces of the Soviet Union to push the Imperial Japanese off the Asian continent. None of the Allied countries could mount a major amphibious landing force against the main islands of Japan. Only Britain offered a substantive force of nearly a million soldiers to complement an American invasion of Japan. Hence, the possibility of the war lasting well into 1946 appeared likely, even with the Soviet Union's potential assault on Imperial Japanese forces on the Asian continent.[5]

Joe Koide, Foreign Agent?

Given the possibility of the war extending into the next year, Joe Koide's efforts to break Japanese morale should have been welcomed. Koide was highly qualified for the task. He was natively fluent in the Japanese language and experienced in writing articles and essays in that language for an educated readership in Japan. From 1933 to 1937, he produced a Japanese language magazine that featured his translations of the writings of Communist Party leaders Harrison George and Rudy Baker. From 1939, Koide was contracted to print up a Japanese translation of *The History of the Communist Party of the Soviet Union*, a project which he continued until the Pearl Harbor attack. Thereafter, Koide shifted his focus back to writing and publishing *Dōhō* (Comrades), the only Japanese-language newspaper in Los Angeles permitted after the Pearl Harbor attack, since their editorial stance was consistently and unconditionally supportive of the Allied cause. Given his active participation in the Communist Party, Morale Operations officials felt reasonably certain that Koide and other Japanese American leftists were loyal to the Allied cause and staunchly opposed to the Imperial Japanese government and its fascist policies.[6]

Yet Koide was unable to satisfactorily dispel suspicions. Doubts about his background, work on behalf of Morale Operations, and above all his loyalty continued to follow him. His Communist Party peers supported the federal government's mass removal and internment of West Coast Japanese Americans in spring 1942 even though all of them, including Koide, would be imprisoned. Koide was sharply critical of the action. His Party superior

Rudy Baker believed Koide had "analyzed the Japanese-American war situation well and adopted the correct line." Koide became further alienated from his Party peers when they accused him of violating organizational security rules. As early as 1938, according to long-time Party leader Karl Yoneda, Koide was accused by another communist of being an undercover agent for the US government. Suspicions dogged Koide, especially after he collected from the forty-six Japanese members of the Communist Party their party name, real names, ages, sex, addresses, and other information—a practice that was considered inconsistent with the Party's policy of maintaining secrecy for its members. That list, minus Joe Koide's name, surfaced among the papers of the Los Angeles Japanese Consulate office years later, fueling suspicions that Koide was an agent of Imperial Japan.

Those suspicions deepened when, contrary to Party policy of support for the Allied war effort, Koide became the perceived opposition leader to Japanese American military conscription at the War Relocation Authority (WRA) camp at Heart Mountain, Wyoming, in 1943. His communist peers enthusiastically declared military service in the US Armed Forces as the duty of all Japanese Americans. Koide, however, insisted that registration for the military draft was an individual, not a group decision. His stance, at variance with Karl Yoneda and others, cast him as *the* leader of the opposition to the military draft at Heart Mountain where forty-one American-born males refused to register for the draft and were arrested, a record high for all ten of the War Relocation Authority camps. In short, they saw Koide as undermining support for Joseph Stalin's Soviet Union. Koide, in contrast, may have seen their uncritical acceptance of Party support for conscription while Japanese Americans were still interned in WRA camps as a poignant reminder of the segregation and anti-Asian discrimination he and other Asians in the Communist International (ComIntern) faced while attending Moscow's International Lenin School.[7]

Koide encountered suspicions from his OSS superiors as well. Was he still a ComIntern agent? When Koide first immigrated to the United States in 1925, his name was Nobumichi Ukai, born in 1903 in the Akashi District of Tokyo. He came to the United States on the recommendation of a missionary schoolteacher after studying English literature at Aoyama Gakuin, a prestigious college in his native Tokyo, and received a scholarship to attend the University of Denver. Ukai earned his degree and then moved to New York City in 1929 to join other young leftists. He met with Communist Party General Secretary Earl Browder who sent him off to the International Lenin School in Moscow for training. Under the false name of "Tanaka," Ukai became an underground ComIntern agent and returned to

New York City in 1933 to await orders for what he labeled the "underground era" of his career. Before long, he was sent to San Francisco to help print Party materials. Ukai moved to Los Angeles after nearly two years of writing and printing, by which time he had adopted a new name, "Teiji Koide," which belonged to a friend from the University of Denver. The real Teiji Koide, a permanent resident, had passed away in 1934, providing Ukai with the chance to adopt an American name—"Joe"—and the last name "Koide" to forge a new identity.

The new Joe Koide's connections with Sanzō Nosaka and the Japan Communist Party raised further concerns, even if they believed in Koide's commitment to the Grand Alliance cause. Nosaka's group was infiltrated by the Japanese police, and the many defections that followed posed a security risk. Nosaka's own Party chairperson (a Central Committee member) abandoned the cause while in prison in 1933. Even though police arrested fewer than 5,000 of the 62,000 Communist Party members from 1928 to 1941, many more defected to avoid imprisonment.[8] Worse, Nosaka's tense relationship with the Japanese Americans in the Japanese Bureau of the Communist Party of the United States raised the possibility of revenge by betrayal. When Nosaka was released from prison in 1931, he fled to Moscow. There he denounced some of the seventeen Japanese American communists deported to the Soviet Union after their 1932 arrests in Long Beach, California. Those communists, along with others once high in Japan's Communist Party, disappeared, leaving many in Japan and the United States to suspect that Nosaka had falsely fingered them as Imperial Japanese agents. Closely associated with Nosaka and having lived most of his adult life under false names while working underground for the ComIntern, could Koide be trusted to faithfully adhere to the federal government's foreign policy vis-à-vis the Soviet Union, considering its entry into the war against Imperial Japan?[9]

Koide was the acknowledged leader of Project Green, a group of twenty-five Japanese Americans who produced 124 propaganda radio broadcasts from April to August 1945. Koide, Project Green member Jin Konomi recalled, possessed a "formidable intellect and irresistible personality" that accompanied his "fiery sense of mission." Others within the OSS questioned the wisdom of utilizing Koide's propaganda materials. Koide, however, felt strongly that his European American superiors' usage of Japanese American personnel merely to translate what they had written was detrimental to the propaganda effort against Imperial Japan. Koide and other Japanese Americans in Morale Operations saw their supervisors' verbal attacks on the emperor and the Japanese public as misdirected: The target of their propaganda, in their estimation, should have been the Japanese political and military leadership. The emperor, Koide and other Japanese Americans in Project Green contended, should be treated with respect to win over the Japanese public.

Propaganda content aside, Koide was a confrontational employee, especially regarding discrepancies in pay or when Japanese Americans received late wages. After Koide complained about unfair treatment, some European American staff members suspected Japanese American personnel and scoured their propaganda materials for covert messages. That distrust dissipated only after Morale Operations learned that the Project Green radio broadcasts beamed from Saipan to Japan had been jammed by Imperial Japanese authorities since their second broadcast. They decided Koide and Project Green members were not, at least, sending covert messages to Japan. But what about the Soviet Union? Had Koide's employer shifted from the Communist International, an organization that Joseph Stalin terminated in 1943, to another agency coordinated with the Soviet Union?[10]

Kunsung Rie, Agent for Imperial Japan?

Similar doubts dogged Kunsung Rie around his involvement in Special Operations. Rie was in training in early 1945 for a covert mission in Japanese-occupied Korea code-named "Napko." This mission, designed by Colonel Carl Eifler, head of the Field Experimental Unit, had as its stated objectives the "organization of an intelligence network in Korea; the rescue of American airmen downed over Korea; clandestine penetration of Japan for intelligence purposes; and organization of resistance, sabotage, and guerrillas in Korea in support of military operations." His commanding officer planned for an initial submarine insertion of eight "clandestine agents" from the Pacific Ocean Area into the Chemulpo Bay (present-day Incheon, South Korea) and Chinnampo (present-day Nampo, North Korea) areas. Rie's group was to establish a radio network to relay intelligence gathered from ground-level observations. Their reports were to be forwarded by radio to two listening posts, one in the Philippines and the other in Okinawa. His rear area support stations were staffed by forty personnel to process and transmit intelligence; many of the staff were Korean residents in America, now no longer defined as enemy aliens by an October 1942 presidential order. Once established, Napko envisioned at least four more landings to extend the spy network farther inland northeast to Pyongyang and south to Moppo (present-day Mokpo, South Korea). Rie's comrade-in-arms, Master Sergeant Sukyoon Chang, was sent by the colonel to recruit additional agents at a Korean prisoner-of-war compound at Camp McCoy, Wisconsin, for Korean men who had served in the Imperial Japanese Army. These prisoners, Chang knew, could never return to their units because all Japanese soldiers, Koreans included, were expected to sacrifice their lives rather than surrender. Chang spent over forty days posing as a Korean POW interpreter for camp commander Colonel Horace J. Rogers in November 1944. After Chang had selected and arranged for the covert transfer of these Korean POWs to Napko, some questioned the advisability of the entire operation, including the loyalty of the personnel.[11]

The Joint Chiefs of Staff and the OSS leadership in Washington, DC, weighed objections to Napko. OSS leaders in the China Theater were unanimously opposed to the entire operation.[12] Richard Heppner, the head of all OSS sections in China, thought Eifler underestimated the Imperial Japanese government's control over Korea. He reported that the Korean underground was nonoperational as of late spring 1945. "By separate radio I am giving you details of information we have recently received," Heppner said, "that the entire Korean underground was smashed recently by [the] Japs." Deputy Director of the China Theater Colonel Willis Bird went even further, advocating operations inside Korea begin with "Eagle," the other OSS insertion team in training at Xian, China. After comparing the profiles of Napko and Eagle team members, Bird assessed Eagle as having a much higher chance of success, given their social and political prestige. "As far as Resistance Groups are concerned," Bird wrote of his own Eagle team, "I believe we are in a better position to get these under way through contacts with the Korean Provisional Government than the agents mentioned in the [Napko] project files." But the voices that mattered most—the Joint Chiefs of Staff, General Albert Wedemeyer, the commander of the China Theater, and William Donovan, the director of the OSS—all favored Napko. Donovan wanted Napko to move forward ahead of Eagle because the Eifler Plan aimed at penetrating the main islands of Japan ahead of other Allied forces.[13]

Despite the OSS director's enthusiastic endorsement of Napko, the objections raised by his China Theater leaders were legitimate. In the first place, Japan's control over Korea was tight, apart from the Imperial Japanese Army's strong presence in northeast Asia, making Napko members' movement difficult. The Japanese police force was well established inside Korea and exercised extensive control. By 1926, the force numbered 18,463 police officers staffing 2,599 police substations. This meant that the colonial police force had at least one police substation for each of the 2,504 townships in Korea. Four years later, with only a slight overall increase in size to 18,811 officers, Japanese authorities increased the Korean composition of the force to 40 percent (7,113 officers). A typical police substation had one native Korean assistant helping two Japanese police officers. Police had jurisdiction over an average of twenty small villages with approximately 800 households. Police officers patrolled their jurisdictional areas on foot (by bicycle in the cities) and knew every man in each village. Most police substations had telephones by the mid-1930s, and so they could swiftly communicate with each other, pair up, and suppress rebels rapidly. Hence, Napko was faced with a formidable foe in a Japanese colonial police force that was, "adequately educated, vigorously trained, closely supervised, and extremely well organized" by 1937, as one historian put it.[14]

Korean "collaborators" compounded Napko's problems of avoiding detection by colonial police. Team members assumed that, with the war turning against Imperial Japan in 1945, the Korean populace would come to side with the Allies. But this assumption was undercut by how many Koreans cooperated with Imperial Japanese authorities through spring 1945. By 1940, 80 percent of the Korean population of over twenty-three million had adopted Japanese surnames, a key sign of acceptance of colonial rule. Their willingness to accept features of Japanese rule was underscored by how many Koreans served in the Imperial Japanese forces from 1937 to 1945—an estimated 360,000 (of whom only 170,000 were conscripted). Those Koreans served in integrated combat units, not segregated as were African Americans and Japanese Americans in the US Army. Some Koreans proved zealous in the execution of their duties and were even decorated by the Japanese emperor. One even sacrificed his own life when he deliberately crashed his aircraft into an attacking American B-29 bomber over the island of Shikoku in late May 1945. Given demonstrated Korean support for Japan, it was reasonable for Napko's critics to point out that local village leaders might reveal team members to Japanese authorities.[15]

The inclusion of Kunsung Rie in the Napko project proved particularly troubling, even though Rie was an indispensable team member. Although not the leader of the small band of agents, he was the fastest at radio communications for his group, having been clocked at a rapid twenty words a minute, a skill that would prove essential for the group's speed in sending intelligence reports without detection by Japanese authorities. Rie was also skilled in demolitions, necessary once the team began its assault on Japanese forces inside Korea. His marksmanship with small arms was another asset. His trainer noted that Kunsung was "at home" with weapons, especially the carbine rifle.[16] Most of all, Kunsung Rie and his colleagues Diamond Kim and Jimmie Pyen were excelling during their training at Catalina Island, California. They were ready for the mission. Napko trainer Vincent Curl rated the group very highly: "Although we are pouring it on this group, they are perfectly capable of taking it, and are showing lots of enthusiasm."[17]

Eifler and others ignored the red flags raised about Rie, sticking to their scheduled deployment as the first American unit to deploy inside Occupied Korea. As one officer reassured William Donovan's executive officer Otto Doering:

> The unfavorable security report, while on its face clearly showing the possibility of disloyalty, does not show any actual acts of disloyalty, and the unfavorable factors are, by their nature, susceptible to explanation. Colonel Eifler and Lieutenant Echols, who are experienced security investigators, have been well aware of the unfavorable factors and after a very intensive investigation over a period of months, are each satisfied that the unfavorable factors are negated by other factors which have been developed in the course of their investigation.

If Rie was an agent for Imperial Japan, the officer reasoned, it was better to keep him under surveillance while in training. He justified this move with the adage, "The best way to catch a thief is to employ one."[18]

Others, however, believed the best way to deal with a "thief" was to throw the criminal out. The Office of War Information took this approach: They conducted a special hearing on Kunsung Rie in July 1943. They heard from fifty-eight witnesses—including college professors, editors, neighbors, landladies, housekeepers, real estate owners, apartment managers, members of the United Korean Committee, staff from the Library of Congress, various hospitals, the Office of Naval Intelligence, the Sino-Korean Peoples' League, the Military Intelligence Service, and employees of the Oriental Importing Co., Japanese Division YMCA, War Department, and Immigration and Naturalization Service. One witness claimed Rie was seeking to avoid combat against Imperial Japanese forces since he feared reprisals against family members in Korea. Others pointed out that Rie failed to report after being served a draft notice. Still others testified that Rie was simply unreliable and had no cause for which he was fighting. Hence, the Office of War Information concluded Rie's reserve officer status in the Imperial Japanese Army, his questionable marriage to federal government employee Clara Kennedy of Washington, DC, and his lack of association with "loyal" Koreans was sufficient evidence to declare him of "questionable loyalty" and thus ineligible for work in the federal government. Even the OSS Security Officer Archbold van Beuren warned against including him in OSS operations since he obviously lacked "basic loyalty to the Allied cause." Worse, van Beuren believed Rie was for hire:

> There is much evidence to indicate that the Subject will always be willing to sell out to the highest bidder and that he cannot be trusted with any type of

confidential information. The Subject is regarded with suspicion by all government departments which have had contact with him, and these suspicions range from allegations that he is a Japanese agent to statements that he is loyal to the Allied cause but very unreliable.[19]

The Office terminated Rie's employment.

Conclusion: A Question of Loyalty

However, the end of the war terminated Napko before the question of Rie's loyalty was resolved. Napko team members were scheduled for departure on 26 August but fighting stopped on 15 August and, three days later, Kunsung Rie received his thirty-day notice of employment termination. Napko itself was canceled on 24 August 1945, and Rie continued on the OSS payroll until mid-September 1945. Once released, he could neither prove nor disprove that he had been an agent of Imperial Japan. OSS officers, however, had themselves assessed Rie as loyal. Rie certainly engaged in some questionable activities prior to his employment with OSS. But, as Carl Eifler pointed out, Rie was committed to carrying out Napko's mission even when the odds of his survival were not high. For the colonel, Rie's pro-Japan leanings before the war made sense. He understood that Immigration and Naturalization Services were returning Rie to Korea; the United States was unconcerned about Korea's postwar fate while the Soviet Union still adhered to its nonaggression treaty with Imperial Japan. In addition, Nationalist China appeared unable to mount a large military offensive against the Japanese forces in northeast Asia as late as spring 1945, leaving Rie vulnerable to Japanese authorities. Eifler further reasoned that a true Korean agent would simply have sat out the war instead of risking his life: The US federal government allowed Korean immigrants whose visas had expired to remain for the duration of the war and lifted all enemy alien restrictions against them on 9 February 1942, except in Hawai'i where martial law was in force. Hence, Eifler determined on this basis that Kunsung Rie was *not* an enemy agent.[20]

The same assessment, however, cannot be made of Joe Koide. He was clearly working as an agent for the ComIntern after he returned from Moscow in the early 1930s. Koide faithfully discharged orders from ComIntern superiors until he, along with over 100,000 West Coast Japanese Americans, were removed and placed in War Relocation Authority camps. Koide supported the removal because he feared that race riots and violence against Japanese Americans were the likely outcome if they remained in the general population on the West Coast. But he was also dismayed by statements made by fellow American Communists who supported military conscription *by ethnic group* when he steadfastly maintained that American-born Japanese males had an *individual* right to determine whether they would obey or refuse the order to register for the draft. That separation between himself and other Party members deepened further when they unjustly accused him of being an agent of Imperial Japan.

Although unsympathetic to the Imperial Japanese government and its military, Koide was probably saddened and somewhat remorseful to witness the destruction of Japanese cities and towns by American aviators dropping incendiary bombs after March 1945. Other Japanese American leftists with whom Koide worked on the propaganda broadcasts may have shared these feelings. The seemingly senseless killing of hundreds of thousands of Japanese civilians to destroy a few small war industry factories may have stirred a "dormant identification with Japan," as historian Howard Schonberger claimed. If true, that would explain why Koide and the other members of the US Strategic Bombing Survey in 1946–47 estimated that some 900,000 civilians were killed by American bombing, instead of favoring lower estimates offered by the Japanese government and others. Although it does not explain why Koide testified at the 1953 hearings of the House Un-American Activities Committee against his former Party colleagues, it suggests that at some point his loyalty narrowed in scope away from the Party down to his own immediate family and ethnic group. It would also explain why, for Koide, loyalty was neither singular nor double, but *serial* with the focal point of his loyalty changing and narrowing over time: His loyalty shifted from the ComIntern (universal) to the United States (national), and then to Japanese Americans (ethnic).[21]

Although neither Kunsung Rie nor Joe Koide were Axis agents, the OSS did have a Trojan Horse in its midst. Before identifying that individual agent, however, it is important to consider the question of why there were so many doubts about the loyalties of the two Asian American OSS agents. Admittedly, the two had pasts that could have and perhaps should have raised questions for anyone trying to secure reliable agents for American intelligence service. However, as early as July 1944, Archbold van Beuren, head of the OSS Security Office, submitted a list of forty-seven employees his investigators believed were communist agents working for the Soviet Union. Donovan was aware he had hired several communists with experience in guerrilla warfare, who had honed their skills during the Spanish Civil War from 1936 to 1939. He was also aware he had individuals like Donald Wheeler on his payroll, an expert on German manpower and a spy for the Soviet Union. He also suspected that Maurice Halperin, the chief of his Latin America section, was an informant for Soviet spy handlers

Elizabeth Bentley (of whom more later) and Mary Price. Yet none of these OSS officers faced the level of scrutiny that Rie did, and none faced a hearing with fifty-eight witnesses criticizing their loyalty and commitment to the Allied war effort.[22]

If "race" played a role at all, it was likely a minor one. A close reading of relevant documents related to the two Asian American agents does not reveal that "race" triggered the criticism of them. Yet the possibility of racial prejudice or racial bias as a motivation against them exists since there were admittedly a few isolated instances of racial discrimination against other Asian Americans working in rear areas. Hitoshi Yamada, for instance, was excluded from entry into OSS facilities in Washington, DC, by a security guard due to his race. Joe Koide and the Project Green Japanese Americans had experienced racial discrimination related to their paychecks and housing, though the latter had much to do with wartime housing shortages in San Francisco and Japanese exclusion from the West Coast. In India, British authorities confined Japanese Americans writing propaganda material inducing Japanese soldiers to surrender to barracks solely because they were of the Japanese "race," while their European American counterparts enjoyed complete freedom of movement in and out of the Morale Operations office.[23] Nevertheless, these instances of racial discrimination that Asian American OSS personnel faced were the exception rather than the rule, and the agency under the leadership of William Donovan was progressive in its hiring and treatment of minority employees.[24]

Hence, loyalty rather than race offers the most plausible explanation for the disparity in treatment some Asian Americans faced while serving in the OSS. Loyalty was a fundamental requirement for all employees of the intelligence agency. It was extensively investigated after an individual applied and monitored after the employee signed his or her Oath of Office. However, many OSS leaders thought of loyalty as static and fixed rather than constructed and fluid; loyalty to the United States was fixed in the same way that identification with America was made permanent by residency and education. That static view of loyalty is best expressed by Columbia University Law professor George Fletcher, who asserted that the idea originates from the idea of the "historical self." That is, an individual or "self" is born into a community of people not of his or her choosing, and adopts an identity rooted in that primary group relationship. After years of socialization, the result is that individuals develop over time (hence "historical") a positive and strong self-identification with and loyalty toward that group. Both Joe Koide and Kunsung Rie were immigrants with minimal time residing in the United States, and both had received only minimal American education, largely at the secondary level. Viewed from this perspective, both men had insufficient time for American "historical selves" to develop, and hence doubts about their loyalties were understandable if not justified.[25]

But Fletcher's understanding of loyalty is flawed. Loyalty is not tied to a particular historical identity, as philosopher Simon Keller points out. Citing the hypothetical example of an abused wife, Keller observes that such an individual may discard loyalty to her husband precisely because she is searching for her true (historical) self. When dealing with loyalty to a nation-state, the philosopher asserts that such loyalty involves "belief" rather than identity. Since belief involves emotional identification, this type of loyalty can prove unstable rather than fixed. Moreover, as other scholars argue, individuals often face competing loyalty claims from different referent groups, resulting in multiple rather than singular loyalty. The multiple rather than singular loyalties of Joe Koide and Kunsung Rie, whether serial as in the case of Koide, or layered as with Rie, makes the most sense as an explanation for the institutional suspicions of these two OSS agents.[26]

OSS emphasis on loyalty over race is demonstrated in the agency's handling of war crimes investigations in the postwar. In Europe, the OSS handled several war crimes cases, with the director himself participating in the Nuremberg Trials. In China, however, the OSS dealt with the additional problem of alleged Asian American collaborators. They did not task anyone to investigate Korean Americans, but they assigned Robert Chin to examine the case of the New York–born Herbert Moy, who became Shanghai's most notorious Axis propagandist, broadcasting over the radio waves from Station XGRS. To deal with Japanese Americans, the OSS assigned Marine Captain Frank Farrell and Army Captain Michael Yasutake to investigate and recommend for prosecution several Japanese Americans accused of collaboration with Imperial Japanese forces. Prominent among them was Los Angeles–born Ray Uyeshima, who many alleged had profited immensely from provisioning the Imperial Japanese forces in Shanghai. In one instance, he was alleged to have supplied 30,000 tons of oil which, according to the Department of Justice, was an established "fact" in a court of law.[27] For Farrell, Uyeshima's birth, nationality, and education in the United States meant he should have remained loyal to the country of his birth rather than "aid and comfort to the enemy," which constituted treason. Michael Yasutake, however, disagreed, finding Uyeshima not guilty since Farrell's evidence was circumstantial and the most reliable eyewitness testimonies demonstrated Uyeshima's innocence. Hence, Yasutake urged the OSS to clear the accused of all charges and concluded his report by assuring his superiors "that he [Uyeshima] is as loyal as I am." The Department of Justice agreed and closed its case against Uyeshima, indicating a triumph of loyalty over race as an explanation for intelligence agency behavior.[28]

But adopting such a static understanding of loyalty could have negative consequences, too. By assuming that loyalty was assured by long familial residency in a given nation-state, the OSS remained blind to a foreign agent in their midst. While casting doubts on the loyalties of Koide and Rie, they missed Soviet informant Duncan C. Lee. He was the chief of the Japan-China Section, Far East Secret Intelligence. Lee was stationed in Washington, DC, and brought in by Director William Donovan. Lee had worked at Donovan's law firm in New York City prior to the war, and served Donovan as his assistant at the OSS Headquarters. This foreign agent had an impressive pedigree, being a direct descendant of Richard Henry Lee (1732–1794) and Francis Lightfoot Lee (1734–1797), both signatories of the Declaration of Independence in 1776. He was also related to Robert E. Lee (1807–1870), Confederate general during the Civil War. Despite (or perhaps because of) Lee's "historical self," having extremely strong ties to the United States, he became attracted to communism after he visited Oxford University in 1935, when the political ideology was at its zenith there. He waited until he and his wife became self-supporting financially in 1939 and then joined the Communist Party of the United States. Lee supported leftist organizations while working for Donovan's law office. After Donovan invited him to join OSS, Lee became an indispensable part of agency leadership.[29]

Despite his deep local roots, Lee also became a spy, providing Soviet intelligence agents with information he picked up at the office. By April 1945, Duncan was working on East Asia and Korea when he became aware of Kunsung Rie and the Napko team. However, he did not provide this information to Soviet intelligence since he feared discovery of his espionage activities (though he was careful never to submit any reports in writing). But the stress of being discovered got the best of him, and he suffered a nervous breakdown that his handler, Elizabeth Bentley, reported to Moscow: Duncan had become "afraid of his own shadow." Lee rightfully feared the future. On November 7, 1945, Bentley defected, became an FBI informant, and helped usher in one of the Communist Party's archenemies, a Wisconsin senator named Joseph McCarthy.[30]

Notes

1. Joseph E. Persico, *Roosevelt's Secret War: FDR and World War II Espionage* (New York: Random House Trade Paperbacks, 2002), 6, 9–13, 56–57, 228, 451; Robin Winks, "'Getting the Right Stuff': FDR, Donovan, and the Quest for Professional Intelligence," in *The Secrets War: The Office of Strategic Services in*

World War II, ed. George C. Chalou (Washington, DC: National Archives and Records Administration, 1992), 20, 24–25, 31.

2. See Sara Castro's chapter 1 in this volume for parallel problems locating those with Chinese language skills.

3. Much has been written on the OSS. For the most recent general studies, see Christopher Andrew, *The Secret World: A History of Intelligence* (New Haven, CT: Yale University Press, 2019); Douglas Waller, *Wild Bill Donovan: The Spymaster Who Created the OSS and Modern American Espionage* (New York: Free Press, 2011); Richard Harris Smith, *OSS: The Secret History of America's First Central Intelligence Agency* (Guilford, CT: Lyons Press, 2005); Burton Hersh, *The Old Boys: The American Elite and the Origins of the CIA* (St. Petersburg, FL: Tree Farm Books, 2002); and Elizabeth P. McIntosh, *Sisterhood of Spies: The Women of the OSS* (Annapolis, MD: Naval Institute Press, 1998). For those including brief accounts of Asian Americans though often indistinguishable from other Asians, see Richard J. Aldrich, *Intelligence and the War against Japan* (New York: Cambridge University Press, 2000); Carolle J. Carter, *Mission to Yenan: American Liaison with the Chinese Communists, 1944–1947* (Lexington: University Press of Kentucky, 1997); and Maochun Yu, *OSS in China: Prelude to Cold War* (New Haven, CT: Yale University Press, 1996). For the availability of OSS records, see Lawrence H. McDonald, "The OSS and Its Records," 78–102; and Bradley F. Smith, "The OSS and Record Group 226: Some Perspectives and Prospects," 359–367, in *The Secrets War: The Office of Strategic Services in World War II*, ed. George C. Chalou (Washington, DC: National Archives and Records Administration, 2002). At present, only two studies on Asian Americans in the OSS are available: Robert S. Kim, *Project Eagle: The American Christians of North Korea in World War II* (Lincoln: University of Nebraska Press, 2017); and this author's book, Brian Masaru Hayashi, *Asian American Spies: How Asian Americans Helped Win the Allied Victory* (New York: Oxford University Press, 2021).

4. Various parts of this story, for example, appear in Timothy L. Savage, "The American Response to the Korean Independence Movement, 1910–1945," *Korean Studies* 20 (1996): 218; and Bruce Cumings, *The Origins of the Korean War: Liberation and the Emergence of Separate Regimes, 1945–1947* (Princeton, NJ: Princeton University Press, 1981), 188. However, for the most complete version, see Robert S. Kim, *Project Eagle: The American Christians of North Korea in World War II* (Lincoln: University Press of Nebraska, 2017), 102–11; and this author's *Asian American Spies*, which the following is based on.

5. D. M. Giangreco, *Hell to Pay: Operation Downfall and the Invasion of Japan, 1945–1947* (Annapolis, MD: Naval Institute Press, 2009), 5, 23; and Edward J. Drea, *Japan's Imperial Army: Its Rise and Fall, 1853–1945* (Lawrence: University Press of Kansas, 2009), 250.

6. Joe Koide, (testimony), December 5, 1953, at the Hearing Before the Committee on Un-American Activities, House Representatives Eighty-Third

Congress, First Session, Investigation of Communist activities in the San Francisco area. Hearing (Washington, DC: US Government Printing Office, 1954), 3423–29, accessed on 27 October 2014 at http://www.archive.org/stream /investigationofcsf195405unit/investigationofcsf195405unit_djvu.txt. Anon., "LA 100–30303," n.d., p. 16, box 8, Jennifer Fowler Papers, Special Collections, University of California, Los Angeles; James Oda, *Secret Embedded in Magic Cables: The Story of a 101-Year-Old Japanese Communist Leader Who Served Japan, KGB and CIA* (Northridge, CA: KNI, 1993), 93–95; Margaret Feldman to Colonel Kenneth Mann, May 4, 1945, folder 6, box 165, entry 139, RG 226 OSS, NARA II.

7. Karl G. Yoneda, *Ganbatte: Sixty-Year Struggle of a Kibei Worker* (Los Angeles: Asian American Studies Center, University of California, Los Angeles, 1983), 94; Joe Grant Masaoka, "Interview with Joe Koide," April 18, 1967, reel 33, box 381, Oral History, Japanese American Research Project 2010, Special Collections, Young Research Library, University of California, Los Angeles; Oda, *Secret Embedded in Magic Cables*, 97–98; Eric L. Muller, *Free to Die for Their Country: The Story of the Japanese American Draft Resisters in World War II* (Chicago: University of Chicago, 2001), 76, 91; Harvey Klehr, John Earl Haynes, and Fridrikh Igorevich Firsov, *The Secret World of American Communism* (New Haven, CT: Yale University Press, 1995), 226–30; Maurice Isserman, *Which Side Were You On? The American Communist Party during the Second World War* (Middletown, CT: Wesleyan University Press, 1982), 143–44; Josephine Fowler, *Japanese and Chinese Immigrant Activists: Organizing in American and International Communist Movements, 1919–1933* (New Brunswick, NJ: Rutgers University Press, 2007), 71–72.

8. In some ways the reverse of the motivation of Soviet defectors in Kevin Riehle's work. See chapter 11 in this volume.

9. Minoru Ōmori, *Sokoku Kakumei Kōsaku* [Revolutionary maneuverings of the ancestral homeland] (Tokyo Kōdansha, 1975), Sengo Hisshi, vol. 3 [postwar secret history], 24–33, 62–65; Joe Koide, *Aru Zaibei Nihonjin No Kiroku Jō* [A record of a Japanese in America, vol. 1] (Tokyo: Yūshindō, 1967), 189–92; FBI, Denver, December 6, 1951, 5–55 NJR, box 8, Jennifer Fowler Papers, Special Collections, University of California, Los Angeles; Shunsuke Tsurumi, *An Intellectual History of Wartime Japan, 1931–1945* (London: KPI, 1986), 5–13; Richard Deacon, *Kempeitai: A History of the Japanese Secret Service* (New York: Berkeley Book, 1985), 159; Yuji Ichioka, "Beyond National Boundaries: The Complexity of Japanese-American History," *Amerasia Journal* 23, no. 3 (Winter 1997–1998): vii. Factional in-fighting characterized Japanese American leftist relations. Police penetration further exacerbated internal tensions and gave rise to differing narratives. See Jennifer Fowler, *Japanese and Chinese Immigrant Activists: Organizing in American and International Communist Movements, 1919– 1933* (New Brunswick, NJ: Rutgers University Press, 2007), 44–48; and Shintarō Shindo, "Reisenki Jōhō sengo no Haikei toshiteno Senkyūhaku Sanjū Nendai

Shanghai" [Intelligence wars during the Cold War Era: The background of 1930s Shanghai], *Shakai Shisutemu Kenkyū* [Social systems research] 18 (March 2015): 155–70.

10. Jin Konomi, "Reminiscences of Joe Koide" (Part 1), *Pacific Citizen*, June 27, 1980, p. 8; Jin Konomi, "Reminiscences of Joe Koide" (Part 2), *Pacific Citizen*, July 4, 1980, p. 8; Office of Strategic Service MO Branch, History of "Blossom" Radio (Green's Project), n.d., 33–37, folder 2500, box 188: Washington and Field Station Files, WASH-MO-RES-10-12, entry 139, RG 226, Records of the Office of Strategic Services, NARA II, College Park, Md.; Oda, *Secrets Embedded in Magic Cables*, 256.

11. OSS, Field Experimental Unit, *The Napko Project*, March 30, 1945, folder 29 Korea, box 3, Washington and Field Station Files Honolulu, entry 139A, RG 226, NARA II; P.G. 108/1, IMPLEMENTATION STUDY FOR THE OVER-ALL AND SPECIAL PROGRAMS FOR STRATEGIC SERVICES ACTIVITIES BASED IN CHINA[:] KOREA, May 15, 1945, p. 21, folder 170, box 29, entry 144, RG 226 NARA II; Thomas N. Moon and Carl F. Eifler, *The Deadliest Colonel* (New York: Vantage Press, 1975), 217; John Whiteclay Chambers, *OSS Training in the National Parks and Service Abroad in World War II* (Washington, DC: US National Park Service, 2008), 462; Peggy Choy, "Racial Order and Contestation: Asian American Internees and Soldiers at Camp McCoy, Wisconsin, 1942–1943," in *Asian Americans: Comparative and Global Perspectives*, ed. Shirley Hune, Hyung-chan Kim, Stephen S. Fujita, and Amy Ling (Pullman: Washington State University Press, 1991), 87–102. Korean immigrants were exempt from Japanese American internment even though they were technically classified as Imperial Japanese nationals. See Wayne Patterson, *The Ilse: First-Generation Korean Immigrants in Hawai'i, 1903–1973* (Honolulu: University of Hawai'i Press, 2000), 196–97; and Lili Kim, "How Koreans Repealed Their 'Enemy Alien' Status: Korean Americans' Identity, Culture, and National Pride," 195–219, in *From the Land of Hibiscus: Koreans in Hawai'i*, ed. Yŏng-ho Ch'oe (Honolulu: University of Hawai'i Press, 2007).

12. See chapter 1 in this volume for further details of OSS work in China.

13. For opposition to Napko, see (Richard) Heppner to 109, May 8, 1945, folder 237, box 16 Field Station Files, Chungking; (Richard) Heppner to Cheston (Info/Chungking), July 14, (1945), folder 237, box 16 Field Station Files, Chungking, RG 226 OSS/NARA II; Willis H. Bird to Richard Heppner, April 27, 1945, Folder 237, box 16 Field Station Files, Chungking, entry 148; Paul L. E. Helliwell to Strategic Services Officer/China Theater, April 26, 1945, folder 3416, box 201 Kunming Office, entry 154, RG 226 OSS NARA II. For support of Napko, see (William P.) Davis to (Richard) Heppner, August 9, 1945, folder 237, box 16 Field Station Files, Chungking; William P. Davis to Commanding General, US Forces CT, August 8, 1945, folder 237, box 16 Field Station Files, Chungking, entry 148; and 109 (William Donovan) to (Richard) Heppner and (Otto) Doering, May

6, 1945, folder 3416, box 201 Kunming Office; William Donovan to Albert Wedemeyer, March 12, 1945, folder 3416, box 201 Kunming Office, entry 154, RG 226 OSS NARA II.

14. Ching-chih Chen, "Police and Community Control Systems in the Empire," in *The Japanese Colonial Empire, 1895–1945*, ed. Ramon H. Myers and Mark R. Peattie (Princeton, NJ: Princeton University Press, 1984), 223–26, 236–39; Bruce Cumings, *The Origins of the Korean War: Liberation and the Emergence of Separate Regimes, 1945–1947* (Princeton, NJ: Princeton University Press, 1981), 30–31.

15. Jun Uchida, *Brokers of Empire: Japanese Settler Colonialism in Korea, 1876–1945* (Cambridge, MA: Harvard University Press, 2011), 380; Glenn T. Trewartha and Wilbur Zelinsky, "Population Distribution and Change in Korea, 1925–1949," *Geographical Review* 45, no. 1 (January 1955): 4; Drea, *Japan's Imperial Army*, 232; Brandon Palmer, *Fighting for the Enemy: Koreans in Japan's War, 1937–1945* (Seattle: University of Washington Press, 2013), 3, 6, 8, 64, 83, 123, 131.

16. C. W. Campbell and H. Kaplan to Paul M. McCallen, Student Progress Report Communications Training, March 31, 1945; (George) Ghecas, Demolitions Evaluation, March 26–31 [1945]; (Robert) Carter, Evaluation, n.d., ca. March 1945; Vincent L. Curl to Eifler, March 25, 1945, folder of Curl's Rpts #1, Box 4, Carl Eifler Papers, The Hoover Institution, Stanford University, Stanford, CA.; Henson L. Robinson to Philip K. Allen, February 20, 1945, Robert Carter Jr. Papers, Catalina Island Museum, Records Center, Avalon, CA.

17. Vincent L. Curl to Carl Eifler, March 25, 1945, folder of Curl's Rpts#1, box 4, Carl Eifler Papers, The Hoover Institution, Stanford, CA.

18. Donald M. Gregory to O. C. Doering, Jr. Executive Officer, February 5, 1945, folder 615 Security, box 79, entry 140, RG 226 OSS/NARA II.

19. FWF to files, January 23, 1945, and CJB to files, January 13, 1945, and Security Officer [A. van Beuren] to Donald M. Gregory, February 1, 1945, folder 615, box79, entry 140, RG 226 OSS, NARA II.

20. Moon and Eifler, *The Deadliest Colonel*, 233; Roby C. Read to Kunsung Rie, Termination of employment notice, August 18, 1945, folder Rie, Kunsung, box 644 OSS Personnel Files, Entry 224; Indiv and Fiser from Stevens, NR 766, August 24, 1945, folder 237, box 16 Field Station files, Chungking, entry 148, RG 226, NARA II; Richard S. Kim, *The Quest for Statehood: Korean Immigrant Nationalism and US Sovereignty, 1905–1945* (New York: Oxford University Press, 2011), 132–33; Robert E. Clark, memo, January 25, 1945, folder 615 Security, box 79, entry 140, RG 226, NARA II.

21. Joe Grant Masaoka, "Interview with Joe Koide," Reel 33; Howard Schonberger, "Dilemmas of Loyalty: Japanese Americans and the Psychological Warfare Campaigns of the Office of Strategic Services, 1943–1945," *Amerasia Journal* 16, no. 1 (1990): 30–31; United States Strategic Bombing Survey, Morale

Division, *The Effects of Strategic Bombing on Japanese Morale* (Washington, DC: US Government Printing Office, 1947), 1; Tomiya Watabe, *"Roy" Nosaka Sanzō Setsu ni Ketsugi wo Tsuketa Gojūnenme no Jijitsu: Soruge Jiken de Gokushita Gaka Miyagi Yotoku wo Nihon ni Hakkenshita Roi to Yobareru Otokowa Nikkei Kyōsantoin Kimoto Denichi da!* [The "Roy" Sanzō Nosaka explanation resolved in the fiftieth year of the truth: the one who sent the artist Yotoku Miyagi to prison for the Sorge Affair was the Japanese American Communist Party member Denichi Kimoto!] (Tokyo: Shakai Undō Shiryō Senta, 2001), 8–12. See also chapter 12 in this volume for another case of complex, shifting state loyalties.

22. Mark A. Bradley, *A Very Principled Boy: The Life of Duncan Lee, Red Spy and Cold Warrior* (New York: Basic Books, 2014), 90–91.

23. Oliver J. Caldwell to Herman Harjes, January 22, 1944, folder 1, box 72 History Office; Robert D. Ellis to Strategic Services Officer, July 27, 1945, folder 2, box 83, History Office files, numbers 106–11, entry 99, RG 226 OSS/NARA II.

24. Bradley F. Smith, *The Shadow Warriors: OSS and the Origins of the CIA* (New York: Basic Books, 1983), 380; Bogart Carlaw to Roger Simpson, February 7, 1945, folder 6, box 165, Central Files, entry 092, RG 226, NARA II; Edward L. Bigelow to Director, OSS, August 30, 1945, folder 6, box 165, entry 092, RG 226 OSS, NARA II; Douglas Waller, *Wild Bill Donovan: The Spymaster Who Created the OSS and Modern American Espionage* (New York: Free Press, 2011), 5, 21, 39, 79, 92, 364; Brian Urquhart, *Ralph Bunche: An American Odyssey* (New York: W. W. Norton, 1993), 101–10.

25. George P. Fletcher, *Loyalty: An Essay on the Morality of Relationships* (New York: Oxford University Press, 1993), 8, 57, 101.

26. Simon Keller, *The Limits of Loyalty* (Cambridge: Cambridge University Press, 2007), 13–14, 21, 64; Michael Waller and Andrew Linklater, "Loyalty and the Post-National state," in *Political Loyalty and the Nation-State*, ed. Michael Waller and Andrew Linklater (London: Routledge, 2003), 2.

27. Waller, *Wild Bill Donovan*, 341–48; Eugenia "Beah" Chen Wing, My Family History Record: A Genealogical Record compiled by Eugenia "Beah" Chen Wing, February 1981, 101 pp., in Jack Young Papers in possession of Jolly Young King, Honolulu, HI; BH-219, report, German Radio Station XGRS, October 7, 1945, folder 123, entry 182A, box 16: X-2 reports from Kunming, Sian, etc.; Memo, 20 March 1947, folder 36, box 8, OSS History Office, entry 216, RG 226; Elwood H. Olsen to Nathan T. Elliff, October 2, 1946, folder 146-28-2057, box 13, Department of Justice, Division of Communications and Records, RG 60 Department of Justice, NARA II, College Park, MD.

28. Walter Winchell, "In New York," March 26, 1947, folder 12, box 43; Jess Stearn, "Phyllis Brooks Meets Old Pal in the Tropics," *New York World-Telegram*, February 3, 1944, folder 12, box 43; (Frank Farrell) to Guy, April 23, 1942, folder 12, box 43; attachment #28: The Shanghai Woosung Garrison, First Investigation Section, n.d., folder 14, box 29; attachment #31: Shigeo Yasutake, To Whom It

May Concern, December 12, 1945, folder 14, box 29, Frank Farrell Papers, Library of Congress, Washington, DC.

29. Bradley, *Very Principled Boy*, 2, 65–69.

30. Bradley, *Very Principled Boy*, 33–35, 43, 91, 98–99; Duncan C. Lee to Chief, SI, OSS, CT, May 14, 1945, Progress Report for April 1945, folder 3, box 81 COI/OSS Central Files Wash-Reg-Ad-7, RG 226, Records of the Office of Strategic Services, NARA II.

11

World War II and Soviet Intelligence and State Security Officer Defectors

Kevin P. Riehle

Thousands of Soviet intelligence and state security officers served during World War II. Today, the Russian Federation honors them with posthumous awards and public glorification; since 1992, fourteen intelligence and state security officers have been among the 115 World War II veterans posthumously awarded the Hero of the Russian Federation medal.[1] However, there were others who, after serving, chose to defect. The Russian government seldom mentions those personnel in the current environment of politically driven historical revisionism in Russia. Nevertheless, they did exist. They chose to defect for a variety of reasons: to save their own lives in the brutal conditions of German prisoner of war (POW) camps; because of political and ideological differences with the Soviet, especially Stalinist, government; and out of fear that the Soviet Union was on the verge of collapse, especially as German forces occupied large portions of Soviet territory.

There is much historical scholarship about Soviet Red Army POWs, with works describing camp conditions and the rationale that led them to cooperate with their German captors.[2] However, few of those works discuss intelligence and state security officers specifically. Thomas Earl Porter details the inhuman conditions of Soviet POWs in German camps, such as summary executions, forced marches, and starvation rations.[3] S. P. MacKenzie describes a Nazi German mentality toward Soviet citizens that equated Bolsheviks with Jews, thus laying the foundation of those atrocities.[4] Mark Edele explains the overall drivers that led Soviet soldiers to give themselves up to German captivity and sometimes to choose collaboration, led by disagreements with the Stalinist system, often resulting from personal losses during earlier Soviet purges.[5] These works, especially Edele's, discuss Soviet soldiers escaping a repressive Soviet state security apparatus, not those who were part of that apparatus themselves. Sergey Chuev discusses Soviet collaboration with the German cause, both by those in German captivity and others elsewhere in Europe.[6] Chuev is unusual among authors for identifying state security personnel among those who collaborated.

Works on Soviet defectors, in general, seldom discuss World War II. The most comprehensive analysis of Soviet defectors, Vladislav Krasnov's 1986 book, *Soviet Defectors: The KGB Wanted List*, is based on a 1969 KGB document that lists Soviet defectors and traitors whom the KGB was instructed to pursue around the world. In its original version, the list included almost 1,200 names, including many who had collaborated with German forces during World War II. However, the list that Krasnov obtained for analysis was redacted, leaving only 470 names, with all World War II defectors removed for privacy purposes.[7] More recently, the unredacted 1969 edition has been released publicly,[8] and the Ukrainian Security Service released the 1979 edition of the same KGB document, which includes 800 names, none of which were redacted. Those documents list over 650 people who were wanted for collaborating with Germany during the war, including intelligence and state security officers.[9] This chapter uses those recently released KGB documents, along with defectors' post-defection debriefings and autobiographical publications, to add to the existing scholarship by discussing that small subset.

Soviet, German, British, and American records identify eighty-six Soviet intelligence and state security officers who served before or during the war and subsequently defected. Forty-two defected during the war, most of whom were captured on the battlefield or surrendered to German or Finnish forces. Forty-four others defected or attempted to defect after the war, waiting until as late as 1964 to defect. These eighty-six officers made up only a small percentage of the thousands of Soviet intelligence and state security personnel who served in the war.

This chapter analyzes those eighty-six defectors, exploring their stories, circumstances, and statements to determine, as much as possible, why they defected.[10] It finds that many defectors experienced personal crises—the death of a family member, troubles in the workplace, or capture on the battlefield—that served as the proximate cause for defection. However, many other Soviet officers experienced similar crises, and few chose to defect. Among those who did defect, personal crises were compounded by simmering anti-Soviet views, often directed at Stalin himself, fueled by prewar experiences of purges and arrests of family members. Postwar defectors viewed the return of repressive measures taken against the Soviet people after the war as a return of 1930s terror. Defectors, regardless of timing, also had in common that they were motivated by fear—fear for their lives in a German POW camp or a recall to Moscow.

Defection during War

World War II was a unique time for defection. Defection requires access to a foreign state to which an aspiring defector can offer himself or herself. Before German forces invaded the Soviet Union, tight control over the Soviet population and severe limitations on interaction with foreigners meant that a defector had to make a considerable effort to approach a foreign power. Opportunities arose either while the officer was posted outside the Soviet Union or when the officer walked across a Soviet-controlled border into a neighboring country. Even diplomats, who had legitimate contact with foreigners for work purposes, were suspect.[11] The organization responsible for monitoring Soviet citizens' interactions with foreigners and preventing their escape was the state security service, making defection from that service particularly bold.

The situation changed with the German invasion of the Soviet Union in June 1941, when millions of Soviet personnel were suddenly exposed to foreigners not by their own choice but by a foreign power's coming to them. As German forces penetrated deep into Soviet territory, thousands of Soviet intelligence and state security personnel fell into German captivity, an unknown number of whom died along with millions of other Soviet POWs. The first Soviet personnel exposed to the German onslaught were border guards and internal troops from the People's Commissariat of Internal Affairs (NKVD). Border guards had regular exposure to foreigners, and a few had defected in the past. NKVD internal troops, on the other hand, were a defector category unique to wartime.

During the war, all three methods of defection existed. Some defected after capture; others voluntarily crossed the line into German-controlled territory; and still others defected while operating clandestinely behind German lines. Whichever method they chose, the German invasion offered Soviet citizens an opportunity to escape Stalin's control. That had been nearly impossible since Stalin had come to power and sowed terror in the Soviet population during various waves of arrests before World War II, including dekulakization—the Soviet government process of arresting small-scale business owners—in the late 1920s and early 1930s and the Great Purge in the late 1930s.[12] During the latter period, in which approximately one million Soviet citizens died during interrogations or in corrective labor camps, any hint of or denunciation about an anti-Stalin statement could mean exile or death.[13] Purges created an environment of fear within the Soviet Union and fostered anti-Stalin views, which the war provided an opportunity to express. Although, according to Edele's analysis, few Soviet soldiers who turned themselves over to German forces were active anti-Stalinists, over a third claimed political disaffection as their motivation, often rooted in the deaths of family members during purges. Edele estimated that Soviet soldiers showed a widespread lack of loyalty to the Soviet system.[14]

Edele estimated that from 1942 to 1945, the number of Soviet military personnel who changed sides could have reached 117,000.[15] Intelligence and state security officers were among them, although available records do not allow precise quantification. They were more thoroughly vetted and were considered the most loyal of Soviet forces and could thus be expected to be the last to defect or collaborate. Nevertheless, a small number—probably on the order of dozens, not thousands—did offer their unique and valuable services to the Germans during the war.

Post-Soviet Russian historians typically portray World War II defectors as Nazi sympathizers to prove their political unworthiness. Dmitriy Prokhorov, for example, proclaims that defectors betrayed the heroism and selflessness that the Soviet people showed in the face of the German invasion. He states, "With that in the background, instances of betrayal and treason appear even more criminal."[16] Chuev called them "cursed soldiers."[17] Vitaliy Karavashkin labels defection a "moral disease of society."[18] But while a few Soviets did support Germany ideologically, many defected due to their opposition to Stalin's policies more than out of sympathy for Germany. They chose to defect to Germany during the war because Germany was the nearest force opposing Stalin and because it initially appeared that Germany might win.[19] Correspondingly, most intelligence and state security officers who defected did so from 1941 to 1943.

Chuev describes four reasons why Soviet citizens collaborated with the Nazi government:

1. The growth of pro-Soviet partisan and covert action in the German rear area prompted Germany to recruit cooperative Soviet citizens into counter-partisan military formations.
2. The horrendous conditions of Soviet POWs in German camps convinced many to accept the German offer of fighting against the Soviet Union to escape the suffering.
3. Nazi Germany used anti-Soviet Russian émigrés to persuade POWs to fight against the Soviet Union.
4. Internal social upheaval caused by Soviet leaders' errors and miscalculations turned some Soviet citizens against their government.[20]

None of these reasons implies a preexisting ideological inclination toward Nazism among Soviet intelligence and state security defectors, which was seldom motivation for collaboration. Reason 4 was most prevalent—they believed their collaboration with Nazi Germany represented the only chance to remove Stalin, whom they had grown to hate. Prominent among the "errors and miscalculations" by Soviet leaders was the Great Purge, which had affected the lives of nearly every Soviet citizen just a few years before the war.

Captured on the Battlefield

Of the forty-two Soviet wartime defectors, at least thirty-two were captured on the battlefield or surrendered to German forces. They may represent only a small portion of the total, but they offer a group for analysis. All but two of those collaborated once in German custody, offering their experience in clandestine tradecraft and knowledge of Soviet security weaknesses, participating in interrogating fellow Soviet POWs, developing propaganda in their native Russian language, and planning sabotage operations behind Soviet lines.

Only a few of those officers expressed support for Germany based on a combination of personal beliefs and survivalist hopes. One who did was Aleksandr Zhigunov, an NKVD counterintelligence officer who got swept up in the German advance into Latvian territory in August 1941. Zhigunov claimed to have deserted his position at the earliest possible moment because he was disenchanted with the Soviet system and looked forward to its replacement with a German protectorate.[21] During his interrogations, Zhigunov spoke critically about the NKVD but in a way that aligned with Nazi German sympathies. He claimed the Great Purge was the result of Jews in charge of the NKVD using "perverted methods" to arrest innocent people.[22] It is unclear whether Zhigunov's emphasis on blaming Jews came from his own analysis or from narratives inculcated into NKVD officers in the post-purge period. Zhigunov tended to repeat Soviet propaganda themes in his interrogations, so his views could have reflected what he heard in NKVD circles. He also possibly held personal views aligning with Nazi antisemitism.

Lidiya Yesenina was arrested as a Soviet penetration agent in Poland in October 1942 and initially resisted German interrogation, giving two false names before finally admitting what was likely her real name. After three months as a POW, she approached German interrogators offering to reveal additional information. She claimed to have been treated well, which convinced her that Soviet propaganda about the Gestapo was untrue.[23] Although nothing is known of her life after her March 1943 interrogation, she apparently impressed the Germans: The Kraków District police commander wrote a letter to the German regional governor recommending Yesenina as an example of the "fabulous human material of the GUGB."[24]

Sixteen of the forty-two officers captured during the war gave their support to Major General Andrey Vlasov, who is often viewed as the primary organizer of German-sponsored anti-Soviet resistance during World War II.[25] Vlasov was captured in July 1942 and soon began to cooperate with German forces, motivated by a belief that Stalin was the real enemy of the Soviet people. Although Vlasov was not the only anti-Soviet leader among POWs, he came to embody the plans of some German officers (although not Hitler himself) to attract deserters from among Soviet troops to fight the Soviet Union.[26] Thus, Vlasov features in the accounts of many wartime Soviet intelligence and state security officer defectors. In some cases, the relationship with Vlasov was cooperative; in other cases, it was competitive or antagonistic.

On the cooperative side were officers who joined military units subordinate to Vlasov, including his intelligence and security team. Ivan Grachev, for example, was serving in the Intelligence Department of the Leningrad Front when he became a POW in fall 1941. He eventually became the chief of the intelligence department of Vlasov's German-sponsored military unit, the Armed Forces of the Committee for the Liberation of the Peoples of Russia (*Военные Силы Комитета Освобождения Народов России;* VS KONR). In a 1951 interview, Grachev disclaimed any predetermination to cooperate with Vlasov, but rather a sense of resignation: "Once having fallen into German hands, my career as a Soviet colonel [*sic*] was over. Either I could perish in the PW camp, or else I could be of some use at least.... But I cannot say that I 'consciously' went over to the Germans in order to fight Bolshevism."[27] Before joining the KONR, Grachev served in a German-sponsored police unit in Mogilev, Belarussia, where he claimed to have helped Russian residents avoid the worst of the German occupation. He later said, "I pride myself on having helped a great many people in Mogilev."[28] He subsequently joined the KONR with his NKVD colleague Petr Kashtanov and supervised another NKVD defector, Nikolay Lapin.

Vyacheslav Artemyev was a former commander of NKVD internal troops and guard troops in a corrective labor camp in Kazakhstan. In 1937, Artemyev fell victim to the purge and was arrested. He was released in 1938; however, he was still not fully trusted and was assigned to an NKVD reserve regiment, where he served as the chief of staff of the military security force at the NKVD Karaganda Camp System in Kazakhstan until fall 1941. After the German invasion, Artemyev was assigned as commander of a cavalry regiment and served at the front until he was captured in September 1943. He soon joined the KONR, assigned as commander of the Second Grenadier Regiment, First Infantry Division, where he served until the unit was disbanded in 1945.[29] After the war, he wrote reverentially of Vlasov and reflected with pride on his time under his command. Artemyev noted in 1951 that when German troops captured him, they treated him respectfully and cared for his wounds, and he was welcomed into Vlasov's fold.[30] He claimed that he had time to reflect on his life while in German captivity, and he became increasingly disillusioned with the Soviet system. However, in the postwar atmosphere, when collaboration with Germany was frowned upon, Artemyev, along with many others who served in the KONR military forces, distanced himself from the Nazis ideologically. He denied that his disillusionment was the product of German propaganda, which he described as "so stupid, so idiotic, so base that it could not have influenced anyone."[31] Artemyev considered it an honor to have served in the KONR military forces, but not necessarily because of German sponsorship.

Aleksandr Anokhin, who joined the NKVD in 1938, was another individual with a tainted past accepted into the NKVD. His father was arrested as a "kulak" in the early 1930s, but Anokhin changed his name to hide his connection to his father. Anokhin himself was arrested in 1941 for violating NKVD rules but escaped in September 1941, when the prison where he was held came under German bombing. He was hiding in Kharkov, Ukraine, when German troops took control of the city in October 1941, at which time he exulted, "We were saved."[32] Because he had NKVD experience issuing Soviet internal passports, the Germans employed him forging documents for German Operation ZEPPELIN, through which the German Army selected Soviet soldiers in POW camps, trained them for operations behind Soviet lines, and dispatched them into Soviet territory. After the war, Anokhin wrote an autobiography using the penname Aleksandr Brazhnev titled Записки Чекиста (Notes of a Chekist), which was highly critical of NKVD methods, comparing them to the tsarist-era *oprichniki*, the sixteenth-century bodyguards of Tsar Ivan IV, the "Terrible," who gained a reputation for their brutality toward opponents of the tsar.[33] Nevertheless, after the war, he also referred to Germans as "pig-headed."[34]

Vlasov's Army was not the only anti-Soviet military formation created under German sponsorship, and not all former state security officers cooperated with Vlasov. Ivan Bessonov, captured in August 1941, almost a year before Vlasov, became one of the leading anti-Soviet voices in German POW camps and established, under German sponsorship, an organization called the Political Center for the Struggle with Bolshevism (Политический центр борьбы с большевизмом; PTsB) to unite anti-Stalinist organizations and prepare for the overthrow of the Bolshevik regime. Alleksandr Sidorov called Bessonov a "Hitlerite chekist."[35] However, Bessonov envisioned himself as a leader in a new Russia freed from Bolshevik rule.[36] His stated goal was to make an agreement under which Germany would recognize Russia's borders as they existed on 1 September 1939, with Bessonov in a leadership role in the post-Bolshevik Russia. He wrote about his view of a future Russia:

> Heavy industry, transport, post and telegraph will be run by the government. Kolkhozes will be dissolved, personal ownership of land will be introduced, and personal initiative permitted: in those circumstances, foreign trade will also be under government control. Russia should retain its full territorial, economic and political independence. After the overthrow of Soviet power, military dictatorship will be introduced until the end of the war, established by leaders of the Liberation forces, and then general elections.[37]

Once Vlasov appeared on the scene, Bessonov viewed himself as senior to Vlasov militarily and politically. Vlasov's views, as articulated in the Smolensk Manifesto of December 1942, aligned closely with Bessonov's: Remove Stalin and the Bolsheviks from power, return to the precepts of the February 1917 revolution (as opposed to the later October Revolution), and reach an honorable peace with Germany.[38] However, rather than drawing them together as partners, the similarity of Vlasov's goals with Bessonov's and both generals' overlapping desire to be the predominant anti-Soviet proponent in Germany created competition between them.

Bessonov was enlisted into Operation ZEPPELIN. Based on his knowledge of the locations and security measures of NKVD prison camps, he proposed a plan, labeled Десант на ГУЛАГ ("Airdrop on the GULAG"), that envisioned parachuting Soviet POWs near prison camps in the far north of Russia, overpowering the camp guards, liberating and arming the prisoners, and turning them against the Soviet Union.[39] The Germans tested Bessonov's plan in June 1943, when twelve Soviet POWs dropped into the Komi Republic in northern Russia dressed as NKVD officers. After only a week, however, actual NKVD troops located the group, killed two outright, and took the rest prisoner.[40] The failure spelled the demise of Bessonov's anti-Soviet insurgent leadership. Dissatisfied Germans disbanded his organization and transferred him to the Sachsenhausen concentration camp, where he remained until the end of the war. Several prominent PTsB officers joined Vlasov's forces.

Other former intelligence and state security officers who enlisted into Operation ZEPPELIN and then joined the KONR included Grachev and

Anokhin, who trained and dispatched POWs into Soviet territory for intelligence and sabotage missions; Rafael Bekker (see below); Vadim Denisov, who led penetration missions himself; and Mikhail Kalugin, a military counterintelligence officer captured on the North Caucasus Front.

Only one of the forty-two officers who defected during the war did so outside the battlefield. Ismail Akhmedov, a Soviet military intelligence officer, arrived in Berlin in May 1941 under TASS cover. A month later, Germany invaded the Soviet Union, severed diplomatic relations, and interned all Soviet diplomatic personnel in Germany. Akhmedov was both anti-Soviet and anti-German. Having been raised Muslim, Akhmedov was circumcised, and thus the Germans treated him as Jewish, assigning him to clean latrines and sweep sidewalks.[41] He was in German custody only a few weeks when Soviet internees were sent to Turkey in exchange for German prisoners. Rather than return home, he was ordered to remain in Turkey to conduct intelligence operations. In November, he learned that his wife had died in the Soviet Union, and he became embittered toward his Soviet employer for not caring for her. After he heard on the radio in December that the United States had entered the war, he approached the US consulate in Istanbul to defect. Akhmedov gave his real name and admitted he was a Soviet military intelligence officer. A consulate official listened politely but responded that he could do nothing.[42] A few months later, after coming under pressure at the Soviet consulate for not actively operating against the Turkish government, Akhmedov approached a British individual, who wished him luck but offered no assistance. Akhmedov then wrote letters of resignation to the Soviet government, renouncing his Party membership and denouncing Soviet domestic and foreign policies. In May 1942, he approached the Turkish police and requested asylum. The Turkish government welcomed him and offered protection.[43] UK and US intelligence services finally noticed him after the war and debriefed him. His UK debriefer was then-MI6 chief of station in Turkey, Kim Philby, who withheld Akhmedov's debriefing information from his own headquarters while likely supplying the complete reports to Moscow.[44] The CIA entered the picture in 1948 and arranged for Akhmedov's immigration to the United States, where he was debriefed in full and became a CIA contractor. He was lucky—others, like Bessonov, were repatriated to the Soviet Union after the war.

Wartime intelligence and state security officer defectors had endured various tragedies, often connected to Stalin's purges. However, their motivation for defection was founded first on opposition to Stalin, which they expressed by supporting various German-sponsored units, especially

Vlasov's. Nevertheless, most such officers distanced themselves from that support in the postwar environment of a defeated Germany.

Real Defectors or Not?

Some former NKVD officers were suspected of either faking defection or having second thoughts. Former NKVD officer Aleksandr Chikalov, who had spent his career as a border guard commander, claimed that the German *Abwehr* tried to recruit him after his capture in November 1943, but he refused.[45] Instead, he used his previous NKVD experience to lead the KONR counterintelligence section, which was responsible for thwarting Soviet penetrations of the KONR.[46] However, he operated under a cloud of suspicion regarding his true loyalties.[47] Boris Morozov, another former NKVD officer serving in the KONR, wrote later that KONR counterintelligence "worked, but was badly led." He implied that Chikalov was disloyal and lacked the skills of a good counterintelligence officer. Grachev, the KONR intelligence chief, went so far as suspecting Chikalov of being a Soviet agent posing as a defector. Nevertheless, Chikalov's section operated well enough to create a sense of insecurity in those who expressed pro-Soviet views or disenchantment with the KONR.[48] He served in the KONR military forces until he was transferred to US custody in 1945.

Like Chikalov, another former NKVD officer, Rafael Bekker, was also suspected of being a Soviet penetration of the KONR. Bekker had been a Soviet military counterintelligence officer until he became a POW in September 1941. In May 1942, Bekker was recruited into collaboration with the Reich Main Security Office (Reichssicherheitshauptamt; RSHA) and he taught intelligence skills in a German Sicherheitsdienst (SD) intelligence school for Russian POWs under Operation ZEPPELIN.[49] In this position, Bekker showed the first signs of lingering loyalty toward the Soviet Union when he approached one of his students and tried to convince him to contact the NKVD after the student was infiltrated into Soviet territory. However, the student reported Bekker's approach, and Bekker was temporarily removed from his duties and placed under investigation in a special block at Sachsenhausen. The investigation established no clear guilt, so Bekker was reassigned to German intelligence duties. He joined the KONR, and from January to April 1945, he was chief of the KONR Marienbad intelligence school. However, Grachev ordered that Bekker be relieved of duties on suspicion of cooperating with the NKVD. The suspicion was justified, first because Bekker caused discord at the school, possibly intentionally, and because Bekker reportedly passed students' questionnaires and application forms to the SMERSH military counterintelligence directorate of the First

Belorussian Front, which led to the neutralization of a KONR intelligence operation.[50]

Deep Penetration Missions

Of the forty-two wartime defectors, eighteen are known to have operated behind German lines—fifteen were dispatched, and three were stay-behind agents ordered to remain in place to conduct sabotage operations and organize partisans as German forces swept over Soviet territory. When the war settled in on the Soviet front, Soviet intelligence services hurriedly trained thousands of officers in radio communications, countersurveillance, intelligence collection, and sabotage, and to organize partisan operations behind German lines.[51] After abbreviated training, many parachuted behind enemy lines into German-occupied Ukraine, western Russia, or Finland. Some were captured or voluntarily turned themselves over to German forces.

In the first year of the German-Soviet war, the average age of deep penetration operatives was in their upper twenties. Aleksandr Kurayev, for example, a stay-behind agent in Ukraine, and Kirill Dovydenko, a dispatched officer in Smolensk Oblast, captured in late 1941 and mid-1942, were twenty-seven and twenty-eight years old, respectively.[52] However, the age of the operatives dropped as the war continued—many were under twenty-five, and some were teenagers. Nina Chaplygina, Yuriy Sedashov, Nikolay Sivtsov, and Aleksandr Kopatskiy, who were dispatched behind German lines in 1942 and 1943; Khelge Vainio, dispatched behind Finnish lines in 1942; and Vladimir Fomenko, a stay-behind agent in Ukraine in 1941, were all twenty-one years old or less.[53] The recruitment of younger people was an indication of the urgent need for intelligence on German and Finnish forces amid increasing personnel shortages. These young officers' surrender to German forces possibly reflected discouragement among the Soviet population about the prospects of a Soviet victory.

In contrast to officers captured by advancing German forces, fewer deep penetration operatives are known to have supported Vlasov, indicating that the ideological training they received had an effect. Viktor Dubkov, a young officer captured while on his first covert mission behind German lines in 1943, expressly denied serving in the KONR under Vlasov. He claimed to view "Vlasov's Army just as he viewed Hitler's Army, not as a liberator of Russia from Bolshevism, but even more of an oppressor and enslaver of the Russian people." Dubkov was among hundreds of thousands of Soviet POWs who were forced to support the German economy; he worked as a common laborer in a brush factory. He enlisted in the US Army Air Corps after being liberated from a German POW camp but did not reveal his experience as an intelligence officer. After being released from US service, he took on a German identity and joined the Communist Party of Germany, hoping to return to the Soviet Union as a German communist to visit his parents. His intelligence affiliation came to light only after he was arrested for a petty crime in 1952 and revealed his past under interrogation.[54]

Aleksandr Kopatskiy, a twenty-one-year-old officer who parachuted into German-held territory in October or December 1943 to conduct partisan operations, similarly expressed continued affinity for communism. His deep penetration operation did not last long; he was wounded as soon as he landed and sent to a German hospital to recuperate.[55] By April 1944, he had reportedly been recruited as a Nazi intelligence officer, and in 1945, he became the only one among the known deep penetration officers to join the KONR.[56] Some have surmised that Kopatskiy was dropped into German territory as a false defector to penetrate German intelligence.[57] Kirill Aleksandrov notes that Kopatskiy was among a few officers within the KONR military forces who retained their Soviet patriotism even after joining KONR. These officers hoped to return someday to the Soviet Union to "atone for their sins to the Motherland."[58] However, expressing pro-Soviet views would be dangerous for a dispatched defector, who would avoid drawing attention to himself to reduce German counterintelligence scrutiny. Nevertheless, Kopatskiy was likely not fully converted to either Nazism or to Vlasov.

Postwar Defections

The NKVD established filtration centers after the war to identify Soviet citizens who had worked for Germany during the war. The centers had some success, especially after the United States repatriated thousands of KONR members who had been held in German POW camps.[59] Yet filtration centers were far from thorough, and many individuals who had tainted family pasts or supported Germany during the war slipped through. Some even received state security jobs.

One such was Aleksandr Trikoz, who had worked as an NKVD operations officer in Ukraine before the war but joined the German cause soon after the German invasion. Whether he did so on his own initiative or after being captured is unclear. Either way, he collaborated with German police in Ukraine during the war but escaped from German control in 1943. Soviet KGB records show that he rejoined Soviet forces "under unknown circumstances" sometime in 1945, was injured, and then deserted from a hospital. He was rearrested for desertion but hid his wartime German service from investigators and then escaped and disappeared in July 1945. His German service became known only after his final disappearance.[60]

Hiding one's wartime service to Germany was not difficult in the early days after the war. That factor, compounded by the Soviet security forces' need for linguists, led to a situation in which people who had served in German units during the war were hired as foreign language interpreters after the war. These included Petr Roze, a Latvian who joined the German Army in 1944 but who was transferred to a Soviet POW camp in March 1945. An NKVD operations unit recruited him as a German interpreter, but he defected to the British zone of Germany in May 1946. Similarly, Yevgeniy Abryutin was living in the Pskov Oblast of Russia when German forces occupied the area in 1942. He offered his Russian language skills to the German Army and participated in anti-Soviet propaganda efforts during the war. It is unclear how he came to the attention of the Soviet Ministry of State Security (MGB) after the war, but an MGB operations unit in eastern Germany hired him as a German language interpreter in December 1945.[61] He defected to the American sector of Berlin less than a year later. Vasiliy Korniyevskiy also actively supported German military intelligence during the war and was reportedly sent behind Soviet lines on clandestine intelligence missions. However, a filtration center cleared him, and he was mobilized into the Soviet Army, eventually working as a German interpreter for Soviet intelligence operations. He defected to the British zone of Germany in April 1948.

Rafail Goldfarb had a tainted past from the time of the Great Purge. Goldfarb's father was arrested in 1931 in what Goldfarb described as an operation to confiscate money, gold, and other valuables from wealthy citizens. Goldfarb and his mother were arrested, and the harsh prison conditions convinced her to surrender her husband's valuables. His father was released and found work in a factory clinic until he was arrested again in 1937; he died in prison in 1938. Goldfarb later described his father as an outspoken opponent of the Soviet system.[62]

Goldfarb was mobilized during the Soviet-Finnish War and again after the German invasion of the Soviet Union. He was required to provide an autobiography but failed to mention his parents' arrest, which would have barred him from service. In June 1943, Goldfarb again hid his family past and was reassigned to the Leningrad Front SMERSH office as a German interpreter, where he worked in recruitment operations among German POWs. From there, he became a full-time counterintelligence officer. However, in June 1949, Goldfarb received an order to return to the Soviet Union. He suspected his father's arrest had finally caught up to him, and he immediately made plans to defect. His defection was mainly to avoid personal punishment, but he provided significant details about Soviet counterintelligence operations during debriefings.[63]

To add to the inefficiencies of filtration centers, several Soviet officers employed in them defected. Enduring the war did not immunize an officer from defection, and some officers who remained loyal during the war defected later. One of those was an officer who wrote a serialized autobiography under the pseudonym "A. A. Petrov" in the Swiss newspaper *La Tribune de Genève* in late 1949 and early 1950. Petrov was captured on the battlefield during the war but never collaborated with the Germans. Instead, he removed his insignia and burned his identity documents. He escaped during a prisoner movement and made his way back to Soviet-held territory. Rather than being welcomed, he was stripped of his Party membership, placed in a disciplinary battalion, and served the rest of the war at the front. His appeals for reinstatement into the Party were fruitless until the NKVD suffered a severe lack of German linguists after the war. Because of his German-language ability, he was reinstated into the Party and assigned to a SMERSH unit.[64]

Petrov's exposure to Vlasov's Army came only after the war when he was assigned to a Soviet repatriation office in Germany. His interaction with members of Vlasov's Army involved hunting them and returning them to Soviet control as criminals. Initially, Petrov's repatriation efforts included telling former KONR personnel that the Soviet government understood the pressures they faced in German POW camps and forgave them for collaborating with the Germans.[65] Petrov's role as a SMERSH officer ultimately led to thousands of Soviet returnees being condemned to forced labor or execution. That mission convinced him to abandon his position and surrender himself to American forces in Germany in 1947.

Another officer involved in filtration operations was Boris Baklanov, a Soviet SMERSH officer who completed training in 1944. After the war, Baklanov was assigned to Soviet occupation forces in Austria, whence he was sent for temporary duty to Hungary. His mission in Budapest was to screen demobilized soldiers for possible future duty with security troops. The soldiers were transiting Hungary on their way back to the Soviet Union, and SMERSH was responsible for identifying politically reliable, physically fit, battle-hardened soldiers who could remain in Europe to fill the special units.[66]

Baklanov published his memoir in 1972 under the name A. I. Romanov, where he claimed to have become disenchanted with the Soviet Union in general and with his job specifically because of the difference he saw between wartime chekists and peacetime chekists. He felt that fighting a foreign enemy was honorable, but forcing Soviet citizens to repatriate and dooming them to Soviet prison camps was more than he could stand.[67] He approached US forces in Austria in July 1947 to defect.

As Soviet state security records were reconstituted after the war and captured German records were integrated into them, filtration centers became more thorough. They began to identify those who had hidden their past lives and recalled them to Moscow to face punishment. The KGB continued to pursue World War II collaborators into the 1980s, listing nearly 300 people who had supported Germany or a German-allied nationalist group in its 1979 list of wanted criminals, including eleven who were affiliated with a Soviet intelligence or security service.[68]

Illegal Intelligence Operations

After the war, Soviet intelligence services translated their success in conducting wartime deep penetration missions into peacetime illegal intelligence operations. Illegal intelligence operations employed operatives who could portray themselves as non-Russians and operate without overt connection to the Soviet Union to avoid drawing foreign counterintelligence scrutiny. For example, two Lithuanians, Bronius Stankaiktis and Simas Pečiulionis, who had both supported German-allied nationalist groups during the war, were recruited as illegal intelligence operatives after the war. Stankaiktis served in the Lithuanian police under German occupation and joined the Lithuanian Territorial Defense Force under Lithuania General Povilas Plechavičius. French forces captured Stankaiktis near the end of the war and repatriated him to Soviet control, but he escaped, adopted a German name, and settled in Germany. The KGB caught him in Berlin in 1954, recruited him, possibly under coercion, and sent him to Moscow for intelligence training; in theory, he was a good candidate for illegal intelligence as a native Lithuanian. However, he did not last long. The KGB sent him back to West Berlin as an intelligence illegal, but he disappeared and was still being sought in 1979.[69]

Pečiulionis likely also served in Plechavičius's forces as a teenager in 1944 but was injured and hospitalized when Soviet forces reoccupied Lithuania. He changed his name and melted into society until he was drafted into the Soviet Army in March 1946. From there, he was recruited into the MGB and received intelligence training. In 1947, he was dispatched to a displaced persons camp in Germany under cover as a Lithuanian refugee. His MGB mission was to cause disorder in the camp and to assassinate anti-Soviet Lithuanians in Germany. But he spent only three months in the camp before he turned himself in and revealed his intelligence and sabotage mission.[70]

The KGB emphasized illegals after the war because of the hostile counterintelligence environment in the primary target countries, the United States and the United Kingdom. Illegals had the advantage of not looking Soviet and thus not drawing counterintelligence attention. But they were risky, especially those with tainted pasts. Although the KGB enjoyed many successes among its illegals after the war, including famous examples like Rudolf Abel (real name William Fisher) in the United States, it also lost several who had wartime experience.

Later Defectors

Postwar defectors reverted to the prewar pattern of either turning to a foreign government while already outside Soviet-controlled territory, such as operating under embassy cover, or by walking across a Soviet-controlled border into foreign territory. While most wartime defectors turned to Germany, most postwar defectors approached the British or American governments, indicating the place those two countries held in Soviet threat perceptions. A defector, especially an intelligence or state security officer, chose a recipient country based on the belief that the country would protect them from Soviet pursuit and use their information effectively against their former employer. Soviet defectors chose the United States and the United Kingdom, believing those countries to be most likely to oppose the Soviet Union.

With the huge number of Soviet personnel who served in World War II, wartime service continued to be a common trait among Soviet intelligence and state security officers for decades after the war. At least thirteen officers with World War II experience defected after 1950, including some of the most famous, like Yuriy Rastvorov in Japan, Petr Deryabin in Austria, Nikolay Khokhlov in Germany, and Vladimir and Evdokia Petrov in Australia. These defections all occurred in 1954 in the wake of Stalin's death, Lavrentiy Beriya's arrest and execution, and the upheaval those events caused in Soviet intelligence and state security services.[71]

Less prominent was Georgiy Salimanov, who chose to defect in May 1950 after being ordered back to the Soviet Union. Recalls to Moscow were frequent catalysts for defection because, after the bitter experiences of the Great Purge, they often signaled punishment. Salimanov joined the NKVD in Dagestan in 1937 and by February 1939 was a commandant in the Dagestan NKVD office. He distinguished himself for cruelty toward arrestees.[72] He was fired from the NKVD in February 1939 for unknown reasons.[73] However, he apparently had a reversal of fortunes because ten years later, he was a colonel in the MGB First Chief Directorate.[74] He arrived in Germany in 1949 as the Deputy Chief of the Soviet uranium mining operation Wismut AG and chief of the Wismut Logistics Directorate in the Soviet zone of Germany.[75] In May 1950, rather than return as ordered, Salimanov fled to West Germany.[76] Then, as suddenly as he had defected, Salimanov disappeared from the US zone in July 1950. Nothing is publicly available about the reasons for this sudden recall, but womanizing might have been a factor. His re-defection may have been the result of an MGB operation to lure him back, using an East German girlfriend as bait. Salimanov was executed in 1952 after his return to the Soviet Union.[77]

The rash of defections following Stalin's death and Beriya's arrest in 1953 resulted from a mix of fear, ideological dissonance, and personal crises. Memories of the Great Purge continued to cast a shadow on intelligence and state security officers well after World War II. Evdokia Petrova (real name Kartseva) was left as a single mother during the Great Purge. In 1936, she moved in with fellow NKVD cipher officer Roman Krivosh and had a daughter with him in June 1937. In July 1937, the NKVD arrested Krivosh because of his foreign connections and because his father had worked for the tsarist Okhrana.[78] Petrova was suspected by association, and her career was put on hold while the NKVD investigated her. She was fortunate: Rather than expulsion, the NKVD Komsomol chairman let her off with a "severe reprimand and serious warning" for entering into a relationship with an "enemy of the people." It took time for the NKVD to expunge her record, but she was eventually accepted back into full Komsomol membership and retained her position in the NVKD.[79] However, in April 1940, her daughter fell ill and, after a few weeks, died of meningitis. Petrova was grief-stricken, and Vladimir Petrov (real name Afanasiy Shorokhov), a work colleague, supported her in the difficult time that followed. By July 1940, they married.[80]

The Petrovs served in the Soviet embassy in Stockholm during the war. Their second foreign assignment began in Australia in 1951, and the Australian Security Intelligence Organization (ASIO) began to monitor Petrov from the moment he arrived.[81] He defected in April 1954 and admitted during debriefings that he had made up his mind to remain in Australia as early as 1952, prompted by what he described as being "persecuted and hounded" by the Soviet ambassador Nikolay Lifanov.[82] After Beriya's arrest in Moscow in July 1953, Lifanov and the embassy Party chief accused Petrov of forming a "Beriya group" in the embassy to undermine the authority of the Party.[83] Petrov endured until April 1954, when he defected to Australian authorities.

Petrova defected several weeks later after a dramatic photo appeared in global press showing her being escorted onto an airplane by two thugs. She later claimed that the distressed look on her face in the photo was more because she was afraid of the crowd yelling at her at the airport than of the couriers who were escorting her.[84] She wrote that she based her decision to defect on a combination of factors: the attitude toward her at the embassy; the knowledge that her husband was still alive and well; and fear for her life.[85]

In November 1954, ASIO compiled a detailed summary of the Petrovs' defection, assessing that they were motivated by a mix of factors: attraction to Western prosperity, fear, and ideology.[86] But ASIO pointed out that, although the couple enjoyed the advantages of living in a Western country, their combined salary was abundant by Soviet standards, and thus Western prosperity was not the primary factor in their defection. They were heavily influenced by dissatisfaction with their position at the embassy and fear about what could happen if their internal enemies denounced them to Moscow. Petrov's position as MGB *rezident*, which placed him outside the ambassador's control, drew enmity from other embassy personnel and created a "tangled skein of intrigue against them."[87]

Their motivations also included ideological disenchantment. Both had begun in the Party as true believers but had experiences that left them embittered toward the Party and the Soviet elite. Petrova remembered the shunning she received because of her relationship with a man arrested as an "enemy of the people" and that her only child died because of the inefficiency of the Soviet medical system. Yet she was less cynical than Petrov, who complained about how collectivization led to the destruction of the peasantry, including his own family; how denunciations ruined many lives; about the injustice and brutality of Stalin's purges, to which he had direct knowledge as a cipher clerk; about the growing elite class that showed no interest in the country's mass poverty; and the contrast between official propaganda and reality.[88] They punctuated their ideological disagreements by publishing a book titled *Empire of Fear*.[89]

Petr Deryabin also defected in 1954. He had served in World War II and entered SMERSH training near the end of the war.[90] He enjoyed a successful ten-year career in state security, spending time in counterintelligence, senior leader security, and human intelligence. However, according to a CIA report of his debriefing, Deryabin defected "for a combination of ideological and personal reasons."[91] His reasons included a failing marriage and feeling overworked and underappreciated. He described his ideological reasons in his public writings: He had become disenchanted with Soviet leaders' attitudes toward the Soviet people, fueled by his close association with the

Soviet elite during his tenure in the Guard Directorate. He went on to co-author multiple books and appeared before the US Congress, testifying about the crimes of the Soviet system.

Yuriy Rastvorov was drafted into the Soviet Army in 1939 and trained as a Japanese linguist working in Soviet signals intelligence against Japan. After complaining about not having a sufficiently operational job, Rastvorov was assigned to case officer training and eventually posted to Japan in 1946 as a source recruiter. Rastvorov's first assignment to Japan ended suddenly when he was recalled to Moscow in December 1946 to face allegations of disloyalty. He was summoned to a board of inquiry because he had failed to mention his father's expulsion from the Party in 1936, even though his father had been restored to full Party membership. Rastvorov was subjected to what he called a three-month "humiliating investigation" but was eventually reinstated in his position in the Japan Section. However, the incident left Rastvorov with bitter feelings toward the Soviet Union.[92] Rastvorov returned to Tokyo in July 1950 and began to recruit Japanese and American sources. He later wrote, "My own life was profoundly influenced by the Beriya crisis. My slowly ripening decision to leave the Soviet mission and to break with the Communist regime and system was hastened by the purge of Beriya, portending as it did dismissals and trials of many high officials."[93]

Nikolai Khokhlov's defection was also heavily publicized in 1954. He had conducted covert operations targeting the German military during World War II and was among the candidates chosen for illegal operations after the war. He worked as an illegal in various countries, including four years in Romania, where his legend included posing as an anti-communist. To maintain that legend, he listened to BBC and Voice of America, through which he began to see the effects of communism on the Romanian state, sowing seeds of doubt about the Soviet system that led to his eventual defection. He later wrote, "During my four years in Bucharest, I saw the deadly origins of a new communist state and was finally revolted. There I watched the progressive wrecking of a free country at the hands of my own leaders."[94] He defected in Germany in 1954 while on an assignment to assassinate a Ukrainian nationalist leader, Georgiy Okolovich. However, when he arrived in the West, the CIA informed him that the agency could not infiltrate him back into the Soviet Union to help his wife and son escape. On 22 April 1954, he spoke to the press and publicly appealed for help. The press conference was broadcast widely and attracted the sympathy of a large viewing audience. It ultimately failed: Khokhlov learned in June that his wife had disappeared in Moscow and was in KGB custody.[95]

The last known Soviet state security officer with World War II experience to defect was Vladimir Ponomarev, who served as a state security officer from 1943 to 1952. He subsequently studied at the Moscow Institute of Foreign Relations and graduated in 1958.[96] Soon after graduating, he started a job in the State Committee for Cultural Exchanges with Foreign Countries, which was created in March 1957 to organize Soviet propaganda efforts abroad.[97] Under the auspices of that state committee, Ponomarev was assigned to the UNESCO Secretariat in Paris in August 1959.[98] By 1964, Ponomarev began to exhibit signs of disenchantment with his Soviet employment, and in spring 1964, the Soviet UNESCO delegation twice requested that he be recalled to the Soviet Union because of "poor" work.[99] He was informed in September 1964 that he would return to Russia in October, but defected to the British consulate in Sweden soon afterward.[100] After his defection, he complained that the Soviet government "taxed" his UNESCO salary, skimming money to bring it into parity with similarly ranked Ministry of Foreign Affairs employees.[101]

A recall to Moscow or the threat of one, with the prospect of punishment for past sins, was a proximate factor in the motivations of multiple defectors. However, personal antipathy toward the Soviet system and its methods grew in prominence among defectors as time passed after World War II.

Conclusion

Russian narratives today look back on World War II as a time of glory for Russia, describing Stalin as the savior of the country. State security officers are portrayed as the most loyal and brave of all. However, Soviet intelligence and state security officers who served during World War II were not immune from defection, even though they were vetted for loyalty. At least eighty-six such officers were driven to defect by fear: fear of purges and their purge-era past catching up to them, fear of dying in a German POW camp, and fear of a recall to Moscow and what awaited them there. Many were captured in battle, while a handful voluntarily crossed the line. They spoke and wrote critically about the Soviet regime, particularly of Stalin. Some even chose to join German and German-sponsored forces despite German policies toward Slavs, hoping to remove Stalin and replace him with a less brutal leader.

For most, even those who cooperated with German forces or German-sponsored Russian forces, their primary motivation was anti-Stalinism rather than pro-Nazism. They applied knowledge and skills obtained in state security employment to support the German fight against Stalin. Many joined Major General Andrey Vlasov's German-sponsored Russian army as one of the few options available to defeat the Soviet regime. However, those who did so downplayed their connections to Germany after the war, describing their wartime collaboration as a last resort to express their opposition to Stalin.

Hiding one's service to Germany was not difficult in the early days after the war, as filtration camps struggled with incomplete information and the urgent need for people competent in the languages of newly occupied Eastern European countries. Some who collaborated with Germany hid their activities sufficiently to be hired into state security positions, especially as foreign language interpreters, but later escaped, most turning themselves over to US and British forces.

Those who persevered through the war found themselves forced to redirect the very state security skills and methods they had used to defeat Nazi Germany back onto their own people, and they questioned their postwar missions. Even though they remained loyal during the war, some even into the 1960s, defection was their way of escaping unhappy lives and expressing their opposition to the Soviet regime. Attempting to do so inside the Soviet system led to time in a labor camp or death.

Notes

1. International Patriotic Internet Project "Heroes of the Country," https://warheroes.ru/main.asp.

2. See, for example, Reinhard Otto, "The Fate of Soviet Soldiers in German Captivity," in *The Holocaust in the Soviet Union: Symposium Presentations* (Washington, DC: United States Holocaust Memorial Museum, 2005), 127–38; Frank Ellis, "Dulag-205: The German Army's Death Camp for Soviet Prisoners at Stalingrad," *Journal of Slavic Military Studies* 19, no. 1 (2006): 123–48; Mareike Otters, "Photographing Soviet Prisoners of War in the Sachsenhausen Concentration Camp: A Study of Anti-Soviet Propaganda Photos," in *Occupation Annihilation, Forced Labour: Papers from the 20th Workshop on the History and Memory of National Socialist Concentration Camps*, ed. Frédéric Bonnesoeur, Philipp Dinkelaker, Sarah Kleinmann, Jens Kolata, and Anja Reuss (Berlin: Metropol, 2017), 101–31; Dmitri Stratievski, "Annihilation through Work or Inhumane Profit-Making? Soviet Prisoners of War as Forced Labourers for the German Reich, 1941–1945," in *Occupation Annihilation, Forced Labour: Papers from the 20th Workshop on the History and Memory of National Socialist Concentration Camps*, ed. Frédéric Bonnesoeur, Philipp Dinkelaker, Sarah Kleinmann, Jens Kolata, and Anja Reuss (Berlin: Metropol, 2017), 132–47; Verena Meier, "'We are the masters, you are the slaves': The economic Exploitation of Soviet Prisoners of War as Forced Labourers in the Propellants Factory at Liebenau," in *Occupation Annihilation, Forced Labour: Papers from the 20th Workshop on the History and Memory of National Socialist Concentration Camps*, ed. Frédéric Bonnesoeur, Philipp Dinkelaker, Sarah Kleinmann, Jens Kolata, and

Anja Reuss (Berlin: Metropol, 2017), 148–67; Thomas Earl Porter, "Hitler's *Rassenkampf* in the East: The Forgotten Genocide of Soviet POWs," *Nationalities Papers* 37, no. 6, published online by Cambridge University Press, 20 November 2018, https://www.cambridge.org/core/journals/nationalities-papers/article/abs/hitlers-rassenkampf-in-the-east-the-forgotten-genocide-of-soviet-pows/19073 02228EDE513F7AA25F3F1DE0DC2; Valeriy P. Ljubin, "Soviet Prisoners of War in Germany, 1941–1945—An Undesirable Topic for German Society?" in *RSUH/RGGU Bulletin*, Political Science, History, International Relations Series, no. 2 (2021): 106–16.

3. Thomas Earl Porter, "Hitler's Forgotten Genocides: The Fate of Soviet POWs," *Elon Law Review* 5 (2013): 359–87.

4. S. P. MacKenzie, "The Treatment of Prisoners of War in World War II," *Journal of Modern History* 66, no. 3 (September 1994): 504–12.

5. Mark Edele, *Stalin's Defectors: How Red Army Soldiers Became Hitler's Collaborators, 1941–1945* (Oxford: Oxford University Press, 2017).

6. Sergey Chuev, Проклятые солдаты. Предатели на стороне III рейха [Cursed soldiers: Traitors to the Third Reich] (Moscow: EKSMO, 2004).

7. Vladislav Krasnov, *Soviet Defectors: The KGB Wanted List* (Stanford, CA: Hoover Institution Press, 1986).

8. Committee of State Security of the USSR (KGB), Алфавитный Список Агентов Иностранных Разведок, Изменников Родины, Участников Антисоветских Организаций, Карателей, и Других Преступников Подлежащих Розыску [Alphabetical list of agents of foreign intelligence services, traitors to the homeland, participants in anti-Soviet organizations, members of punitive units, and other criminals under search warrant] (Moscow: KGB, 1969), https://imwerden.de/pdf/alfavitny_spisok_agentov_izmennikov_antisovetchikov_v%20rozyske_1969__ocr.pdf.

9. KGB, Алфавитный Список Изменников Родины, Агентов Иноразведок, Карателей и Других Государственных Преступников, Подлежащих Розыску [Alphabetical list of traitors to the homeland, agents of foreign intelligence services, punitive units, and other state criminals under search warrant] (Moscow: KGB, 1979), fond 13, file 885, State Security Archive, Kyiv, Ukraine.

10. For another close analysis of the ideas of POWs, see Derek R. Mallett's essay, chapter 4 in this volume.

11. Robert Conquest, *The Great Terror: Stalin's Purges of the Thirties* (New York: Collier, 1973), 609–12.

12. Aleksandr Solzhenitsyn, *The Gulag Archipelago* (New York: Harper and Row, 1973), 24–92.

13. Michael Ellman, "Soviet Repression Statistics: Some Comments," *Europe-Asia Studies* 54, no. 7 (November 2022): 1151–72. Other estimates place the deaths in the Great Purge as much as three times higher; see Robert Conquest, *The Great Terror: A Reassessment* (New York: Oxford University Press, 1990), 485–96.

14. Edele, *Stalin's Defectors*, 95–119. For another angle on the Soviet system at war, and civilian support for it, see Erina Megowan's essay, chapter 6 in this volume.

15. See Edele, *Stalin's Defectors*, 21.

16. Dmitriy Prokhorov, Сколько Стоит Продать Родину [What is the cost of betraying one's homeland?] (Moscow: Neva, 2005), 151.

17. Sergey Chuev, Проклятые Солдаты. Предатели на Стороне III Рейха [Cursed soldiers: Traitors on the side of the Third Reich] (Moscow: EKSMO, 2004).

18. Vitaliy Karavashkin, *Кто Предавал Россию* [Who betrayed Russia] (Moscow: Olimp, 2008), 4.

19. For more insight into the radicalization of German military behavior in 1941, see Rutherford's essay, chapter 3 in this volume.

20. Chuev, *Проклятые Солдаты* [Cursed soldiers].

21. "Testimony of the NKVD Official Zhigunov," 25, German file number EAP 3-a-11/2; NARA, RG 242, entry UD 282AV, box 18.

22. Aleksander Zhigunov, "NKVD-VChK-OGPU-NKVD-NKBG-NKVD," in "Testimony of the NKVD Official Zhigunov," 57, 59, 64. Zhigunov's debriefing materials are also in captured German records in the National Archives, Kew, London, GFM 3/259.

23. Yesenina's interrogation reports are among Gestapo records that fell into US custody after World War II and are stored in the US National Archives; Gestapo/RSHA file number 173-b-16-12/126; NARA, RG 242, entry UD 23B, box 13.

24. Letter from Kraków District Police to Kraków District Governor, 8 April 1943, NARA, RG 242, entry UD 23B, box 13. GUGB is the abbreviation for the Главное Управление Государственной Безопасности (Main Department of State Security), the intelligence element of the NKVD during WWII.

25. See, for example, Joachim Hoffmann, *Die Geschichte der Wlassow-Armee* [History of the Vlasov army] (Freiburg im Breisgau: Rombach, 1984); and Wladyslaw Anders, "Russian Volunteers in the German Wehrmacht in WWII," ed. Antonio Munoz, Feldgrau.com, https://www.feldgrau.com/WW2-German-Wehrmacht-Russian-Volunteers. See also Kirill Aleksandrov, Генералитет и Офицерские Кадры Вооруженных Формирований Комитета Освобождения Народов России *1943–1946 гг.* [General and officer corps of the armed formations of the committee for the liberation of the peoples of Russia 1943–1946] (dissertation for the Russian Academy of Sciences, Saint Petersburg History Institute, 2015). Aleksandrov published two additional works on the KONR Military Forces: Офицерский Корпус Армии Генерал-Лейтенанта Ал. Власова, *1944–1945* [Officer corps of the army of General Lieutenant Vlasov, 1944–1945] (Saint Petersburg: Russko-Baltiiskiy Information Center "БЛИЦ," 2001); and Армия Генерала Власова 1944–1945 [General Vlasov's army, 1944–1945] (Moscow: Yauza EKSMO, 2006).

26. Anders, "Russian Volunteers in the German Wehrmacht in WWII."

27. Harvard Project on the Soviet Social System (HPSSS). schedule B, vol. 10, case 219 (interviewer A.D.), 4. Other sources indicate that Grachev had only reached the rank of major in the Soviet Army, not colonel.

28. HPSSS, schedule B, vol. 10, case 219 (interviewer A.D.), 3.

29. HPSSS, schedule B, vol. 15, case 136 (interviewer H.B.), 12.

30. HPSSS, schedule B, vol. 15, case 136 (interviewer H.B.), 11.

31. HPSSS, schedule A, vol. 11, case 136 (interviewer A.P., type A4), 15–16.

32. Aleksandr Brazhnev, *Записки Чекиста* [Notes of a Chekist], typescript in Hoover Institution Archive (HIA), Boris Nicolaevsky Collection, box 294, folder 11 (microfilm reel 253), 254.

33. David Nicolle and Vyacheslav Shpakovsky, *Armies of Ivan the Terrible: Russian Troops 1505–1700* (Oxford: Osprey, 2006), 9–10.

34. HPSSS, schedule B, vol. 10, case 147, 1–3.

35. Alleksandr Sidorov, "Мюнхгаузен 'в законе': история одного предательства" [Munchausen "in law": The story of one betrayal], *Index*, no. 27 (2007), http://index.org.ru/journal/27/sid27.html.

36. For other cases of those who creatively reimagined political loyalties in wartime, see Brian Masaru Hayashi's essay, chapter 10, and Katrin Paehler's essay, chapter 12, both in this volume.

37. "Десант на ГУЛАГ" [Airborne assault on the GULAG], Новая Газета [New Journal], 1 March 2004, http://2004.novayagazeta.ru/nomer/2004/14n/n14n-s31.shtml.

38. Aleksandrov, Армия Генерала Власова 1944–1945 [General Vlasov's army, 1944–1945], 38–39.

39. Chuev, *Проклятые Солдаты* [Cursed soldiers]. See also Counter Intelligence War Room London, *Amt VI of the RSHA, Situation Report No. 8*, 28 February 1946, 17, NARA, RG 263, box 36, folder 1, German Intelligence Service WWII, volume 2.

40. Aleksandr Petrushin, "Призраки Приполярного Урала" [Ghosts of the polar Urals], Тюменский курьер [Tyumen courier], no. 104 (16 June 2011), http://tm-courier.ru/archives/61524.

41. Ismail Akhmedov, *In and Out of Stalin's GRU: A Tatar's Escape from Red Army Intelligence* (Frederick, MD: University Publications of America, 1984), 149.

42. Akhmedov, *In and Out of Stalin's GRU*, 159.

43. Akhmedov, *In and Out of Stalin's GRU*, 168–71.

44. Center for the Study of Intelligence, *Of Moles and Molehunters: A Review of Counterintelligence Literature, 1977–92* (Washington, DC: Center for the Study of Intelligence, 1993), 53.

45. Manuscript biography of Almazov (A. Repin; pseudonyms of Chikalov), HIA, Boris Nicolaevsky Collection, box 497, folder 35 (microfilm reel 386). The manuscript is undated, but Chikalov mentions the biography in a letter dated 30

March 1949 in the same file. See also memo titled "Operation HAGBERRY," 24 December 1947, NARA, RG 319, entry A1 314B, box 810.

46. Aleksandrov, Генералитет и Офицерские Кадры [General and officer corps], 636.

47. See Brian Masaru Hayashi's discussion of parallel Asian American figures accused of double and triple loyalties in chapter 10 in this volume.

48. Aleksandrov, Генералитет и Офицерские Кадры [General and officer corps], 633–34; Aleksandrov, Армия Генерала Власова 1944–1945 [General Vlasov's army, 1944–1945], 47, 49.

49. For an explanation of Operation ZEPPELIN, in the words of RSHA Amt VI Chief Walter Schellenberg, see Office of United States Chief of Counsel for Prosecution of Axis Criminality, *Nazi Conspiracy and Aggression*, Supplement B (Washington, DC: US Government Printing Office, 1948), 1623.

50. Aleksandrov, Армия Генерала Власова 1944–1945 [General Vlasov's army, 1944–1945], 53–55.

51. Nikolay Smirnov, "Первые часы, первые дни . . . " [The first hours, the first days . . .], in Очерки истории российской внешней разведки [Essays on the history of Russian foreign intelligence], ed. V. I. Trubnikov, vol. 4 (Moscow: Mezhdunarodnye Otnosheniya, 1999), 26.

52. KGB, Алфавитный Список Изменников Родины [Alphabetical list of traitors to the homeland], 1979, 95, 174.

53. KGB, Алфавитный Список Изменников Родины [Alphabetical list of traitors to the homeland], 1979, 48, 285, 298, 333, 347.

54. Headquarters Region VI, 66th Counterintelligence Corps Group, 24 March 1953, NARA, RG 319, entry 134A, box 173, Dubkov file.

55. David E. Murphy, Sergei A. Kondrashev, and George Bailey, *Battleground Berlin: CIA vs. KGB in the Cold War* (New Haven, CT: Yale University Press, 1999), 111, says October; Christopher Andrew Vasili and Mitrokhin, *The Sword and the Shield: The Mitrokhin Archive and the Secret History of the KGB* (New York: Basic Books, 1999), 149, says December.

56. Andrew and Mitrokhin, *The Sword and the Shield*, 149.

57. James Angleton, CIA chief of counterintelligence from 1954 to 1975, was among these; see David Wise, *Molehunt: The Secret Search for Traitors That Shattered the CIA* (New York: Random House, 1992), 273.

58. Aleksandrov, Генералитет и Офицерские Кадры [General and officer corps], 628–29.

59. Julius Epstein, *Operation Keelhaul; The Story of Forced Repatriation from 1944 to the Present* (Greenwich, CT: Devin-Adair, 1973); Donna E. Dismukes, "The Forced Repatriation of Soviet Citizens: A Study in Military Obedience" (thesis, Naval Postgraduate School, Monterey, CA, December 1996).

60. KGB, Алфавитный Список Изменников Родины [Alphabetical list of traitors to the homeland], 1979, 318–19.

61. For an analysis of the prominence of linguists among Soviet intelligence defectors, see Kevin Riehle, *Soviet Defectors: Revelations of Renegade Intelligence Officers, 1924–1954* (Edinburgh: Edinburgh University Press, 2020), 174, 176.

62. High Commission for Occupied Germany (HICOG) Frankfurt, "Soviet Defector Interrogation Report (Sponge No. 5)," 11 February 1950, 10, NARA, RG 59, Central Decimal file 1950–1954, box 3800, serial 761.00/2-650.

63. Rafael Goldfarb, "Autobiography," 1 August 1949, 15, NARA, RG 319, entry 134B, box 236.

64. "Les souvenirs d'un agent Soviétique" [The memories of a Soviet agent], *Le Tribune de Genéve*, 6 January 1950.

65. "Les souvenirs d'un agent Soviétique" [The memories of a Soviet agent], 7 January 1950.

66. A. I. Romanov, *Nights Are Longest There* (Boston: Little Brown, 1972), 198–99.

67. Romanov, *Nights Are Longest There*, 239–41.

68. KGB, Алфавитный Список Изменников Родины [Alphabetical list of traitors to the homeland], 1979.

69. KGB, Алфавитный Список Изменников Родины [Alphabetical list of traitors to the homeland], 1979, 301–2.

70. Headquarters, Sub-Region Kassel, Counterintelligence Corps Region III memo, 8 March 1948, NARA, RG 319, entry 134B, box 600, Peciulionis.

71. Riehle, *Soviet Defectors*, 215–17.

72. Sagim Suleymanov, Книга памяти жертв политических репрессий 20–50-х гг. XX в. в Дагестане [Memory book of the victims of political repression, the '20s–'50s of the twentieth century in Dagestan] (Makhachkala, Dagestan, 2015), 144–46.

73. "Салиманов, Георгий Васильевич" [Salimanov, Georgiy Vasilyevich], Кадровый Состав Органов Государственной Безопасности СССР, *1935–1939* [Staff personnel of the organs of USSR state security, 1935–1939], https://nkvd.memo.ru/index.php/Салиманов,_Георгий_Васильевич.

74. Murphy, Kondrashev, and Bailey, *Battleground Berlin*, 15.

75. Georgiy Andreyev, Списки Советских Специалистов, Работавших в САО 'ВИСМУТ' 1945–1953, Часть III [Lists of Soviet Specialists working at SAO "VISMUT" 1945–1953, Part III], 415. This list is part of Уран и люди. история СГАО 'ВИСМУТ' в двух томах [Uranium and people: The history of SGAO "VISMUT" in two volumes] (Moscow: Spets-Adress, 2012).

76. O. S. Smyslov, Генерал Абакумов. Палач или жертва? [General Abakumov: Executioner or victim?] (Moscow: Veche, 2012).

77. Nikita Petrov, Почётные граждане ГУЛага [Honored citizens of the GULAG] (Moscow: International "Memorial" Foundation, 2015), http://ipvnews.org/hegemon_article13042011.php.

78. Vladimir Petrov and Evdokia Petrov, *Empire of Fear* (London: Andre Deutsch, 1956), 138–39.

79. Petrov and Petrov, *Empire of Fear*, 142–47.

80. Petrov and Petrov, *Empire of Fear*, 155.

81. Australian surveillance and agent reports regarding Petrov, 1950 to 1954, are in National Archives of Australia (NAA), A6119, vols. 1–5.

82. "The Year 1953," 12 May 1954, NAA, A6283, folder 1, item number 4104669, 127; duplicate in NAA, A6283, folder 14, item number 4104675, 30.

83. Petrov and Petrov, *Empire of Fear*, 251–52.

84. Statement by Petrova, 22 April 1954, NAA, A6283, folder 14, item number 4104675, 50.

85. "Copy of Statement in the Handwriting of Mrs. Petrov Setting Out the Reasons for Her Departure," 7 May 1954, NAA, A6283, folder 14, item number 4104675, 55–56; "Exhibit 63," NAA, A6283, folder 14, item number 4104675, 58.

86. "Defection of Vladimir Mikhailovich Petrov @ Proletarski, and Evdokia Alexeevna Petrova @ Kartseva," undated but probably November 1954, NAA, A6283, folder 15, item number 4104676, 132–54.

87. "Defection of Vladimir Mikhailovich Petrov @ Proletarski, and Evdokia Alexeevna Petrova @ Kartseva," 136.

88. "Defection of Vladimir Mikhailovich Petrov @ Proletarski, and Evdokia Alexeevna Petrova @ Kartseva," 135.

89. Petrov and Petrov, *Empire of Fear*.

90. Peter Deriabin and Frank Gibney, *The Secret World* (New York: Doubleday, 1959), 55–57.

91. CIA Report, "Economic Enterprises of the MVD," 13 July 1955, NARA, RG 319, entry 134A, box 138

92. 441st CIC Detachment Report of Investigation, "RASTVOROV, Yuriy A.," 2 February 1954, NARA, RG 319, entry A1 314B, box 627.

93. Yuri Rastvorov, "Beria's Plot," HIA, Boris Nicolaevsky Collection, box 295, folder 21 (microfilm reel 255), 21–22.

94. Nikolai Khokhlov, as told to Milton Lehman, "I Would Not Murder for the Soviets," *Saturday Evening Post*, 27 November 1954, 72.

95. Khokhlov, "I Would Not Murder for the Soviets," 11 December 1954, 130.

96. KGB, Алфавитный Список Изменников Родины [Alphabetical list of traitors to the homeland], 1979, 250.

97. N. A. Trebugov, "Государственный комитет по культурным связям с зарубежными странами как орган советской культурной дипломатии (1957–1967 гг.)" [The state committee for cultural ties with foreign countries as an organ of Soviet cultural diplomacy (1957–1967)], Управление в современных системах [Management in modern systems] 11, no. 4 (2016): 61–67.

98. Vladimir Ilich Ponomarev, Letter to UNESCO Director-General René Maheu, 15 October 1964, UNESCO Archives, AG 8: CAB/1/8.

99. Louis H. Porter, "Cold War Internationalisms: The USSR in UNESCO, 1945–1967" (PhD diss., University of North Carolina, 2018), 337–38.

100. State Archives of the Russian Federation (GARF), fond 9519, opus 2, delo 28, 67.

101. Vladimir Ilich Ponomarev, Letter to UNESCO Director-General René Maheu, 15 October 1964, UNESCO Archives, AG 8: CAB/1/8.

12

The Space Between
Hildegard Beetz, Espionage, and Gender, 1944–1949

Katrin Paehler

The American SCI (Special Counterintelligence) Detachment arrived at the house in Weimar in mid-June 1945. The men had learned from Wilhelm Hoettl, a ranking member of the SS political foreign intelligence service—designated as Office VI of Heinrich Himmler's Reich Security Main Office, RSHA, and sometimes referred to as the SD (Sicherheitsdienst)—that "an important woman executive and agent" who likely "had in her possession . . . the personal diaries of the late Count Ciano" lived there. The woman in question, Hildegard Beetz, did not have the diaries, but she had the Americans dig up copies of some of Ciano's other documents as well as documents dealing with her wartime activities in Italy from her mother's garden.[1] One is left to wonder what surprised the Americans more: the document bonanza or the self-possessed and prepared twenty-five-year-old greeting them?

Within days of her first encounter with American counterintelligence, Hildegard Beetz began to work with the US intelligence services, a relationship that would last, in a formal fashion, until the early 1950s.[2] In the following, I focus on Beetz's interactions with her US handlers and her second career in espionage between the summer of 1945 and 1950/51, that is, between the end of the war and shortly after the establishment of the Federal Republic of Germany (FRG). How did a woman who had worked for the SS foreign intelligence service remake herself into a well-respected American asset? How did Beetz navigate her personal and political *Zeitenwende* (turn of the times)?

Allied intelligence services were initially interested in Beetz for her role in the so-called Ciano Affair. In fall 1943, after Italy's surrender, Office VI had meant to use Ciano's writings as ammunition in Germany's intramural fights. Beetz had played a leading role in the efforts to obtain Ciano's diaries. After Ciano's execution in January 1944, Beetz was charged with keeping tabs on his widow, Edda Mussolini. Over the course of the Ciano Affair, Beetz's role became increasingly ambiguous: Committed to the broad outlines of Office VI's mandate, Beetz tried to spare Ciano's life, and aided his widow's escape, with the prized diaries, to Switzerland. At the same time, Beetz procured the vast majority of Ciano's other documents for Office VI, thus scoring an undeniable victory. Charged with translating the documents, she kept copies for herself—and handed them over when the SCI Detachment came knocking.

Beetz had come to Office VI in a roundabout way. Born in 1919 to a middle-class family, a talented linguist, industrious, and ambitious, Beetz had sought employment in fall 1939, landing a position with the local office of the RSHA's domestic intelligence service in her hometown. Fluent in several languages, she eventually won a transfer to Office VI's headquarters in Berlin. Technically in an administrative position as a secretary and translator, she took on analytical responsibilities as well. She was then posted to Rome as a secretary to Office VI's Main Representative; eventually, after several Main Representatives blundered themselves back to Germany, Beetz—officially still a secretary—took over. It was after her recall from Rome, in the aftermath of the Italian surrender, that she became involved in matters relating to Ciano.[3] She was, indubitably, an intelligence insider, if an unusual one.

There exist numerous studies on German officials who transitioned seamlessly into the postwar period.[4] This also holds true for intelligence officials who were taken on by the occupation powers' services for their self-professed—rarely actual—intelligence and counterintelligence knowledge.[5] Recent studies have also heeded the active roles these men played in their "recasting." Much less is known about women both on the individual and the collective level.[6]

Beetz's story has, despite the extraordinary elements, broader implications. Elsewhere, I have proposed the existence of "New Nazi Women": modern, ambitious women who, in the words of Wendy Lower, saw "a professional opportunity and a liberating experience" and were comfortable in Nazi Germany; used its racist and imperial designs to their fullest advantage; and ably worked the system, and its commonly understood notions of acceptable female roles and behaviors, which could diverge from official, more ideologically orthodox pronouncements, to their benefit.[7] In the following, I argue that Beetz's experiences in Nazi Germany—in particular her ability to navigate complicated administrative structures, her industriousness and ambition, and her ability to adhere to and subvert gendered expectations—equipped her to navigate the end of Nazi Germany and to thrive in the postwar era. Put differently: Nazism made her, grounded, and made possible, her later careers.

Beetz was adept at managing the "the spaces between" and working them to her advantage: both the liminal, politically unstable space between the end of the war and the establishment of the Federal Republic of Germany (West Germany) as well as the liminal space of contradictory gender(ed) expectations that the Americans brought with them. Beetz both conformed to and confounded American gendered norms and illusions, which, incidentally, shifted toward a restoration of more traditional gender roles at the end of the period under investigation. It was at that point that Beetz lost some of her luster in the eyes of her American handlers. German historians of gender have coined the term *Handlungsräume*—scopes for action—open to women in subaltern positions.[8] I am interested in gauging these scopes for action, both in terms of concrete historical moment but also in terms of thinking about how gender undergirded them, creating an ever-changing terrain.

This work is based on US records on Beetz, namely her CIA file. Declassified in the early 2000s, the file is exhaustive—even if it remains unlikely that it is complete—and allows for detailed, intriguing insights into Beetz's life and career.[9] After she was picked up by US counterintelligence, Beetz was questioned extensively, mostly about the Ciano Affair. Beetz also spoke rather freely about her life in Nazi Germany, and her frankness occasionally puzzled her interrogators; she likely anticipated that her role in the Ciano Affair, her officially subaltern position, her youth, and her gender would offer a measure of protection. Thereafter, she worked for and with US intelligence; the file includes reports on and by her. And even when she was not formally active anymore, her file kept growing, as she would "pop up" in other contexts, necessitating the inclusion of materials into her file. In sum, Beetz's CIA file offers a decent window into her life, career, and subjectivities, frequently in her own words, and allows for valuable insights into a smart and ambitious woman negotiating her way out of Nazi Germany and into a new professional and personal life.

In this chapter, I first discuss Beetz's initial interactions with US intelligence agencies, focusing on her ability to serve the needs of the United States while establishing her own credentials and employment. I then detail her role in the high-stakes Berlin spy-games, showing her as an able asset and operative and an outspoken if self-proclaimed intelligence expert, whose handlers quickly accepted her as such. Last, I touch on the beginnings of Beetz's journalistic career, which was a side effect of her work for US intelligence. Liminal spaces and gendered expectations, adhered to and subverted, play a starring role throughout.

In the summer of 1945, Beetz fell under Automatic Arrest policies, but it appears that counterintelligence's initial interest in her stemmed from interrogations of Wilhelm Hoettl. He had suggested that she might have copies of the Ciano Diaries and divulged her whereabouts.[10] Counterintelligence questioned Beetz, but she was well-positioned: Her roles in the political foreign intelligence service and in the Ciano Affair made her a useful source, while her ostensibly low-level administrative position, her youth, and her gender rendered her unthreatening. Beetz actively fastened on these advantages; she was forthright and detailed about her past but also claimed that "in a sense [she] double-crossed the SD." There was truth to that: During the war, she had kept information from her office, and she was the reason that Ciano's diaries, which Allen Dulles was in the process of obtaining, remained with Ciano's widow, Edda Mussolini, whom Beetz had allowed to slip into Switzerland in early 1944.[11]

Beetz's relationship with Hoettl added to her importance and was emblematic of her role as a reliable source. US counterintelligence was deeply suspicious of the man and his motives. Hoettl had occupied numerous important positions in Office VI and was a close associate of Ernst Kaltenbrunner, the last head of the RSHA. In the custody of the Third Army at that time, Hoettl was also rumored to have extensive intelligence connections, and although he was keen to work for a Western intelligence service, he was considered willing to look elsewhere. He was also full of himself. When he disclosed Beetz's location, he also asked the—bemused—Americans to deliver a letter revealing his plans to work for the Americans, and he asked Beetz to join him, as he "trusted [her] implicitly." Beetz did not return the sentiment and listed four instances in which she had double-crossed him for her interrogators. She also warned that Hoettl "was not ... to be completely trusted," and counseled "that ... if we saw to use him we should beware of his retaining connections with the underground; that she had on several occasions heard RSHA officials—though probably not the doctor himself—discussing post defeat plans such as using the American service as a cover for their own operations."[12] In sum, Beetz portrayed Hoettl as both dangerous, which was to be expected, and, presumably unexpectedly to the Americans, as gullible. Herself she painted as an expert on the man.

Beetz's first American mission took shape in this context with her subtly steering it and anticipating American needs. In a "general conversation,"

Beetz "suggested that if she went to work for Hoettl . . . she would be in an excellent position to watch him on our behalf." Playing both coy and her cards right, she also claimed little willingness "to enter this type of work again." Beetz's suggestion "curiously [accorded] exactly [with] the mission that Capt. Schriever and the undersigned had thought best for her."[13] After this meeting of minds, preparations began.

In the meantime, Beetz continued to provide testimony on the Ciano Affair, burnishing her credibility, and gaining a measure of trust. Her gender and her looks, combined with her knowledge and her willingness to give precise information, took in her interrogators. In what must have been a refreshing change of pace, Beetz's statements lacked the self-aggrandizing innuendo found in the interrogations of SD men. The Americans swiftly concluded that Beetz was an "attractive young woman" and an "extremely intelligent person with an excellent memory," whose statements checked out.[14] A notable disconnect developed between Beetz's self-portrayal and the American view of her. In an early *Lebenslauf*, a detailed, prose curriculum vitae—Beetz rendered herself as a capable woman with agency, smarter and more professional than many of her male superiors; she also spoke frankly about her early enthrallment with Nazism. She likely reasoned that her gender, her youth—then and now—and her roles in the Ciano Affair protected her from being painted a Nazi. The US summary of the *Lebenslauf* subtly reconfigured Beetz's frank and self-assured statements and made them cohere with American assumptions about women's roles in Nazi Germany: Beetz appeared younger, less confident, less qualified, and void of much of her agency. Keen to rely on her, the Americans thus created an asset that was magically both eminently capable and largely innocent. And compared to just about anyone else foreign intelligence services were recruiting in Germany at the time, Beetz was exactly that. Yet in the process, the Americans lost interest in information Beetz could have provided.[15] The present and the future trumped the past.

In July 1945, US intelligence used Beetz for a short-range exploitation. She was to meet with Hoettl, held at the Third Army Intelligence Center, and find out his plans. The mission's setup betrayed Beetz's special status: Not only was she fully aware of the meeting's purpose, she was actively cooperating with and advising the SCI officers. However, the Americans did not rely "on her good faith alone," but installed recording devices to double-check her reporting.[16] Beetz passed the test with flying colors and in fall 1945, she became a penetration agent in Munich. A vetting request summarized the allure she held for the Americans after numerous interrogations and a minor counterintelligence operation: Fluent in several languages, she was deemed "highly intelligent," trustworthy, and no "disciple of Nazi ideals." Trusted by her former colleagues, it was expected that they would contact her, and, owing to her knowledge and "insight into the German mind," she would be able to evaluate them and their information. However, US intelligence also had control: Her ongoing freedom was dependent on her collaboration, as was the fate of her POW husband.[17]

Beetz thus established her credentials and standing with US intelligence within weeks. Her ambiguous role in the Ciano Affair recommended her, and her knowledge about SS intelligence and its personalities made her an asset. And her youth, frankness, and looks made her interrogators disinclined to probe too deeply into all of her knowledge and made them adjust her biography to American understandings of female life in Nazi Germany. Language mattered as well: Beetz's English was excellent and must have made interrogations less cumbersome and casual conversations more likely and more pleasant.[18]

US intelligence had pressure points—her and her husband's fate—but there is no indication that they resorted to them. Rather, much like in 1943/1944, Beetz showed agency, if in unthreatening "womanly" fashion: She was prepared when the Americans arrived and anticipated her interrogators' moves thereafter. She had squirreled away not only Ciano's Italian documents but also materials documenting her role. She suggested spying on Hoettl, an idea her interrogators had also been pondering. Hildegard Beetz was in charge of her own destiny. She knew how to play (with) the big boys, did so well, and paved her path forward. And—as Hoettl surely noticed—she even settled a score or two along the way.

They did not call Berlin "kidnap city" for nothing, and by the summer of 1946—at an auspicious time and a year after claiming that she had little interest "to enter this type of work again"—Beetz found herself at the center of a daring scheme. In fall 1945, the plan had been to use her as a penetration agent in the American Zone, but nothing came of it; Beetz remained in "protective custody pending the appearance of a new project fitted to her special talents."[19] That project, which dovetailed with the new focus of US counterintelligence on Soviet intelligence services, rather than on German wartime organizations, was Operation "Sitting Duck."[20]

In Berlin, the double agent "Savoy," the former *Abwehr*—military intelligence—member Hans Kemritz, was becoming notorious. Savoy had worked for Soviet intelligence since May 1945 but was eventually doubled by the Americans with the goal of learning about Soviet penetration plans and of getting to his case officer, a certain Captain Skurin. However, by 1946, too many German men in contact with Savoy had been abducted by the Soviets for him to remain in the shadows. Savoy also ran afoul of his Soviet handlers, and in November US intelligence exfiltrated him to the Western Zone.[21] Subsequently, the Americans relied on another double agent of Skurin's, code-named "Ford." Skurin remained the target, and that was where Beetz came in.

"Sitting Duck" was rather a misnomer for the operation envisioned by the Berlin Field Station of the Security Control Branch of the SSU. The original plan was to place Beetz in OMGUS (Office of the Military Government), the main target of Soviet intelligence, and to use her as a cutout, a middle(wo)man, "to give the Soviet controlling officer the illusion that their agent has in fact contacted well-placed sources of information." Thus far "secure American officers" had been used for that purpose, but the project planners reasoned that the Soviets would find "a well-placed German secretary" more trustworthy. A draft noted that such a "decoy" or "sitting duck"—the imprecise language already implies a potentially broader role for Beetz—would make Soviet intelligence overconfident and possibly also easier to penetrate.[22]

US intelligence considered Beetz perfect for the assignment. Beetz would be able to secure her cover job based on her professional qualifications—her experience as a secretary and her skill in English and German shorthand. The Americans were as excited about her intelligence qualifications. Noting her "extensive experiences with Amt VI, RSHA," they regarded her as a "professional able to handle the intricate relationships involved in top-level double agent operations." They had also concluded that she held "anti-Nazi convictions developed prior to and during the war" and a "westward orientation." In addition, they stressed their "complete" control over Beetz, since her husband remained in US custody. Control notwithstanding, Beetz was neither a pawn nor pressed into service but on-board with the plan, well, and happy.[23]

The operation raised red flags regarding security. Beetz was a former German intelligence operative and, as US intelligence had concluded and eagerly touted, a capable one. Vetting materials emphasize that "extraordinary pains to examine the agent's background were taken . . . because of the extremely delicate—vis-à-vis OMGUS—project she is undertaking and the possibility that her association with Ciano might someday lead someone, through misunderstanding, to believe us to be harboring a wicked internationally notorious queen of spies."[24] The thick irony aside, the employment of a former Nazi operative under the fake name "Hildegard Blum," provided by US intelligence, violated security regulations, even if OMGUS security personnel—but security personnel only—were aware of her true identity. Beetz had clearly managed to persuade the Americans of both her anti-Nazi credentials and of the excellence of her work for Nazi Germany. Her new posting was predicated on both, and it turned her Nazi past, a liability, into a postwar asset.

"Sitting Duck" developed in an unexpected fashion.[25] The initial plan had been to use her as a cutout, but not much happened. Beetz made herself useful—and showed initiative—in other ways. She commented on the notebook of one of her former Amt VI associates in Italy. She kept an eye open for Soviet penetration attempts of OMGUS, detecting none. And she used her contacts in her hometown of Weimar in the Soviet Zone to collect information on Soviet intelligence activities there. US intelligence considered her information reliable and emphasized that this was only the second time that they had received any information out of Weimar.[26] However, these activities, possibly driven by Beetz's intent to show her usefulness, were no reason to have her working at OMGUS. Already in early November, there was talk about moving her to the Refugee Control Unit.[27] It is unclear why US intelligence considered pulling the plug so quickly. It might have been impatience, but there were also concerns about Beetz's sensitive position at OMGUS. By mid-November, Henry Hecksher, one of the "Sitting Duck's" nonlocal masterminds, took stock of the operation and made clear that it had been misunderstood and mishandled. With tart annoyance, Hecksher spelled out that while code-named "Sitting Duck," the expectation had been "that steps would be taken to direct the attentions of the SIS [Soviet Intelligence Service] in the direction of Gambit [Beetz's new code name] rather than reducing the operation to an altogether passive 'playing possum.'" Handily ignoring that the initial proposal had talked of cutouts and decoys, Hecksher upped the ante:

> Here you have an OMGUS employee, placed in a position of trust and with access to classified material, who falsified her Fragebogen and concealed the fact that at one time she had been a member of the SD in a fairly prominent position and that her husband is a German General Staff officer. Any outsider cognizant of Gambit's secret would be in the ideal position to blackmail her. The consequences, if found out, would be rather serious, because under the ruling of the Nuremberg Tribunal Gambit is a former member of an organization declared criminal. Put yourself in the position of an imaginative Soviet intelligence officer who has learned through one of his informants of Gambit's double life. Is it not reasonable to expect that he would try to apply his knowledge as a means of coercion against Gambit?

Consequently, Hecksher counseled "that before throwing in the towel, you try to think out this operation to its logical conclusion" and suggested subtly alerting Soviet intelligence to Beetz's presence at OMGUS. However, he also made it very clear that the operation could only succeed if Beetz were on-board; explicitly acknowledging her expertise, he advised, "you may therefore want to obtain her views on its practicability before making up your mind."[28] In short: if she was willing and found the plan feasible, Beetz was to be a proper sitting duck, ready to be blackmailed.

But things had started to move already. A few days before Hecksher's exasperated missive, a report by Ford indicated that Skurin had asked after Beetz—whom he considered "one of the outstanding RSHA operators of the war" and believed to be "still at large in the British Zone"—and had tasked Ford to locate her. As the Soviets knew that she was still registered in Weimar, Ford was to "make personal inquiries" there. US intelligence, for its part, "advised" Ford that it shared Soviet sentiments about Beetz and deemed her a war criminal, instructing Ford to report his findings, as US intelligence wanted to catch her first.[29]

Ford's account likely played into the decision to follow Hecksher's plan. On 25 November, Toivo Roswall, Beetz's temporary and Ford's permanent case officer took stock of the operation and suggested how to proceed. He noted that Soviet penetration of OMGUS had not been as deep as expected; consequently, one needed to draw attention to Beetz. Despite Skurin's recent interest in Beetz and Ford's trips to Weimar, Roswall was certain that neither Ford nor Skurin knew about Beetz's name change and position. Ford was therefore instructed "to report to Captain Skurin that Hildegard Beetz, formerly of the RSHA, is now Hildegard Blum, confidential secretary in an important division in the US Military Government Headquarters," and given a cover story to explain his knowledge. Ford was told "not to facilitate" Beetz's arrest, but US intelligence was not unduly worried about this possibility; one expected greater Soviet interest in blackmailing her. Roswall saw only positives: Skurin would "enlist the services of one of the best known RSHA operatives," well established in an agency Soviet intelligence was keen to penetrate. "Gambit"—Beetz—could finally be activated, and Ford, one of Skurin's "oldest and most trusted agents," would burnish his credentials.[30] Clearly, there were only advantages.

Seemingly offered up on a silver platter, Beetz was no pawn in the developments. Hecksher had advised his colleagues in Berlin "to obtain [Beetz's] views on [the operation's] *practicability* [emphasis mine]," an intriguing suggestion, as this alluded to more than a simple inquiry as to whether she was willing to fulfill her role.[31] Rather, it intimated an exchange between professionals to ascertain whether Beetz, as an intelligence operative, found the operation professionally sound. Roswall struck a similar chord, noting that "the project has been thoroughly discussed with Gambit, who agreed to every phase of it." Indeed, she was "looking forward to a more exciting and active role."[32] But for all her excitement, Beetz also hoped that by "working" for Soviet intelligence she would divert Soviet attention from her family in Weimar. She had learned about the inquiries in Weimar but seemed unaware that Ford was their source: She was not privy to all the operation's details.

The operation entered into its active phase in early 1947. Ford had given the information about Beetz's new name and position to Skurin in early December; Skurin then tasked him to locate Beetz in Berlin and meet with her.[33] By early January, Beetz's residence was under intermittent Soviet surveillance, and there were peculiar events, such as alleged German policemen—from "the Alex," police headquarters on Alexanderplatz in the Eastern part of the city—inquiring about her. Tom Polgar, the operation's apparent new point person, was pleased: It made Beetz cautious and confirmed Soviet interest in her. There was, however, concern about confirmed Soviet intentions to "lure" Beetz into the Soviet sector to kidnap her; US intelligence was taking "maximum precautions" against this.[34]

US intelligence, for its part, planned to use Beetz to get ahold of Skurin and to double him. A visit by Ford and Beetz to a "musicale," a house concert, in the French Zone in April 1947 was the operation's crescendo: US intelligence expected that Skurin would try to nab Beetz then, as the location was close to the sectional border; the US plan was to get Skurin. However, something spooked the Soviets. No attempt was made to grab Beetz, which derailed American plans. The operation petered out in early summer 1947.

Beetz had been at the center of this daring scheme, which easily could have gone south in different ways. But she clearly saw herself—and was seen by her handlers—as a professional, able to handle a complex and dangerous mission and its cast of characters. In particular, she did not suffer easily men she deemed unqualified fools, as separate reports by her and Ford indicate. Ford was clearly at a disadvantage in these interactions. Different from him, she was a privileged US asset: She knew about the overall plans and expected Ford's call. Ford's report on his visit opened with a comment on Beetz's "disorderly room"; he then related that he admitted that he was working for the "Russians" and "told her that the Russians were well aware of who she was and what she had done during the war and were consequently much interested in her." He warned Beetz that Soviet interest in her was such that she should be wary of attempts to lure her into the

Soviet sector and, if she did not cooperate, they would move against her mother in Weimar. Ford noted that Beetz liked his frankness and shared information with him to give to the Soviets; he told her that "undoubtedly ... the Russians would insist on further and closer contact." Ford's initial take on Beetz was not "particularly favorable"; he pointedly evaluated her as "rather sharp" and opined that she was "a 'cat,' who is morally probably quite loose."[35] He had presumably deduced this from the state of her room.

Beetz's report on the meeting differed notably. She reported on Soviet interest in her and detailed Ford's interactions with her, which, in her view, combined barely disguised threats and unprompted confidentialities. Ford told her that the Soviets "of course" knew about her wartime activities, but that he was not to tell her about this and asked about her current work "to satisfy the Russians." He also conveyed that "the Americans would be informed first of what she had said and would censor it before it was given to the Russians." In short: He revealed that he was a double agent. He also suggested that Beetz use "him as a cutout for any dealing with the Russians"; Beetz could thereby avoid trips to the Soviet sector and possible abduction, while his "reputation and value" would be enhanced. As an added tit-for-tat, Ford proposed that if the Russians arrested her, he would "volunteer himself" to the Americans for a prisoner exchange. Ford then invited Beetz to the theater with him. Beetz chose to understand this invitation as a way to alert the Soviets to their acquaintanceship, but as Ford thanked her for the "professional tip," his intent might have been different. Indeed, Ford settled in and regaled Beetz with his life story, mentioning his "real name, work with the AND [Allgemeine Deutsche Nachrichtendienst, the press service in the Soviet Zone], and about his wife turning pottery in the English zone." Ford seemed taken with Beetz and eventually apologized for his "garrulousness," noting that "seldom had he met anyone who on first meeting inspired so much confidence." During their first meeting, Ford divulged a few trade secrets and his status as a double agent, fashioned himself as Beetz's protector, and unburdened his heart. Unsurprisingly, Beetz's assessment of Ford was highly critical. It also demonstrates her belief in her professional acumen and special status. Self-assured and comfortable enough to be scathing, she pronounced Ford "well meaning, reliable, but not too intelligent" and opined: "As for his professional qualifications ... it was too bad he had not had the benefit of Amt VI [SS intelligence] schooling."[36] In short, she reminded her American handlers of her value as an asset due to her SS training and painted Ford as a well-intentioned bore.

Beetz also reported on another, unexpected visit by Ford some days later, which cast him in a dubious personal, professional, and political light. She recounted that he arrived at 8 a.m. on a Tuesday, staying for two hours and "pour[ing] out quite a portion of his soul." On the professional side, Ford noted the Soviets' interest in her and their wish to "have her directly in their hands." Ford emphasized that he was unwilling to facilitate her abduction, as they were both "first of all Germans, [who] should act together to prevent it, whatever else may happen." Ford then aired his dislike of the "Russians" and noted that he "did not like the Americans much better." Most damningly, Beetz reported that Ford had "praised Hitler and the Führer principle, which he still believed in, lamenting only a few of its excesses." In Beetz's expert opinion, Ford thereby "showed himself ... as an idealistic Nazi." Maybe concerned that this unprompted, negative report on a fellow, male asset would backfire, Beetz proffered her justification: Ford was too interested in her personally; too fearful for (t)his line of work; and, disconcertingly, probably also unwilling to take risks—"he might try to veto any aggressive plans we may have."[37] Her subtext was clear. Beetz fashioned herself as Ford's polar opposite: She was a consummate professional, willing to embrace risk, and an anti-Nazi committed to US goals.

Her minders agreed. Even though the plan to abduct Skurin had come to naught, US intelligence was pleased with it, labeling the—failed—operation the "highlight of the month." Ford eventually disclosed that the Soviets had, indeed, been on the scene on 12 April 1947 but were unsettled "by the large number of French vehicles in the general neighborhood." The Americans had clearly been on the right path. And they were equally pleased with the people involved. Ford "continue[d] satisfactorily." And Beetz, engaged in an operation not for the faint of heart—but then she had proven in 1943/44 that she was all but unflappable—had failed to yield, but by no fault of hers.[38] She remained the golden child, although without an immediate objective.

Arno Scholz was the editor of the Berlin daily *Der Telegraf*, commonly considered a "social democratic-leaning" paper, which began publication under British license in March 1946.[39] Scholz also worked for US intelligence. Under the code name Camlet he used the paper to collect information on the SPD (Sozialdemokratische Partei Deutschlands) and related issues, so-called "Alcatraz materials." However, his output had "decreased considerably," and Scholz also lacked a solid channel to get his materials to the Americans. His designated cutout had, per request of US intelligence, distanced himself from Scholz. Frequent meetings with his case officers were out of the question for security reasons, but also because Scholz was busy. This is where Beetz came in. She was to become Scholz's "confidential secretary," a position with "ready access" to the editor. Scholz was not privy to all the details. Beetz had been suggested to Scholz in July, and, having been advised that US intelligence trusted her, he had eagerly accepted the offer. But he neither knew her real name and identity nor her Nazi intelligence background. To him, she was Hilde Blum. Scholz was also in the dark about the scope of her brief: to "supply [US intelligence] with information on inside happenings... allow us to observe closely Camlet's activities, and act as a high-class cutout between Camlet and [US intelligence]."[40] Beetz was spying on Scholz.

Beetz was glad about her new role and so were her handlers. She found her position at OMGUS "uninteresting and routine," and the Americans regarded Beetz's work at the *Telegraf*, which began in September, as a first step in a future "journalistic career."[41] At the paper, she was to focus on "Alcatraz" materials, but her different targets—Camlet, the paper's *Ostbüro* (East-[German] Office) as well as "German officials and civilians coming from the Russian Zone"—indicated an ambitious scheme. US intelligence was pleased that her cover was, again, "legitimate employment" and that beginning in January 1948, Beetz "would head her own research department at the *Telegraf*." Deemed under "ideological control," Beetz's case officer contacted her at her residence in the US sector of Berlin, reporting that Beetz was aware that she was working with American intelligence and, due to "continuity of control since August 1945," understood that the organization was related to the—meanwhile disbanded—OSS, the Office of Strategic Services.[42] She was still married, but her husband lived in Darmstadt; her brother and mother resided in Weimar in the Soviet Zone. She was also inexpensive: Her salary was paid by the newspaper. Beyond that, she received a monthly package of supplies, which, in addition to gender-neutral products, included sanitary pads. The Americans also assisted with a yearly travel permit. But US intelligence felt little responsibility toward her. There were "no disposal costs" if she were dropped; had to flee and resettle; or were to be killed.[43] Here, then, are visible the limitations of American appreciation of Beetz.

Over the next year, Beetz focused on the objectives laid out for her. Helped along by Scholz and her handlers in service of her intelligence work, she moved from "editorial assistant" to head of her own research department to editor of the political pages of *Telegraf*'s Germany-wide edition.[44] Her handlers saw her as a "valuable and usually reliable source," who, unlike Scholz, "require[ed] little guidance." Based on "her drive and ability" and "our sponsorship," the Americans noted, Beetz was "groomed for an important position" at the paper. They had great plans for her: Beetz was to supersede Scholz/Camlet, and she would use "to the full the information gathering facilities" of the paper and its East Office.[45]

As always, Beetz hit the ground running. In late October 1947, her case officer met with Scholz. Scholz reported that he had sent Dr. Grunner, the head of *Telegraf*'s political desk, to Vienna. He regarded the Austrian Grunner as well-positioned to learn about a potential Soviet-controlled underground movement in the Austrian Social Democratic Party (SPÖ) but did not fully trust him. The case officer, for his part, noted rumors that Grunner shared information with the Soviet press service. Scholz doubted this, but thought Beetz, with whose work he was "very well satisfied," a good person to keep an eye on Grunner. The Field Comment noted approvingly: "Beetz is at present assigned to the political desk, and it appears that she has already rendered herself indispensable to Grunner."[46]

Beetz's work was both in the background, crucial, and predicated on gendered dynamics. She filed reports with US intelligence—for example when she relayed information about a dinner meeting between Grunner, with whom she later had a romantic relationship, and the head of TASS (Soviet press service)—but she also became a veritable "Scholz-whisperer."[47] She helped the Americans cement their relationship with Scholz, an "invaluable service" that turned him into a "very valuable contact" for "spot intelligence" as well as for long-term penetration of the SPD. She also became the facilitator—and more: Scholz turned over materials he collected to Beetz, who then selected what went to the Americans. In addition, Beetz ensured that the reportedly overworked Scholz produced concrete results. Yet her work went further: Close to Scholz, she kept the Americans "conscientiously" apprised of his thinking. US intelligence thus learned, for example, that Scholz, despite his confidence in the Americans' "discretion and sense of fairness," had never been completely open with them. He particularly loathed to divulge top-level SPD information or to reveal his sources. Indeed, Beetz and Scholz's handlers had an agreement in which she let the Americans know when Scholz withheld information. The Americans then inquired about these issues and, tickled in his vanity, Scholz would be "unable to hold back that information any longer." Alternatively or additionally, Beetz pushed Scholz into divulging information by committing "studied indiscretion[s]," exclaiming, for example, "but you told me only yesterday . . . ."[48] The gendered structures of these arrangements were as effective as they are hard to miss: they range from the superbly organized assistant who enables her supposedly overworked male superior to meet his professional commitments; to the omniscient secretary who knows how to expertly exert pressure and to play to a man's vanity; and, finally, to the slightly ditzy, junior colleague who inadvertently, but charmingly, spills the beans about her boss's knowledge.

The US service's appreciation of Beetz's work led to an increasing sense of obligation toward her—as did the realization of how deeply knowledgeable she was about American intelligence efforts, past and present, in Berlin. A memorandum dated 22 June 1948, two days before the beginning of the Berlin Blockade, included Beetz among the people to be evacuated in case of an American withdrawal from Berlin. Prima facie, the reasoning was simple: "Camise has been under our control since spring [sic!] 1945. During her period of service her devotion to our cause and discretion has always been exemplary." But a general sense of obligation for a valued asset was not the entire story. An earlier, embarrassing American snafu had provided Beetz with a card she knew not to play: in 1945, one of her minders had mistakenly handed her a complete operational file instead of her private papers. She had studied it with "bated attention" before handing it back. In addition, her initial Berlin case officer "became deeply infatuated with her," which had led to a perceptible "drop in security consciousness." And to make her effective with Scholz, she had been given extensive briefings on American objectives. In short, Beetz knew more than her share: "She is probably better acquainted with the history of our organization and its personnel than any other agent this base has ever run."[49] Hidden behind the careful wording was both a fond appreciation of and deep concern about Beetz's undeniable smarts.

Beetz's journalistic and intelligence careers continued hand in hand, a testament to her abilities and industriousness. By late spring 1949, she was the editor of the Western German edition of the *Telegraf*, soon to be published out of Frankfurt, planning to split her time between Berlin and Frankfurt. US intelligence intended to exploit her in her overt position in Frankfurt, in her covert tasks regarding Scholz, and in a new project. Her loyalty was unquestioned: She was deemed pro-American, convinced that Germany's future was tied to the United States, and "uncompromisingly hostile" toward the Soviet Union. Only her "duties as a German" might override this. US intelligence had far-reaching plans for her, even if the Acting Chief of the Berlin Operations Base (BOB), considered specifics "premature." There was no doubt that Beetz was "professional agent caliber" and should eventually, "once political conditions in Germany have sufficiently crystallized," receive "sufficient operational latitude to organize her own information net."[50]

Concerns about Beetz's legend mounted, though. Her personal and professional background as well as decisions taken by her handlers when she became involved with US intelligence had created a difficult mess to disentangle. Her real identity remained secret, but there were many who could unmask the increasingly prominent journalist "Hilde Blum." It was, however, common wisdom that she was less likely to be recognized in Berlin, as most "persons with an activist Nazi record" tended to stay away from Berlin with its Soviet presence and its history of abductions. However, Beetz was perturbed by the lenient sentence that Walter Schellenberg, the head of Amt VI, received during his trial. What would he do with his knowledge? Then there was the husband, now a student in West Germany, who knew of her new identity. Beetz was keen to divorce him, but divorce proceedings could reveal that she was not Hilde Blum. Another question was what both rival and Allied intelligence services knew or suspected: US intelligence was certain that British intelligence had scrutinized all personnel at the *Telegraf* but remained confident that Beetz's cover was intact. The Soviets were another matter. In 1949, American intelligence was unsure whether Ford had been told about Beetz's actual identity, incidentally a question the files could have easily answered. All concerns aside, US intelligence was pleased with its creation and gestured to the idea that Beetz's transformation made her unrecognizable: Beetz's "new identity fits her to perfection, so much so that the case officer in dealing with her is most of the time oblivious to the fact that [Beetz] and the girl he interrogated in 1945 are one and the same."[51] Hildegard Beetz, formerly of the Amt VI of Himmler's Reichssicherheitshauptamt, had come a long way.

In Frankfurt, Beetz's scope extended further. As a journalist, she oversaw the *Westdeutsche Redaktion* (West German Editorial Office), coordinating the *Telegraf*'s correspondents in West Germany; she was also advising her boss on the Berlin-related interests of West German readers. In her "free" time, she attended press conferences and wrote articles, burnishing her reputation as a journalist. She liked being her own boss but missed Berlin.[52] Her intelligence brief was ambitious, too. Under her cover as a "well-known reporter of a large German newspaper," Beetz was to keep tabs on the "a. Western Federal Government. Political targets of opportunity. b. SPD parliamentary representation, SPD party executive, various key government officials." She had also been "briefed to pay particular attention to extreme rightist and leftist activities within or against the present German government."[53] The bureaucratic language obscures its importance: Beetz had been made—and made herself—into the perfect agent to keep tabs on an SPD-led government based in Frankfurt. However, the West German election of August 1949 created a Christian Democratic Union (CDU)-led government in Bonn. Beetz was now not only in the wrong place but had the wrong connections.

Over the next two years, the formal relationship between Beetz and the CIA petered out. In December 1949, US intelligence took stock of the situation and, intriguingly, Beetz's gender and her emotional state began to matter. The report asserted that Beetz was loyal and that the operation's general setup, using a well-known journalist to gather information difficult for Allied representatives to attain, was sound. But circumstances conspired against it. The influence of the *Telegraf* and the SPD had declined and so had, with Bonn's designation as the capital, the importance of Frankfurt. Beetz wanted her newspaper to move her to Bonn, but Scholz held that "the head of the Bonn bureau must be an older man with well-developed political connections of his own." Heading a large staff and holding an important position in Frankfurt, Beetz had initially been "satisfied intellectually and materially," and her work had "[made] her forget her unhappy love affair with Dr. Joseph Grunner." However, once the Frankfurt office faltered and the staff was reduced—all for reasons outside of her control—Beetz grew discouraged and her "emotional problems" became "aggravated." This, the assessment suggested, led to a decline in her reporting. Simultaneously, Beetz also found herself "greatly disappointed by her ideological love, i.e., the SPD," but this had led to a stronger bond with her case officers. She remained eager to work for the Americans, but her "good intentions are continually frustrated by her depressive mental state due to the Grunner affair." In this crucial moment then, in the midst of professional, political, and personal problems, Beetz was reduced to a love-sick woman. "Thus we have a situation where we have a controlled agent with the necessary intellectual qualifications in a desirable position, who is unable to produce because of emotional difficulties which are completely beyond our control. An unsatisfactory and unreasonable situation, we are sure you will agree with us, but we must remember that [Beetz] is not merely an agent—she is also a woman."[54] Classic misogynist structures masqueraded as paternalism, which, in turn, masqueraded as agent handling. Times, roles, and personnel were changing.

Beetz remained officially involved with US intelligence, but her role diminished. She provided information not readily available to the Americans; acted yet again as a cutout; also as a bird dog, identifying members of former Nazi organizations; and introduced American intelligence personnel to potential agents. Documents describe Beetz's output as small—she submitted only three reports in 1950 and four in 1951—but well received. They also note that she "helped," "assisted," and "facilitated," thereby describing Beetz in clearly subaltern and female terms.[55]

A critical view of Beetz gained traction during the American reevaluation of intelligence operations in West Germany. Her performance was a minor element, even though the Chief of Station Karlsruhe noted that she "cannot readily distinguish between overt and covert intelligence and ... tends to regard all political information as 'hot stuff,'" but stressed that an experienced case officer could easily solve that problem.[56] The larger issue was her emotional makeup and her habits, evaluated and discussed in strikingly gendered terms. The idea that Beetz was emotionally unstable, or "very" unstable, became accepted. Her emotional state was linked, first, to her failing relationship with Grunner and later to the beginning of a new liaison, condescendingly labeled her "sixth grand amour." She was also judged to be suffering from "fits of depression," "often despondent," and prone to talk about suicide, "but probably not seriously." Assessments emphasized that she "consumes a fair amount of liquor," effectively self-medicating "to off-set her complicated personal life," but also held her alcohol well; the person filling out the questionnaire emphasized that he had never seen her drunk.[57] An image of Beetz as an emotionally unstable, love-sick woman prone to desperate drinking bouts took shape and, eventually, held.

This new view of Beetz fed into two main concerns. One was that she could be turned. Beetz "depends on us ideologically," a report counseled, but the notion that she could come "under the influence of a man who would be able to undo whatever loyalty she has to us," or who espoused a different ideology, or was Italian, was a recurring theme. However, one was also certain that the contact with Beetz was close enough to notice a change.[58] The other was a growing uneasiness about her knowledge of US intelligence operations in postwar Germany—"installations, our precise identity, eight of our staff officers and several of our agents."[59] Clearly, Beetz was disconcertingly well-informed about US intelligence in West Germany.

The official relationship between Hildegard Beetz and US intelligence was nevertheless terminated in December 1951. The primary reason was not the growing concerns about Beetz, but the reevaluation and reorganization of US operations and the lack of a case officer available to work with her in an operation under consideration. At the same time, Beetz remained interested in working with the Americans, and US intelligence planned to "maintain casual contact" with her.[60] Even the most critical assessments of her emotional state noted her smarts, her contacts in Berlin and Bonn, and her position as a respected, female newspaper correspondent.[61] And occasionally, reports nodded to the elephant in the room: "We know to what ends she was willing to go to for the RSHA [during the war]."[62]

Beetz's personal situation also changed. In late 1951, she married Karl Heinz Purwin, an editor of *Welt der Arbeit*, a paper associated with the trade union Deutsche Gewerkschaftsbund (DGB). The Americans noted his impeccable anti-fascist credentials and, with puzzled approval, that, despite belonging to the "socialist wing of the SPD," Purwin "wholeheartedly enjoyed" and paid for a champagne breakfast.⁶³ A seasoned, unidentified intelligence officer friendly with Beetz, taking stock of the situation after her, in his words, "suspension," pointed out that her marriage should make her more valuable as an asset. She now had "access to the higher levels of the DGB," while her new marital status gave her "additional prestige and respectability." "A girl reporter," he explained, even though Beetz was in her early thirties in 1951, "is still not quite accepted in conservative Bonn. A husband-wife team much more so." Considering her long-term potentials, he promised to stay in contact and keep his Washington superiors apprised. But then he was her champion. He tempered the more negative assessments of Beetz that had become de rigueur since 1950 and defended her private life and emotional stability with a mixture of gravitas and nonchalance:

> I think Camise's [Beetz's] present husband . . .] is her fifth "grand amour" [*sic*]. Considering her age, occupation, professional background, and other factors against the backdrop of the last decade in Europe, I would say that her personal life was rather normal considering the circumstances. I think "frequent emotional attachment" conveys the idea that she is emotionally unstable. I don't think so, but that is a matter of opinion.⁶⁴

One cannot avoid the sense of an experienced practitioner politely reading a "desk jockey" the riot act.

Conclusion

Beetz built her postwar career not out of the ashes of her wartime career, but directly from it. It was the education and expertise she acquired as a "New Nazi Woman" that allowed her to thrive in subaltern positions. She had dealt with the likes of Hoettl and Kaltenbrunner, playing them and keeping her cool, while using her gender and gendered norms to create *Handlungsräume*—scopes for action—that suited her.⁶⁵ In the liminal spaces of post–May 1945, she adapted to new circumstances, while also showing calculated disdain for a system—and its men—that she had served diligently for years. And she clearly held her Nazi spy background in esteem, so much so that she reminded her US handlers of it. Especially in the early years that accorded with the US view of the SS intelligence service; its epic failure was not realized in the field quickly.⁶⁶ That the US service was all too happy to rely on former Nazis, using them against each other and ultimately also against democratic politicians in West Germany, is not news. Beetz, however, attained, with American assistance but based on her own ambition and smarts, a position in political journalism from which she could have informed on West German politicians for years.

Similarly to her situation in Nazi Germany, Beetz benefited from contradictory gender expectations and norms in the immediate postwar period. These the Americans brought with them, and she simultaneously conformed to and confounded those norms. She was young and pretty and in need of protection. She was attractive, smart, wily, and a source of good reporting—a veritable femme fatale, if formerly a Nazi. Later still—at a point when both US intelligence structures and gender norms settled in the postwar period—these traits were used to discredit her and to explain away the failure of an ambitious US intelligence scheme. Beetz, for her part, came out on top: as an established journalist with far-reaching contacts. Continuities between Nazi Germany and the postwar period came in many shapes. One was Hildegard Beetz and her transition from espionage to journalism. But maybe her undeniable successes were based primarily "on the ease with which she handled case officers for her own benefit."[67] She never found *Handlungsraum* she did not use.

Notes

1. Headquarters 12th AG, SCI Detachment to Chief, CIB, G-2, 12th AG, Hildegard Beetz, nee Burckhardt, SD Executive and Agent, 18 June 1945, NARA, RG 263, entry ZZ-16, box 5, File: Beetz, Hildegard, vol. 3. See Howard McGaw Smyth, *Secrets of the Fascist Era: How Uncle Sam Obtained Some of the Top-Level Documents of Mussolini's Period* (Carbondale: Southern Illinois University Press, 1975), 57.

2. In the latter part of this article, I use "US intelligence" as a catchall. For a broad overview, see Tim Weiner, *A Legacy of Ashes: The History of the CIA* (New York: Doubleday, 2007), 8–27; on Germany: Kevin C. Ruffner, "Eagle and Swastika: CIA and Nazi War Criminals and Collaborators (U)" (unpublished manuscript, History Staff, Central Intelligence Agency, Washington, DC, April 2003), chap. 3.

3. For the most comprehensive information on Beetz's early years see Katrin Paehler, "Gender and Espionage: Hildegard Beetz, the Ciano Affairs, and Female Agency," in *Gender and the Second World War: Lessons of War*, ed. Corinna Peniston-Bird and Emma Vickers (London: Palgrave Macmillan, 2016), 73–87; Katrin Paehler, *The Third Reich's Intelligence Services: The Career of Walter Schellenberg* (Cambridge: Cambridge University Press, 2017), chaps. 6 and 7. For a less scholarly work but by one of her handlers see Richard W. Cutler, "Reminiscence: Three Careers, Three Names: Hildegard Beetz, Talented Spy," *International Journal of Intelligence and Counterintelligence* 22 (2009): 515–35. Beetz makes an appearance in Ray Mosely, *Mussolini's Shadow: The Double Life*

of Count Galeazzo Ciano (New Haven, CT: Yale University Press, 1999); Edda Ciano, *My Truth*, as told to Albert Zarca (New York: William Morrow, 1977); and Smyth, *Secrets*. All of these pieces take an intriguingly gendered view of Beetz, which I highlight in "Gender and Espionage."

4. See, for example, Norbert Frei et al., *Flick: Der Konzern, die Familie, die Macht* (Munich: Blessing Verlag, 2009); Philipp Gassert, *Kurt Georg Kiesinger, 1904–1988: Kanzler zwischen den Zeiten* (Stuttgart: DVA, 2006); Norman Goda, *Tales from Spandau: Nazi Criminals and the Cold War* (Cambridge: Cambridge University Press, 2008); Lutz Hachmeister, *Der Gegnerforscher: Die Karriere des SS-Führers Franz Alfred Six* (Munich: Beck, 1998); Lutz Hachmeister and Friedemann Siering, *Die Herren Journalisten: Die Elite der deutsche Presse nach 1945* (Munich: Beck, 2001); and Lutz Hachmeister, *Schleyer: Eine deutsche Geschichte* (München: Beck, 2004); Ulrich Herbert, *Best: Biographische Studien über Radikalismus, Weltanschauung und Vernunft* (Bonn: Dietz, 1996); Ernst Klee, *Was sie taten, was sie wurden: Ärzte, Juristen und andere Beteiligte am Kranken- und Judenmord* (Frankfurt: Fischer TB, 2004).

5. See, for example, essays by Goda, Naftali, and Wolfe in Richard Breitman et al., eds., *US Intelligence and the Nazis* (Washington, DC: National Archives Trust Fund for the Nazi War Crimes and Imperial Japanese Records Interagency Working Group, 2004) and Peter Hammerschmidt, *Deckname Adler: Klaus Barbie und die westlichen Geheimdienste* (Frankfurt: S. Fischer, 2014).

6. For case studies, including one on a woman, see David Messenger and Katrin Paehler, eds., *A Nazi Past: Recasting German Identity in Postwar Europe* (Lexington: University of Kentucky Press, 2015). For a fascinating book that uses the biography of and active mythmaking by Beate Uhse to explore changing sexual morals in postwar West Germany, see Elizabeth Heinemann, *Before Porn Was Legal: The Erotica Empire of Beate Uhse* (Chicago: University of Chicago Press, 2011). In this volume, see also Cookson-Hills's essay on the limited agency of German women at the end of the war in chapter 8 of this volume.

7. Paehler, "Gender and Espionage," 73–87; Wendy Lower, *Hitler's Furies: German Women in the Nazi Killing Fields* (Boston: Houghton Mifflin Harcourt, 2013), 9. I distinguish between officially prescribed female roles and behaviors, laid out in speeches, and the realities of life, which were defined by policy prescriptions, political developments, and by men and women constantly (re-)negotiating acceptable female behaviors in both the public and private spheres. A flavor of these differences can be found in the oral histories assembled by Margarete Dörr, *"Wer die Zeit nicht miterlebt hat . . . ."* in *Frauenerfahrungen im Zweiten Weltkrieg und in den Jahren Dannach*, 3 vols. (Frankfurt: Campus Verlag, 1998). See also Dagmar Herzog, *Sex after Fascism: Memory and Morality in Twentieth-Century Germany* (Princeton, NJ: Princeton University Press, 2005), chap. 1.

8. Kirsten Heinsohn, Barbara Vogel, and Ulrike Weckel, eds., *Zwischen Karriere und Verfolgung: Handlungsräume von Frauen im nationalsozialistischen Deutschland* (Frankfurt: Campus, 1997), 13.

9. NARA, RG 263, entry ZZ-16 and ZZ-18. ZZ-16 was the first, incomplete release of the CIA Name Files; NARA subsequently released "ZZ-16 plus x," designated as entry ZZ-18. See Norman W. Goda, "The Gehlen Organization and the Heinz Felfe Case," in *Nazi Past*, ed. Messenger and Paehler, 288n7.

10. Hoettl made a production of "finding" her address; see Statement by Dr. Wilhelm Hoettl, Location of the Ciano Diaries in Germany, no date. On Beetz's initial detention, see SCI Detachment Weimar to CO, SCI, Germany, Subject: Interrogation Reports on Frau Hildegard Burkhardt Beetz, 17 June 1945. A later document holds that she fell under Automatic Arrest: SCI Munich to Chief X-2 Germany, Subject: Frau Hildegard Beetz, 11 August 1945, all documents in NARA, RG 263, entry ZZ-16, box 5, file: Beetz, Hildegard, vol. 3. On Automatic Arrest policies and women, see Kathrin Meyer, *Entnazifizierung von Frauen: Die Internierungslager der US-Zone Deutschlands 1945–1952* (Berlin: Metropol-Verlag, 2004), chap. 1, esp. 49; and Kristen J. Dolan, "Isolating Nazism: Civilian Internment in American Occupied Germany, 1944–1950" (PhD diss., University of North Carolina, Chapel Hill, 2013), 37, 119.

11. Headquarters 12th AG, SCI Detachment to Chief, CIB, G-2, 12th AG, Hildegard Beetz, nee Burckhardt, SD Executive and Agent, 18 June 1945, NARA, RG 263, entry ZZ-16, box 5, file: Beetz, Hildegard, vol. 3. In an essay published before declassification of the CIA Name Files, Charlesworth and Salter refer to a 29 June 1945 telegram in which Dulles calls Beetz "our agent," raising the possibility that "at some point [during the war], [Beetz] became a double agent controlled by the OSS." Lorie Charlesworth and Michael Salter, "Ensuring the After-Life of the Ciano Diaries: Allen Dulles' Provision of Nuremberg Trial Evidence," *Intelligence and National Security* 21, no. 4 (2006): 576n89.

12. SCI Detachment Weimar to CO, SCI, Germany, Subject: Interrogation Reports on Frau Hildegard Burkhardt Beetz, 17 June 1945, NARA, RG 263, entry ZZ-16, box 5, file: Beetz, Hildegard, vol. 3. For this sort of intelligence agency double dealing on the Soviet side, see Kevin Riehle's essay in chapter 11 of this volume.

13. SCI Detachment Weimar to CO, SCI, Germany, Subject: Interrogation Reports on Frau Hildegard Burkhardt Beetz, 17 June 1945, NARA, RG 263, entry ZZ-16, box 5, file: Beetz, Hildegard, vol. 3.

14. Headquarters 12th AG, SCI Detachment to Chief, CIB, G-2, 12th AG, Hildegard Beetz, nee Burckhardt, SD Executive and Agent, 18 June 1945, NARA, RG 263, entry ZZ-16, box 5, file: Beetz, Hildegard, vol. 3; SCI Munich to Chief X-2 Germany, Subject: Frau Hildegard Beetz, 11 August 1945 NARA, RG 263, entry ZZ-16, box 5, file: Beetz, Hildegard, vol. 2.

15. Untitled Document, no date, NARA, RG 263, ZZ-16, box 5, Beetz, Hildegard, vol. 3; Addendum to Lebenslauf written by H.B., 28 May 1946, NARA, RG 263, ZZ-16, box 5, Beetz, Hildegard, vol. 3. On Beetz's potential knowledge, see Paehler, *Third Reich's Intelligence Service*, chaps. 6 and 7. On American preconceptions about female life in Nazi Germany, see Ramona M. Rose, *Position and Treatment of Women in Nazi Germany: As Viewed from the Perspective of the English Language Press, 1933–1935* (Vancouver: Tantalus Research, 1973). She concludes: "German women were generally presented in a sympathetic, if not favorable light. The position . . . was defined as a subordinate one, and it was agreed by most members of the press that the Nazis manipulated and exploited German women in order to further their own aims" (76). On US gendered assumptions and professional women, see Deborah Barton, "Rewriting the *Reich*: German Women Journalists as Transnational Mediators for Germany's Rehabilitation," *Central European History* 51 (2018): 570.

16. OSS Mission for Germany to SCI, Third Army, Subject: Exploitation of Frau Hildegard Beetz, 6 July 1945, NARA, RG 263, ZZ-16, box 5, Beetz, Hildegard, vol. 3.

17. SCI Munich to Chief X-2 Germany, Subject: Frau Hildegard Beetz, 11 August 1945 NARA, RG 263, entry ZZ-16, box 5. file: Beetz, Hildegard, vol. 2. The vetting request notes "his future is a matter of great concern to her. She is willing to perform any duty that she feels may be of assistance in his future well being." Beetz had married in June 1943; her husband had been a General Staff member. Compare this with the behavior of Joe Koide in Brian Masaru Hayashi's essay, chapter 10 of this volume.

18. Beetz wrote her *Lebenslauf* in English. Even assuming that she took great care, it is an excellent piece of writing.

19. AB 16 [Cutler], Berlin to AB 51 [Hecksher], Amzon, Project Proposal for CIB: Gambit, 13 July 1946. Details on Beetz's time in Munich remain hazy; she might have worked as a secretary for the Bavarian Red Cross and "with a translating establishment in Munich." SC Berlin, Camise, 15 June 1947. Both documents NARA, RG 263, entry ZZ-18; box 9, file: Beetz, vol. 2, 1 of 2. Cutler provides the "clear names," and I follow his lead; see "Three Careers, Three Names," 515–35.

20. Ruffner, "Eagle and Swastika," 92–93.

21. See David E. Murphy, Sergei A. Kondrashev, and George Bailey, *Battleground Berlin: CIA vs. KGB in the Cold War* (New Haven, CT: Yale University Press, 1997), 408–9; and Arthur Lee Smith Jr., *Kidnap City: Cold War Berlin* (Westport, CT: Greenwood Press, 2002), chap. 5. Smith raises the question of what Kemritz achieved for the US that made officials willing to weather a public relations storm and call in high-level "favors."

22. Hecksher to O'Neal, Project "Sitting Duck," 16 July 1946; AB 16 [Cutler], Berlin to AB 51 [Hecksher], Amzon, Project Proposal for CIB: Gambit [Beetz's new

code name], 13 July 1946, NARA, RG 263, entry ZZ-18; box 9, file: Beetz, vol. 2, 1 of 2.

23. AB 16 [Cutler], Berlin to AB 51 [Hecksher], Amzon, Project Proposal for CIB: Gambit, 13 July 1946; Hecksher to O'Neal, Project "Sitting Duck," 16 July 1946, NARA, RG 263, entry ZZ-18; box 9, file: Beetz, vol. 2, 1 of 2. Note that the latter document focuses on the "cut out."

24. AB 16 [Cutler] to AB 17 [Wilma Tabe], Gambit's Lebenslauf and Analysis by AB 16, 5 June 1946, NARA, RG 263, entry ZZ-18; box 9, file: Beetz, vol. 2, 1 of 2.

25. Clearance was granted on either 26 or 27 July 1946. For AB 16 [Cutler], 30 July 1946; Route Slip, SSU Project "Sitting Duck," 24 July 1947, NARA, RG 263, entry ZZ-18; box 9, file: Beetz, vol. 2, 1 of 2.

26. AB 52 [Roswall] to AB 51 [Hecksher], The Zimmer Notebooks, 21 August 1946; Gambit, Miscellaneous Information on MVD Weimar, 18 October 1946; [Reference AB 52], Gambit Project, 25 November 1946, NARA, RG 263, entry ZZ-18; box 9, file: Beetz, vol. 2, 1 of 2.

27. Communication, 6 November 1946; there were security concerns about placing her with the Refugee Control Unit as well: 14 November 1946, NARA, RG 263, entry ZZ-18; box 9, file: Beetz, vol. 2, 1 of 2.

28. AB 51 [Hecksher] Amzon to AB 52 [Roswall], Future Employment of Gambit, 12 November 1946, NARA, RG 263, entry ZZ-18; box 9, file: Beetz, vol. 2, 1 of 2.

29. [Reference AB 52, Roswall] Report: Agent Security—Gambit, 9 November 1946, NARA, RG 263, entry ZZ-18; box 9, file: Beetz, vol. 2, 1 of 2. While it remains possible that Skurin was aware of Beetz and her position at OMGUS and feeling out Ford, the Americans were pleased with Ford's reporting.

30. [Reference AB 52, Roswall], Gambit Project, 25 November 1946, NARA, RG 263, entry ZZ-18; box 9, file: Beetz, vol. 2, 1 of 2.

31. AB 51 [Hecksher] Amzon to AB 52 [Roswall], Future Employment of Gambit, 12 November 1946, NARA, RG 263, entry ZZ-18; box 9, file: Beetz, vol. 2, 1 of 2.

32. Reference AB 52 [Roswall], Gambit Project, 25 November 1946, NARA, RG 263, entry ZZ-18; box 9, file: Beetz, vol. 2, 1 of 2.

33. [Reference AB 36, Polgar], Ford Project, 6 December 1946, NARA, RG 263, entry ZZ-18; box 9, file: Beetz, vol. 2, 1 of 2. AB 36 was Tom Polgar; he took over for Roswall. According to Cutler, Hecksher disliked Roswall's handling of the Gambit Project. Cutler, "Three Careers, Three Names," 526.

34. To Saint, 11 January 1947; [Reference AB 36, Polgar; Source Ford], Ford-Gambit Project, 17 January 1947; [Reference AB 36, Polgar], Gambit Project, 20 January 1947; [Reference AB 36, Polgar; Source Ford], Ford Project, 28 January 1947, NARA, RG 263, entry ZZ-18; box 9, file: Beetz, vol. 2, 1 of 2.

35. [Reference AB 36, Polgar; Source Ford], Ford Meeting with Gambit, 11 January 1947, NARA, RG 263, entry ZZ-18; box 9, file: Beetz, vol. 2, 1 of 2. Polgar noted that Ford himself decided on the direct approach.

36. [Reference AB 36, Polgar; Source Gambit] Meeting with Ford, 17 January 1947, Registry No. 1943, NARA, RG 263, entry ZZ-18; box 9, file: Beetz, vol. 2, 1 of 2.

37. [Reference AB 36, Polgar; Source Gambit] Gambit Project: Meeting with Ford, 17 January 1947, Registry No. 1945, NARA, RG 263, entry ZZ-18; box 9, file: Beetz, vol. 2, 1 of 2. Note the ambiguous usage of "we" in the memo. As Polgar wrote it, "we" might refer to US intelligence. Alas, it might also include Beetz. Beetz reported security violations with seeming regularity; for example: Chief of Station Heidelberg to Chief Foreign Branch "M," Calesa Security Violation, Berlin 23 September 1947, NARA, RG 263, entry ZZ-18; box 9, file: Beetz, vol. 2, 1 of 2.

38. Extract Berlin Operations Report, 1–30 April 1947, 18 April 1947, NARA, RG 263, entry ZZ-18; box 9, file: Beetz, vol. 2, 1 of 2.

39. On Scholz, see https://de.wikipedia.org/wiki/Arno_Scholz. His closed *Nachlass* is at the Archiv der sozialen Demokratie at the Friedrich Ebert Stiftung. On the paper, see Susanne Grebner, *Der Telegraf: Entstehung einer SPD-nahen Lizenzzeitung in Berlin 1946 bis 1950* (Berlin: LIT Verlag, 2002). Having reviewed several years of the paper, I consider the early *Telegraf* more than "SPD-nah." The party did not own the paper, but it was, for all intents and purposes, an SPD paper, representing the part of the party that opposed any cooperation with the SPD, as the British occupation authorities intended. Its other license holders and editors were luminaries of the prewar SPD: Otto Löbe and Annedore Leber.

40. Chief of Station Heidelberg to Chief Foreign Branch "M," Project for Camise [Beetz's new code name], 30 September 1947, NARA, RG 263, entry ZZ-18; box 9, file: Beetz, vol. 2, 1 of 2. For changes of the US intelligence structure and nomenclature, see https://www.cia.gov/library/readingroom/docs/CIA%20AND%20NAZI%20WAR%20CRIM.%20AND%20COL.%20CHAP.%201–10,%20DRAFT%20WORKING%20PAPER_0004.pdf, page 16, accessed 13 March 2019.

41. They also held that her cover as a journalist would come in handy, "should her services be required as investigator or interrogator." Chief of Station Heidelberg to Chief Foreign Branch "M," Project for Camise, 30 September 1947, NARA, RG 263, entry ZZ-18; box 9, file: Beetz, vol. 2, 1 of 2.

42. For more on the OSS, see in this volume Castro's essay in chapter 1 and Hayashi's essay in chapter 10.

43. SC Operations Base, Project Camise, no date [late 1947/early 1948?], NARA, RG 263, entry ZZ-18; box 9, file: Beetz, vol. 2, 1 of 2.

44. Project Camise, 22 June 1948, NARA, RG 263, entry ZZ-18; box 9, file: Beetz, vol. 2, 1 of 2.

45. Progress Report Dec–Jan 48, 20 February 1948, NARA, RG 263, entry ZZ-18; box 9, file: Beetz, vol. 2, 1 of 2. The exploitation of Scholz's Ostbüro contacts is described as "a private undertaking [*sic!*] designed to exploit Camlet's [Scholz's] covert sources in the Soviet Zone."

46. Chief of Station, Heidelberg to Chief, Foreign Branch "M," Subject: Meeting with Camlet, 1 November 1947, NARA, RG 263, entry ZZ-18; box 9, file: Beetz, vol. 2, 1 of 2.

47. SC to WASHF, Source Camise, 30 March 1948, NARA, RG 263, entry ZZ-18; box 9, File: Beetz, vol. 2, 1 of 2. It is unclear whether Beetz attended the dinner.

48. Chief of Station, Karlsruhe to Chief, Foreign Branch "M," Subject: Camise—Progress, 4 May 1949, NARA, RG 263, entry ZZ-18; box 9, file: Beetz, vol. 2, 1 of 2.

49. SC, Berlin Operations Base, Project Camise, 22 June 1948; Chief of Station, Karlsruhe to Chief, Foreign Branch "M," Subject: Camise—Progress, 4 May 1949, NARA, RG 263, entry ZZ-18; box 9, tile: Beetz, vol. 2, 1 of 2.

50. The new project, "Educator" involved someone whose name is redacted, assembling content analyses of *Der Telegraf*'s East edition. Beetz translated them into English and, if need arose, drafted rebuttals. Chief of Station, Karlsruhe to Chief, Foreign Branch "M," Subject: Camise—Progress, 4 May 1949, NARA, RG 263, entry ZZ-18; box 9, file: Beetz, vol. 2, 1 of 2.

51. Chief of Station, Karlsruhe to Chief, Foreign Branch "M," Subject: Camise—Progress, 4 May 1949; CoS [Chief of Station] Karlsruhe to CFBM [Chief, Foreign Branch M], SS Sturmbannführer Dr. Wilhelm Höttl, 12 June 1949, NARA, RG 263, entry ZZ-18; box 9, file: Beetz, vol. 2, 1 of 2. Hoettl was an additional problem for Beetz's legend and livelihood.

52. Chief of Station Karlsruhe to Chief Foreign Branch "M," Camise—Progress Report, 7 June 1949, NARA, RG 263, entry ZZ-18; box 9, file: Beetz, vol. 2, 1 of 2. Item 1 in this document is almost completely redacted.

53. Chief of Station Karlsruhe to Chief Foreign Division "M," Field Project Outline Camise, 25 November 1949; NARA, RG 263, entry ZZ-18; box 9, file: Beetz, vol. 2, 1 of 2. Beetz's file begins to include documents with substantial redactions as well as Withdrawal Notices.

54. Chief of Station, Karlsruhe to Chief, Foreign Division "M," Camise—Progress Report, 27 December 1949, NARA, RG 263, entry ZZ-18; box 9, file: Beetz, vol. 2, 1 of 2.

55. Chief of Station, Karlsruhe to Chief, Foreign Division "M," Transmittal of Unemployment Statistics, 27 January 1950; teletype, 28 February 1950; extract, 16 March 1950; Chief, Frankfurt Operations Base to Chief of Station, Karlsruhe, 17 May 1950; Chief Foreign Division "M" to Chief of Station Karlsruhe, Operational Camise, 5 November 1951, NARA, RG 263, entry ZZ-18; box 9, file: Beetz, vol. 2, 1 of 2. Ruffner, "Eagle and Swastika," 129.

56. Chief of Station, Karlsruhe to Chief, Foreign Office Branch "M," Camise, 3 October 1951, NARA, RG 263, entry ZZ-18; box 9, file: Beetz, vol. 2, 1 of 2. Her habit of regarding all information as relevant was a function of her work with Amt VI, see Paehler, *Third Reich's Intelligence Services*, passim, esp. chap. 6.

57. Chief of Station, Karlsruhe to Chief, Foreign Division "M," Field Project Outline 1 July–31 December 1950, 12 June 1950; Chief of Station, Karlsruhe to Chief, Foreign Division "M," Operational Personal Record Questionnaire, 18 August 1950; Chief, Foreign Division "M" to Chief of Station, Karlsruhe, Operational Camise, 5 November 1951, NARA, RG 263, entry ZZ-18; box 9, File: Beetz, vol. 2, 1 of 2. In other words, she drank like the "ideal" man.

58. Chief of Station, Karlsruhe to Chief, Foreign Division "M," Field Project Outline 1 July–31 December 1950, 12 June 1950; Chief of Station, Karlsruhe to Chief, Foreign Division "M," Project Approval for Camise, 16 March 1951, NARA, RG 263, entry ZZ-18; box 9, file: Beetz, vol. 2, 1 of 2.

59. Chief, Foreign Division "M" to Chief of Station, Karlsruhe, Operational Camise, 5 November 1951; Chief of Station, Karlsruhe to Chief, Foreign Division "M," Operational Personal Record Questionnaire, 18 August 1950; Chief of Station, Karlsruhe to Chief, Foreign Division "M," Project Approval for Camise, 16 February 1951, NRA, RG 263, entry ZZ-18; box 9, file: Beetz, vol. 2, 1 of 2. US intelligence stressed that Beetz was also at risk due to her many SPD contacts.

60. Memorandum for the AD/SO, Project Camise, 23 July 1951, NARA, RG 263, entry ZZ-18; box 9, file: Beetz, vol. 2, 1 of 2. See also the attached Project Outline, Camise, 1 July 1951–31 March 1952.Chief of Station, Karlsruhe to Chief, Foreign Division "M," Camise, 3 October 1951; Chief, Foreign Division "M" to Chief of Station, Karlsruhe, Operational Camise, 5 November 1951, NARA, RG 263, entry ZZ-18; box 9, file: Beetz, vol. 2, 1 of 2.

61. Chief of Station, Karlsruhe to Chief, Foreign Division "M," Operational Personal Record Questionnaire, 18 August 1950; Chief of Station, Karlsruhe to Chief, Foreign Office Branch "M," Camise, 3 October 1951, NARA, RG 263, entry ZZ-18; box 9, file: Beetz, vol. 2, 1 of 2.

62. Chief, Foreign Division "M" to Chief of Station, Karlsruhe, Operational Camise, 5 November 1951, NARA, RG 263, entry ZZ-18; box 9, file: Beetz, vol. 2, 1 of 2.

63. Chief of Station, Karlsruhe to Chief, Foreign Division "M," Marriage of Hildegard Blum and Karl Heinz Porwin [sic], 14 December 1951, NARA, RG 263, entry ZZ-18; box 9, file: Beetz, vol. 2, 1 of 2. The couple had a child together; the marriage ended in divorce.

64. Chief of Station, Karlsruhe to Chief, Foreign Division "M," Camise, 14 December 1951, NARA, RG 263, Entry ZZ-18; Box 9, File: Beetz, Vol. 2, 1 of 2.

65. Heinsohn et al., eds., *Zwischen Karriere und Verfolgung*, 13.

66. Paehler, *Third Reich's Intelligence Services,* chap. 8.

67. Cable, April 1982, NARA, RG 263, entry ZZ-18; box 9, file: Beetz, vol. 2, 2 of 2. This 1982 report is damning.

Acknowledgments

This project has been several years in development and has drawn on a wide community of scholars for support. We thank all the chapter authors for their hard work over the years, the entire Second World War Research Group membership, and a few people in particular: Mary Kathryn Barbier, SWWRGNA co-director; Robert Engen, who got this volume off the ground; Jonathan Fennell; Jacob Stoil; and all the participants in our first three research workshops. Thanks go to the Society for Military History (SMH), to Mississippi State University in Starkville, Mississippi, and the National World War II Museum in New Orleans, Louisiana, for hosting our events, and to Sam Houston State University in Huntsville, Texas, for providing technology support and subvention funding for our diagrams and maps. For their support of this project at various stages we are grateful to Robert Citino, Joyce Harrison, and the entire team at Fordham University Press, especially Kurt Piehler and Fredric Nachbaur, and Teresa Jesionowski for her excellent editing. Thanks also to our generous anonymous readers who provided both helpful critique and validating support for our volume. We are grateful to Kelly Sandefer at Beehive Mapping for designing the map and Basia Nowak for indexing.

This project would also have not been possible without the love and support of our families, to whom we hold the ultimate gratitude.

Jadwiga Biskupska
Sara B. Castro
Co-Editors

Acronyms and Abbreviations

AA40	Army Act 40, British military legal code for non-fraternization orders
AA41	Army Act 40, British military legal code for rape
ALO	Area Liaison Officers (UK)
BSC	British Security Coordination (UK)
CBI	China-Burma-India Theater
CCP	Chinese Communist Party
CICI	Combined Intelligence Centre Iraq and Persia (UK)
CSDN	Conseil Supérieur de la Défense Nationale (National Defense Superior Council) (France)
CIC	US Counterintelligence Corps
CMHQ	Canadian Military Headquarters
COMINTERN	Communist International (USSR)
DSC	Distinguished Service Cross
DSO	Defence Security Offices (UK)
FO	Foreign Office (UK)
FSS	Field Security Sections of the Intelligence Corps (UK)
GI	General Infantryman (US)
GlavPURKKA	Main Political Administration of the Red Workers and Peasants Army (USSR)
GUGB	Главное Управление Государственной Безопасности (Main Department of State Security, the intelligence section of the Soviet NKVD)
HUMINT	human intelligence
IDP	internally displaced person
ISLD	Baghdad station of MI6, known in the Middle and Far East as the Inter-Services Liaison Department (UK)
JAG	Judge Advocate General (US/UK)
KGB	Komitet Gosudarstvennoy Bezopasnosti (Committee for State Security)

KONO	Kriegsorganisation Nahost (German Abwehr Near East War Organization)
KPDI	Committee on Artistic Affairs (USSR)
MEC	Middle East Command (UK)
MEIC	Middle East Intelligence Centre (UK)
MEW	Ministry of Economic Warfare (UK)
MGB	Ministerstvo gosudarstvennoy bezopasnosti Ministry of State Security, successor to the NKVD and KGB (USSR)
MI5	Security Service (UK)
MI6	Secret Intelligence Service (SIS) (UK)
MOFA	Movements of Foreign Agents (UK)
MOI	Ministry of Information or Mininform (UK)
MP	military police
NCM	non-commissioned member, military personnel (Canada)
NKVD	Наро́дный комиссариа́т вну́тренних дел (People's Commissariat of Internal Affairs) (USSR)
NWOA	Loi sur l'organisation de la nation pour le temps de guerre (National Wartime Organization Act) (France)
OMGUS	Office of the Military Government (US in Germany)
OSA	Official Secrets Act (UK)
OSS	US Office of Strategic Services, forerunner of the CIA
OSS-SI	OSS Secret Intelligence Branch
PAIC	British and Indian Armies' Persia and Iraq Command (UK)
PGC	US Persian Gulf Command
POW	prisoner of war
PWE	Political Warfare Executive (UK)
RAF	Royal Air Force (UK)
RSHA	Reichssicherheitshauptamt (Reich Security Main Office) (Germany)
RSHA VI	SS Foreign Intelligence Service
SCI	Special Counterintelligence (US)
SHAEF	Supreme Headquarters Allied Expeditionary Force (US/UK)
SIME	Security Intelligence Middle East (UK)
SMERSH	(СМЕРШ) "Death to Spies" Combined Soviet wartime Counterintelligence agencies (USSR)
SNOPG	Senior Naval Officer Persian Gulf (UK)

SOE	Special Operations Executive (UK)
TASS	Информационное агентство России ТАСС (State News Agency) (USSR)
T&P	tribal and political (UK)
USAFFE	United States Forces in the Far East
USO	United Services Organization (US)
VC	Victoria Cross (UK)
VS KONR	*Военные Силы Комитета Освобождения Народов России* (Armed Forces of the Committee for the Liberation of the Peoples of Russia, or the Vlasov Army) (USSR)
WRA	War Relocation Authority (US)

Contributors

Jadwiga Biskupska is an associate professor of military history at Sam Houston State University and co-director of the Second World War Research Group, North America. She completed her PhD at Yale University and is the author of *Survivors: Warsaw under Nazi Occupation* (Cambridge, 2022), which won the 2022 Heldt Prize of the Association for Women in Slavic Studies.

Sara B. Castro is an associate professor of history at the US Air Force Academy in Colorado Springs, Colorado, where she teaches global, military, and East Asian history. She served as president of the Society of Intelligence Historians (SIH), 2022–2024. She completed her PhD at the University of North Carolina, Chapel Hill and is the author of *Mission to Mao: US Intelligence and the Chinese Communists in World War II* (Georgetown, 2024).

Robert Citino is a Distinguished Fellow at The National World War II Museum in New Orleans. He is the author of eleven books, including *The German Way of War* (2005) and *The Wehrmacht's Last Stand* (2017). He has won the Society for Military History's Distinguished Book Award twice, one of the very few historians to have done so. In 2021, he received the Samuel Eliot Morison Prize, the Society's lifetime achievement award and its highest scholarly recognition.

Claire Cookson-Hills is a professional historian who has worked in Canada and is currently a freelance academic living in Canberra, Australia. She holds a BA (Hons) from the University of Calgary and graduate degrees from Queen's University.

Elena M. Friot is a contract historian with the National Guard Bureau in Arlington, Virginia. She completed her PhD at the University of New Mexico in 2020 and is currently working on a book project exploring the meaning of surrender in America during World War II. Her research examines how

Americans responded to defeat in the Pacific, the ways communities and the nation commemorated surrender, and the development of US prisoner of war policies.

Brian Masaru Hayashi is a professor in the History Department of Kent State University. He was formerly a professor at Kyoto University and assistant professor at Yale University. His research work on Japanese Americans resulted in *For the Sake of Our Japanese Brethren* (Stanford University Press, 1995), winner of the Kenneth Scott Latourette Award; *Democratizing the Enemy* (Princeton, 2004), winner of the Robert Athearn Award; and his co-edited volume with Yasuko Takezawa, *New Waves* (Kyoto, 2004). His new book, *Asian American Spies* (Oxford) is now available.

Derek R. Mallett is an associate professor of history at the US Army Command and General Staff College in Fort Belvoir, Virginia. He received his PhD in History at Texas A&M University in 2009. He is the author of, among other publications, *Hitler's Generals in America: Nazi POWs and Allied Military Intelligence* (Kentucky, 2013), and the editor of *Monumental Conflicts: Twentieth-Century Wars and the Evolution of Public Memory* (Routledge, 2017).

Erina Megowan is a historian of the USSR who specializes in the social and cultural history of World War II. She is a visiting lecturer in history at Northeastern University. Her current book examines the relationship between Soviet cultural institutions, morale, and propaganda during World War II. Related articles have appeared in *Kritika* and *Neprikosnovennyi Zapas*.

Adrian O'Sullivan is an honorary professor of intelligence history at Bishop Grosseteste University in Lincoln, UK. He received his doctorate in intelligence history from the University of South Africa. He is the author of, among other works, *Nazi Secret Warfare in Occupied Persia (Iran)* (Palgrave Macmillan, 2014); *Espionage and Counterintelligence in Occupied Persia (Iran)* (Palgrave Macmillan, 2015); and *The Baghdad Set* (Springer Nature, 2019). O'Sullivan is a fellow of the Royal Historical Society, a fellow of the Royal Asiatic Society of Great Britain and Ireland, and a member of the Irish Association of Professional Historians.

Katrin Paehler is a professor of history at Illinois State University. She specializes in Nazi Germany, the Holocaust, foreign intelligence, genocide, and mass violence. She is the author of *The Third Reich's Intelligence Services: The Career of Walter Schellenberg* (Cambridge, 2017) and the coeditor of *A Nazi Past: Recasting German Identity in Postwar Europe* (Kentucky, 2015). She is currently working on a book on Hildegard Beetz's life and careers.

Kevin P. Riehle is a lecturer in intelligence and international security at Brunel University London. He spent more than thirty years in the US government as a counterintelligence analyst studying foreign intelligence services. He received a PhD in War Studies from King's College London, an MS of Strategic Intelligence from the Joint Military Intelligence College, and a BA in Russian and political science from Brigham Young University. He has written on a variety of intelligence and counterintelligence topics, focusing on Soviet and Eastern Bloc intelligence services.

Jeff Rutherford is a teaching professor of history at Xavier University. He is the author and co-author of several books, including: *The German Army on the Eastern Front: An Inner View of the Ostheer's Experiences of War* (Pen & Sword, 2018); *Combat and Genocide on the Eastern Front: The German Infantry's War, 1941–1944* (Cambridge, 2014); and co-editor of *Nazi Policy on the Eastern Front: Total War, Genocide, and Radicalization* (Rochester, 2012).

Victoria Sotvedt is currently a PhD candidate in history at the University of Calgary in Alberta, Canada. Her dissertation research focuses on Canadian armored field reconnaissance, but she also works in Canadian military and social history.

Cameron Zinsou is an assistant professor of military history at the US Army Command and General Staff College (CGSC) in Fort Leavenworth, Kansas. He received his PhD in history at Mississippi State University. His dissertation, "Occupied: The Civilian Experience in Montélimar, 1939–1945," earned the Allan R. Millett Dissertation Research Fellowship Award in 2017 from the Society for Military History. He has bylines in the *New York Times* and *War on the Rocks*. His first manuscript, based on his dissertation, is currently under contract with the University Press of Kansas.

Index

"A" Force, 37, 43, 51
AA40, 187–88
AA41, 187–88
Abbott, Ambrose: background, 179, 184; buddy rape, 5, 179, 183, 194–97; charges, 187–88, 193; conviction, 189, 197; court martial, 184, 186, 196–97; motivations for rape, 179, 191, 197; plunder, 183, 185, 190, 192–94, 197–98; rape, 179, 182–84, 186, 191, 193–94, 197–98, 201n32; sentence, 189; sexual violence, 179, 182, 184, 196–97; trial, 5, 179–80, 183, 188–90, 203n64; trinket offering, 183–84, 190, 193, 197; victims, 182–83, 188–89, 191–94, 196–97, 201n32
Abel, Rudolf, 265
Abryutin, Yevgeniy, 262
Abwehr, 37, 49, 87, 259, 283
Akhmedov, Ismail, 258
"Alcatraz materials," 289–90
Aleksandrov, Georgii, 146
Al-Husayni, Mohammed Amin, 52
All-Union Guestrole-Concert Organization, 140
All-Union Theatrical Organization, 140–42
Anglo-Iraqi War, 37, 45, 47, 52
Anokhin, Aleksandr, 256, 258
Arab Legion, 36, 43, 44
Armed Forces of the Committee for the Liberation of the Peoples of Russia. *See* KONR
Army Act 40, 187–88
Army Act 41, 187–88
Arnold, Henry "Hap," 96
Artemyev, Vyacheslav, 255–56
ASIO, 266–67

Australia, 163, 214–15
Australian Security Intelligence Organization, 266–67
Austria, 66–67

Bad Zwischenahn, 185–86, 197
Baghdad, 35–39, 41–42, 44–48, 51, 53
Baker, Rudy, 232–33
Baklanov, Boris, 263–64
Balkans, 38, 51, 71–72, 76
Bard, Ralph A., 221
Barrett, David, 16, 23
Barrow, Henry, 212–13
Basra, 35–36, 42, 46, 48
Bataan: Alamo comparisons, 216–19; Battle of Bunker Hill comparisons, 216–19; conditions, 211, 214–16, 222–23; defense of, 207, 213, 217, 220–24, 227n36; Senate Bill 1374, 208, 220–23; surrender, 6, 207–8, 211–13, 215–16, 219–24; surrender/heroism media narratives, 212–13, 215–17. *See also* home front, US
Battle of France, 120, 128
BBC, 100–4, 161, 268
Beetz, Hildegard: Ciano Affair, 278–84; concerns about, 292, 294–96; early life, 279; family, 287–88, 290; gender, 8, 279–83, 291, 294–97; husbands, 283–85, 290, 293, 295–96, 300n17; intelligence, German, 7, 278–79, 282–86, 288, 290, 293, 295–97; intelligence, US, 7, 278–83, 289–97, 299n11; as journalist, 280, 289–97; and Nazism, 7–8, 279–80, 285, 289, 293–94; in OMGUS, 284–86, 290, 301n29; and Operation "Sitting Duck," 283–89

316 | Index

Bekker, Rafael, 258–59
Belgrade, 66–67, 72
Bentley, Elizabeth, 241, 243
Beriya, Lavrentiy, 265–66, 268
Berlin, 42, 51, 101; intelligence, US, postwar, 279–80, 283, 287, 290, 292–93, 295
Bessonov, Ivan, 256–58
billeting: in Germany, 179, 184–86; in Montélimar (France), 113–114, 117–20, 123, 126
Bird, Willis, 236
Bishop, H. F. "Adrian," 43–45, 48, 57n25, 58n35
Blum, Hildegard. *See* Beetz, Hildegard
Bolshevism, 255, 257, 260. *See also* Judeo–Bolshevism
bombing offensive (Allies), 86–87, 89, 95–100, 102
Bonn, 293–95
Brazhnev, Aleksandr. *See* Anokhin, Aleksandr
British Army, 46, 187, 190, 198
British Broadcasting Corporation. *See* BBC
British Council, 40, 57n24
Brotherhood of Freedom, 43, 45, 53
Browder, Earl, 233
Bulgaria, 66–67

Caen, 166, 168–70, 174, 178n67
Cairo, 3, 36–40, 44, 53, 56n8
Camlet. *See* Scholz, Arno
Canadian Army: and sexual violence, 179, 184–89, 195, 197–98. *See also* reconnaissance, armored
Carpiquet, 168–71, 177n47
Catholic Center Party, 103–4
CBI. *See* China-Burma-India (CBI) Theater
CCP. *See* Chinese Communist Party
censorship, 24, 288; in intelligence, British, 42, 50, 52; mail, 160, 180, 191–92, 198n6; news, 162–66, 174, 209–11, 226n17; reports, 180, 182, 190–92, 198n6
Central House of the Actor, 135
Central House of Workers of Art, 140
Chang, Sukyoon, 235–36

Chaplygina, Nina, 260
Chávez, Dennis, 208, 220–23
Chengdu, 13, 22
Chiang Kai-shek, 15, 17–18, 24; and Chinese Communist Party, 14–15, 18, 21–22; and Dixie Mission, 19, 21, 24; and Stilwell, Joseph, 14, 18, 25, 31n21
Chikalov, Aleksandr, 259
Chin, Robert, 242
China: and intelligence, US (*see* Dixie Mission; mish kids); and Japan tensions, 2, 18–22, 24–25, 28, 239; occupation of, 15, 18–19, 22–25, 232
China-Burma-India (CBI) Theater, 2, 14–15, 18, 23, 28, 230; and Dixie Mission, 19, 21, 27; and mish kids ,16, 23
China Theater, 230, 236
Chinese Communist Party, 32n29; and Dixie Mission, 4, 14, 16, 18–29; guerrilla fighters, 18–19, 24; and Nationalist Party, 14–15, 21, 24–25, 30n8
Chongqing, 14, 15, 18–19, 21, 23, 31n23
CIA, 7, 258, 267–68, 280, 293
Ciano Affair, 278–84
Ciano (count), 278; diaries/documents, 278–79, 281, 283
CIC, 41, 43
CICI. *See* Combined Intelligence Centre Iraq and Persia
Clark, Gerald, 168–71
Clarke, Dudley, 51
Clarke, E. L., 190–91
Claus, P. J., 192
Clive, Nigel, 44
Cold War, 4, 8, 41
Colling, John, 25
Colonial Pioneer Infantry Regiment, 117–119, 131n34
Combined Bomber Offensive, 85, 95–100
Combined Intelligence Centre Iraq and Persia, 36–37, 39, 41, 46–48, 50–51, 56n7
ComIntern, 233–35, 239–40
Commission on Evaluating Requisitions, 116
Committee for Artistic Affairs, 135–36, 140–41, 143–45, 155n45, 157n82

Index | 317

Committee for State Security. *See* KGB
Communist Party of the Soviet Union, 258, 263, 266–68; and concert brigades, 139, 141, 145–46
Communist Party of the United States, 232–34, 239–40, 243
concert brigades, German, 134, 138, 148
concert brigades, Soviet: centralization, 5–6, 135, 137–38, 140–41, 143–44, 148–51; draft exemption, 137, 153n20, 155n45; history, 135, 138, 149; numbers/size, 5, 134, 152n6; objectives, 135–38, 144, 151; reception, 139, 141–51; spontaneity, 5, 137–39, 143, 150; venues, 134, 136, 139–40, 142, 147
concert brigades, Soviet, repertoire, 142; agitation/propaganda, 5, 136–39, 143–48, 151; *chastushki*, 135, 146, 149; comfort/leisure, 5, 137–38, 144–46, 151; contestation of, 5, 137–39, 143–46, 150–51; *estrada*,135, 143, 155n46–47; types, 134–35, 138, 142–46, 148–51
concert brigades, Soviet, troupes/members: Beiul, Olga, 147; Bolshoi theater, 148; Cheliabinsk theater, 140; Diner, Akiva, 142, 147; Dorokhin, Nikolai, 148; First Front Theater, 142; Iartsev, Konstantin, 136; Iskra Theater, 135, 145, 151n1; Kirov theater, 148, 153n20; Kutasova, Tatiana, 144, 147; Leningrad Children's Theater, 140, 148; Magdesian, Sara, 149; Mariinsky theater, 149–50; Moscow Art Academic Theater (MXAT), 146, 148; Nemirovich–Danchenko theater,135, 140, 148; Orlov, Georgii, 149–50; Pushkin theater, 140; Ruslanova, Lidiia, 142, 148; Shul'zhenko, Klavdiia, 148, 153n20; Stanislavsky theater, 140; Sverdlovsk theater, 140; Tarasova, Alla, 146; Tomskii, Aleksandr, 135, 147; Vakhtangov theater, 148, 150, 152n6; Zhukovskaia, Garen, 147; Zueva, Anastasia, 146
concert brigades, US. *See* USO

Connolly, Donald, 41
Conseil Superieur de la Defense Nationale, 115–116
Cornwallis, Kinahan, 45, 48, 53
Corregidor, 207–9, 213–14, 216, 218, 228n36
Counter Intelligence Corps, 41, *43*
courts martial (Canadian), 180, 192, 198n6; for sexual violence/rape, 180–81, 184–90, 192, 195–97, 199n8. *See also under* Ambrose, Abbott; McGill, Jack
CPMB. *See under* Military Intelligence Service
CSDN, 115–116
Curl, Vincent, 237
Currie, David Vivian, 172–73

Daladier, Edouard, 122–23
Darbyshire, Norman, 40–41
Davies Jr., John Paton, 27; in Dixie Mission, 15, 17–18, 20–21, 23–26, 28, 31n23, 32n30; early life, 15, 23; as mish kid, 15, 21, 28; skills/qualifications, 17, 23–24
Dawson-Shepherd, Hanbury K., 39, 53
defectors/defection, Soviet officers: collaboration, 251, 253–55, 259–61, 263–64, 269–70; fake, 259, 261; and KONR, 255–57, 259–60, 263, 269; methods, 7, 252, 265, 269; motivations, 7, 250–54, 258, 265–70; and Nazism, 7, 253–54, 256, 261, 269; and NKVD, 254–57, 259, 261, 263, 265–67; numbers, 251, 269; and opposition to Stalinism, 7, 250–54, 256–58, 267–70; postwar, immediate, 251, 261–65, 270; postwar, from 1950s, 265–70; as prisoners of war, 7, 250–52, 254–56, 258–60; repatriation, 258, 261, 263–64; during war, 251–58
Defence Security Officers, 39-40
Defence Security Offices, 37, 42, *43*, 44, 46–48, 52–53
Denisov, Vadim, 258
Der Telegraf, 289–90, 292–94, 302n39, 303n50
Deryabin, Petr, 265, 267–68

318 | Index

Deutsche Gewerkschaftsbund, 295–96
DGB, 295–96
Dieppe raid, 163, 176n16
Dixie Mission, 14, 19; and Chiang Kai-shek, 17, 21, 24; and China-Burma-India (CBI) Theater, 19, 21, 27; and Chinese Communist Party, 4, 14, 16, 18–29; concerns about, 20–21, 26; failure, 27; location, 14–15, 19–20, 26–27; mish kids in, 14–15, 17, 20–21, 23, 26–29, 34n55; and Nationalist Party, 17, 24; objectives/plans, 19–20, 22, 24, 28; and Office of Strategic Services, 18, 22, 25, 28, 31n23; origins, 15, 18–19, 31n23; reports, 19, 24–26
Dixon, Ken, 211
DKA. *See* House of the Red Army
Doering, Otto, 238
Domvile, Pat, 45, 59n43
Donovan, William, 22–23, 236, 238, 240–41, 243
double agents, 7, 239–40, 242–43, 283–84, 288. *See also* Beetz, Hildegard
Dovydenko, Kirill, 260
Downey, Sheridan, 220
DSOs. *See* Defence Security Officers; Defence Security Offices
Dubkov, Viktor, 260
Dyess Story, 216, 227–28n36

Edelweiss Pirates (*Edelweiss Piraten*), 103–4, 109n47
Edmonds, C. J., 45, 48
Eglseer, Karl, 68, 75
Ehrenburg, Ilya, 136, 145
Eifler, Carl, 231, 235–36, 238–39
8th Canadian Reconnaissance Regiment, 159, 165, 172
82nd Armored Reconnaissance Battalion, 160, 167, 170, 176n29
Eisenhower, 166, 176n27
Eisenstaedt, Alfred, 162–63
Emmerson, John, 15, 30n10

Farrell, Frank, 242
Federal Republic of Germany, 278, 280, 293–96

Field Security Sections of the Intelligence Corps, 46–47
Field Security Wing, 43, 46
Fifteenth Infantry Regiment, 16
Filippov, Boris, 142
Filippov, Vladimir, 135, 145
First Canadian Army, 184–85
Fisher, William. *See* Abel, Rudolf
Floyd, Nat, 209
FO. *See* Foreign Office
Fomenko, Vladimir, 260
Ford (double agent), 284, 286–89, 293, 301n29
Foreign Office, 40, 43, 45, 48, 50, 57n24
Fort Hunt, Virginia, 3, 85–88, 90–92, 95–96, 101–4
482nd Régiment Pionniers Infanterie Coloniaux (RPIC), 117–119, 131n34
4th Canadian (Armored) Division, 185–86, 196–97
4th Mountain Division: establishment, 64–66; hostages, 72–74; invasion of Yugoslavia, 66–69, 72, 75; objectives, 67, 70, 73, 77; occupation of Yugoslavia, 62, 69–75, 78; during Operation Barbarossa, 78–79; plunder, 68–70, 72–75, 77; as prelude to Operation Barbarossa, 3, 62–63, 70, 72, 75, 77–79; and prisoners of war, 70–71, 73; problems, 63–65, 67–69, 74–77; and Serbs, 63, 67, 71–74, 78; tasks/policies, 70–71, 73–74; and total war, 3, 66, 70–71, 79; Yugoslav campaign duration, 62, 69, 75, 77, 79
France: conscription, 114, 116, 124; mobilization, 113–116, 124–26, 128; occupation of, 6, 102, 113–114, 122, 128–29, 133n100; requisition policies, 115–117, 124, 128. *See also* Montélimar; Normandy; Phony War
Frankfurt, 292–94
French Army, 4, 114, 117, 119–20, 125, 128
FRG. *See* Federal Republic of Germany
FSS, 46–47
FSW, 43, 46

Gambit (code name). *See* Beetz, Hildegard
Gaspich, Frederick, 195, 201n42
Gauss, Clarence, 26
George, Harrison, 232
German Army, 85, 93, 95, 100, 190–91; total war, 3, 61–64, 66. *See also* 4th Mountain Division; Operation Barbarossa; *Wehrmacht*
German Communist Party, 102–3, 261
Germany: American Zone, 262, 266, 283, 290; British Zone, 262, 286, 288; French Zone, 202n51, 287; German way of war, 3, 61–64, 67–69, 73, 75–76, 78–79; occupations of, 89–91, 102, 104–5, 186–87, 192; Soviet Zone, 266, 285, 288, 290, 302n45. *See also* Operation Barbarossa
Gestapo (RSHA IV), 51, 96, 99, 104, 254
Gladue, Charles, 185
GlavPURKKA, 137–38, 141, 146–47, 149
Glubb, John Bagot, 44–45
Goldfarb, Rafail, 262–63
Grachev, Ivan, 255, 257, 259
Greece, 66–67, 71
Grunner, Joseph, 291, 294–95
Guam, 208, 222
Guderian, Gunther, 85
Guderian, Heinz, 85
Guomindang. *See* Nationalist Party, China

Halder, Franz, 71
Halperin, Maurice, 240
Hamburg "Penny Club," 103–4
Hamburger, Wilhelm, 52
Hammill, Charles, 42
Handlungsräume, 280, 296–97
Harris, Arthur, 96
Hartung, Jules, 120
Hecksher, Henry, 285–86
Heppner, Richard, 236
Hersey, John, 212, 226nn20–21; *Men on Bataan*, 212–13
Hewlett, Frank, 209–10, 213–16
Hill Project, 85, 87

Himmler, Heinrich, 278, 293
Hitler, 39, 42, 66, 127, 255, 260, 289; and prisoners of war, German, 89–90
Hitler Youth, 103–4
Hodgkin, E. C. "Teddy," 44
Hoettl, Wilhelm, 278, 281–83, 296, 299n10
Holocaust, 9, 62, 181
home front, German, 64, 98–99
home front, North American, 5–6, 158, 160, 162, 164–65, 167–68, 173–74
home front, Soviet, 5, 136, 144–45, 147, 149
home front, US, 207–8, 210–12, 214, 216–17, 223–24, 225n11; and Senate Bill 1374, 219–23. *See also* home front, North American
Hope–Gill, Cecil, 45
Household Brigade, 36
Household, Geoffrey, 46
House of the Red Army, 135, 141, 144, 148
Hurley, Patrick, 26

Ikhwan-al-hurriya, *43*, 45, 53
Imperial Japanese forces, 232, 235–38, 240, 242
India, 35–37, 241
intelligence, British, 4, 41, 258, 293. *See also* Intelligence, British (Iraq)
intelligence, British (Iraq); and Cairo, 3, 36–40, 44, 53, 56n8; composition/structure, 35–37, 41; functions, 36–38, 42, 44, 48–51, 53; interservice collaboration, 3, 9, 37–40, 42, 44–48; "nonoperational," 37, 42, 50; "operational," 42, 49–50; origins, 36–37; outcomes, 9, 52–53; tribal and political (T&P), 35, 37, 42, 50
intelligence, German, 101, 162, 166, 259–62; in Middle East, 37–38, 41, 51–52. *See also* Abwehr; Beetz, Hildegard; SS Foreign Intelligence Service
intelligence, "nonoperational," 37, 42, 50, 86
intelligence, "operational," 42, 49–50

320 | Index

intelligence, Soviet, 243, 260; deep penetration missions, 260–61, 264; illegal operations, 264–65, 268; and Operation "Sitting Duck," 283–89. *See also* defectors/defection, Soviet officers

intelligence, US, 42, 258. *See also* Beetz, Hildegard; Dixie Mission; Koide, Joe; Rie, Kunsung; Office of Strategic Services; reconnaissance, armored

intelligence officers, Soviet. *See* defectors/defection, Soviet officers

Inter-Services Liaison Department, *43*, 44, 47–48, 50

Iraq, 35–36; factions, 35, 53; Hashemite monarchy, 35, 53; and Nazi Germany, 41–42, 44, 46–47, 51–52. *See also* intelligence, British (Iraq)

Iraqi Army, 36, 52, 53

Iraqi Police, 46, 52

Iran. *See* Persia (Iran)

ISLD. *See* Inter-Services Liaison Department

Istanbul, 38, 51–52

Italy, 38, 46–47, 66; armed forces, 62, 67, 88; surrender, 278–79

Jacoby, Annalee, 209, 212, 215, 226n20

Jacoby, Melville, 209, 212, 215, 226n20

JAG, 187, 195–96

Japan: and China tensions, 2, 18–22, 24–25, 28, 239; Imperial, 7, 231–40; invasion of, 231–32, 236; surrender, 24, 231–32. *See also* Bataan; Koide, Joe; Rie, Kunsung

Japan Communist Party, 234

Japanese internment, 232–33, 239, 246n11

Jews, 42, 62, 64, 71, 73, 254. *See also* Judeo-Bolshevism

Johnson, Douglas, 169

Jones, Edgar, 218

Jones, Ellis, 214–215

Journal de Montélimar, 120, 126

Judeo-Bolshevism, 42, 62, 64, 71, 78, 250

Judge Advocate General, 187, 195–96

Kaltenbrunner, Ernst, 281, 296

Kalugin, Mikhail, 258

Kampfverband Gegen Faschismus (Fighters against Fascism), 102–3

Kartseva, Evdokia. *See* Petrova, Evdokia

Kashtanov, Petr, 255

Kellar, A. J. "Alex," 39, 54

Kemritz, Hans. *See* Savoy (double agent)

Kennedy, Clara, 238

KGB, 251, 261, 264–65, 268

K.g.F., 102–3

Khokhlov, Nikolay, 265, 268

Kim, Diamond, 237

Kisters, Gerry H., 173

Kleczkowski, Karl, 52

Knatchbull-Hugessen, Hughe, 48

Koide, Joe: and ComIntern, 233–35, 239–40; and Communist Party of the United States, 7, 232–33, 239–40; and draft, 233, 239–40; early life, 232–34; and House Un-American Activities Committee, 240; and Imperial Japan, 7, 231–34, 240; and Japanese internment, 232–35, 239; loyalty, 7, 231–32, 240, 242–43; and Office of Strategic Services, 7, 231, 233–34, 240, 242; and Project Green, 234–35, 241; radio broadcasts, 231, 234–35, 240; skills, 232; suspicions about, 7, 231–35, 240, 242–43

Koide, Teiji. *See* Koide, Joe

Kolm, Henry, 87

Komitet Gosudarstvennoy Bezopasnosti. *See* KGB

KONO, 51–52

Konomi, Jin, 234

KONR, 255–57, 259–61, 263, 269

Kopatskiy, Aleksandr, 260–61

Korea 231; Operation Napko in, 231, 235–37, 239, 243. *See also* Rie, Kunsung

Korniyevskiy, Vasiliy, 262

KPDI. *See* Committee for Artistic Affairs

Krivosh, Roman, 266

Kuomintang. *See* Nationalist Party, China
Kurayev, Aleksandr, 260
Kvasnitskii, Lev, 146, 155n47

Lamb, Harold, 40
Lanquetin, Marcel, 124
Lapin, Nikolay, 255
Le Nail (captain), 120, 123
L'Echo Montilien, 127
Lee, Clark, 207, 209–12, 214, 217
Lee, Duncan C., 243
Leonard, Malcolm, 185
Leverkuehn, Paul, 52
Lewis, T. C., 170
Lewiston Evening Journal, 170–71
Liddell, Guy, 37
Lifanov, Nikolay, 266
Life magazine, 209, 211, 215
List, Wilhelm, 67
Lloyd, Seton, 45, 59n43
Long March, 15, 21
Loubet, Emile, 114
Lovell, Stanley, 28
Ludden, Raymond, 15, 26–27, 30n10

MacArthur, Douglas, 208–15, 217–19, 225n11
Main Political Directorate of the Red Army. *See* GlavPURKKA
Malgré Nous, 103
Mao Zedong, 18, 23, 26–27
Marshall, Howard, 161
masculinity: heterosexual, 196–97; martial, 212, 217, 223
Maunsell, Raymond "RJ," 39
Maxwell, Elsa, 218
McGill, Jack: background, 184, 194; buddy rape, 5, 179, 183, 194–97; conviction, 190, 192; court martial, 184, 186, 189, 196; motivations for rape, 179, 191, 197; plunder, 183, 185, 190, 192–94, 197–98; rape, 179, 183–84, 186, 193, 198; sentence, 190; sexual violence, 179, 182, 196–97; trial, 5, 179–80, 190, 203n64, 204n84; trinket offering, 183–84, 190, 193–94; victims, 182–83, 192–94, 196

McNearnie, Hugh, 47
MEC. *See* Middle East Command
MEDC, 49–50
MEIC, 36, 56n8
Mendardiere, Arnault de la, 125–26
Menzies, Stewart, 45
MEW, 40
MGB. *See* Ministry of State Security
Middle East: "true" (location), 36, 48, 51, 54; and Nazi Germany, 41–42, 51–52. *See also* intelligence, British (Iraq)
Middle East Command, 38
Middle East Defence Council, 49–50
Middle East Intelligence Centre, 36, 56n8
Middleton, Drew, 171
MI5, 37, 39–40, 44, 53–54, 56n7
Military Intelligence Service, 3, 86–89, 238
Ministry of Economic Warfare, 40
Ministry of Information, 40, *43*, 44–45, 48
Ministry of State Security, 262, 264, 266–67
MIS. *See* Military Intelligence Service
mish kids, 2, 4; and China-Burma-India (CBI) Theater, 14, 16, 23; definition, 13; in Dixie Mission, 14–15, 17, 20, 27–29, 34n55; early life, 14, 20; and Office of Strategic Services, 7, 16, 23; recruitment, 14, 21–23, 28; skills, 2, 14–16, 23, 28; values, 14, 17, 20–21, 26–29. *See also* Davies Jr., John Paton; Service, John S.; Stelle, Charles
MI6, 39–41, 43–45, 47–48, 58n29, 258; Section D, 39–40, 44, 47. *See also* Inter-Services Liaison Department (ISLD)
missionaries, Christian, 16–17, 27–28; China Inland Mission, 15; and Dixie Mission, 21, 24, 26, 28; and mish kids, 2, 13–16, 20, 26; missionary cosmopolitanism, 21, 24, 26; and Office of Strategic Services, 23, 28
Mitford, Terence Bruce, 47
MOFA, 37, *49*
MOI. *See* Ministry of Information

Montélimar, 128; Catholicism in, 126–27; Chateau de Milan, 117–118; colonial troops in, 125–26; history, pre–World War II, 114–115; location, 4, 114; mobilization center, 114; patriotism, 4, 113, 124, 127; population, 114; Quartier de Beausseret, 117–118, 131n34. *See also* Phony War; Piollet (captain, lieutenant colonel); Tardieu, Edouard
Morehead, Richard, 219
Morozov, Boris, 259
Moscow: recalls to, 251, 264–66, 268–69
Moscow Administration for Artistic Affairs, 140
Movements of Foreign Agents, 37, *49*
Moy, Herbert, 242
Moyzisch, Ludwig, 52
Munich crisis, 116, 125
Mure, David, 37, 51
Mussolini, Edda, 278, 281
Mydans, Carl, 209, 212, 226n20
Mydans, Shelley, 209, 212

National Defense Superior Council, 115–116
National Wartime Organization Act, 116, 123, 128
Nationalist Party, China, 30n8, 232, 239; and Chinese Communist Party, 14–15, 21, 24–25, 30n8; and Dixie Mission, 17, 24. *See also* Chiang Kai-shek
Nazi Party, 90, 102–3
Near East War Organization, 51–52
New Mexico, 207–8, 211, 220, 222–23
New York Times, 166, 171, 173, 209, 212
NKVD: arrests, 254, 256, 265–66; defectors, 252, 254–57, 259, 261, 263, 265–67; filtration centers, 261–64, 270; in Persia (Iran), 41
Noble, Robert, 214–15
nonfraternization orders, 180–81, 184, 187–88, 192, 195, 197, 200n21
Normandy, 89–90, 160–61, 166–68, 170, 172, 176n27, 178n67
Nosaka, Sanzō, 234
NSDAP, 90, 102–3

NWOA. *See* National Wartime Organization Act

O'Connor, James, 220
Office of Strategic Services, 8, 22, 32n33, 242, 290; Asian Americans in, 230–31, 240–42 (*see also* Koide, Joe; Rie, Kunsung); and Dixie Mission 18, 22–23, 25, 28, 31n23; double agents in, 240–43; and Eagle team, 236; loyalty, 230, 242–43; in Middle East, 38; and mish kids, 7, 16, 22–23, 28; Morale Operations, 231–32, 234–35, 241; and Operation Napko, 236; and PO Box 1142, 86; racial discrimination in, 230, 241; Secret Intelligence Branch (OSS-SI), 40–41. *See also* Donovan, William
Office of the Military Government, 284–86, 290, 301n29
Office of War Information, 238
Official Secrets Act, 40
Okolovich, Georgiy, 268
Oldenburg, 179, 182, 184–86
OMGUS. *See* Office of the Military Government
Operation Barbarossa, 3, 61–63, 69; failure, 79; and German way of war, 78–79; and intelligence, British, 36, 52; plunder, 62, 64, 69, 78–79; preparation, 63–65; problems, 62, 77–79; resistance, 78–79; total war, 61–64; violence in, 78–79. *See also under* 4th Mountain Division
Operation KINO, 42
Operation MAMMUT, 52
Operation Napko, 231, 235–37, 239, 243
Operation REISERNTE, 42
Operation "Sitting Duck," 283–89
Operation TEL AFAR, 42, 52
Operation ZEPPELIN, 256–57, 259
OSA, 40
OSS. *See* Office of Strategic Services

PAIC. *See* Persia and Iraq Command
PAIFORCE. *See* Persia and Iraq Force
Paine, Bayard H., 217
Palestine, 42, 44, 53

Index | 323

panzer divisions, 63–69, 71, 75, 79
PAS, 48, 50
Patterson, Paul, 185
Patton, 160, 167
Pearl Harbor, 2, 14–15, 36, 41, 52, 207, 226n21, 232
Pečiulionis, Simas, 264–65
People's Commissariat of Internal Affairs. *See* NKVD
People's Republic of China, 18–19, 26, 30n8
Perowne, Stewart, 45, 59n43
Perry, Wallace, 215–16
Persia (Iran), 36, 41, 55n4; and intelligence, British, 39, 41–42, 46–48; and Nazi Germany, 41–42, 51–52; Soviet occupation of, 40–41
Persia and Iraq Command, 37–38, *43*, 55n7
Persia and Iraq Force, 42–43, 46, 48, 50–51, 55n7
Persian Gulf Command, 41
Petrov, A. A., 263
Petrov, Vladimir, 265–67
Petrova, Evdokia, 265–67
PGC, 41
Philby, Kim, 258
Philip, Aidan, 44
Philippines, 207, 235; and Japanese invasion, 209–10, 212–14. *See also* Bataan
Phony War: billeting, 113–114, 117–20, 123, 126; colonial troops, 126; conscription, 114, 121; damage during, 117–20, 123–24; donation drives, 124–28; duration, 4, 113, 117; indemnities, 118–20, 122–23, 131n34; mobilization, 120–24, 127–28; as occupation, 113, 129, 131n34; requisition orders, 113–114, 117–24, 127–28; resistance/complaints, civilian, 4–6, 114, 117–24, 128; Syrian reinforcements (renfort de Syrie), 119
Piollet (captain, lieutenant colonel), 117–21, 123, 126
Plechavičius, Povilas, 264
PO Box 1142, 3; duration, 86; intelligence categories, 88; interrogators, 87–91, 93–95, 97–98, 100, 102–5, 106n14; numbers of prisoners of war, German, 86; reasons for, 85–86, 89–90; weaknesses, 97
PO Box 1142, reports, 3, 97; Allied states, 90; bombing offensive, 86–87, 89, 95–100; civilian morale, 88–89, 95–99; militaries, 88–89, 91–96, 105; Nazi infiltration, 104–5; Nazism/Hitler, 89, 90, 93–94; numbers of, 88; propaganda, Allied, 86–87, 89–91, 100–2; propaganda, German, 89, 91, 100–1; "Trends" report, 89–92, 95, 100–1, 106n8; underground movements, 89, 102–4; United States 3, 90–91
Poland, 4, 62–63, 66, 76, 78, 103, 151; Free Polish troops 46–47
Polgar, Tom, 287
Political Advisory Staff, 48, 50
Political Center for the Struggle with Bolshevism, 256–57
Political Warfare Executive, 40, 55n5
Ponomarev, Vladimir, 269
Price, Mary, 241
prisoners of war, American, 208, 216, 220–23, 227–28n36
prisoners of war, Filipino, 216
prisoners of war, German, 186, 191, 262, 283; treatment 91, 101. *See also* PO Box 1152
prisoners of war, Japanese, 26, 213
prisoners of war, Korean, 235–36
prisoners of war, Soviet, 7, 70; collaboration, 250, 253–59, 263; conditions, 250, 253–54, 256, 258; officers, 251–52, 254–56, 258–60, 263; in POW camps, German, 250–51, 253, 256, 260–61, 263, 269; repatriation, 261, 264
prisoners of war, Yugoslavian, 70–71, 73, 102
Project Green, 234–35, 241
propaganda: Allied, 85, 90, 100–2, 104; American, 87, 91, 161, 230; "black," 40, 42, 45, 50, 57n25; German, 91, 100–1, 187, 256; "grey," 42, 45, 57n25; and intelligence, British (Iraq), 40, 42, 44–45, 50, 52; Soviet, 53, 100,

propaganda *(continued)*
254, 266, 269 (*see also under* concert brigades, Soviet, repertoire); "white," 40, 42, 45, 57n25
PTsB, 256–57
purges, Soviet, 250–53, 255, 258, 266, 268–69; Great Purge, 252, 254, 262, 265–66
Purwin, Heinz, 295–96
PWE, 40, 55n5
Pyen, Jimmie, 237

RAF. *See* Royal Air Force
rape, 180; accusations of, 187, 190; and alcohol consumption, 193, 196; attempted, 180, 188–89; buddy rape, 195–96, 204n92; camaraderie, 184, 195–97; by Canadian soldiers, 185, 187–88, 192, 194–98; charges, 188–89, 192; convictions, 188–89, 196, 204n92; courts martial, 184, 188, 190, 192, 195; mass, 197, 200n19; nonfraternization orders, 187–88; numbers, 181, 187, 190; and plunder, 192, 195, 197, 203n76; prosecution, 180, 187, 196, 198, 204n92; reports, 180, 186–88, 195; sentences, 189–90, 196, 204n92; by Soviet soldiers, 181, 195, 197, 199n9, 200n19; trials, 180, 195–96. *See also* Abbott, Ambrose; McGill, Jack
Rastvorov, Yuriy, 265, 268
recce. *See* reconnaissance, armored
reconnaissance, armored: casualties, 169; combat, 158–59, 164, 167–75; role, 158–59, 168, 174–75; and scouting, 158–59, 167, 175; secrecy, 158–59, 161–62, 164–67, 170–71, 174; security, 162, 164, 166–67, 170; structure/size, 159–60
reconnaissance, armored, reporting of, 161; after-action, 159–60, 172; censorship, 162, 165–66, 174; disconnect/gap, 5–6, 159–60, 162, 167–75; newspaper, 5–6, 158–62, 165–66, 168–74; photographs, 164, 166, 174; radio, 158, 161–62, 165; timing, 158–59, 162, 166, 168, 172

Red Army: and Operation Barbarossa, 62–63, 79. *See also* concert brigades, Soviet
Reich Security Main Office, 259, 278–79, 281, 284, 286, 295; Amt VI, 284–85, 288, 293
Remer, C. F., 23, 33n40
Reynolds, Robert, 221
Reziapkin, Aleksandr, 148
Rie, Kunsung: hearing, 238, 241; and Imperial Japan, 7, 231, 238–39; loyalty, 7, 231, 238–43; and Office of Strategic Services, 7, 231, 238–42; and Operation Napko, 231, 235, 237, 239, 243; skills, 237; suspicions about, 7, 231, 235, 237–43; termination of employment, 239
Rogers, Horace J. 236
Romania, 61, 66–67, 78
Romanov, A. I. *See* Baklanov, Boris
Roosevelt, 217; and China, 13, 17; and Dixie Mission, 19, 26; and Office of Strategic Services, 22; and Pacific theater, 208–9, 214, 217
Roswall, Toivo, 286–87
Rotmistrov, Pavel, 144
Rouanes (captain), 113
Royal Air Force: Bomber Command, 96; Habbaniya Base, 35–36, 47; in Iraq, 36–37, 56n7; "I" Branch, 35–36, 43, 44; Levies, 43, 47; Shaiba Base, 46–47
Roze, Petr, 262
RSHA. *See* Reich Security Main Office
RSHA IV. *See* Gestapo
RSHA VI. *See* SS Foreign Intelligence Service

Sainte-Croix Catholic Church, 126–27
Salimanov, Georgiy, 265–66
Sandburg, Carl, 216
Savoy (double agent), 283–84, 300n21
Saylor, Harry, 217
Sayre, Frank, 209
Schellenberg, Walter, 293
Scholz, Arno, 289–92, 294, 302n45
Schriever (captain), 282
SCI Detachment, 278–79, 282

Index | 325

scouting, 158–59, 167, 175
SD. *See* Sicherheitsdienst
2nd Armored Division, 160, 167
Second Army (German), 66–67, 71
2nd Canadian Infantry Division, 164, 184–86, 176n16, 201n45
Secret Intelligence Service. *See* MI6
Security Intelligence Middle East, 37–39, 42, 43, 44, 46–48
Security Service. *See* MI5
Sedashov, Yuriy, 260
Senate Bill 1374, 208, 220–23
Senior Naval Officer Persian Gulf, 42, 43, 47, 49
Serbia/Serbs, 62–63, 67, 69, 71–74, 76, 78; occupation of, 72, 74
Service, John S. "Jack," 16; arrest, 32n30; in Dixie Mission, 15, 18, 20–21, 23–26, 28; early life, 13, 22–23; as mish kid, 13–15, 21, 28; postwar 26–27; skills/qualifications, 13, 17, 23–24
7th Canadian Reconnaissance Regiment, 159, 168–71, 178n67
sexual violence: American soldiers, 6, 181–82; Canadian soldiers, 179–81, 184, 186, 195–98, 200n19; courts martial, 184–89, 196–97; courts martial, numbers, 180–81, 184–85, 199n8; definition, 180; German soldiers, 181; indecent assault, 180, 188–89; motivations, 182, 190; and nonfraternization orders, 180–81, 184, 187–88, 195; and plunder, 181–82, 184, 186; prosecutions, 181, 186–87, 198, 202n52; and prostitution, 180, 193; sexual misconduct, 181, 185, 188–89, 192, 196; trials, 180, 187, 190, 199n8; trinket offering, 184, 190. *See also* Abbott, Ambrose; McGill, Jack; rape
Shatilov (general), 144, 147
Shcherbakov, Aleksandr, 146
Shorokhov, Afanasiy. *See* Petrov, Vladimir
Sicherheitsdienst, 87, 259, 278, 281–82, 285
Sichuan Province, 13, 15, 21

Sicily, 160, 171–72, 174, 180, 198
Sidorov, Alleksandr, 257
SIME. *See* Security Intelligence Middle East
Sino-American Cooperative Organization (SACO) Treaty, 18
Sivtsov, Nikolay, 260
Skurin (captain), 283–84, 286–87, 289, 301n29
SMERSH, 259, 262–63, 267
Smith, Arthur, 53
Smith, Joe, 211–13
SNOPG. *See* Senior Naval Officer Persian Gulf
SOE. *See* Special Operations Executive
Song Mei-ling, 17
SPD (Sozialdemokratische Partei Deutschlands), 289, 291, 293–96, 302n39, 304n59
Special Counterintelligence Detachment, 278–79, 282
Special Operations, 231, 235
Special Operations Executive, 38–45, 47–48, 50, 52; Force KALPAK, 47
Spencer, E. L. "Joe," 39
SS Foreign Intelligence Service, 42, 49, 51, 278, 281, 296; Office VI, 278–79, 281
SS (Schutzstaffel), 64, 71, 87, 283, 288
Stalin, Joseph, 233, 235, 251–52, 265–66, 269; opposition to, 251–55, 269–70; and purges, 251–52, 258, 266
Stalingrad, 41, 52, 147
Stalinism, 5, 42, 53; opposition to, 7, 250, 257, 269–70
Stankaiktis, Bronius, 264
Stark, Freya, 44–45, 53
State Department (US), 30n10; and Dixie Mission, 15, 18–19; and mish kids, 16, 22, 28
state security officers, Soviet. *See* defectors/defection, Soviet officers
state security service, Soviet, 250, 252, 261, 265. *See also* defectors/defections, Soviet officers

326 | Index

Stelle, Charles, 16; in Dixie Mission, 15, 18–19, 21–26, 28, 31n23; early life, 23; as mish kid, 15, 21, 23, 28; and Office of Strategic Services, 23; skills/qualifications, 23–24, 33n40

Stilwell, Joseph "Vinegar Joe," 16, 22; and China-Burma-India (CBI) Theater, 2, 13–16, 18, 27; and Chiang Kai-shek, 14, 18, 26, 31n21; and Chinese Communist Party, 18; and Dixie Mission, 15, 18, 24, 26–27; and mish kids, 2, 13–16, 22

Stimson, Henry, 221–22
Strobing, Irving, 213
Sweet-Escott, Bickham, 39
Sykes, Christopher, 40
Syria 45, 47, 119

Tanaka. *See* Koide, Joe
Tardieu, Edouard, 113, 115, 118–24, 126
Tehran, 37–41, 43, 47
3rd (Canadian Infantry) Division, 185
3rd Reconnaissance Troop, 173
Time magazine 209, 214–15
total war, 3–4, 6, 61–64, 66, 79, 204n61
Trikoz, Aleksandr, 261
Trujillo, Alfredo, 222
Tunisian Tirailleur Regiment, 125–27
Turkey, 36, 47, 51–52, 258
Twelfth Army (German), 66–67
28th Regiment de Tirailleurs Tunisiens (RTT), 125–27
29th Armoured Reconnaissance Regiment, 169

Ukai, Nobumichi. *See* Koide, Joe
Ukraine, 79, 251, 260–61
underground movements, 89, 102–4, 109n47, 233–34, 236, 281, 291
Underwood, H. John, 48
United Service Organizations. *See* USO
US Army, 237; and Dixie Mission, 15, 19, 22; and PO Box 1142, 4, 86, 88, 92–95, 105; size, 232. *See also* Bataan; reconnaissance, armored
US Army Air Forces, 96–97, 227n36
US Army Historical Division, 85, 87

US Army Observer Group. *See* Dixie Mission
US Army Observers Mission. *See* Dixie Mission
US Foreign Service, 13, 15, 26–27, 32n30
US Navy, 4, 86, 105, 221
US Persian Gulf Command, 41
US Strategic Bombing Survey, 240
USO, 5, 134, 138, 148
Uyeshima, Ray, 242–43

Vainio, Khelge, 260
Valence, 114, 119, 123
Van Beuren, Archbold, 238, 240
Vermehren, Erich, 52
VGKO, 140
Vlasov, Andrey, 255–57, 259–61, 263, 269
Vlasov's Army. *See* KONR
Vokes, Christopher, 186
VTO, 140–42

Wagner, Eduard, 71
Wainwright, Jonathan, 214, 218, 227n29
Wake Island, 208, 222
Wallace, Henry, 19
war correspondents, 163, 226n17; Bataan/Philippines, 207, 209–10, 224; and reconnaissance, armored, 165–66, 171, 175n6. *See also* Clark, Gerald; Hewlett, Frank; Lee, Clark
War Department (US), 208, 210, 221, 226n17, 238
War Relocation Authority, 233, 239
War Report (BBC), 161–62, 175n6
war reports, after-action, 89, 105, 159–60, 172
war reports, films, 160–62, 164; *The Memphis Belle: A Story of a Flying Fortress*, 161
war reports, newspapers/magazines: about Bataan/Philippines, 207–18; censorship, 162–66, 174, 209–11, 226n17; content, 158, 167–68; errors 166–67; and morale, 167–68; photographs, 162–64, 210. *See*

also reconnaissance, armored, reporting of
war reports, newsreels, 160–61, 164; *Canadian Army Newsreel*, 164
war reports, radio, 158, 160–62, 165–66, 213; *War Report* (BBC), 161–62, 175n6
Waybur, David C., 173
Wedemeyer, Albert C., 26, 236
Wehrmacht, 3, 8, 74, 85–86; and sexual violence, 6, 181, 196–97
Weichs, Maximilian von, 66, 71–72, 74
Weimar, 278, 285–88, 290
West Germany, 278, 280, 293–96
Wheeler, Donald, 240
Womack, Paul, 211–12
women, German, 300n15; and accusations of prostitution, 180, 183, 193; "New Nazi Woman," 279, 296; rape, 5–6, 179–80, 182–85, 187, 194–95, 197–98, 201n32; reports of rape, 180, 186–87, 190, 195. *See also* Abbot, Ambrose; Beetz, Hildegard; McGill, Jack

Wood, E. K. "Chokra," 39
WRA, 233, 239
Wren, Walter "Freckles," 39–40

Yamada, Hitoshi, 241
Yan'an, 31n23; Chinese Communist Party in, 18, 21; Dixie Mission in, 14–15, 18–21, 23–29; Long March to, 15, 21; and Office of Strategic Services, 23
Yasutake, Michael, 242
Yesenina, Lidiya, 254–55
Yoneda, Karl, 233
Yugoslavia, 3; ethnic groups, 73; prisoners of war, 70–71, 73, 102; resistance, 67–68, 71–73, 75, 78–79; surrender, 72; total war in, 62. *See also* 4th Mountain Division

Zaehner, R. C. "Robin," 40–41, 58n29
Zagreb, 67, 72
Zentrum Party, 103–4
Zhigunov, Aleksandr, 254
Zhou Enlai, 18, 23

World War II: The Global, Human, and Ethical Dimension
G. Kurt Piehler, *series editor*

Lawrence Cane, David E. Cane, Judy Barrett Litoff, and David C. Smith, eds., *Fighting Fascism in Europe: The World War II Letters of an American Veteran of the Spanish Civil War*

Angelo M. Spinelli and Lewis H. Carlson, *Life behind Barbed Wire: The Secret World War II Photographs of Prisoner of War Angelo M. Spinelli*

Don Whitehead and John B. Romeiser, *"Beachhead Don": Reporting the War from the European Theater, 1942–1945*

Scott H. Bennett, ed., *Army GI, Pacifist CO: The World War II Letters of Frank and Albert Dietrich*

Alexander Jefferson with Lewis H. Carlson, *Red Tail Captured, Red Tail Free: Memoirs of a Tuskegee Airman and POW*

Jonathan G. Utley, *Going to War with Japan, 1937–1941*

Grant K. Goodman, *America's Japan: The First Year, 1945–1946*

Patricia Kollander with John O'Sullivan, *"I Must Be a Part of This War": One Man's Fight against Hitler and Nazism*

Judy Barrett Litoff, *An American Heroine in the French Resistance: The Diary and Memoir of Virginia d'Albert-Lake*

Thomas R. Christofferson and Michael S. Christofferson, *France during World War II: From Defeat to Liberation*

Don Whitehead, *Combat Reporter: Don Whitehead's World War II Diary and Memoirs*, edited by John B. Romeiser

James M. Gavin, *The General and His Daughter: The Wartime Letters of General James M. Gavin to His Daughter Barbara*, edited by Barbara Gavin Fauntleroy et al.

Carol Adele Kelly, ed., *Voices of My Comrades: America's Reserve Officers Remember World War II*, foreword by Senators Ted Stevens and Daniel K. Inouye

John J. Toffey IV, *Jack Toffey's War: A Son's Memoir*

Lt. General James V. Edmundson, *Letters to Lee: From Pearl Harbor to the War's Final Mission*, edited by Dr. Celia Edmundson

John K. Stutterheim, *The Diary of Prisoner 17326: A Boy's Life in a Japanese Labor Camp*, foreword by Mark Parillo

G. Kurt Piehler and Sidney Pash, eds., *The United States and the Second World War: New Perspectives on Diplomacy, War, and the Home Front*

Susan E. Wiant, *Between the Bylines: A Father's Legacy*, Foreword by Walter Cronkite

Deborah S. Cornelius, *Hungary in World War II: Caught in the Cauldron*

Gilya Gerda Schmidt, *Süssen Is Now Free of Jews: World War II, The Holocaust, and Rural Judaism*

Emanuel Rota, *A Pact with Vichy: Angelo Tasca from Italian Socialism to French Collaboration*

Panteleymon Anastasakis, *The Church of Greece under Axis Occupation*

Louise DeSalvo, *Chasing Ghosts: A Memoir of a Father, Gone to War*

Alexander Jefferson with Lewis H. Carlson, *Red Tail Captured, Red Tail Free: Memoirs of a Tuskegee Airman and POW, Revised Edition*

Kent Puckett, *War Pictures: Cinema, Violence, and Style in Britain, 1939–1945*

Marisa Escolar, *Allied Encounters: The Gendered Redemption of World War II Italy*

Courtney A. Short, *The Most Vital Question: Race and Identity in the U.S. Occupation of Okinawa, 1945–1946*

James Cassidy, *NBC Goes to War: The Diary of Radio Correspondent James Cassidy from London to the Bulge*, edited by Michael S. Sweeney

Rebecca Schwartz Greene, *Breaking Point: The Ironic Evolution of Psychiatry in World War II*

Franco Baldasso, *Against Redemption: Democracy, Memory, and Literature in Post-Fascist Italy*

G. Kurt Piehler and Ingo Trauschweizer, eds., *Reporting World War II*

Kevin T Hall, *Forgotten Casualties: Downed American Airmen and Axis Violence in World War II*

Chad R. Diehl, ed., *Shadows of Nagasaki: Trauma, Religion, and Memory after the Atomic Bombing*

Raffaella Perin, *The Popes on Air: The History of Vatican Radio from Its Origins to World War II*

Daniel McKay, *Beyond Hostile Islands: The Pacific War in American and New Zealand Fiction Writing*, foreword by Patrick Porter

Robert Sommer, *The Concentration Camp Brothel: Forced Sexual Labor under Nazi Rule*, translated by Dominic Bonfiglio, foreword by Annette F. Timm

Lawrence R. Samuel, *The World War II Bond Campaign*

Douglass K. Daniel, *Kill–Do Not Release: Censored Marine Corps Stories from World War II*

Jadwiga Biskupska and Sara B. Castro, eds., *Shots in the Dark: Experimentation, Success, and Failure in the Second World War*

www.ingramcontent.com/pod-product-compliance
Lightning Source LLC
Chambersburg PA
CBHW020351080526
44584CB00014B/985